ST Disk Drives:
Inside and Out

Uwe Braun • Stefan Dittrich • Axel Schramm

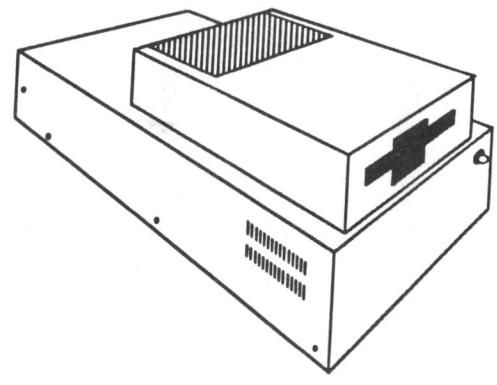

A Data Becker Book

Published by

First Printing, May 1987
Printed in U.S.A.
Copyright © 1986

Copyright © 1987

Data Becker GmbH
Merowingerstraße 30
4000 Düsseldorf, West Germany
Abacus Software, Inc.
P.O. Box 7219
Grand Rapids, MI 49510

This book is copyrighted. No part of this book may be reproduced, stored in a retrieval system, or transmitted in any form or by any means, electronic, mechanical, photocopying, recording or otherwise without the prior written permission of Abacus Software or Data Becker, GmbH.

Every effort has been made to ensure complete and accurate information concerning the material presented in this book. However, Abacus Software can neither guarantee nor be held legally responsible for any mistakes in printing or faulty instructions contained in this book. The authors always appreciate receiving notice of any errors or misprints.

ATARI, ST, 520ST, 1040ST, TOS, SH204, SF354, SF314 and ST BASIC are trademarks or registered trademarks of Atari Corp. GEM and GEMDOS are registered trademarks of Digital Research Inc. GFA BASIC is a trademark of Gfa-Systemtechnik. MS-DOS is a registered trademark of Microsoft Corp. ST PASCAL Plus is a trademark of CCD. Lattice C is a trademark of Metacomco. Pro FORTRAN-77 is a trademark of Prospero Software Ltd.

ISBN   0-916439-84-4

Table of Contents

1	**Introduction**	**1**
2	**Files and programs**	**5**
2.1	File structures and access by high-level languages	11
2.1.1	An overview of GEMDOS functions	11
2.2	File access in BASIC	14
2.2.1	BASIC command overview	14
2.2.2	The sequential file in BASIC	15
2.2.3	The random-access file in BASIC	16
2.3	File handling in Pascal	19
2.3.1	The sequential file in Pascal	19
2.3.2	Random-access files in Pascal	22
2.4	File access in C	24
2.4.1	The sequential file in C	27
2.4.2	The random-access file in C	29
2.5	File handling in FORTRAN	32
2.5.1	The sequential file in FORTRAN	32
2.5.2	The random-access file in FORTRAN	33
2.6	A simple database	35
3	**Data structures**	**43**
3.1	Diskette format	45
3.2	The boot sector	47
3.2.1	Formatting program	50
3.2.2	The BIOS parameter block	58
3.3	The directory	65
3.4	The FAT	68
3.5	Program construction	69
3.5.1	The program header	70
3.5.2	The relocation table	72
3.6	Hard disk format	73
4	**The disk drives**	**75**
4.1	Floppy diskette functions	77
4.2.1	The DMA chip	79
4.2.2	The disk controller	80
4.2.2.1	Pinout	83
4.2.2.2	Organization	88
4.2.2.3	Command description	96

4.2.2.4	Status interpretation	126
4.2.3	The floppy interface	132
4.3	Connecting the disk drives	133
5	**The SH204 hard disk**	**137**
5.1	Function and design	138
5.1.1	The hard disk controller	139
5.1.1.1	Command structure	141
5.1.1.2	List of commands	147
5.1.1.3	HDC tools	153
5.1.1.4	Partition analyzer	158
5.2	Connecting the hard disk	167
5.3	Print the complete directory	168
6	**The RAM disk**	**177**
6.1	An easy-to-use RAM disk program	181
6.2	Disk to RAM disk copy	193
7	**Programming a disk monitor**	**199**
7.1	The TOS functions for disk access	202
7.2	Listing and operation of the disk editor	210
7.2.1	The main menu	303
7.2.2	The TRACK menu	304
7.2.3	The TRACK with SYNC menu	305
7.2.4	The SECTOR menu	305
7.2.5	The CLUSTER menu	306
7.2.6	The FORMAT menu	307
7.2.7	The GAP menu	307
7.2.8	The OPTIONS menu	308
7.3	Sample use of the disk editor	309
7.3.1	File Allocation Table	313
7.3.2	Subdirectories and folders on diskette	315
7.3.3	Formatting in non-Atari format	316
7.4	Assembling with different assemblers	318
8	**Machine language utilities for BASIC**	**319**
8.1	Calling and passing parameters	321
8.2	Some example programs	323
8.2.1	BASIC/TOS interface	323
8.2.2	Directory reader	325
8.2.3	Read/write sectors	328
8.2.4	Any disk format	330
8.2.5	Searching for data	334

8.2.6	Sort data	336
8.2.7	Reading the date and time	338
8.3	Programming the FDC in BASIC	341
8.3.1	The BASIC/FDC interface program	342
8.3.2	Demo 1—All FDC commands	361
8.3.3	Demo 2—Copying disks	370
8.3.4	Demo 3—Creating standard and foreign formats	374
8.4	Creating BASIC loaders	380

Appendices — 385

Appendix A: BASIC loader for `disk editor` — 387

Appendix B: ASCII character set — 398

Index — 401

Chapter One

Introduction

Introduction

The Atari ST computers are ideal for professional applications with their fast 16/32-bit processors and their large memory capacities. But equally as important as internal memory are the methods of external data storage. The floppy disks and hard disks used for storage are very interesting, complex storage media which can do much more than you would guess from reading the manuals.

If you want to make optimal use of your ST, it's important to know the capabilities of the individual ST components. That is the purpose of this book. It first gives you an overview of mass storage methods and describes the procedures for writing application programs. Later chapters detail the secrets of the Atari floppy disk drives, hard disk drives and even RAM disks.

All of this software and hardware knowledge lets you make the best use of these storage media. You can increase the capacity of the disks, develop a method of copy protection for your programs, and create a RAM disk to meet your own needs. With the help of the example and utility programs listed in this book, you'll be able to access your floppy or hard disk much faster and much more efficiently.

In addition, this book and its optional program diskette contain some very useful programs. They include a program that prints out a complete directory, including the contents of all folders, and one that allows you to analyze diskettes or the hard disk. A special feature of this book is a complete disk monitor—a program that gives you direct access to disks, thereby allowing you to apply all of your new knowledge. You can use this disk monitor to recover deleted files, to read "foreign" disk formats and much more.

You will find information in this book that doesn't appear in any ST manual or user's guide. These commands or relationships were discovered after much work with the ST disk systems. You'll soon find out that the ST disk drives can do more than you might have thought.

We hope that this book helps you answer any questions you may have about mass storage on the ST, and that you find this information useful.

Uwe Braun, Stefan Dittrich, Axel Schramm   October, 1986

Chapter Two

Files and programs

Files and programs

The two terms *file* and *program* really mean the same thing: Computer data stored on some form of external storage medium. It's true that internal memory capacity in computers is growing; for example, the Atari 1040 ST has 1 megabyte of RAM. However, the computer still must store data that is not immediately needed—whether it's a word processing program, the population of the city of Chicago, or the price of tea in China—on some external medium. Otherwise this data would be lost when the computer's power was turned off.

Magnetic tape, diskettes, hard disks and CD ROMs are used as external storage media. With all of the devices that handle these media, the data is first encoded on the storage medium, and later read back into the computer's memory using electronic circuitry. A group of data stored under one name is called a *file*, regardless of the type of mass storage.

It is imporant for the user to have at least fundamental knowledge of how the computer stores a file, whether it's an address list, a letter, or executable program code. For example, a file of stored program code may not have any separators between the individual data items. This is different from a file of stored text, where separators are often used between individual sentences such as carriage returns (i.e., the <Return> key) and punctuation marks.

The type of file is indicated by its *extension*. An extension is three additional characters following the name, separated from the name by a period. The ST operating system distinguishes between programs and files by means of this extension. If you were to change the extension of a program from .PRG to .DAT, clicking on this name would only result in this dialog box:

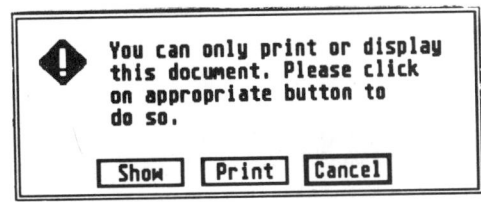

The extensions which the Atari can directly distinguish are:

- `.PRG`   Designates an executable machine language program that can run with GEM support.

- `.TOS`   Designates an executable machine language program, but GEM will be disabled while it is running.

- `.TTP`   Abbreviation for TOS Takes Parameters; same as `.TOS`, except that before the program is executed a dialog box appears, into which you can enter parameters (such as a filename for editors).

- `.ACC`   Special machine language programs known as accessories are loaded after the computer is turned on. These programs remain in memory and can be called as accessories from the **Desk** menu of the Desktop.

- `.INF`   Used by the Desktop for `DESKTOP.INF`. This file contains information about the positions and sizes of the windows, the values set for the Control Panel, etc. This file is created by selecting `Save Desktop` from the **Options** menu.

Other files such as BASIC programs are equipped with the extension `.BAS`, but this is not vital to the ST operating system. You can load a `.TXT` file into the BASIC interpreter, for instance, if it contains the text of a BASIC program. The other extensions are therefore not important, but they can be useful for keeping your files in order.

The actual differences between file types are found in the internal construction of the files themselves. Most high-level languages distinguish between various file forms, such as those with or without separators between strings and numbers, special text modes, etc. We will look first at data files which contain only strings and numbers—that is, ASCII data. We can use various methods for finding and processing certain data in the file.

The speed of access to given data on the diskette or hard disk depends largely on the "intelligence" of the file management system.

This can best be shown through a concrete example. Let's say we have a file containing the addresses of all of the female inhabitants of Escanaba, Michigan.

The block of information that contains complete data on an individual, like the first and last names, street address, city, state, and zip code, is called a *record*. A single piece of information, like the first name, is a *field* in the record.

Breen	Candace	15 Main Street	Escanaba MI	49829	555-1213
Olafsson	Marian	13 Mine Street	Escanaba MI	49829	555-1212
Psmith	Laureen	1 Mime Street	Escanaba MI	49829	555-1234
Taber	Rosalyn	1562 120 Mi. Rd	Escanaba MI	49829	555-5555

A few of the women of Escanaba

The simplest form of file is a *sequential file*, in which the data is stored in linear sequence, one field after the other. The program which reads this data from the file must be able to recognize the end of a record, because a separator is used only between the individual fields.

Generally, every record has a different length. If you want to access the 10th record, you must read through the file from the 1st record to the 10th record. This procedure is acceptable for small files, but what if you had to find the address of Willem Zygonze from Wawatosa in a sequential file containing every inhabitant of Wisconsin?

If large quantities of data must be managed, you would generally use records of a set length and *random-access files*. In random-access files, each field of a record has a set, predetermined size, such as 12 characters for the last name, 10 for the first name, 20 for the street address, 15 for the city, 2 for the state, and 5 for the zip code—a total of 64 characters per record.

Now if you want to access the 10th record, you can calculate the start of the 10th record relative to the start of the file through simple multiplication. You then need only start to read at the $10*64=640$th byte of the file. At this byte you can immediately read your data. This calculation applies only if the numbering of the data records starts with 0 and you want record number 10.

This trick works only if an arbitrary location in the storage media can be directly accessed, which is not possible with audio tape, for example. This kind of access is possible with diskettes or a hard disk, because the disks themselves are divided into individual, numbered sections called *tracks*.

Let's return to our address file example. If we know in which sector the first record (record number 0) begins, we can also calculate where the 640th byte of the file is located. Let's say that our file starts in sector number 10. On the Atari ST, each sector contains 512 bytes. Accordingly, our 10th record, or the 640th byte, is found in the 11th sector at byte 640-512, or byte 128.

You don't need to bother with all this arithmetic if you're writing in a high-level language. A high-level language is any programming language except machine or assembly language. Assembly language programmers can also perform these sector calculations using the ST's operating system, because the operating system offers such a function (but more about this in Chapter 7).

Building on this simple principle of direct access, there are several forms of file organization. For instance, you can sort the entire file according to one important field, such as the last name, and then write the sorted names into a separate file together with the numbers of the corresponding records. This type of file is called an *index file*. The result is an *index-sequential file* (index file with sequential access) for which there are some very advanced search procedures. An index-sequential file can be used to find and access a given record very quickly.

2.1 File structures and access by high-level languages

The operating system of a computer manages the basic operations for file handling. The various high-level languages build their file forms around this operating system management. As we already mentioned, the Atari ST disk operating system GEMDOS supports random-access files. These GEMDOS file functions will now be covered briefly, and then discussed in more detail as they are used with each high-level language. The programs which follow in BASIC, Pascal, C and FORTRAN all have the same effect: They create and read a sequential file and a random-access file.

2.1.1 An overview of GEMDOS functions

Every file must be given a *filename* by the user. The maximum length of a filename is 11 characters. The first eight characters represent the actual filename. The last three characters after the period (which serves as a separator) represent the file extension.

Extensions are necessary for the use of high-level language compilers, i.e., programs which convert the language's source text into an executable program in machine code. As the complier converts from source text to finished program, up to four files are created that have the same name, but different extensions. For example, you would write a C sourcecode with an editor and call it `test1.c`. When you compile and link the program, files with the names `test1.o` (compiled object code) and `test1.prg` (the final linked running program) are created.

To create a new file, GEMDOS offers the CREATE function (function number $3C). The programmer passes the desired filename to the function, as well as a special mode word that contains information about the type of file. If the file is successfully created (the disk is not write-protected, etc.), GEMDOS returns a file number which will be used for all subsequent file access. This number is called a *handle*.

The CREATE function is called only before the very first access to a file. Later access to an existing file can be prepared for by a call to the function OPEN ($3D). When calling CREATE, an empty file with the given name is created on the current drive, and this file can then be accessed for writing.

Many high-level languages incorporate the CREATE function into their OPEN commands, so that if a file is opened and it does not already exist, it will be created.

To write to a file, a programmer uses the GEMDOS function WRITE ($40), passing it the filename or handle returned by CREATE or OPEN, the number of characters to be written, and the characters themselves. Once all of the data has been written to the file, it must be closed before that data can be accessed. The CLOSE function ($3E) accomplishes this. If the CLOSE function is not called, data will probably be lost, or the file's distribution on the disk will not be properly marked on the diskette.

After the file has been created with CREATE, filled with WRITE, and then closed again with CLOSE, it can be opened again for reading with the OPEN function ($3D). Like CREATE, OPEN is given the filename as well as a mode word between 0 and 2.

A 0 passed as the mode word opens the file for reading only. This means that data may only be read from the file. Any attempts to write to the file will result in error messages. A mode of 1 opens the file for writing only, and a 2 allows both reading and writing. The function READ ($3F) is used to read data from a file. Like WRITE, this function is given the handle and the number of characters to be read.

File access with READ and WRITE is completely sequential. This means that when you open the file with CREATE, the operating system creates a *pointer* to the file, which is always set to zero each time the file is opened. This pointer always points to the current position in the file.

For example, if you write 14 characters in this file, the operating system moves this internal pointer 14 positions farther. When the next write access occurs, the new characters will be appended to the 14 existing characters. You must therefore either specify a given number of characters per field, or else a given character must be inserted between fields, so that the end of a field can be recognized when the file is read.

For our address file, which represents a pure text file, we really don't need all of the 256 characters which can be represented by 8 bits. All we need are the uppercase and lowercase letters, numbers and some punctuation. The American Standard Code for Information Interchange (ASCII), the code the ST uses to represent characters, has several control characters which mark the end of the file or the end of a field, for example.

The internal pointer advances by the number of characters read from a file, just like when we write to a file. Every character can be read this way, but to read the last character in a file, all of the previous characters must be read first. The GEMDOS function LSEEK ($42) makes it possible to position the internal data pointer to an arbitrary character relative to the start of the file, the end of the file, or the current pointer. Again, the parameters must include the file handle, the mode word and the desired change to the pointer position.

If the LSEEK mode word has a value of 0, the pointer's position is calculated relative to the start of the file. A value of 1 calculates the new position of the pointer relative to the current pointer, meaning that negative values are also allowed. A value of 2 as the mode word calculates the pointer's position relative to the end of the file, and only negative values are allowed. With the LSEEK function it is possible to program a random-access file using fixed field lengths, such as 12 for the name and 64 characters for an entire record. This way you can compute the number of characters by which the internal data pointer must be moved to get to the desired record.

There are three more GEMDOS functions important for file handling which we haven't yet discussed.

SETDTA ($1A) sets up a buffer for the two functions SFIRST ($4E) and SNEXT ($4F). These latter two functions make it possible to read all the files on a diskette from the directory and to determine the lengths of these files.

In the following sections, we'll turn to the individual high-level languages and take a closer look at the file handling features for each language. These examples are not introductions to the languages themselves, nor do they illustrate a complete file management system. They are only intended to show concrete examples of how simple it is to create and access a disk file in these languages.

After this semi-theoretical treatment of access techniques, you will find a simple but complete database program written in BASIC in Section 2.6. It illustrates the practical application of what you will have learned by then.

2.2 File access in BASIC

The ST BASIC language included with the Atari ST provides both sequential and random file access. The programs below will run in the GFA BASIC© interpreter without alterations. However, the line numbers must first be removed with the ST-KILL program included with GFA BASIC©.

2.2.1 BASIC command overview

Use the command OPEN to create a disk file. The disk file offers three different file options. Here is the command syntax:

```
OPEN "mode",#file number,"filename",record length
```

The following options, which must be in capital letters, exist for mode:

"I" = open file for sequential reading (input)
"O" = open file for sequential writing (output)
"R" = open file for random access

#file number is any number between 1 and 15. filename can contain a maximum of eight letters followed by a period and three more letters (the extension). record length has an effect only when opening a random-access file (mode = "R"); it specifies the size of each record in bytes. In contrast to the operating system function, you must specify when the file is created whether it will use sequential or random access.

The use of sequential files is severely limited in ST BASIC, because there is no way to append data to an existing file. This can only be done with a rather roundabout trick. For example, if you have a sequential address file with 100 addresses stored, and you want to add an address to the list, you would have to read all 100 addresses into memory, add the new address, and write the 101 addresses back to disk.

OPEN"O" erases an existing file with the same name and creates a completely new, empty file on the disk. Because of the limited file handling capabilities, and the fact that the maximum size of a sequential file is dependent on the size of the random access memory (RAM) in the ST itself, we will not spend a lot of time on sequential files under ST BASIC.

2.2.2 The sequential file in BASIC

ASCII strings and numbers can be written to a sequential file. Writing special characters can cause problems because it is possible that the end of a field may not be found, so we'll keep to the ASCII standard. For example, this type of file can be opened for writing by the following command:

```
OPEN "O",#1,"TEST1.DAT"
```

This newly created file is given the filename `TEST1.DAT`. The `WRITE#1` and `PRINT#1` commands handle writing to the file. `WRITE` outputs a comma between the data to be written, while `PRINT` uses the same formatting characters as are used in screen output, such as spaces following a comma.

`PRINT#1` and `WRITE#1` have the same syntax:

```
PRINT#file number,data[,data,...]
WRITE#file number,data[,data,...]
```

The following command sequence opens the file `TEST1.DAT` for writing and writes data to it:

```
10   open "O",#1,"A:TEST1.DAT"
20   a$ = "Harry"
30   b$ = "Hirsch"
40   for i = 1 to 10
50   write#1,a$
60   write#1,b$
70   next i
80   close #1
```

This program creates the file `TEST1.DAT` on the diskette in drive A and writes `Harry Hirsch` to the file ten times.

The `WRITE#` function encloses a string in quotation marks and places the characters $0D (CR = Carriage Return) and $0A (LF = Line Feed) at the end of the output. The character $1A is used by BASIC as the end-of-file (EOF) character, and gives the programmer a way of recognizing the end of the file.

There are two commands in ST BASIC for reading from a sequential file. These commands differ only in the way they handle control characters in the text to be read:

The `INPUT#` function skips preceding spaces, CR's, LF's, and special characters. The function starts at the first ASCII character and reads until it finds a space, a comma, the end-of-line character (EOL, consisting of $0A and $0D [LF and CR]), the EOF character, or a maximum of 255 characters. The `LINE INPUT#` function reads all characters from the first to the EOL character, or up to 254 characters. Both commands must be passed a variable in which to place the characters read, as well as the file number. `INPUT#1,a$` reads a string from the file numbered 1 into the variable `a$`.

The following program fragment opens the file `TEST1.DAT` created on the last page, and reads all strings up to the EOF character. The function `EOF(filenumber)` is used to recognize this. It returns a logical value: TRUE if the end of the file was reached, or FALSE if this was not the case.

```
10    open "I",#1,"A:TEST1.DAT"
20    if eof(1) goto 100
30    input #1,a$
40    print a$
50    goto 20
100   close #1
```

2.2.3 The random-access file in BASIC

Random-access file manipulation is implemented much better in ST BASIC than sequential access. However, you must learn several commands first, because the creation and handling of a random-access file is proportionately more complex.

Opening and creating a random-access file is not much different from opening a sequential file. `OPEN "R",#1,"TEST2.DAT",64` opens the file `TEST2.DAT` as a random-access file, and declares a record length of 64 characters for the file. When you later access the file with `GET#` and `PUT#`, these accesses will always take place in 64-character "segments."

The only characters allowed in this type of file are ASCII characters. For this reason, all numbers to be written to a random-access file must be converted to ASCII codes first. When the file is being read, these codes must then be converted back into numbers. There are several BASIC functions available for this purpose.

Generally a random-access file record will contain several fields, e.g., for the last name, the first name, etc. This division of available space (in this case the 64 characters) is accomplished with the command FIELD #.

```
FIELD #1, 10 AS a$, 12 AS b$, 20 AS c$, 15 AS d$, 2 AS e$, 5 AS f$
```

The preceding instruction reserves 10 characters for a$ (first name), 12 for b$ (last name), 20 characters for c$ (street address), 15 for d$ (city), 2 characters for e$ (state), and 5 characters for f$ (zip code). These string variables are not accessed directly, but only by way of the functions LSET and RSET. LSET a$ = "Harry" transfers the string Harry to the string variable a$ and left-justifies it in a$, which can contain 10 characters. The remaining five characters not used by the word are filled in with spaces ($20).

The command RSET a$ = "Harry" fills the buffer variable right-justified; that is, the word Harry will be formatted to the right margin of the variable, and the spaces will be placed to the left of the word.

To write numbers into a random-access file, they must first be converted to byte strings. The functions MKD$, MKI$, and MKS$ take care of this:

MKI$ (number) returns a 2-byte string for integers
MKS$ (number) returns a 4-byte string for real numbers
MKD$ (number) returns an 8-byte string for double-precision numbers

Numbers are converted to ASCII strings by one of these functions before they are written to the desired buffer variable and later converted to "normal" numbers by another set of functions (CVI, CVS, CVD).

After the desired buffer variables of the record have been set up with FIELD, strings have been placed in the buffer variables with LSET, and numbers have been converted by one of the above converters then put in place with LSET, the entire record can be written to the file with the PUT command. PUT #5, 1 writes the data contained in the buffer variables of file number 5 as record number 1.

The following BASIC program creates a random-access file with the name TEST3.DAT on the disk in drive A, specifies 6 fields for the buffer variable, fills the buffer variable with values, and then writes these values to the file as records 1 and 2.

```
10   open "R",#1,"A:FILE3.DAT,64
20   field #1,10 as a$,12 as b$,20 as c$,15 as d$,2 as e$,5 as f$
30   lset a$= "Harry"
40   lset b$= "Hirsch"
60   lset c$= "2222 Oak Dr."
70   lset d$= "Portland"
80   lset e$= "OR"
90   b = 94750
100  lset f$=mks$(b)
110  put #1, 1
120  put #1, 2
130  close #1
```

In line 100, the number 94750 is converted to a 4-byte string by mks$ before it is assigned to the buffer variable f$.

Reading the data in from a random-access file is similar to writing. You open the file, define buffer variables, and read a complete record with the command GET #1. The individual fields can be accessed directly through the corresponding buffer variables. However, numbers must be converted back to the normal format, because they are stored in a random-access file as strings. The following BASIC program opens the file created above and reads all of the records from it, printing the data on the screen.

```
10   open "R",#1,"A:FILE3.DAT",64
20   field #1,10 as a$,12 as b$,20 as c$,15 as d$,2 as e$,5 as f$
30   get #1,1
40   print a$,b$
50   print c$,d$,e$
60   print cvs(f$)
70   close 1
```

The sizes of the fields may not differ between writing and reading. That means that if 13 characters are reserved in the buffer variables for a$ before writing, then 13 characters must also be defined for the buffer variable in the same position as a$ when the file is read. But the names of the buffer variables do not have to be the same when reading as when writing.

2.3 File handling in Pascal

This description of file functions in Pascal is based on the ST PASCAL Plus© compiler by CCD. This compiler is a very good implementation of Pascal on the Atari ST—it goes far beyond the Pascal standard. ST PASCAL Plus supports both sequential and random-access files.

The data type `file of` or the predefined type `text` (which can be used only for sequential files and which corresponds to the type `packed array of char`) can be used. For example:

```
var dat: file of integer
```

This instruction declares a file which will hold integer numbers and the corresponding pointer as the variable `dat`, which points to the element currently being accessed in the file.

2.3.1 The sequential file in Pascal

After declaring a file variable of type `file of`, a new file will be created by the function `rewrite(internal filename, 'external name')`, which is similar to the BASIC command `OPEN "O"`. This command will create a file with the given filename and assign it an external name. The filename must be declared as a variable of type `file of` in the declaration section. The file can be accessed via the filename or the buffer variable defined by `rewrite` (same name with an appended ^).

`internal filename` represents the file within the Pascal program and the `external name` in single quotes represents the same file on the mass storage medium (disk file). For example, if you declare the file `dat` with:

```
var dat: file of integer;
```

and open it with `rewrite(dat,'a:sfile.dat')` for sequential writing, the buffer variable `dat^` will be defined at the same time which can accept an integer, and which points to the first element in the file. In addition, the file `sfile.dat` will be created on the disk in drive A and opened for writing. All subsequent input and output refers to this disk file.

To read an existing file, it must be opened with `reset(internal filename, 'external name')`. This command opens an existing file for reading and transfers the first record into the buffer variable. If an attempt is made to open a nonexistent file, `eof()` will be TRUE.

The function `eof(internal filename)` returns a value of type `boolean` (TRUE or FALSE). TRUE is returned if the file pointer points to the end of the file. `eol(file variable)` is also a function of type `boolean`, but it can only be used on files of type `packed array of char` or `text` and returns TRUE when the end of the line is reached.

Access to the data in the file is made via `put(internal filename)` for write access and `get(internal filename)` for read access.

`put(dat)` writes the value of the buffer variable `dat^` in the file. The buffer variable represents a pointer to the file, which is set to zero by `rewrite` or `reset` and is incremented by one with `get` or `put` upon each access. This sets the pointer to the next element in the file. After opening the file for reading with `reset(dat, 'name')`, the first file element is transferred to the buffer variable `dat^`. A subsequent `get(dat)` increments the file pointer by one and transfers the value to which the pointer points to the buffer variable `dat^`. The function `eof(file variable)` is used to recognize the end of the file. This function returns a value of type `boolean`. In the example, we must test for the end of the file before the access with `get`, because `get` increments the file pointer and tries to read the next file element into the buffer variable. With files of type `text` it is also possible to recognize the end of the line with the function `eol(file variable)`, which returns a value of type `boolean`.

All available data types in Pascal, including records, can serve as possible file elements. After a file has been opened with `rewrite`, the buffer variable can be assigned a value, which can then be written to the file with `put`. For pure text files, those of type `packed file of char (text)`, the command sequence necessary for writing a file element, assigning a value to the buffer variable through `dat^ := value;` and writing this value to the file with `put(dat);` can be abbreviated to the command `write(dat, value);`. Similar to this, the command `read(dat, value)` reads from a `text` file and replaces the commands `value := dat^` and `get(dat)`.

The following Pascal program creates a file on the diskette in drive A and writes 20 strings to it. In CCD Pascal, `string[20]` defines a variable of type `packed array of char` which can hold 21 characters. The Pascal compiler stores the length of each string at the start of each string, inserting it in the null character.

```
(* Writing a sequential file in Pascal. U.B. 9.86 *)

program sfile ;

var    dat1  :    file of string[20] ;
       t1,t2 :    string[20] ;
       i     :    integer ;

begin
   rewrite (dat1, 'a:seqfile.dat' );
   t1 := 'Harry';
   t2 := 'Hirsch';

   for i:= 1 to 10 do
      begin
         dat1^ := t1;
         put (dat1);
         dat1^ := t2;
         put (dat1);
      end;  (* for loop *)

end.  (* program *)
```

If you look at the created file `seqfile.dat` with the disk monitor presented in Chapter 7, you can clearly see the organization of a sequential Pascal file with string variables (21 characters per string, string length at the start of the string). The following program reads the file created by the program above:

```
(* Reading a sequential file in Pascal. U.B. 9.86 *)

program readfile ;

var    dat1  :    file of string[20] ;
       t1,t2 :    string[20] ;
       i     :    integer ;

begin
   writeln (' Read file ');
   reset (dat1,'a:seqfile.dat');
```

```
      while not eof(dat1) do
        begin
           t1 := dat1^;
           get (dat1);
           writeln (t1);
        end;  (* while loop *)
      writeln;
      writeln (' Press the Return key ');
      readln (t2);

end.  (* program *)
```

After opening the file with `reset(dat1, 'a:seqfile.dat')`, the first file element will be assigned to the buffer variable `dat1^`, so that the buffer variable can process a variable immediately after opening the file. This variable must naturally be the same type as the buffer variable defined along with the declaration of the file variable, or errors can occur. Moreover, no attempt may be made to read data beyond the end of the file. The function `eof(dat1)` checks to see if the end of the file has been reached. The read loop will be exited in this case.

As in BASIC, there is no way to append data to an existing sequential file in Pascal. If you want to expand an existing file, you will have to read in the entire file, add the new file elements and write it all out to a new file.

Creation of and access to files of other data types (`file of integer`, `file of real`) is done in the same way as the examples given here.

2.3.2 Random-access files in Pascal

Creating random-access files and opening them for reading uses the same commands that are used for sequential files (`rewrite`, `reset`). Even the access to individual pieces of data is similar. There is only one additional parameter for `get` and `put`: the number of the record which is to be read or written. The numbering of records starts with 0, whereby all records between 0 and the largest number must first be created. For example, if the last record has the number 8, then record number 10 cannot be created until record number 9 has been written. The short example program below demonstrates the flexibility of this file type. The program creates a small address file to which the same address is written 10 times.

```
(* Random-access file writing in Pascal.  U.B. 9.86 *)
program ranfile ;

type addr =
   record
      fname   : string[10];
      lname   : string[12];
      street  : string[20];
      city    : string[15];
      state   : string[2];
      zip     : string[5];
   end; (* record *)

var   dat1  :  file of addr;
      t1,t2 :  addr;
      i     :  integer;

begin
   rewrite(dat1,'a:random1.dat');
   t1.fname   := 'Harry';
   t1.lname   := 'Hirsch';
   t1.street  := '2222 Oak Dr.';
   t1.city    := 'Portland';
   t1.state   := 'OR';
   t1.zip     := '94750';

   for i:= 0 to 9 do
      begin
         dat1^ := t1;
         put (dat1,i);
      end; (* for loop *)

end. (* program *)
```

In CCD Pascal, the command `dat1^ := t1;` passes the entire address record (with first name, last name, etc.) to the buffer variable, which is then written to the file as record number 1 with `put (dat1, i)`.

As you can see, the number of characters in a string is stored before the first character of the string, simple integers are stored as 2-byte hexadecimal numbers. Pascal uses the number $F5 as the end-of-file character.

2.4 File access in C

The C language can be considered the native language of the Atari ST. Large parts of the TOS are written in this language. Therefore it's not surprising to find the GEMDOS functions described in the introduction to this chapter in the language description of C, although in a modified form.

From the user's point of view, C is an incomplete language. That's because many functions, including the functions for file management, are omitted from the C language, and the user has to design them himself. However, all C compilers come with the standard I/O library—the #include file stdio.h as described by C authors Brian W. Kernighan and Dennis M. Ritchie. To use the file functions, this file must be integrated into the C program at its beginning with the command #include "stdio.h".

One of the problems for someone learning C on the Atari ST, other than the chaotic appearance of the operators and abbreviations (&, !=, ~, ||, etc.), is the initial version of the Digital Research C compiler for the ST. An inexperienced C programmer can never be sure whether a given problem or error lies was caused by his program or by the Digital Research compiler itself. For this reason, all of the C programs presented here have been compiled with the Lattice C© compiler from Metacomco. It shouldn't be difficult to adapt the program to other C compilers, because only the standard functions from the stdio.h library are used.

Communication with files in C is accomplished by a data structure of type FILE, which is defined in the stdio.h library along with the functions for accessing this data structure. Here is an overview of the individual access functions with the data types of their parameters:

```
pointer = fopen(name, mode)

FILE *fopen()
FILE *pointer
char *name
char *mode
```

Here are the possible mode words:

"w" : create a file and open for writing
"a" : open an existing file for appending data
"r" : open an existing file for reading data

In addition to these, there are other mode words which have different functions depending on the compiler used, but they are not of importance to us in this case.

The above function opens a file with subsequent access dependent upon the mode word. If an error occurs and the file cannot be opened, the pointer will equal NULL, or else it will contain the pointer to the file.

```
code = fclose(pointer)

int code
FILE *pointer
```

This closes the file to which `pointer` points.

```
fprintf(pointer, format, arguments)

FILE *pointer
char *format
char *arguments
```

This function writes multiple arguments, separated by commas, to the file with the format described by `format`. The format parameters correspond to the those of the normal `printf` function.

```
code = fscanf(pointer, format, chpointer)

FILE *pointer
char *format
char *chpointer
int code
```

This function reads strings from the file specified by pointer in the format specified by `format` into the variable `chpointer`. The format options are identical to those of the `scanf` function.

```
code = fputs(buffer, pointer)

FILE *pointer
char *buffer
int code
```

This function writes a string to which `buffer` points, to the file to which `pointer` points. If an error occurs, `code` will equal EOF. The zero byte which terminates a C string is not written, but the string is terminated with a NEWLINE character.

```
code = fgets(buffer, number, pointer)

FILE *pointer
char *chpoint
char *buffer
int number
int code
```

This code reads `number` characters from the file to which `pointer` points into the buffer to which `buffer` points. It will stop reading when the end-of-line character (EOL) is encountered. A zero-byte will be appended to the string and the pointer to the buffer will be returned in `chpoint`. After an error-free access, `chpoint` points to `buffer`, otherwise `chpoint` will contain a 0, which is expressed as null in C.

```
code = fputc(chr, pointer)

FILE *pointer
char chr
int code
```

A single character, contained in `chr`, is written into the file to which `pointer` points. After an error, `code = EOF`, otherwise `code` contains the character written.

```
code = fgetc(pointer)

FILE *pointer
int code
```

The above function reads a single character from the file to which `pointer` points. The code of the character read will be returned in `code`, `EOF` if the end of the file was reached.

```
code = fseek(pointer, position, mode)

FILE *pointer
long position
int mode
int code
```

Sets the file pointer of the file to which `pointer` points to a new value. The `mode` parameter specifies the new position of the pointer and can have the following values:

   0 : set new position relative to the start of the file
   1 : set new position relative to the current position
   2 : set new position relative to the end of the file

2.4.1 The sequential file in C

The following C program opens the file `SEQFILE.DAT` for writing and writes `Harry Hirsch` into this file 10 times.

```
/* Writing to a sequential file in C.  U.B. 9.86 */

#include <math.h>
#include <stdio.h>

main()
{
   int i, k;
   FILE *dat1, *fopen();

   char *t1 = "Harry";
   char *t2 = "Hirsch";

   dat1 = fopen("a:seqfile.dat","w");

   for (k=1; k<11; k++)
   {
      fprintf(dat1,"%13s",t1);
```

```
        fprintf(dat1,"%13s",t2);
    }  /* end of the for loop */

    i = fclose(dat1);
    printf("Press a key\n");

    getchar();
}  /* End main */
```

The following program reads the file just written and displays the contents of the entire file on the screen:

```
/* Reading a sequential file in C. U.B. 9.86 */

#include <stdio.h>

main()
{
    int i, k;
    FILE *dat1, *fopen();

    char space[14];
    char *p;

    dat1 = fopen("a:seqfile.dat","r");

    while (p = fgets(space,14,dat1) != NULL)
    {
        printf("%s\n",space);

    }  /* End of while loop */

    i = fclose(dat1);
    printf("\n\n");

    printf("Press key");

    getchar();
}  /* End main */
```

2.4.2 The random-access file in C

The function `fseek()`, which allows positioning of the file pointer to a specific character within the file, is required to make random-access files possible in C. Each field receives a set length as a result of the formatted output to the file with `fprintf()`. As a result, each complete record (such as an address) also has a precise, set length (which, in our case, is 64 characters). To read the 10th record, you need only multiply the length of a record with the number of the desired record, set the file pointer to the computed value, and the desired record can be processed. In C the numbering of the records starts with zero.

```
/* Writing a random-access file in C.  U.B. 9.86 */

#include <math.h>
#include <stdio.h>

char *fname = "Harry";
char *lname = "Hirsch";
char *street = "2222 Oak Dr.";
char *city = "Portland";
char *state = "OR";
int zip = 94750;

main()
{
   int i, k;
   FILE *dat1, *fopen();

   dat1 = fopen("A:random2.dat","w");

   for (k=1; k<11; k++)

   {
      fprintf(dat1,"%10s",fname);
      fprintf(dat1,"%12s",lname);
      fprintf(dat1,"%20s",street);
      fprintf(dat1,"%15s",city);
      fprintf(dat1,"%2s",state);
      fprintf(dat1,"%5d",zip);

   } /* End for loop */
```

```
    i = fclose(dat1);

    printf("Press a key\n");
    getchar();

}   /* End main */
```

The following program reads all of the data from the file and displays it on the screen, including the record number and relative position within the file:

```
/* Reading a random-access file in C.   U.B. 9.86 */

#include <math.h>
#include <stdio.h>

#define LENGTH 64L

main()

{
    int k, i1, i;
    FILE *dat1, *fopen();
    long pos;

    char space[80], *p;

    dat1 = fopen("a:random2.dat","r");

    k = 0;
    pos = k*LENGTH;

    while ((i = fgetc(dat1)) != EOF)

    {
        i = fseek(dat1,pos,0);

        printf(" Record number     = %8d\n",k);
        printf(" Byte pos. in file = %8d\n",pos);
        printf("\n");

        p = fgets(space,11,dat1);
        printf(" First name = %s\n",space);

        p = fgets(space,13,dat1);
        printf(" Last name  = %s\n",space);
```

```
        p = fgets(space,21,dat1);
        printf(" Street = %s\n",space);

        p = fgets(space,16,dat1);
        printf(" City   = %s\n",space);

        p = fgets(space,3,dat1);
        printf(" State  = %s\n",space);

        p = fgets(space,5,dat1);
        i1 = atoi(space);
        printf(" Zip code = %8d\n",i1);

        k+=1;
        pos=k*LENGTH;
        printf("*****************************\n\n");

    }   /* End WHILE loop */

    i = fclose(dat1);
    printf("\n\n");

    printf("Press a key\n");

    getchar();

}   /* End main */
```

2.5 File handling in FORTRAN

All of the examples using FORTRAN here refer to the Pro FORTRAN-77© compiler from Prospero. Like CCD Pascal, this FORTRAN allows both sequential and random-access files. The Atari implementation is quite good, and all language definitions meet FORTRAN-77 standards. In comparing the speed of compiled code, at least in terms of mathematical computations, this compiler is substantially faster than the C and Pascal compilers.

2.5.1 The sequential file in FORTRAN

The OPEN function is used to create a sequential file as well as open a file. OPEN (5, FILE = 'a:fdat1.dat') opens a file on access unit 5 with the name "fdat1.dat" on drive A. This file will be created if it does not already exist.

The normal I/O command WRITE, with optional parameters, can be used to write to this file. WRITE (5) "Harry" writes to file unit 5. The WRITE command also supports the standard FORTRAN formatting options, although we do not have the space to discuss them here.

Here is the FORTRAN version of our example program which creates a sequential file and writes the name Harry Hirsch into the file 10 times:

```
        PROGRAM SEQ1

        CHARACTER*13 LNAME, FNAME

        FNAME = "Harry"
        LNAME = "Hirsch"

        OPEN (2, FILE='A:FSEQ1.DAT', FORM='UNFORMATTED')

        DO 100 N = 1,10
        WRITE (2) FNAME
        WRITE (2) LNAME
100     CONTINUE
        CLOSE (2)
        END
```

The following program reads the data from the sequential file:

```
      PROGRAM SEQ2
      CHARACTER*2 T1
      CHARACTER*13 TEXT

      OPEN (2, FILE='A:FSEQ1.DAT', FORM='UNFORMATTED',STATUS='OLD')

100   CONTINUE
      READ (2,END=200) TEXT
      WRITE (*,*) TEXT
      GOTO 100

200   CONTINUE
      CLOSE (2)
      END
```

2.5.2 The random-access file in FORTRAN

Back to our standard random-access file program, this time in FORTRAN:

```
C     Write a random-access file in FORTRAN.  U.B. 9.86

      PROGRAM RAND1
      INTEGER*4 ZIP

      CHARACTER*10 FNAME
      CHARACTER*12 LNAME
      CHARACTER*20 STREET
      CHARACTER*15 CITY
      CHARACTER*2 STATE

      FNAME = 'Harry'
      LNAME = 'Hirsch'
      STREET = '2222 Oak Dr.'
      CITY = 'Portland'
      ZIP = 94750

      OPEN (2, FILE = 'A:\FRAND1.DAT', REC1 = 64, ACCESS = 'DIRECT')
      DO 100 N = 1,10
      WRITE (2,REC = N) FNAME, LNAME, STREET, CITY, ZIP
100   CONTINUE
      CLOSE (2)
      END
```

The next program reads the data from the file:

```fortran
C Read a random-access in FORTRAN.   U.B. 9.86

      PROGRAM RAND1
      INTEGER*4 ZIP, STAT

      CHARACTER*10 FNAME
      CHARACTER*12 LNAME
      CHARACTER*20 STREET
      CHARACTER*15 CITY
      CHARACTER*2 STATE

      OPEN (2, FILE = 'A:\FRAND1.DAT', REC1 = 64, ACCESS = 'DIRECT',
     -  STATUS = 'OLD)

      N=1
10    CONTINUE

      READ (2, REC = N, IOSTAT = STAT) FNAME, LNAME, STREE, CITY, ZIP
      IF (STAT .EQ. 0) THEN

      WRITE (*,*) ' Record number: ',n
      WRITE (*,*)
      WRITE (*,*) ' First name = ' , FNAME
      WRITE (*,*) ' Last name  = ' , LNAME
      WRITE (*,*) ' Street     = ' , STREET
      WRITE (*,*) ' City       = ' , CITY
      WRITE (*,'(a,i6)') ' Zip code   = ' , ZIP
      WRITE (*,*)
      WRITE (*,*)
      N = N+1
      GOTO 10

      ELSE
      WRITE (*,*)
      WRITE (*,*)
      WRITE (*,*) ' Press a key'
      CLOSE (2)
      ENDIF
      END
```

2.6 A simple database

After all of this theory, we want to demonstrate some practical data/file management techniques with a simple database program. This program probably isn't the best thing to use for warehouse inventory, but it will work well for listing telephone numbers or managing your record collection.

The program is written in ST BASIC, which is included with the Atari ST.

When creating such a program, you should consider what a database program should be able to do. This program has some of the most important functions:

- Create a new database
- Input new data or correct old entries
- Load an existing database into memory
- Output data on the screen or printer
- Search for given keywords
- Sort data according to a field
- End the program

These functions are accessible from a simple menu displayed on the screen. To select a function, simply enter the function number and press <Return>.

Before we take a closer look at the individual functions, it would be a good idea to enter the program first:

```
10      '*** Mini-Database   S.D. ***
20      dim d$(5),i$(5),l(5),p$(500),r(500)
30      for i=1 to 500: r(i)=i: next i
40      for i=1 to 5: d$(i)=space$(100)
50      i$(i)="" : next i
60      start:
70      fullw 2: clearw 2: gotoxy 0,0
80      ? "**** Mini-database from ST Drive Book ****
90      ? d;" Data sets available in file ";f$
100     for i=1 to 5
110     gotoxy 28,1+i: ?i;") ";i$(i)
120     next i
130     if so then gotoxy 21,1+so: ?">"
140     gotoxy 0,6
150     ?: ? "1) Create a database"
```

```
160     ? "2) Input the data"
170     ? "3) Load the data"
180     ? "4) Sort the data"
190     ? "5) Search"
200     ? "6) Output the data"
210     ? "7) End"
220     ?: input "Your choice ";w
230     on w gosub create,enter,lading,sort,search,output,ende
240     goto start
250     '
260     '** create the database  **
270     create:
280     ? " ** Database create  : 500 items with 5 fields free  **"
290     sum=0
300     ?: for i=1 to 5
310     ? i;". Field name,Length ";
320     input i$(i),l(i)
330     sum=sum+l(i)
340     next i
350     ?: input "OK ";o$
360     if o$="n" or o$="N" then create
370     gosub getfn
380     open "O",#1,fi$
390     for i=1 to 5
400     print#1,i$(i)
410     print#1,l(i)
420     d$(i)=space$(l(i))
430     next i
440     close #1
450     open "R",#1,fd$,sum
460     field #1, l(1) as d$(1), l(2) as d$(2), l(3) as d$(3), l(4)
480     return
490     '
500     '** Enter the data  **
510     enter:
520     clearw 2: gotoxy 0,0: ? " *** Data entry ***
530     ? d;" Data sets available"
540     gotoxy 0,3:? "Number ";d+1
550     gotoxy 0,4: input "Number ";d$
560     if len(d$)>0 then d1=val(d$) else d1=d+1
570     if d1=0 then return
580     if d1>d+1 then enter
590     if d1<d+1 then gotoxy 0,5: o$="b": gosub output1
600     for i=1 to 5
610     gotoxy 0,4+i
620     ?i$(i);:: gotoxy 20,4+i
630     input d$
```

```
640     if len(d$)>0 then lset d$(i)=d$
650     next i
660     ?: input "OK (y/n) ";o$
670     if o$="n" or o$="N" then enter
680     if d1=d+1 then d=d+1
690     put #1,r(d1)
700     goto enter
710     '
720     '** Database load   **
730     lading:
740     gosub getfn
750     close #1
760     sum=0
770     open "I",#1,fi$
780     for i=1 to 5
790     input#1,i$(i)
800     input#1,l(i)
810     sum=sum+l(i)
820     d$(i)=space$(l(i))
830     next i
840     close #1
850     open "R",#1,fd$,sum
860     field #1, l(1) as d$(1), l(2) as d$(2), l(3) as d$(3), l(4) as
        d$(4),l(5) as d$(5)
870     d=0
880     while not eof(1)
890     d=d+1
900     get #1,d
910     wend
920     return
930     '
940     '** Data output   **
950     output:
960     if d=0 then ? "No data available !": goto waitkey
970     ? " ** Data output **"
980     input "S)creen or P)rinter ";o$
990     for d1=1 to d
1000    gosub output1
1010    if o$="p" or o$="P" then lprint else ?
1020    next d1
1030    waitkey:
1040    gotoxy 30,16: input "----Press 'Return'----",w$
1050    return
1060    output1:
1070    get #1,r(d1)
1080    for j=1 to 5
1090    if o$="p" or o$="P" then lprint i$(j),d$(j) else ? i$(j),d$(j)
```

```
1100    next j
1110    return
1120    '
1130    '** Search **
1140    search:
1150    if d=0 then ? "No data available!": goto waitkey
1160    ?: input "Field number,Text ";f,t$
1170    for d1=1 to d
1180    get #1,d1
1190    if instr(d$(f),t$) then gosub output1: ?
1200    next d1
1210    goto waitkey
1220    '
1230    '** Sort **
1240    sort:
1250    if d=0 then ? "No data available!": goto waitkey
1260    ?: input " Which field to sort on ";so
1270    if so=0 or so>5 then return
1280    for i=1 to d
1290    get #1,i
1300    p$(i)=d$(so)
1310    next i
1320    for i=1 to d
1330    for j=i to d
1340    if p$(r(i))>p$(r(j)) then swap r(i),r(j)
1350    next j
1360    next i
1370    return
1380    '
1390    '** End **
1400    ende:
1410    close #1
1420    ?: ? "**** End Program ! ****"
1430    end
1440    '
1450    '** subroutines    **
1460    getfn:
1470    ?: input "Filename ";f$
1480    fi$=f$+".idx"
1490    fd$=f$+".dat"
1500    return
```

Now we'll discuss the individual functions:

1) Creating a database

After calling this function, you will be asked five times to enter two parameters: field name and field length. Here you enter the name of the field, followed by a comma and the maximum length of this entry in characters. For an address database, this might look like this:

```
First name,10
Last name,15
Street address,25
City,16
Telephone,13
```

Once you have entered these, you will be asked if the information is correct (`OK?`). If it is, enter `Y` here (the program accepts upper or lower case lettering).

You will then be asked for the filename under which the database will be stored on the disk. The drive may be included along with the name, as in `A:TEST`. You may not enter an extension (like `.DAT`) because the program creates two files with the same name but different extensions. After the program is run you'll find one file with the extension `.IDX`. This file contains the names and lengths of the data fields, as well as one with the extension `.DAT`, which contains the records themselves.

Once the data items are entered and stored on the disk, the main menu will be displayed again.

2) Enter data

After selecting this function, you will be told how many records currently exist, and you will be asked to enter the name of the record to enter or modify. The number of the next available record is supplied behind the question mark, so you just have to press <Return> to enter a new record.

If you want to change a record, enter its number and you will be shown the old contents of the record as well as a question mark requesting that you enter new data. If you want to keep the old contents of a data field, just press <Return>.

Additional data is entered in the same way. If you want to stop entering data, enter 0 for the record number.

3) Load a database

Here you are asked for the name of the database. Again, you can enter only the drive and the filename without an extension. The main menu will be displayed again once the database is loaded, and the menu will list the name of the file, the number of entries in it and the field names.

4) Sorting the data

If you want to sort the records based on a specific field, choose this function. You will be asked for the number of the field by which the records are to be sorted. For example, you can use this to sort your address list by name, print it out, and then sort by zip code and print it out again.

The sort function does not contain any output function. A > character will be placed in front of the field name with which you last sorted the file.

5) Search

This function asks you to enter a field number and a search string. For example, if you want to output all the addresses in Wawatosa, you would enter "4,Wawatosa" in the previous example. All records whose city field (field number 4) contains the string Wawatosa will be displayed. You can also enter just part of search string.

6) Output data

This function allows you to output all records to the screen or printer. Answering the question regarding the destination of the output with P sends it to the printer, while all other input sends it to the screen.

The records are output in the order they were entered, unless you first call the sort function.

7) End

The opened data channel is closed (CLOSE #1) and the program ends.

The program uses both sequential and random-access files. The field names and lengths of the fields are stored sequentially (name.IDX), and the records themselves are placed in a random-access file (name.DAT). For small databases and with the large memory capacity of the Atari ST, you could also store all data sequentially in an appropriate string array and manage it directly in memory. However, this takes more time to load, and works only if everything is saved again after it is accessed and edited.

Chapter Three

Data structures

Data structures

Writing to disk is basically a matter of taking a large set of data and placing it on diskette. It sounds simple enough, but when we look at the procedures more closely, certain areas present some difficulties.

First of all, the diskette must be organized in such a way that the data can be found again. Some preparations are necessary for this. You don't have to bother much with the details, but the operating system and the computer and disk drives must execute many complex steps.

A diskette must be *formatted* before it can be used. During formatting, the surface of the diskette is divided into individual sectors whose positions are determined by the format used.

The computer must be able to recognize this format, because it can work with different formats. The number of sides of the diskette used is as important as the number of sectors and their length. This information is contained in the *boot sector*, which we'll examine in detail.

The sectors used for every file or program stored on the diskette must be assigned and marked. This information is stored in the File Allocation Table (FAT) of the disk directory. This will be discussed in the next chapter.

3.1 Diskette format

As we explained before, when a diskette is formatted it is divided into individual sections. The diskette is first divided into *tracks*. These tracks are concentric rings on the diskette and are numbered from the outside in. There are 80 such tracks on a normally formatted diskette, numbered from 0 to 79. It is possible to format up to 82 tracks, but the data security decreases toward the center because of the reduced available space. For this reason tracks 80 to 82 are not used. They can be used if formatted appropriately.

The individual tracks are in turn divided into *sectors*. The sectors represent segments of the track rings. These sectors are combined into *clusters*, usually two sectors per cluster. Clusters are not very significant, so we will ignore them and discuss only sectors.

In the normal diskette format there are 9 sectors on every track, and each sector comprises 512 bytes. This results in a storage capacity of 80*9*512=368640 bytes on a single-sided disk.

However, 368640 is not the actual number of bytes stored on the diskette. Additional information is placed on each track and each sector during formatting. This data is required by the *disk controller*, the chip that controls the disk drive in the Atari ST. The disk controller uses the information to find the proper sector in the track. Let's look at the complete construction of a normal track.

Number	Bytes	Comments
60	$4E00	Start of track

per sector:

Number	Bytes	Comments
12	$00	
3	$F5	will be written as $A1
1	$FE	ID address mark
1	track #	track number 0 to 79
1	side #	side number 0 or 1
1	sector #	sector number 1 to 9
1	$02	*$100=512 bytes per sector
1	$F7	CRC checksum (will be 2 bytes)
22	$4E	filler bytes
12	$00	"
3	$F5	become $A1
1	$FB	marker (data address mark)
512	Data	the actual sector data
1	$F7	write CRC checksum
40	$4E	filler bytes

end of track:

Number	Bytes	Comments
1401	$4E	filler bytes

If you add all of these bytes together, you get 6969 bytes per track, which corresponds to an unformatted diskette capacity of 557520 bytes. Unfortunately, this capacity cannot all be used for data, or else the controller wouldn't be able to find the data again (how would it recognize the start and end of a sector?).

However, it is possible to use the last 1401 bytes of each track for an additional sector. This would increase the usable diskette capacity to 409600 bytes. If we also use the three additional tracks (80 to 82), the total storage space increases to 424960 bytes. But as we said, the security of the data decreases.

We'll need a short program to create this custom disk format. Before we take a look at such a program, we must take a closer look at the individual steps that comprise the formatting process. It isn't enough just to format the tracks. The parameters used, like the number of tracks and sectors, must be written on the diskette or the ST will not be able to determine how the diskette is formatted. This is where the boot sector comes in.

3.2 The boot sector

The boot sector always lies at the very beginning of a diskette or hard disk: track 0, side 0, sector 1 of a diskette, or sector 0 of a hard disk. Like all the other sectors, the boot sector is 512 bytes long and is checked by the operating system every time the diskette is changed.

In addition, the boot sector plays a decisive role in *booting* the diskette. Booting refers to loading the operating system from diskette after the computer is turned on. First the boot sector of the diskette in drive A is loaded and checked to see if the diskette contains an operating system. The boot sector also contains additional information.

The boot sector contains the serial number of the diskette, a parameter block for the BIOS of the computer, and possibly a boot program with boot parameters. If this program is present, the sum of all the bytes in the sector (checksum) must yield the "magic number" $1234. If the checksum equals $1234, the program at the start of the sector, which usually contains a BRA (branch always) command, is executed. The program must be written so that it can run at any memory location.

Normally, a boot sector does not contain such a boot program. More important are the various parameters which are found in the sector. These parameters are loaded by a GETBPB operating system call into the BPB (BIOS parameter block). If these parameters are not valid, the GETBPB function returns a 0 instead of the address of the BPB.

The additional information in the boot sector is the serial number of the diskette. This is a 24-bit number that's determined and written to the diskette during formatting. This number is used to verify when the diskette has been changed.

Here is the complete construction of the boot sector:

	Byte#	Name	Significance	
	$00	BRA	Branch command to boot program (if present)	
	$02	filler	Reserved fill bytes or loader	
	$08	serial #	Serial number	
*	$0B	BPS	Bytes per sector	(512)
*	$0D	SPC	Sectors per cluster	(2)
*	$0E	RES	Reserved sectors	(1)
*	$10	NFATS	Number of FATs (File Allocation Tables)	(2)
*	$11	NDIRS	Number of possible directory entries	(112)
*	$13	NSECTS	Number of sectors on the diskette	(720/1440)
*	$15	MEDIA	Medium description (unused)	
*	$16	SPF	Sectors per FAT	(5)
*	$18	SPT	Sectors per track	(9)
*	$1A	NSIDES	Number of sides of the diskette	(1/2)
*	$1C	NHID	Number of hidden sectors	(0)
	$1E	EXECFLG	Flag for COMMAND.PRG	
	$20	LDMODE	Flag for file or sector boot	
	$22	SSECT	First sector to be loaded	
	$24	SECTCNT	Number of sectors to be loaded	
	$26	LDADDR	Load address	
	$2A	FATBUF	FAT address	
	$2E	FNAME	Filename (usually TOS.IMG)	
	$39	RES	Reserved	
	$3A	BOOTIT	Boot program	
	$1FD			
	$1FE		Comparison word for the checksum	

The entries marked with an asterisk (*) correspond to the BPB of the diskette. These entries are identical to those of MS-DOS, the operating system of the IBM PC. We should note that a 16-bit word is stored here, in the byte order low byte-high byte (for example, BPS = $00 $02 means $200 bytes per sector). This makes it possible for the Atari ST to read IBM PC diskettes. However, the ST cannot do any more than read these files, because the data distribution on the diskette is organized differently on the PC.

A couple of comments about the entries in the boot sector:

- The numbers in parentheses found behind some of the entries indicate the normal contents of these entries on a single-sided diskette.

- NHID, the number of hidden sectors, is not used by the ST BIOS for diskettes.

The data at $1E are of interest only if the diskette is bootable. Such a diskette normally contains the operating system in the form of data files called image files (.IMG). An executable boot sector can also be recognized by the text LOADER at the 3rd byte. The boot program, which is stored in two ROMs in older Atari STs, also recognizes such a boot sector by the checksum—it must be $1234 for an executable boot sector. If this is the case, the additional data in the boot sector has the following meaning:

EXECFLG will be copied in the system variable cmdload. This flag determines whether or not the program COMMAND.PRG will be loaded after loading the operating system.

LDMODE determines the loading mode. If this flag is zero, the file specified by FNAME will be loaded. This file is usually TOS.IMG. If LDMODE is not zero, sectors will be directly loaded, depending on SECTCNT and SSECT.

SSECT is the logical sector at which booting starts. This variable is valid only if LDMODE is not zero.

SECTCNT specifies the number of sectors to be booted. This is also valid only if LDMODE is not zero.

LDADDR is the address at which the file or sectors will be loaded.

FATBUF specifies the address at which the FAT and the directory sectors will be loaded.

FNAME is the filename of the image file to be loaded (LDMODE = 0). It is constructed just like a normal filename, with eight characters for the name and a three-character extension.

BOOTIT is a boot program that will be executed after the boot sector has been loaded.

That is the basic construction of the boot sector. Together with what we have learned about the diskette format, we can start putting some of our knowledge into practice by writing a program for formatting diskettes.

We can already use the Format option in the **File** menu to format disks. As we mentioned earlier, the format used by the Atari operating system TOS is set to 80 tracks and 9 sectors per track. However, we can physically fit more tracks and sectors on a diskette.

3.2.1 Formatting program

The program below offers some options for increasing the capacity of a normal diskette. It displays a menu which shows the parameters for formatting:

```
    *** Formatting program   S.S. ***

    [F1]   Sides(s) ........:  2
    [F2]   Tracks ..........: 80
    [F3]   Sectors/track ...:  9
    [F4]   Drive ...........:  A
    [F8]   Format ...
    [F10]  Quit !
```

Pressing a function key changes a setting or performs a function. The following settings are available:

<F1>:   This key toggles between one and two sides. If you are using a single-sided disk drive, only one side can be formatted.

<F2>:   Here you can select 80 (normal setting) or 82 tracks. It is also possible to use 83 tracks, but we have not included this option because of data loss problems. You can add this capability by making a minor change to the program.

<F3>:   This function key toggles between 9 and 10 sectors per track.

<F4>: This key allows you to select either drive A or drive B. Always check this parameter before you start the formatting, to prevent accidentally erasing important data on the diskette in the other drive...

<F8>: Formatting begins immediately after this key is pressed, indicated by the following message:

   Formatting. Please wait...

If an error occurs, the following message appears:

   ** An error occurred !! **

You should check the diskette to make sure that it is not write-protected. The error message remains onscreen until you press a key.

<F10>: When are finished formatting disks, you can exit the program by pressing this key.

Disks of varying storage capacities can be created by the selections possible with this program. Here are some values for single-sided formats:

Tracks	Sectors per track	Capacity in bytes
80	9	357376
82	9	366592
80	10	398336
82	10	408576

As you can see from the table above, it is possible to increase the capacity of a single-sided diskette by up to 51200 bytes. For double-sided disks, it is possible to gain more than 100K.

Here is the program. It was created with the *AssemPro* assembler, which has few differences from the DRI assembler. If you want to assemble the program with the DRI assembler, you must start each comment line with an asterisk (*), and change the ALIGN.W instruction to EVEN.

```
;** Formatting-Program S.D. **

run:
        move.l    #menue,d0
        bsr       print           ;Menu output
        bsr       getkey
        cmp.b     #$3b,d0
        blt       run             ;false key
        cmp.b     #$44,d0
        bgt       run             ;false key

        cmp.b     #$3b,d0         ;F1 ?
        bne       notf1
        eor       #3,sds          ;1/2 Side
        eor       #1,sdsf
        bra       run

notf1:
        cmp.b     #$3c,d0         ;F2 ?
        bne       notf2
        eor       #2,trs          ;80/82 Tracks
        eor       #2,trsf
        bra       run

notf2:
        cmp.b     #$3d,d0         ;F3 ?
        bne       notf3
        eor       #3,sptf
        eor       #$1109,spt      ;9/10 Sectors per Track
        bra       run

notf3:
        cmp.b     #$3e,d0         ;F4 ?
        bne       notf4
        eor       #3,lw
        eor       #1,lwf          ;Drive A/B
        bra       run

notf4:
        cmp.b     #$42,d0         ;F8 ?
        bne       notf8
        bsr       format          ;=> Formatting
        bra       run

notf8:
        cmp.b     #$44,d0         ;F10 ?
        bne       run
```

```
            clr     -(sp)
            trap    #1                  ;Quit, return to Desktop
format:                                 ;* Formatting *
            move.l  #wait,d0
            bsr     print               ;"Formatting drive.."
            move    trsf,trsf1
            subq    #1,trsf1

floop:
            move    sdsf,side           ;Side

floop1:
            bsr     fmttr               ;format one Track
            bne     error
            subq    #1,side             ;Get other side
            bpl     floop1              ;format
            subq    #1,trsf1
            bpl     floop               ;next Track
setboot:                                ;Boot-Sector create
            clr     -(sp)               ;Execute-Flag: not set
            moveq   #2,d0
            or      sdsf,d0
            move    d0,-(sp)            ;Disk type and number of sides
            move.l  #$1000000,-(sp)     ;Serial number
            pea     buffer              ;Buffer address
            move    #$12,-(sp)
            trap    #14                 ;Boot-Sector create
            add.l   #14,sp

            lea     buffer,a0           ;number of Boot-Sector-buffer
            clr.l   d0
            cmp     #9,sptf             ;9 Sectors per Track ?
            beq     sok                 ;yes
            move.b  #10,24(a0,d0)       ;set 10 SPT value
            move    trsf,d1             ;number of Tracks in D1
            tst     sdsf                ;1 Side ?
            beq     sd11                ;yes
            lsl     #1,d1               ;else set two sided
sd11:
            bsr     addsec              ;SEC + number of  Tracks (D1)

sok:
            cmp     #80,trsf            ;80 Tracks ?
            beq     trok                ;yes
            move    #18,d1
            tst     sdsf                ;1 Side ?
```

```
        beq     sd12                ;yes
        lsl     #1,d1               ;else double sided
sd12:
        bsr     addsec              ;SEC + 2*9 or 4*9

trok:
        move    #1,-(sp)            ;1 Sector
        clr.l   -(sp)               ;Side 0, Track 0
        move    #1,-(sp)            ;Sector 1
        move    lwf,-(sp)           ;Disk drive
        clr.l   -(sp)
        pea     buffer              ;Buffer
        move    #9,-(sp)
        trap    #14                 ;flopwr, Boot-Sector write
        add.l   #20,sp
        tst     d0                  ;Error test?
        bne     error               ;yes: error routine
        bra     run                 ;New start

addsec:                             ;SEC = SEC + D1
        move.b  20(a0,d0),d2        ;HI
        lsl     #8,d2
        move.b  19(a0,d0),d2        ;LO
        add     d1,d2
        move.b  d2,19(a0,d0)        ;set LO
        lsr     #8,d2
        move.b  d2,20(a0,d0)        ;set HI
        rts

error:
        move.l  #errtxt,d0
        bsr     print               ;Error message output
        bsr     getkey              ;wait for key press
        bra     run                 ;and new start

fmttr:                              ;one track formatting
        clr     -(sp)               ;Virgin data
        move.l  #$87654321,-(sp)    ;Magic-number
        move    #1,-(sp)            ;interleave
        move    side,-(sp)          ;Side
        move    trsf1,-(sp)         ;Track
        move    sptf,-(sp)          ;Sectors/Track
        move    lwf,-(sp)           ;drive
        clr.l   -(sp)
        pea     buffer              ;Track-Buffer
        move    #10,-(sp)
        trap    #14                 ;flopfmt, Track format
```

```
        add.l    #26,sp
        tst      d0                 ;Test for Error
        rts

print:                              ;Text output from (D0)
        move.l   d0,-(sp)
        move     #9,-(sp)
        trap     #1
        addq.l   #6,sp
        rts

getkey:                             ;wait for key press,
        move.w   #1,-(sp)
        trap     #1
        addq.l   #2,sp
        swap     d0                 ;key code in D0.b
        rts


; Text and Variables:

menue:  dc.b    $1b,"E***** Formatting--Program S.D. *****"
        dc.b    10,13,10,13
        dc.b    " [F1] Side(s) ........: "
sds:    dc.b    " 2",10,13
        dc.b    " [F2] Tracks .........: "
trs:    dc.b    "80",10,13
        dc.b    " [F3] Sectors/track ..: "
spt:    dc.b    " 9",10,13
        dc.b    " [F4] Drive ..........: "
lw:     dc.b    " A",10,13
        dc.b    " [F8] Format ...",10,13
        dc.b    "[F10] Quit !",10,13,10,13,0

wait:   dc.b    "Formatting. Please wait...",10,13,0
errtxt: dc.b    "** An error occurred !! **",10,13,0

 align.w
sdsf:   dc.w 1
trsf:   dc.w 80
trsf1:  dc.w 80
sptf:   dc.w 9
lwf:    dc.w 0
side:   dc.w 0
 BSS
buffer: DS.B 8000
 END
```

The program is divided into the following segments:

1) Menu control: The screen is cleared and the menu is printed. After a key is pressed, the key code passed in D0 is evaluated. If one of the `CMP.B #$xx,D0` comparisons match, the selected function will be executed. For the switch function (<F1>-<F4>), the switch is accomplished with the EOR command in the menu text and the corresponding parameter line. After the switch, the program branches back to `start` (run), except for the <F10> key, which ends the program via the GEMDOS TERM function.

2) Formatting: After outputting the message `Formatting...`, the diskette will be formatted from the set maximum track-1 to track 0. If double-sided formatting is enabled, the tracks on side 1 (back) are formatted first, followed by the tracks on side 0.

3) Creation of the boot sector: First a normal boot sector is created by the XBIOS PROTOBT function. Only the number of sides is taken into account.

4) Correction of the boot sector: If nonstandard settings are used (10 sectors per track, 82 tracks), the boot sector will be corrected accordingly. First the number of sectors per track is tested. If it is 10, this will be placed in the SPT cell of the boot sector and then the number of tracks will be added to the number of sectors on the diskette. The selected number of tracks will then be tested and the sector number increased if required.

5) Saving the boot sector: The new boot sector will be written to side 0, track 0, sector 1 with the help of the FLOPWR XBIOS function. If an error occurs, it will be displayed.

6) Data area: This is where the strings for the menu, messages and variables are stored. The length of the buffer is set, but the buffer is not written on the diskette because it is in the `.bss` area.

Here is a BASIC program which generates the formatting program on the diskette, storing it under the name `bigfmt.prg`:

```
1000    open"R",1,"a:bigfmt.prg",16
1010    field#1,16 as bin$
1020    a$="":for i=1 TO 16:read d$:if d$="*"then 1050
1030    a=val("&H"+d$):s=s+a:a$=a$+chr$(a):next
```

```
1040 lset bin$=a$:rec=rec+1:put 1,rec:goto 1020
1050 data 60,1A,00,00,03,00,00,00,00,00,00,00,1F,40,00,00
1060 data 00,00,00,00,00,00,00,00,00,00,00,20,3C,00,00
1070 data 01,FC,61,00,01,DC,61,00,01,E4,B0,3C,00,3B,6D,EC
1080 data B0,3C,00,44,6E,E6,B0,3C,00,3B,66,00,00,14,0A,79
1090 data 00,03,00,00,02,3E,0A,79,00,01,00,00,02,F4,60,CC
1100 data B0,3C,00,3C,66,00,00,14,0A,79,00,02,00,00,02,5A
1110 data 0A,79,00,02,00,00,02,F6,60,B2,B0,3C,00,3D,66,00
1120 data 00,14,0A,79,00,03,00,00,02,FA,0A,79,11,09,00,00
1130 data 02,76,60,98,B0,3C,00,3E,66,00,00,16,0A,79,00,03
1140 data 00,00,02,92,0A,79,00,01,00,00,02,FC,60,00,FF,7E
1150 data B0,3C,00,42,66,00,00,0A,61,00,00,12,60,00,FF,6E
1160 data B0,3C,00,44,66,00,FF,66,42,67,4E,41,20,3C,00,00
1170 data 02,B9,61,00,01,3C,33,F9,00,00,02,F6,00,00,02,F8
1180 data 53,79,00,00,02,F8,33,F9,00,00,02,F4,00,00,02,FE
1190 data 61,00,00,E2,66,00,00,CC,53,79,00,00,02,FE,6A,F0
1200 data 53,79,00,00,02,F8,6A,DE,42,67,70,02,80,79,00,00
1210 data 02,F4,3F,00,2F,3C,01,00,00,00,48,79,00,00,03,00
1220 data 3F,3C,00,12,4E,4E,DF,FC,00,00,00,0E,41,F9,00,00
1230 data 03,00,42,80,0C,79,00,09,00,00,02,FA,67,00,00,1E
1240 data 11,BC,00,0A,00,18,32,39,00,00,02,F6,4A,79,00,00
1250 data 02,F4,67,00,00,04,E3,49,61,00,00,50,0C,79,00,50
1260 data 00,00,02,F6,67,00,00,16,32,3C,00,12,4A,79,00,00
1270 data 02,F4,67,00,00,04,E3,49,61,00,00,30,3F,3C,00,01
1280 data 42,A7,3F,3C,00,01,3F,39,00,00,02,FC,42,A7,48,79
1290 data 00,00,03,00,3F,3C,00,09,4E,4E,DF,FC,00,00,00,14
1300 data 4A,40,66,00,00,1E,60,00,FE,84,14,30,00,14,E1,4A
1310 data 14,30,00,13,D4,41,11,82,00,13,E0,4A,11,82,00,14
1320 data 4E,75,20,3C,00,00,02,D6,61,00,00,46,61,00,00,4E
1330 data 60,00,FE,5A,42,67,2F,3C,87,65,43,21,3F,3C,00,01
1340 data 3F,39,00,00,02,FE,3F,39,00,00,02,F8,3F,39,00,00
1350 data 02,FA,3F,39,00,00,02,FC,42,A7,48,79,00,00,03,00
1360 data 3F,3C,00,0A,4E,4E,DF,FC,00,00,00,1A,4A,40,4E,75
1370 data 2F,00,3F,3C,00,09,4E,41,5C,8F,4E,75,3F,3C,00,01
1380 data 4E,41,54,8F,48,40,4E,75,1B,45,2A,2A,2A,2A,2A,20
1390 data 46,6F,72,6D,61,74,74,69,6E,67,2D,2D,50,72,6F,67
1400 data 72,61,6D,20,53,2E,44,2E,20,2A,2A,2A,2A,2A,0A,0D
1410 data 0A,0D,20,5B,46,31,5D,20,53,69,64,65,28,73,29,20
1420 data 2E,2E,2E,2E,2E,2E,2E,2E,3A,20,20,32,0A,0D,20,5B
1430 data 46,32,5D,20,54,72,61,63,6B,73,20,2E,2E,2E,2E,2E
1440 data 2E,2E,2E,2E,3A,20,38,30,0A,0D,20,5B,46,33,5D,20
1450 data 53,65,63,74,6F,72,73,2F,74,72,61,63,6B,20,2E,2E
1460 data 3A,20,20,39,0A,0D,20,5B,46,34,5D,20,44,72,69,76
1470 data 65,20,2E,2E,2E,2E,2E,2E,2E,2E,2E,2E,3A,20,20,41
1480 data 0A,0D,20,5B,46,38,5D,20,46,6F,72,6D,61,74,20,2E
1490 data 2E,2E,2E,0A,0D,5B,46,31,30,5D,20,51,75,69,74,20,21
1500 data 0A,0D,0A,0D,00,46,6F,72,6D,61,74,74,69,6E,67,2E
```

```
1510  data 20,50,6C,65,61,73,65,20,77,61,69,74,2E,2E,2E,0A
1520  data 0D,00,2A,2A,20,41,6E,20,65,72,72,6F,72,20,6F,63
1530  data 63,75,72,72,65,64,20,21,21,20,2A,2A,0A,0D,00,00
1540  data 00,01,00,50,00,50,00,09,00,00,00,00,00,00,00,02
1550  data 24,08,12,08,12,08,12,08,26,0A,04,06,06,04,0E,08
1560  data 0C,0E,12,0A,10,06,12,0E,1A,08,34,1E,06,06,06,08
1570  data 00,00,00,00,00,00,00,00,00,00,00,00,00,00,00,00
1580  data *
1590  close 1:if s<> 48541 then print"ERROR IN DATA!":end
1610  print "Ok."
```

Some comments about the program:

- The only way to copy a normal diskette to an extended-capacity diskette is file by file. The operating system will not copy the disks directly because of the different disk formats.

- It is not directly possible to use an extended-capacity diskette as a TOS system disk, because there is no loader in the boot sector. To make such a diskette bootable, the boot sector of another diskette must be copied and modified with a disk monitor to take into account the parameters of the extended-capacity diskette.

- Do not use extended-capacity diskettes for storing very important and unique data. If the diskettes are not very high quality, one or more sectors can go bad in the inner tracks.

3.2.2 The BIOS parameter block

Back to theory. As we mentioned before, the BIOS parameter block (BPB) is made up of a variety of information. Let's take a closer look at this BPB.

Some entries in this parameter block will look familiar, because they are also present in the boot sector. The BPB is created by calling the BIOS command GETBPB (number 7), provided the diskette was changed in the meantime. Unlike the boot sector, the data in the BPB is in the normal 16-bit format. It is in the following order:

recsize	- Sector size in bytes	(512)
clsiz	- Cluster size in sectors	(2)
clsizb	- Cluster size in bytes	(1024)
rdlen	- Number of directory sectors	(7)

fsiz	- FAT size in sectors	(5)
fatrec	- Start sector of the second FAT	(6)
datrec	- First data sector	(rdlen+fsiz+fatrec=18)
numcl	- Number of data clusters	(711)
bflags	- FAT entry size in bit 0: 0=12 bits, 1=16 bits	(0)

The numbers in parentheses are the typical contents of the entries for a double-sided diskette.

Now we'll take a look at a program that reads the BIOS parameter block and analyzes it. The construction of the program is fairly simple. First a prompt that contains the title is displayed. This prompt asks you to enter a letter from the keyboard. This letter is either a drive specifier (a, b, c, or d) or the letter q. Pressing <q> ends the program and returns you to the Desktop.

After this input, the program tests to see if a valid letter was entered. If not, the program is restarted. (If a <q> is entered, the program will end).

The valid letter entered will then be converted to the value required for the GETBPB call (0-3) by subtracting a. The GETBPB will then be called. The address of the BPB will be returned in register D0.

The entries in the BPB can now be read, printed in hexadecimal, and given appropriate labels. All of the information about the diskette can then be seen at a glance.

Here is the program, written with the *AssemPro* assembler:

```
;** BPB-Analyzer S.D. **

run:
        move.l  #prompt,d0
        bsr     pmsg                ;Prompt output
        bsr     getkey              ;input the drive A-D
        cmp     #'q',d0             ;Quit ?
        beq     quit                ;yes => Desktop
        move    d0,d6               ;save charavter
        bsr     pcrlf               ;CR output

        sub     #'a',d6             ;value to small
        bmi     run                 ;false input
        cmp     #3,d6
        bgt     run                 ;false input
```

```
        move    d6,-(sp)            ;Device-Nr.
        move    #7,-(sp)
        trap    #13                 ;GETBPB-Function
        addq.l  #4,sp

        tst.l   d0
        beq     run                 ;Error !
        move.l  d0,a5               ;store BPB-Address

        bsr     pnext
        move.l  #bps,d0
        bsr     pline               ;"Bytes per Sector"

        bsr     pnext
        move.l  #spc,d0
        bsr     pline               ;"Sectors per Cluster"
        bsr     pnext
        move.l  #bpc,d0
        bsr     pline               ;"Bytes per Cluster"

        bsr     pnext
        move.l  #dirsec,d0
        bsr     pline               ;"Directory-Sectors"

        bsr     pnext
        move.l  #fatsec,d0
        bsr     pline               ;"FAT-Sectors"

        bsr     pnext
        move.l  #fat2s,d0
        bsr     pline               ;"Start-Sector of 2. FAT"

        bsr     pnext
        move.l  #datsec,d0
        bsr     pline               ;"Start-Sector of Data"

        bsr     pnext
        move.l  #datc,d0
        bsr     pline               ;"Data cluster"
        move    #'$',d0
        bsr     pchar               ;"$" output
        move    #12,d0              ;12 Bit
        btst    #0,(a5)             ;correct ?
        beq     bits12              ;yes
        move    #16,d0              ;else 16 Bit
```

```
bits12:
        bsr     phexbyt
        move.l  #fatbit,d0
        bsr     pline           ;"Bits per FAT-entry"
        bra     run             ;ready => New start

quit:                           ; Exit to Desktop
        clr     -(sp)
        trap    #1

getkey:                         ;Get Key -> D0
        move    #1,-(sp)
        trap    #1
        and.l   #$ff,d0
        addq.l  #2,sp
        rts

pline:                          ;Print Line/CR
        bsr     pmsg
pcrlf:                          ;Print CR,LF
        move    #10,d0
        bsr     pchar
        move    #13,d0
pchar:                          ;Print Character D0
        move    d0,-(sp)
        move    #2,-(sp)
        trap    #1
        addq.l  #4,sp
        rts

pmsg:                           ;Print Line (D0)
        move.l  d0,-(sp)
        move    #9,-(sp)
        trap    #1
        addq    #6,sp
        rts

pnext:                          ;get next word and output
        move    #'$',d0
        bsr     pchar           ;"$" output
        move    (a5)+,d0

phexword:                       ;Print Hex-Word D0
        moveq   #3,d1
        bra     phex1
```

```
phexbyt:                        ;Print Hex-Byte
        moveq   #1,d1
        rol.l   #8,d0

phex1:
        rol.l   #4,d0
        move.l  d0,-(sp)
        move.l  d1,-(sp)
        bsr     phexnib         ;one Nibble (0-F) output
        move.l  (sp)+,d1
        move.l  (sp)+,d0
        dbra    d1,phex1
        rts

phexnib:
        and.l   #$7f,d6
        swap    d0
        and.l   #$0f,d0
        add.b   #$30,d0
        cmp.b   #$3a,d0
        bcs     phexn
        add.b   #7,d0

phexn:
        bra     pchar           ;Nibble output

prompt:     dc.b "*** BPB-Analyzer S.D. ***",10,13
            dc.b "Input disk drive (a-d) or",10,13
            dc.b "'q' for Quit : ",0
bps:        dc.b " Bytes per Sector",0
spc:        dc.b " Sectors per Cluster",0
bpc:        dc.b " Bytes per Cluster",0
dirsec:     dc.b " Directory-Sectors",0
fatsec:     dc.b " FAT-Sector",0
fat2s:      dc.b ": Start-Sector 2.FAT",0
datsec:     dc.b ": Start-Sector of data",0
datc:       dc.b " Data-Cluster",0
fatbit:     dc.b " Bits per FAT-entry",10,13,0

    end
```

Here is the BASIC loader. It creates the BPB analysis program as **BPBANA.TOS** on the diskette:

```
1000   open"R",1,"a:bpbana.tos",16
1010   field#1,16 as bin$
1020   a$="":for i=1 TO 16:read d$:if d$="*"then 1050
```

```
1030  a=val("&H"+d$):s=s+a:a$=a$+chr$(a):next
1040  lset bin$=a$:rec=rec+1:put 1,rec:goto 1020
1050  data 60,1A,00,00,02,44,00,00,00,00,00,00,00,00,00,00
1060  data 00,00,00,00,00,00,00,00,00,00,00,00,20,3C,00,00
1070  data 01,54,61,00,00,FA,61,00,00,CA,B0,7C,00,71,67,00
1080  data 00,BE,3C,00,61,00,00,D0,9C,7C,00,61,6B,DE,BC,7C
1090  data 00,03,6E,D8,3F,06,3F,3C,00,07,4E,4D,58,8F,4A,80
1100  data 67,CA,2A,40,61,00,00,D4,20,3C,00,00,01,9A,61,00
1110  data 00,A2,61,00,00,C6,20,3C,00,00,01,AC,61,00,00,94
1120  data 61,00,00,B8,20,3C,00,00,01,C1,61,00,00,86,61,00
1130  data 00,AA,20,3C,00,00,01,D4,61,00,00,78,61,00,00,9C
1140  data 20,3C,00,00,01,E7,61,00,00,6A,61,00,00,8E,20,3C
1150  data 00,00,01,F4,61,00,00,5C,61,00,00,80,20,3C,00,00
1160  data 02,09,61,00,00,4E,61,00,00,72,20,3C,00,00,02,20
1170  data 61,00,00,40,30,3C,00,24,61,00,00,48,30,3C,00,0C
1180  data 08,15,00,00,67,00,00,06,30,3C,00,10,61,00,00,5A
1190  data 20,3C,00,00,02,2E,61,00,00,1A,60,00,FF,30,42,67
1200  data 4E,41,3F,3C,00,01,4E,41,C0,BC,00,00,00,FF,54,8F
1210  data 4E,75,61,00,00,1A,30,3C,00,0A,61,00,00,06,30,3C
1220  data 00,0D,3F,00,3F,3C,00,02,4E,41,58,8F,4E,75,2F,00
1230  data 3F,3C,00,09,4E,41,5C,4F,4E,75,30,3C,00,24,61,E2
1240  data 30,1D,72,03,60,00,00,06,72,01,E1,98,E9,98,2F,00
1250  data 2F,01,61,00,00,0C,22,1F,20,1F,51,C9,FF,F0,4E,75
1260  data CC,BC,00,00,00,7F,48,40,C0,BC,00,00,00,0F,D0,3C
1270  data 00,30,B0,3C,00,3A,65,00,00,06,D0,3C,00,07,60,A2
1280  data 2A,2A,2A,20,42,50,42,2D,41,6E,61,6C,79,7A,65,72
1290  data 20,53,2E,44,2E,20,2A,2A,2A,0A,0D,49,6E,70,75,74
1300  data 20,64,69,73,6B,20,64,72,69,76,65,20,28,61,2D,64
1310  data 29,20,6F,72,0A,0D,27,71,27,20,66,6F,72,20,51,75
1320  data 69,74,20,3A,20,00,20,42,79,74,65,73,20,70,65,72
1330  data 20,53,65,63,74,6F,72,00,20,53,65,63,74,6F,72,73
1340  data 20,70,65,72,20,43,6C,75,73,74,65,72,00,20,42,79
1350  data 74,65,73,20,70,65,72,20,43,6C,75,73,74,65,72,00
1360  data 20,44,69,72,65,63,74,6F,72,79,2D,53,65,63,74,6F
1370  data 72,73,00,20,46,41,54,2D,53,65,63,63,74,6F,72,00
1380  data 3A,20,53,74,61,72,74,2D,53,65,63,74,6F,72,20,32
1390  data 2E,46,41,54,00,3A,20,53,74,61,72,74,2D,53,65,63
1400  data 74,6F,72,20,6F,66,20,64,61,74,61,00,20,44,61,74
1410  data 61,2D,43,6C,75,73,74,65,72,00,20,42,69,74,73,20
1420  data 70,65,72,20,46,41,54,2D,65,6E,74,72,79,0A,0D,00
1430  data 00,00,00,02,3C,0E,0E,0E,0E,0E,0E,26,00,00,00
1440  data *
1450  close 1:if s<> 40341 then print"ERROR IN DATA!":end
1470  print "Ok."
```

When the computer is turned on, the BPB data are not available. The operating system doesn't create the BPB until after booting, when the number of connected drives and their designations are known.

If you have an early model of the ST (without TOS in ROM), the System Disk must first be booted. Booting also occurs if the computer contains an operating system but the disk contains a bootable operating system (TOS.IMG) and the boot sector is executable.

Booting takes place in four steps:

1) The boot sector is loaded and the boot program contained in it is executed.

2) The FAT and the directory are loaded from the current diskette. The loader searches for the given filename (usually TOS.IMG). If it is not found, it will return an error message.

3) TOS.IMG is loaded at memory address $40000.

4) The loaded program is started.

The file TOS.IMG, for its part, consists of three parts:

- A *relocator*, which is a program that moves the operating system to the address at which it was intended to run ($6100). This program clears the screen, moves the TOS image block to its original address and then starts it there.

- The operating system data (BIOS, XBIOS).

- The GEM data and the Desktop program.

As you can see, the construction of the operating system in the file TOS.IMG is pretty complicated. The built-in TOS, which is contained in 6 PROM chips (Programmable Read Only Memory), is naturally somewhat shorter because it contains only the operating system with GEM and no relocator.

Let's continue looking at data structures on the disk with a discussion of the construction and management of the directory.

3.3 The directory

On single-sided disks the directory starts at track 1, sector 3 and occupies 7 sectors. In each entry it stores a whole set of data in addition to the filename and extension, data which is more or less important for the management of the diskette.

Each entry in the directory consists of 32 bytes, which contain all of the information about the file. These 32 bytes are divided into eight data fields, which are constructed as follows:

1) Filename   8 bytes
2) File type (extension) 3 bytes
3) Attribute   1 byte
4) Reserved   10 bytes
5) Time   2 bytes
6) Date   2 bytes
7) First cluster   2 bytes
8) File size   4 bytes

The first field contains the filename. This name consists of ASCII characters, letters and numbers only. Furthermore, only uppercase letters are used. The name is limited to eight characters. If the name has fewer than eight characters, the remaining characters will be blank spaces.

If the first byte of a name is zero, it means that the entry has never been used. If the file was already used and then erased, this byte will contain a 229 ($E5). If the first character of the name is a period (.), the entry is for a special subdirectory: a *folder*.

The following field contains the file type, also called the *extension*. This extension is limited to three characters (such as PRG, TOS, BAS, etc.) and is also padded with spaces. Again, only uppercase letters are used.

After this comes the file attribute byte. It contains a bit code for the status of this entry or file. The meanings of these bits are as follows:

Bit	Meaning when set (1)	Bit	Meaning when set (1)
0	read only	1	hidden file
2	system file	3	entry is the disk name
4	entry is a file	5	file was changed

After this byte are 10 bytes which are not used. They are reserved and may be used by later versions of TOS.

Following these are two bytes which contain the time of the last modification of the file. The time is specially coded to save space. The 16 bits of the time entry are divided into three sections: hours, minutes, and seconds. This division looks like this:

```
Example:   19:21:34

Hour   Minute  Second/2
10011  010101  10001
```

The clock in the ST reports the time only in two-second increments, which is why the lowest five bits of the time contain a 17.

The next field in the directory contains the date of the last modification of the file. The division into year, month, and day is done like the time. Only seven bits are reserved for the year, which is why the number 1980 must be added to the value returned.

```
Example:  5/12/1986

Year     Month Day
0000110  0101  01100
```

The seventh field of the directory contains the number of the first cluster on the disk which can be used by a file. Files are stored on the disk starting with this cluster, which usually consists of two sectors. More information about what happens after this can be found in the next section.

The last field contains the length of the file in bytes. It should be noted that fewer bytes may be read than are indicated here, which also depends on the FAT. The file length should only be seen as the maximum file length.

With this information about the construction of the directory on the diskette, you can now analyze the division of the diskette using a disk monitor. Many results can be obtained by changing the values, but most of these manipulations lead to unpleasant results. For this reason, it is a good idea to work with a copy of the diskette rather than risk destroying the original.

If we wanted to write a program which read the directory of a disk, we would have to prepare a buffer for the expected data before the corresponding operating system function was called. The address of this buffer is designated the Disk Transfer Address (DTA).

This buffer is 44 bytes long and must be specified to the operating system by calling a special function. Once this is done, the search for directory entries can begin. The function SFIRST (Search FIRST) looks for the first matching entry in the directory, and SNEXT (Search NEXT) looks for additional entries. Entries which are found by either function are loaded into the buffer at the DTA.

After calling one of these functions, the buffer contains all of the information that also appears in the directory window on the Desktop. The division of the data is as follows:

Byte(s)	Contents
0...20	Reserved
21	File attribute
22,23	Time of modification
24,25	Date of modification
26...29	File size in bytes (LO, HI)
30...43	Filename and extension

The machine language routine below sets the DTA and then searches the directory for the specified filename. If the name given is simply *.*, the first entry that corresponds to the given attribute will be returned. If no matching entry is present, the function will return error number -33 (File not found) in register D0. Otherwise this register will contain zero.

```
        MOVE.L  #BUFFER,-(SP)    * Pass DTA
        MOVE    #$1A,-(SP)       * SETDTA function number
        TRAP    #1               * Call operating system
        ADDQ.L  #6,SP            * Repair stack
        MOVE    #%11001,-(SP)    * File type: all files
        MOVE.L  #NAME,-(SP)      * Address of the filename
        MOVE    #$4E,-(SP)       * SFIRST function number
        TRAP    #1               * Call operating system
        ADDQ.L  #8,SP            * Repair stack
        TST     D0               * Found
        BNE     NOTHING          * no
        etc.

BUFFER: .ds.b   44               * Space for the data
NAME:   .ds.b   "*.*",0          * All names allowed
```

To search for the next entry, all we need is:

```
MOVE     #$4F,-(SP)      * SNEXT function number
TRAP     #1              * Call operating system
ADDQ.L   #2,SP           * Repair stack
TST      D0              * Found
BNE      NOTHING         * no
```

We can easily write a program to output the directory of a diskette to the printer, for example. Such a program, which prints the entire directory including the contents of all folders, is found in section 5.3.

If you look at the directory in the Desktop, you will see the name, extension, date, time, and length of the file. When you then click a program, the operating system needs to know not only where the file begins on the disk, but also where the rest of the file is located. This information is contained in the FAT, which we'll look at next.

3.4 The FAT

The FAT (File Allocation Table) normally occupies five sectors on a single-sided diskette. It usually starts at track 0, sector 2 of side 0. The size of this table varies depending on the format used. The table is used to store the distribution of each file on the disk.

The reason for this lies in the fact that a file does not necessarily consist of consecutive sectors. Sectors which used to belong to a deleted file are released for storing new data. A new file being written to the disk would be assigned to such free sectors. Occupied sectors are simply skipped.

Each sector must therefore have an entry in the FAT to be recognized as either free or allocated. In order to keep the size of the FAT down, every two sectors are grouped together and designated as a cluster. Clusters are numbered from 2 to the end of the disk, and the FAT then contains only one entry for every two sectors.

Each entry in the FAT is normally 12 bits long. Some formats use 16-bit entries, but we will not go into that here. Twelve-bit FAT entries mean that two entries occupy three bytes.

The first two entries of the FAT contain format information, which is why the numbering starts at 2. Every other entry represents a cluster. A zero in an entry means that the corresponding cluster is free.

Naturally, this does not mean that the sectors don't contain any data, since a deleted file isn't actually removed from the disk. When a file is deleted, all that happens is that the first letter of the name in the directory is changed to $E5 and the cluster belonging to the file are released with zeroes in the FAT. The data itself is still present, but hard to find.

If a FAT entry contains $FF7, the cluster is unusable. Such clusters are recognized and marked during formatting. If a disk is physically damaged in some way (e.g., scratched), you will notice that the capacity announced after formatting is less usual. However, if such an error occurs in track 0 or 1, the entire diskette is unusable, because these tracks are supposed to contain the boot sector, the FAT, and the directory.

When a file is to be loaded, the operating system takes the number of the first cluster of the file from the directory entry. The FAT entry of this cluster then contains the number of the next cluster in the file. The FAT entry of this cluster in turn contains the next number, and so on, until an entry contains $FF. This means that this cluster is the last in the file.

A disk monitor can also be used to make changes to the FAT. However, the probability of data loss from doing this is extremely high—be sure to make a copy of the disk before you change anything in the FAT.

3.5 Program construction

The Atari ST has a large amount of memory which can hold more than one program at a time. In fact, it is possible to place several programs in memory at the same time and execute them. Simple examples are the desk accessories, which run in the "background" while an application is running.

This open memory division causes a problem. When we used to program 8-bit computers, we were used to writing machine language programs that would be stored at a specific location in memory and would run there. This is because the machine language program would address the memory directly or branch via a specific address.

But this is impossible on the Atari ST. How can a programmer know in advance where his program will be loaded, and whether or not another program is already resident?

Another problem is that the operating system must know the size of the program and how much memory it needs to run. If the program needs additional memory for storing information, this memory may not be overwritten by other programs.

As you can see, it won't work if a program file on the disk contains nothing more than the program data themselves. The construction of such a file is the subject of this section.

An executable program on the disk (.PRG, .TOS, and .TTP files) is divided into four segments. These segments are the file header, the program with data field, the symbol table (if one exists) and relocation data (if present).

Let's look at the first part: the header.

3.5.1 The program header

The header is 14 bytes long and contains the lengths of the individual segments. The construction of the header is as follows:

Byte #	Contents
$00,$01	$601A, the machine language command BRA *+$1A
$02-$05	Length of the program segment (text)
$06-$09	Length of the data segment (data)
$0A-$0D	Length of the additional storage segment (bss)
$0E-$11	Length of the symbol table
$12-$1B	00, reserved

The first entry is a machine language command which branches the program execution to the start of the program segment. Following this is the length of the program segment. This segment, generally called the "text" segment, contains the program itself. All addresses which the program uses are set up so that the start of the program is taken as address 0. Data contained in this segment are not changed.

The next entry contains the length of the data segment. This segment must follow the program immediately. In a machine language program, the separation between the text and data segments is made with a `data` instruction. The initialized data, such as strings or tables, are stored here. Uninitialized data, like buffers for disk operations or temporary storage, are contained in the next segment.

The fourth entry of the header contains the length of this additional storage. This memory area is called `bss`. After the program is loaded this memory area will be made available to the program. At the same time, other applications will be prevented from using it. Its contents are not defined—it must be filled by the program. The advantage of the `bss` segment over the data segment is that this area does not have to be stored in the disk file.

Entry number five contains the length of the symbol table. Such a table is seldom present, because it plays no role in the function of the program. A symbol table is appended to the program by a compiler or assembler if the you desire. The symbols correspond to the labels used in the source program for routines or variables. The advantage of such a table is that a symbolic debugger like SID can include labels in a disassembly of the program. Once the test and development phase of a program is completed, the symbol table should be left off to save space.

Each entry in the symbol table is seven words long, and contains the name, type, and value of the symbol:

Byte	Contents
$0-$7	Symbol name, ends with zero
$8-$9	Symbol type: relocatable, global, or external
$A-$C	Value, such as address, register number, direct value, etc.

The entire symbol table of a program can be read and printed with the program `NM68`. To do this, enter the follwing line from the command prompt:

`NM68 `*`filename`*

By adding `>prn:` to the command line, the output of `NM68` can be directed to the printer. Otherwise the output is displayed on the screen.

Back to the construction of the program header: The remaining bytes from $12 to $1B are reserved for later use, and must be zero.

Immediately following the header is the program. As we said, the program can really only work at address $0000. In order to make it run at the address at which it was loaded, all absolute addresses which occur in the program must be changed by adding the actual starting address of the program to the addresses contained in the program. But how does the operating system know that it has to make these changes, or where the absolute address are located in the program? The answer is called a *relocation table*.

3.5.2 The relocation table

Following the symbol table in the program file is the relocation table. This table contains the distances between the longwords which must be relocated. The first longword in this table specifies the offset of the first longword to be changed from the start of the program. After this, bytes are used whose values give the distances between the current longword and the next longword to be changed. If the distance between two such longwords is greater than 254, bytes of value 1 will be inserted until the distance to the next longword is less than 255.

The first byte which contains a zero indicates the end of the relocation table. This is also the end of the entire program file on the disk.

When a program is loaded, the operating system places the program at a free location in memory and then relocates it. The distribution of the program in memory is somewhat different than it was on the disk. Before the actual program (which the `data` and `bss` segments follow) lies what is called the *base page*. This 256-byte-long base page is another header, which contains information about the actual distribution of the program in memory. The base page is laid out as follows:

Byte	Length	Contents
00	4	Start address of the working memory
04	4	HI address of the working memory + 1
08	4	Start address of the program
0C	4	Length of the program segment in bytes
10	4	Start address of the data segment
14	4	Length of the data segment in bytes
18	4	Start address of the `bss` segment
1C	4	Length of the `bss` segment in bytes
2C	4	Pointer to the "environment string"
80	80	Command line text (for `.TTP` programs)

All other entries in the base page are reserved.

The computer isn't the only one that needs the information in the base page. A program can also make good use of it. The best example of this is the command line. If the program is of type .TTP, the operating system displays a dialog box when the program is called in which the user can enter the command line. This line can then be evaluated by the program.

To get the address of the command line, a command sequence like the following must be at the start of the program:

```
run:   MOVE.L  4(SP),A0      ;Address of the base page
       LEA     $80(A0),A0
```

A0 now contains the address of the command line, and the line can be processed.

3.6 Hard disk format

Now let's turn to the hard disk. Because of its enormous storage capacity, the hard disk's organization is not quite so simple as that of the diskette. A hard disk is divided into four individual sections, each of which contains a boot sector. These individual sections are called *partitions*.

The first sector on the hard disk (logical sector 0) contains the information about the partitioning of the hard disk. This information is stored as follows:

Byte	Name	Meaning
$1C2	hd_siz	Total size of the hard disk in logical sectors
$1C6	p0_flg	Partition 0 exists if p0_flg>0 If bit 7, booting starts here
$1C7	p0_id	Partition ID (GEM)
$1CA	p0_st	Logical sector # of the first sector in the partition
$1CE	p0_siz	Size of the partition in sectors
$1D2	p1_flg	
$1D3	p1_id	see above, partition 1
$1D6	p1_st	

Byte	Name	Meaning
$1DA	p1_siz	
$1DE	p2_flg	
$1DF	p2_id	see above, partition 2
$1E2	p2_st	
$1E6	p2_siz	
$1EA	p3_flg	
$1EB	p3_id	see above, partition 3
$1EE	p3_st	
$1F2	p3_siz	
$1F6	bsl_st	Starting sector of the bad sector list
$1FA	bsl_cnt	Number of defective sectors

The bad sector list is created when the diskette is formatted. It contains a list of the defective sectors which could not be formatted. The table is usually stored at the end of the hard disk.

The operating system uses the variable `p*_flg` to determine whether the given partition exists or not (`p*_flg` not equal to zero). The first sector of each partition contains a boot sector which contains the BPB. The operating system boots from the first boot sector whose `p*_flg` has bit 7 set.

Note: A program for analyzing and displaying the partition parameters is found in Section 5.1.1.4.

Chapter Four

The disk drives

The disk drives

Probably the most common media for data storage are floppy diskettes. These disks, measuring 3 1/2 and 5 1/4 inches in diameter have certain advantages. The first is the price. If a 3 1/2" diskette costs about two dollars and stores 360K of data, this comes out to a little over a half a cent per kilobyte. The price per kilobyte is even less with 5 1/4" diskettes. Since no technical problems prevent the use of 5 1/4" diskettes on the Atari, this cost advantage might play a role in which diskette format you'll select. Some ST owners have connected both 3 1/2" and 5 1/4" drives to their computers.

Another advantage that diskettes have over hard disks is that you can easily switch between different diskettes. This means that, at least in theory, a disk drive can manage an unlimited amount of data. Also, diskettes are well-suited for copying, exchanging and backing up programs and data.

But we should also mention the disadvantages. Except for storage on audio cassette tapes, diskettes are the slowest form of data storage. The Atari ST drives compare favorably with the competition because they allow relatively fast data transfer, using various technical tricks in the ST.

Let's look at floppy diskettes in detail.

4.1 Floppy diskette functions

When the ST computer needs data from a floppy diskette in one of its drives, various functions are initiated within the disk drive itself. First of all the *drive motor* is switched on. If two drives are connected, both of them will run, because the signal line responsible for the motor control from the ST is connected to both drives. The advantage of this is that copying from drive to drive is faster—time isn't wasted waiting for the motors to reach the correct speed.

The next step is to select a single drive's address. This is done via the *drive select line*. If a disk drive detects that it is being accessed, the BUSY light goes on and shows that the device is operating.

Now comes the decision whether data should be read from or written to the diskette. First the ST must specify the exact track on which the data lies.

These tracks are rings that are organized concentrically on the diskette. The read/write head is then moved to a location on the diskette by a small arm, gliding above the rotating diskette to this track's location.

The stored data is distributed on these tracks with a system that records and reads the data items as tiny magnetic pulses on the surface of the diskette. To make the distribution of data on a track a little easier to manage, the tracks are divided into *sectors*. Each track has nine such sectors. In turn, each sector contains 512 bytes of actual data. A sector really contains more data than stated, but this additional data is not immediately accessible. (We'll discuss these special bytes in a later section).

The read/write head moving over the rotating magnetic diskette contains a small coil. This coil serves as a magnetic receiver, and recognizes the magnetic pulses that represent the data bits. This method is similar to that used by an audio tape recorder—but much greater precision is required for a diskette. The read/write head can exactly locate every one of almost three million bits on a disk of about 30 square centimeters—the surface area of a 3 1/2" diskette. A single byte, which consists of 8 bits, is stored in a surface of only 0.008 square millimeters!

If the computer needs data from the diskette, it requests an individual sector from the disk. Through a complicated process, the disk controller built into the computer decides which of the stream of bits arriving at the read/write head belong to the sector. These data bits are then selected, and its resulting 512 bytes are sent to the computer.

All of these procedures present many technical problems for the disk drive manufacturers. The mechanism that positions the head must place it exactly on the desired track (approximately 0.2 mm wide). Then the magnetic pulses which come from the rotating disk must be recognized as zeros or ones. At 300 rotations per minute, there are only about 0.5 microseconds available to read each bit. It's the job of the drive's electronics to sort through the desired information from a huge pool of bits. This is achieved through what are called *synchronization bytes*. The synchronization bytes are stored at the start of each sector on the disk.

As we have seen, a disk drive is an extremely complicated device. We'll only look at the rudimentary construction of the system that processes the information on the diskettes.

4.2.1 The DMA chip

Let's start with the ST computer itself. The disk drive sends the requested data through the cable, which arrive at the computer as a flood of bytes. This data must be placed somewhere in memory to be able to use it again. Most computers use their Central Processing Unit (CPU) to receive the data and place it in memory. This means that the speed at which data can be received is limited by the speed of the microprocessor.

The Atari ST does things differently, however. Data is received and distributed in memory by a special component which has direct access to the memory just like the CPU. This component is the DMA (Direct Memory Access) chip. The DMA chip is under the control of the CPU, but it performs its task completely independent of the processor. As a result, the CPU can perform other tasks while data is being transferred. Moreover, the DMA chip can move data much faster than the CPU could.

The result of this advanced feature is that a very high data transfer rate for diskette operations can be achieved—especially for hard disk operations.

The DMA chip occupies the following memory locations in the Atari ST:

$FF8604   FDC access/sector count. This is where the registers of the DMA chip or the FDC chip are accessed, the selection of which is determined by $FF8606

$FF8606   DMA mode/status. Bits 0-2 reflect the status of the DMA and FDC chips when reading. Writing to this 16-bit register sets the mode of the DMA chip.

$FF8609   DMA memory vector HI byte

$FF860B   DMA memory vector MID byte

$FF860D   DMA memory vector LO byte

These three bytes make up the 24-bit address at which or from which data is to be transferred by the DMA chip. These bytes must be stored in the order LO, MID, HI.

The DMA chip used in the ST is connected directly to the hard disk interface. The connection to the floppy disk drives is not tied directly to the DMA chip. Between this connection and the DMA chip is a component that prepares the serial data arriving from the disk drive or sends the data to the drive serially. This component is the *floppy diskette controller*, which also controls the functions of the drive. The next section explains the programming of these two devices.

4.2.2 The disk controller

This lengthy section deals with the WD1772 floppy diskette controller (hereafter referred to as the FDC, or simply the controller) used in the Atari ST. For the description of this component, we gathered all of the available information and data sheets on the chip that we could find. Naturally, this alone wasn't good enough for a comprehensive treatment, because theory and practice often differ from each other. It was necessary to experiment with the WD1772 ourselves to verify the information we had—and to discover deviations from this information.

As a result, this section contains more than enough information for those who just want an overview of the controller. This section also contains information for programmers who want to know how the FDC works, and want to control it directly from their own programs.

It's not necessary to program the FDC yourself for normal data exchange between the disk drive and the ST. Appropriate calls to the BIOS or XBIOS will handle this.

However, the operating system does not support all of the capabilities of the FDC. For programmers who want to develop a fast copy program or devise some form of copy protection, for example, these missing functions are quite important. If you want to create special disk formats, you cannot use the existing operating system routine for track formatting—you will have to write your own.

To use these functions in an application program, the controller must be programmed directly. This is only possible if you have a good knowledge of the FDC commands and the way they work.

This knowledge can save you hours of programming and debugging, only to find out that your idea would never work. An example of such an idea:

"If I read all of the tracks of a diskette into the computer with the READ TRACK command and then write all of the tracks onto another diskette with the WRITE TRACK command, I'd have the fastest copy program imaginable. And I could use this to make 'backups' of copy-protected disks. The READ TRACK command reads all of the information on the track (including the copy protection), and the WRITE TRACK command will write all of it back out again!"

If you actually wrote a program that worked this way, however, you would find that the copies that it created were unusable—and it wouldn't even copy an unprotected diskette.

After you have worked through this section and know how the FDC commands work and what they do, you'll see why the copy program above won't work. We are reasonably sure that the description of the controller is comprehensive enough to inhibit "ideas" of this sort.

Now to the description of the WD1772 (finally!). Developed by Western Digital, this chip incorporates all of the functions necessary for controlling a 5 1/4" drive. As the Atari ST demonstrates, the WD1772 can also control 3 1/2" drives. This capability of the WD1772 comes thanks to Sony, the developer of the 3 1/2" drive. Sony decided that a faster market introduction would be possible if the 3 1/2" drives were equipped with an interface compatible with 5 1/4" drives. From an ST owner's point of view, this means that you can also connect 5 1/4" drives to your computer.

But be careful with older disk drives—especially rebuilt or used ones—which can be had for very low prices. If you want to connect this type of device as a foreign drive, you may run into problems for the following reason:

The standard version of the WD177x series (the WD1770) is software compatible with the older FDC series WD179x and WD279x. But the WD1772 uses shorter *stepping rates* than these other models. The stepping rate is the time the controller waits between tracks when moving the read/write head across the disk. The four programmable times of the WD1772 are 2, 3, 5 and 6 ms, while on the WD1770 they are 6, 12, 20, and 30 ms. This means that the drive must be capable of changing tracks in a maximum of 6 ms. You should find the stepping rate information in the documentation for the drive under "TRACK TO TRACK."

Let's look at the FDC now and start with a brief summary of the features of this chip:

- 28-pin Dual-Inline-Package
- single 5V supply
- integral digital data separator
- integral write precompensation
- single and double write density
- integral motor control
- sector lengths of 128, 256, 512, or 1024 bytes
- fast stepping rates (2, 3, 5, and 6 ms)

We want to explain two of these points right now and we'll get to the rest in the following sections, in connection with the individual functions of the FDC.

1) The fact that the WD1772 is contained in a 28-pin package is important only for the development of a system in which an FDC is required. Since a 28-pin chip means less layout work than a 40-pin device, system developers are more likely to choose devices with fewer pins (assuming the features are equivalent).

2) The ability to operate the WD1772 in single or double density will not be treated in the course of the controller discussion. The reason for this is simple: In the Atari ST, the FDC is used in double-density mode. To use the controller in the single-density mode, the computer must be opened and wiring of the FDC changed. The result of this undertaking would be that only 50% as much information could be stored on a disk as before. Although it doesn't seem like there would be any reason to do this (after all, why would anyone throw away half the storage capacity?), it might be useful to do this in practice to create a disk format compatible with some other computer. Special cases like this are not of general interest, however. Since the FDC is already complicated enough, we won't burden you with capabilities which will probably never be used in the ST.

4.2.2.1 Pinout

We will start our detailed examination with the pinout of the FDC.

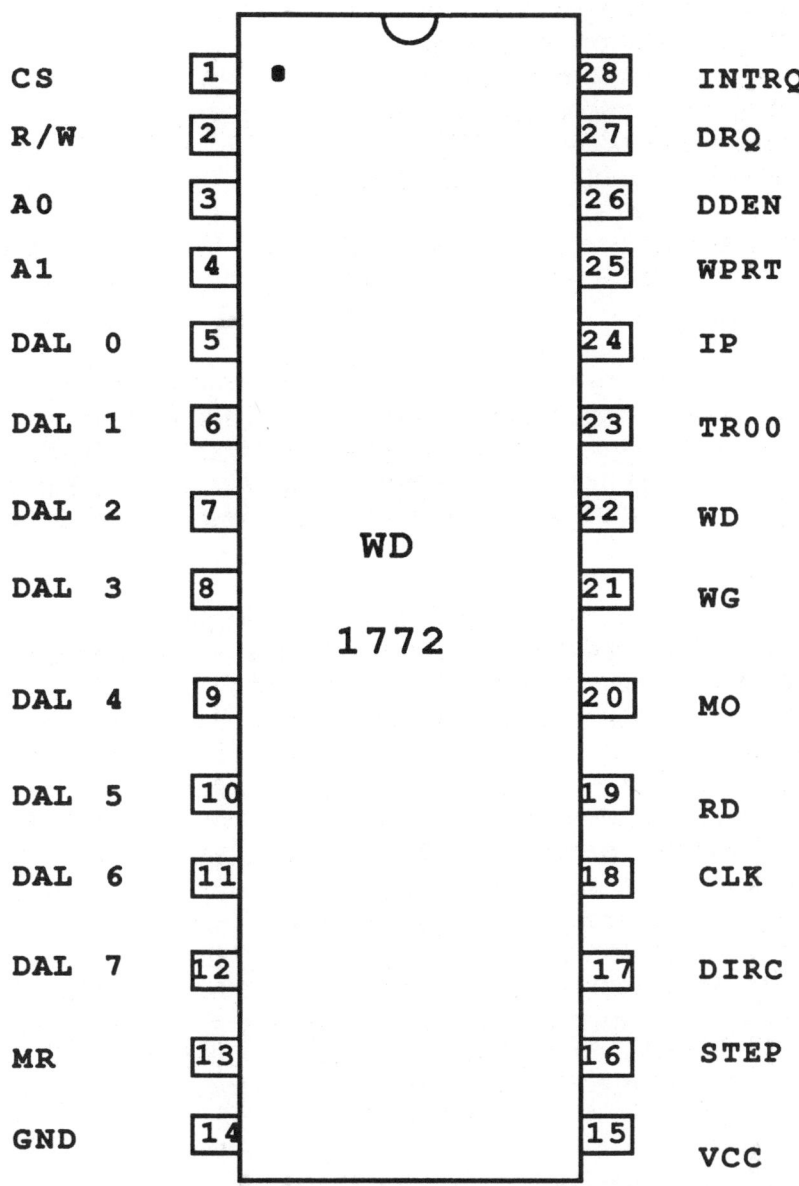

PIN 1   CS (CHIP SELECT)
A low signal on this input selects the chip and allows access to the registers. The CHIP SELECT connection is found on all peripheral components including the memory chips. Since they are all connected to the data bus of the processor, there has to be some way of keeping them from all trying to use the bus at once. The CHIP SELECT lines enable just one device for data transfer. In the ST, the FDC is selected by the DMA controller.

PIN 2   R/W (READ/WRITE)
The signal at this input controls the data direction. If it is high, the contents of the selected register are output on DAL0-DAL7, while if it is low, the data on DAL0-DAL7 is placed in the selected register.

PINS 3,4   A0,A1 (ADDRESS 0,1)
These two inputs select the FDC register. The WD1772 has 5 registers which are addressable by the computer system. But since two address lines can select only four registers, one address has two registers (A0=0 and A1=0). The signal on the R/W pin is used to decide between these two registers.

CS	A1	A0	R/W = 1	R/W = 0
0	0	0	Status reg.	Command reg.
0	0	1	Track reg.	Track reg.
0	1	0	Sector reg.	Sector reg.
0	1	1	Data reg.	Data reg.

The result is that the command register cannot be read and the status register cannot be written.

These pins are connected to the DMA controller and not the processor address bus. The FDC registers are selected via a control register in the DMA controller.

PINS 5-12   DAL0-DAL7 (DATA ACCESS LINE 0-7)
These eight lines make up the bidirectional data bus. The data between the computer system and the FDC registers are transferred over this bus. These lines, like the address lines, are connected to the DMA controller. The FDC registers are accessed indirectly via the data registers of the DMA controller, which is selected via the control register of the DMA controller.

PIN 13   MR (MASTER RESET)
After power is supplied to the FDC, the contents of its registers are purely random and the registers must be placed in a defined initial state. This is achieved by a low pulse (of at least 50µs) at this input.

This is usually done after the ST is turned on. Naturally, it is always possible to reset the FDC with the 68000's RESET command. But remember, the other devices connected to this common line will also be reset if you execute this command.

PIN 14   GND (GROUND)
Ground connection.

PIN 15   Vcc (POWER SUPPLY)
The +5V supply connection.

PIN 16   STEP (STEP)
This output sends a pulse to the drive for each step the read/write head is to be moved.

PIN 17   DIRC (DIRECTION)
The FDC uses the signal on this line to tell the drive the direction in which to the move when it encounters a STEP pulse. If this pin is high, a STEP pulse moves the head toward the center of the disk, while if it is low, a STEP pulse moves the head one track out.

PIN 18   CLK (CLOCK)
Like a microprocessor, a command issued to the FDC executes microprograms within it. This is why the FDC is supplied with a clock, just like a microprocessor, which controls the execution. This clock is also required for the timing of the serial data stream.

The clock is not created by the FDC itself but is taken from the outside via the CLK input. The clock frequency is 8 MHz.

PIN 19   RD (READ DATA)
The signal which the read/write head of the drive sends is connected to this input of the FDC. The data separator in the FDC separates the clock and data pulses, which are both contained in the signal.

PIN 20   MO (MOTOR ON)
          This output is used for motor control. The drive motors are started by the FDC for read, write, and seek operations.

PIN 21   WG (WRITE GATE)
          The data pulses which the FDC sends to the drive are first sent to a write amplifier instead of directly to the read/write head. If no data items are sent by the FDC, the input of this amplifier is open. Amplifiers with open inputs have the unpleasant property of being sensitive to stray voltages that might enter the connection cable. To keep such voltages from reaching the read/write head and thereby destroying data on the disk, the drives have a circuit which controls the write amplifier. For write operations, WRITE GATE is set to a high signal by the FDC. This enables the write amplifier, and the data pulses that arrive over the WRITE DATA line can be processed.

PIN 22   WD (WRITE DATA)
          The information to be written to the disk, consisting of data and clock pulses, is sent to the drive via this line.

PIN 23   TR00 (TRACK 00)
          The disk drives have a light barrier which detects when the read/write head is over track zero. When the head is over track zero, this input of the FDC is set to low.

PIN 24   IP (INDEX PULSE)
          The drive sends a pulse to this pin on each revolution of the disk, which the controller then uses for its operations. For example, it uses this signal to detect the start of track when reading or writing.

          The speed of the drive motor can also be measured by counting the index pulses in a given length of time.

          The index pulse on the 3 1/2" drives is created independent of the diskette. 3 1/2" diskettes, unlike 5 1/4" diskettes, do not have an index hole.

PIN 25   WPRT (WRITE PROTECT)
          This input is tested before the FDC attempts a write operation. If this input from the drive is placed low (write-protected diskette), the controller will terminate the write operation.

PIN 26   DDEN (DOUBLE DENSITY ENABLE)
The signal at this input determines the recording format with which the FDC works. A low signal at this pin puts the controller in the double-density mode, while a high places it in the single-density mode. In the Atari ST the WD1772 is always operated in the double-density mode because DDEN is connected to ground.

PIN 27   DRQ (DATA REQUEST)
This output, the condition of which is indicated by a bit in the status register, has the following meaning when it is placed high by the FDC:

a) For a read operation, a byte is in the data register which must now be read (data register full).

b) For a write operation the data register is empty and must be filled with the next byte to be written.

Reading or writing the data register resets the DRQ output and the DRQ status bit.

The DMA capability of the WD1772 rests on the existence of this output. In the Atari ST, this pin is connected to the DMA controller. During read and write operations, the DRQ status bit must be read to recognize when a data transfer takes place. The DMA controller handles this through the DRQ output.

PIN 28   INTRQ (INTERRUPT REQUEST)
After each command, this FDC output is set high. It is reset when the status is read. This connection is connected to the I/O port (bit 5) of the MFP 68901. To recognize when the FDC has finished a command, this port bit is read in a loop. It should be noted that this bit is inverted. The command is ended when the port bit is cleared.

It is possible to program the MFP so that a high on the INTRQ output generates an interrupt. This saves having to poll the port bit continually. The interrupt control is not used by the operating system.

4.2.2.2 Organization

To better understand the programming of the FDC, which is explained in detail later, it's a good idea to take a look at the function diagram of the WD1772 and then talk about the individual function blocks.

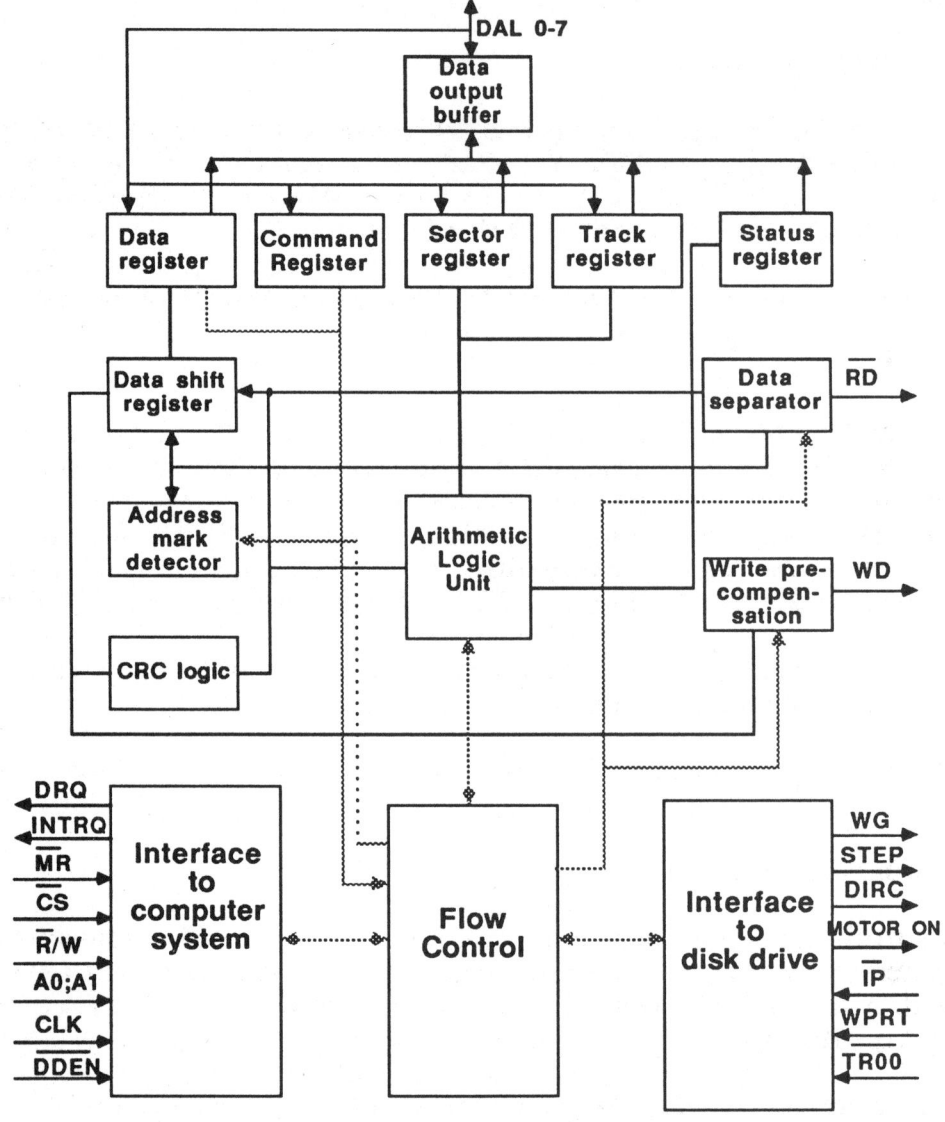

WD1772 organization

Data shift register (DSR)

During a read operation, the serial data which arrive over the READ DATA input (RD) are collected in this 8-bit shift register. For write operations the contents of this register are sent out in serial over the WRITE DATA output (WD). For some operations the data shift register is also used for temporary storage.

Data register (DR)

For a read/write operation, this register is used as temporary storage. When the DSR has received eight bits after a read operation, this information is transferred to the data register. For write operations, the next byte is transferred to the DSR after the DSR has sent a byte.

For a seek operation, the data register contains the number of desired track.

Track register (TR)

This register normally contains the track over which the read/write head is located—but there are exceptions to this. To keep the track register up to date, it is incremented by one for each step in and decremented by one for each step out. The commands RESTORE and SEEK increment or decrement the register every time. However, this is only true for the commands STEP, STEP IN and STEP OUT if the update flag (U bit) is set.

For write, read, and verify operations, the contents of the track register are compared with the track number recorded in the ID field.

The track register can be read and written, but it should not be loaded during an operation.

Sector register (SR)

For read and write operations, this register contains the number of the desired sector, which is compared with the sector number recorded in the ID field. After a READ ADDRESS command, the sector number from the ID field is in the register.

The sector register can be read and written, but it should not be loaded during an operation.

Command register (CR)

This register contains the command currently being executed. It can only be written because reading automatically selects the status register. The command register should not be loaded during an operation, except when the command is FORCE INTERRUPT.

Status register (STR)

The information found in this register indicates the status of the FDC/drive. The individual bits are partially dependent on the command being processed. The status register can only be read, whereby the byte read has the following meaning(s):

Bit 7 MOTOR ON
: This bit reflects the status of the MOTOR ON output. It is set for about one to two seconds after a command, if the busy bit is already cleared.

Bit 6 WRITE PROTECT
: After write operations, this bit indicates whether or not the diskette in the drive is write protected. If it is set, it also means that the desired write operation was not executed. The WPRT bit is set (in the case of a write-protected diskette) after a type 1 command. This bit is reset when an operation with a non-write-protected diskette takes place.

Bit 5 SPIN UP / RECORD TYPE
: SPIN UP: For type 1 commands this bit is set at the conclusion of the spin up sequence. This shows that the drive motor has (probably) reached its nominal rotation rate.

    RECORD TYPE: After a READ SECTOR command, this bit indicates whether the data field starts with a "normal" or an "erased" data mark.

    Bit 5 = 0, "normal" data mark ($FB)
    Bit 5 = 1, "erased" data mark ($F8)

Bit 4 RECORD NOT FOUND (RNF)
: If no correct ID field was found, this bit is set. This could be the case after a READ SECTOR, WRITE SECTOR, or READ ADDRESS command. However, after a READ

SECTOR command, the RNF bit can be set despite a correct ID field. This is the case if no data mark was found within the 43 bytes which follow the last CRC byte in the ID field.

Bit 3 CRC ERROR
This bit is set if the contents of the CRC field in the data field or the ID field do not match the contents of the CRC register.

Bit 2 LOST DATA / TRACK 00
LOST DATA: If no action is taken after a data request (indicated by the DRQ output or DRQ status bit) within the required time for a type 2 or type 3 command, this bit is set.

TRACK 00: For type 1 commands this bit is set when the read/write head is on track zero.

Bit 1 DATA REQUEST / INDEX
DATA REQUEST: This bit is set when data is ready or required for type 2 and type 3 commands. It is reset by reading or writing the data register.

INDEX: For type 1 commands this bit is set during an index pulse.

Bit 0 BUSY
This command is set during the execution of a command.

CRC Logic

To avoid read errors, a process must be used that supports high data security. The process used here generates 16-bit checksum from the written data according to a specific algorithm and this checksum is written after the data on the diskette.

When these data items are read again the checksum is generated again according to the same algorithm. If this checksum matches the recorded checksum, you can be almost 100 percent certain that the data was read correctly. The complicated algorithm makes it highly improbable that the checksums would match if there were read errors.

These 16-bit checksums are called Cyclic Redundancy Checks (CRC). The CRC logic is responsible for the creation and control of the checksums. The calculation is performed in hardware to speed the operation up. The hardware calculates the sum using the following polynomial:

$$CRC(x) = x^{16} + x^{12} + x^5 + 1.$$

Arithmetic Logic Unit (ALU)

The ALU is used for register modification (increment, decrement). The ALU is also used for comparisons between registers and the information contained on the disk in the ID fields.

Address Mark Detector

This detector is probably the most important part of the FDC. As its name indicates, this part is capable of recognizing an address mark. This mark designates the start of an ID field (index address mark) or the start of a data field (data address mark).

But why do we need a special detector? As an example, let's take the value $FE. The controller interprets this value as an index address mark. Even without a special detector it isn't difficult to find this $FE. However, the problem becomes clear when we consider that this value can occur in a data field, where it must not be evaluated as an index address mark. How is it possible to distinguish one $FE from the other $FE? The address mark detector takes care of this for us.

As we mentioned before, the recorded information consists of more than just data pulses—clock pulses are also found in it. For read operations these are filtered out of the signal by the data separator and sent to the address mark detector.

For a WRITE TRACK command, values which are larger than $F4 require special handling. The common feature of these values is that they are written without clock pulses. Values written like this consist only of data pulses. When this information is read, no clock pulses will arrive from the data separator because none are present in the signal. The address mark detector is activated by the absence of clock pulses. It can only recognize an address mark when it is written without clock pulses.

There is another problem, however. This one you probably didn't know anything about, because we have always talked about "complete" data bytes. These bytes are recorded in serial, but the start of a byte is not marked in any way. When eight bits are collected in the DSR by a read operation, we can't just assume that they belong to a single data byte. They could just as well be four bits from each of two different data bytes.

The address mark detector will recognize an address mark only if the collection of data bytes happens to be byte-synchronized. It's easy to see that we can't leave this up to chance—there has to be a way of recognizing the start of a byte. This is done through the synchronization byte. These are written (three of them) before each address mark when formatting a track. The SYNC bytes, like the address marks, don't contain any clock pulses, and therefore they activate the address mark detector.

The controller, informed of the status of the address mark detector, reads the serial data bits until the contents of the DSR correspond to a SYNC byte. After this, the next bit must be the first bit of the following byte.

One thing should be noted, however. The bytes read can be corrupted while the detector is enabled (see the READ TRACK command). When and why are the bytes corrupted? If the detector is activated by missing clock pulses, the FDC assumes that SYNC bytes and an address mark follow. In the synchronization phase (following the reconstruction of a SYNC byte), some of the data bits are discarded. If the detector "accidentally" trespasses on a data field looking for an address mark, the data up to the time the "false alarm" is recognized and changed. Since the address mark detector is so sensitive, it overreacts to missing clock pulses, and is switched off when ID or data fields are being read.

Data Separator

The data separator was actually described along with the address mark detector. We will mention here again that the data separator's job is to remove the clock pulses from the signal read and to send them to the address mark detector.

The interface to the computer system

The processor interface consists of eight bi-directional data lines (DAL0-DAL7), the two address lines (A0, A1), the data request (DRQ), the interrupt request (INTRQ), the chip select (CS), the read/write line (R/W), the clock input (CLK), and the master reset input (MR). These connections carry the exchange of data and control signals between the processor and the FDC.

The interface to the drive

The controller receives the following information:

    1) whether a write-protected diskette is inserted (WPRT=1)
    2) whether the read/write head is over track 0 (TR00=0)
    3) whether the diskette completed a 360° revolution (IP=0)
    4) the serial data that was read

The signals which the controller sends to the drive are:

    1) turn the drive motor on (MOTOR ON=1)
    2) step the read/write head (STEP=1)
    3) the direction of the step (DIRC=0 or 1)
    4) turn on the write logic (WG=1)
    5) the serial data to be written (WD)

Process control

When a command is performed by the FDC, the individual functions must be turned on and off in a certain order. Moreover, data items are transferred between the FDC registers, calculations are made, input lines are read, and output line status is changed. The entire process, depending on the command, is controlled or supervised by the process control.

Read operations

Read operations generally take place only as a result of the READ SECTOR command. The other commands, which can also be used to read data from the diskette, are used only for diagnostic purposes and have no meaning for normal operation.

The sectors can be 128, 256, 512, or 1024 bytes long. The sector length is determined at formatting by the *length field* (the fourth byte in the ID field).

When a sector is to be read, the controller uses the length field to figure out how many bytes must be after the data address mark. An precondition for error-free reading of the data byte is that the address mark detector is turned off during this time. Otherwise it may create read errors.

Write operations

Before data can be written to the diskette with a write command, the WRITE GATE output of the FDC must be activated. As protection against accidental writing, this is not done until the data register is loaded as a reaction to the DRQ output set by the FDC.

If this is not done, the command execution is completed, INTRQ is set, the LOST DATA status bit set, and the BUSY status bit is cleared. If a reaction is made to the first data request, the write command will be executed. If the FDC does not transfer another data in response to a subsequent data request, the command will not be terminated and a "zero-byte" is written instead. The LOST DATA bit is also set after the command is completed. If only 112 bytes were transferred by a WRITE SECTOR command, the controller would fill the remaining 400 bytes with zeroes (assuming a sector size of 512 bytes).

This should not be used to erase part of a sector. Since the LOST DATA bit is set in any event, there is no way to tell if an error occurred when writing actual data or not.

Writing is usually suppressed when the WRITE PROTECT input is marked low. In this case, any write command is terminated immediately, INTRQ is placed high, the WRITE PROTECT status bit set, and the BUSY status bit cleared.

To increase the data security when the write density increases (on the inner tracks), it is possible to enable what is called *write precompensation*. If the write precompensation bit is cleared in the write command, the data stream over WRITE DATA is sent 125 nanoseconds earlier or later, depending on the bit pattern to be written. The following table shows the cases:

```
        X    1    1    0       earlier
        X    0    1    1       later
        0    0    0    1       earlier
        1    0    0    0       later
        |    |    |    |
        |    |    |    |_____ next bit to be transferred
        |    |    |_____ bit currently being sent
        |____|_____ previously transferred bit
```

The write precompensation is normally enabled on the inner tracks of 5 1/4" diskettes, where the write density is the highest. The precompensation is usually constantly enabled for 3 1/2" diskettes—the data density on their outer tracks already reaches the density of the middle tracks on a 5 1/4" diskette.

4.2.2.3 Command description

Now that we have seen the internal construction of the FDC and gone into some of the basic processes involved in read and write operations, we will talk about the commands.

The WD1772 recognizes eleven commands, and these are divided into four groups or types. The following table gives an overview of the commands:

Type	Command	Bit 7	6	5	4	3	2	1	0
I	Restore	0	0	0	0	h	V	r1	r0
I	Seek	0	0	0	1	h	V	r1	r0
I	Step	0	0	1	u	h	V	r1	r0
I	Step in	0	1	0	u	h	V	r1	r0
I	Step out	0	1	1	u	h	V	r1	r0
II	Read sector	1	0	0	m	h	E	0	0
II	Write sector	1	0	1	m	h	E	P	a0
III	Read address	1	1	0	0	h	E	0	0
III	Read track	1	1	1	0	h	E	P	a0
III	Write track	1	1	1	1	h	E	P	0
IV	Force interrupt	1	1	0	1	I3	I2	I2	I0

These commands have several flag bits which have the following meanings:

h = Motor On Flag   h = 0, enable motor-on test
h = 1, disable motor-on test

When the drive motor is switched on, the operating system should delay until the motor has reached its operating speed. The WD1772 accomplishes this delay by waiting 6 index pulses after the motor is turned on. With an operating speed of 300 RPM, this delay time is at least one second. This process, called the *spin-up sequence*, ensures that the motors have reached their required speed by the time the read/write operations take place.

After ending a command, the drive motors will not be turned off until ten more disk rotations are counted (about 2 seconds). If another command occurs during this time, it would be just a waste of time to go through another spin-up sequence. This is why a motor-on test was implemented in the controller. If this test is enabled (h=0), the MOTOR ON output will first be tested. If it is low, the FDC goes through the spin-up sequence. If MOTOR ON is high, however, the controller assumes that the motors are at their operating speed and continues processing the command.

If the FDC receives a command (with the h-bit set), it first turns on the drive motors by placing MOTOR ON high. This is regardless of whether the MOTOR ON output is high already or not. It then begins executing the command immediately and does not wait until six index pulses have been received.

V = verify flag $V = 0$, disable verify
    $V = 1$, enable verify

This flag bit exists only in type-I commands. If it is set, the controller performs a track verification after a step command or after the last step in a restore or seek command. It does this by searching for a correct ID field after the step, whose track number matches the contents of the track register.

Whether or not a verify is executed should be determined by the subsequent command, because a verify is not necessarily required and not always sensible.

If a READ or WRITE SECTOR command follows and the read/write head is not on the desired track, an incorrect sector will never be written or read because these commands executed a verify.

A verify doesn't make sense in certain situations, such as when a new diskette is being formatted. The verify after each STEP command would be negative. Since the controller searches for a correct ID field for the time of five revolutions, about one minute would be wasted while formatting the diskette.

If you format a single track on a diskette that already contains data, use a verify to be safe. The WRITE TRACK command, which is used for formatting, does not perform any tests on the track before it is executed. The track over which the read/write head is positioned is formatted.

r1, r0 = stepping rate
        0 0   2ms
        0 1   3ms
        1 0   5ms
        1 1   6ms

The step rate of the drives can be programmed with these two bits. This is the delay time between the individual step pulses for a SEEK or RESTORE command. This feature is used to adapt the FDC to the physical limitations of the drive.

As an example let's take a drive whose head mechanism requires 6ms per step. If the step rate is set to 3ms and the head is moved with a SEEK command from track 0 to track 40 (which corresponds to 39 step pulses), the head would only reach track 20—every other pulse would be lost due to the mechanical limits.

The drive will probably be correctly controlled by individual step pulses (STEP, STEP IN, STEP OUT) because the duration of the step pulse is not affected by the stepping rate. This pulse is determined by the internal timing of the FDC and is about 4µs long.

u = update flag   u = 0, do not update track register
                              u = 1, update track register

If the u-bit is set for a STEP, STEP IN, or STEP OUT command, the track register is incremented or decremented by one, as appropriate, after the operation. This does not mean that the contents of the track register match the actual track. Two conditions must be met for this to happen:

1) The actual track number must have matched the contents of the track register before the step.

2) No attempt can be made to access a track number greater than 82. If the read/write head is on track 82 (the last track the drive can reach), for example, the track register would contain the number 87 after five STEP IN commands, while the head would stay at track 82.

m = multiple sector m = 0, read or write one sector
m = 1, read or write multiple sectors

This bit lets you read or write a maximum of all of the sectors on a track at once. It is assumed that the sector numbers are in a continuous sequence. The number of the first sector to be read or written is written to the sector register beforehand. After the FDC has read/written this sector, it increments the sector register and attempts to read/write the next sector. This continues until no more sectors are found or the command is terminated with a FORCE INTERRUPT command.

a0 = data address mark a0 = 0, write normal data mark ($FB)
a0 = 1, write erased data mark ($F8)

The data address mark designates the start of the data field. The capability to write different data address marks with the a0 bit (depending on whether it is set or cleared) allows you to easily mark a sector. The type of data address mark is indicated in the RECORD TYPE status bit after a READ SECTOR command.

E = 30ms settling delay E = 0, no head settling time
E = 1, 30ms head settling time

Some drives have read/write heads that are not constantly in contact with the magnetic disk surface. These drives raise or lower the head with a solenoid. This setup, called *head load*, is intended to reduce the wear and tear on the diskette by lowering the head only when read or write operations are actually taking place. Lowering the head causes vibrations in the head mechanism, which prevents optimum contact between the head and the storage medium for a given length of time. Setting the E-bit results in a delay that takes this settling time into account.

P = write precompensation P = 0, enable write precompensation
P = 1, disable write precompensation

I0-I3 = interrupt conditions I0 = 1, no meaning
I1 = 1, no meaning
I2 = 1, interrupt on next index pulse
I3 = 1, immediate interrupt
I0-I3 = 0, terminate current command without interrupt

The type-I commands

The type-II and type-III commands, which are responsible for reading and writing data, always refer to the track that the read/write head is located over at the time. The group of commands consisting of RESTORE, SEEK, STEP, STEP IN, and STEP OUT is responsible for positioning the head.

RESTORE (seek TRACK 0)

```
Command word:  7   6   5   4   3   2   1   0
               ----------------------------
               0   0   0   0   h   V   r1  r0
```

When the FDC is sent this command, it first tests the TR00 input. If the TR00 input is low (because the read/write is already over track 0), the track register will simply be set to zero.

If the read/write is not over track 0, STEP OUT pulses will be created until the TR00 input goes low. If this is not the case after 255 step pulses, the command is terminated. The end of the command is indicated by the setting of the INTRQ output and the clearing of the BUSY status bit.

SEEK

```
Command word:  7   6   5   4   3   2   1   0
               ----------------------------
               0   0   0   1   h   V   r1  r0
```

This command moves the read/write head directly over a given track. The number of the desired track is first written to the data register. For this command to work properly, the contents of the track register must be the current track number. If more than one drive is used, the track register may have to be loaded so that it points to the current track number.

When the FDC receives a SEEK command, it compares the track register with the data register, which tells it whether a STEP IN or STEP OUT is necessary. Step pulses are then generated for the appropriate direction. The track register is UPDATEd after each step pulse. Once the contents of the track register and the data register are equal, the destination track has been reached and the command is ended. This is indicated by setting the INTRQ output and clearing the BUSY status bit.

STEP

```
Command word:   7   6   5   4   3   2   1   0
               ---------------------------------
                0   0   1   u   h   V   r1  r0
```

This command causes the FDC to output a step pulse. The direction is the same as that used for a previous step pulse, because the state of the DIRECTION output is not changed. The INTRQ output is set high afterwards, and the BUSY status bit is cleared.

STEP IN

```
Command word:   7   6   5   4   3   2   1   0
               ---------------------------------
                0   1   0   u   h   V   r1  r0
```

A STEP IN command sets the DIRECTION output to high, regardless of what it was before, and sends out a step pulse. This moves the read/write head one step toward the center of the disk. The INTRQ output is set high and the BUSY status bit cleared.

STEP OUT

```
Command word:   7   6   5   4   3   2   1   0
               ---------------------------------
                0   1   1   u   h   V   r1  r0
```

A STEP OUT command sets the DIRECTION output to low, regardless of what it was before, and sends out a step pulse. This moves the read/write head one step toward the edge of the disk. The INTRQ output is set high and the BUSY status bit cleared.

The verify sequence for type-I commands

If the V-bit is set in a command, the following sequence is executed when the desired track is reached and after a 30 millisecond delay:

The track number from the first ID field read is compared with the contents of the track register. If they match, the CRC byte of the ID field is tested. If this matches the byte generated by the CRC logic, the verify sequence is terminated without error. The INTRQ output is placed high and the BUSY status bit is cleared.

If either the track number or the CRC checksum in the ID field is wrong, the next ID field is read and a new test made. If an ID field with the correct track number and valid checksum is not found within five revolutions, the RECORD NOT FOUND bit is set in the status register. The command terminates, as indicated by the set INTRQ ouput and the cleared BUSY status bit.

Flow chart of the type-I commands

To clarify the operation of the type-I commands, here are some flowcharts which demonstrate the processes:

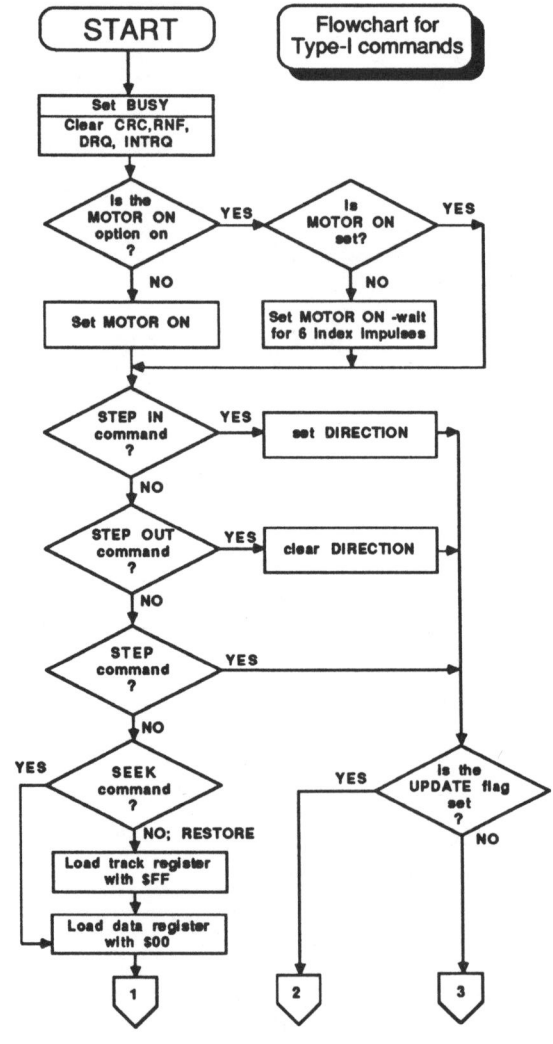

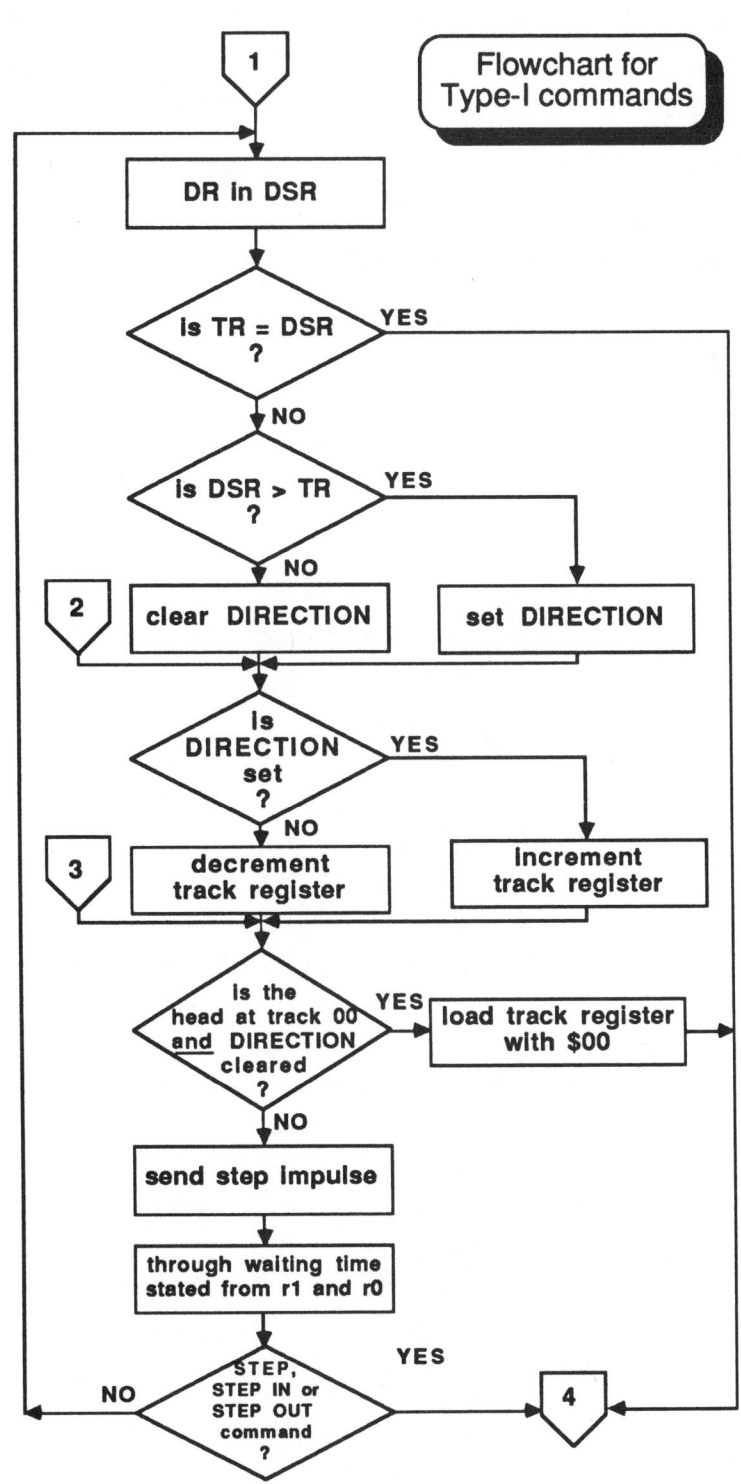

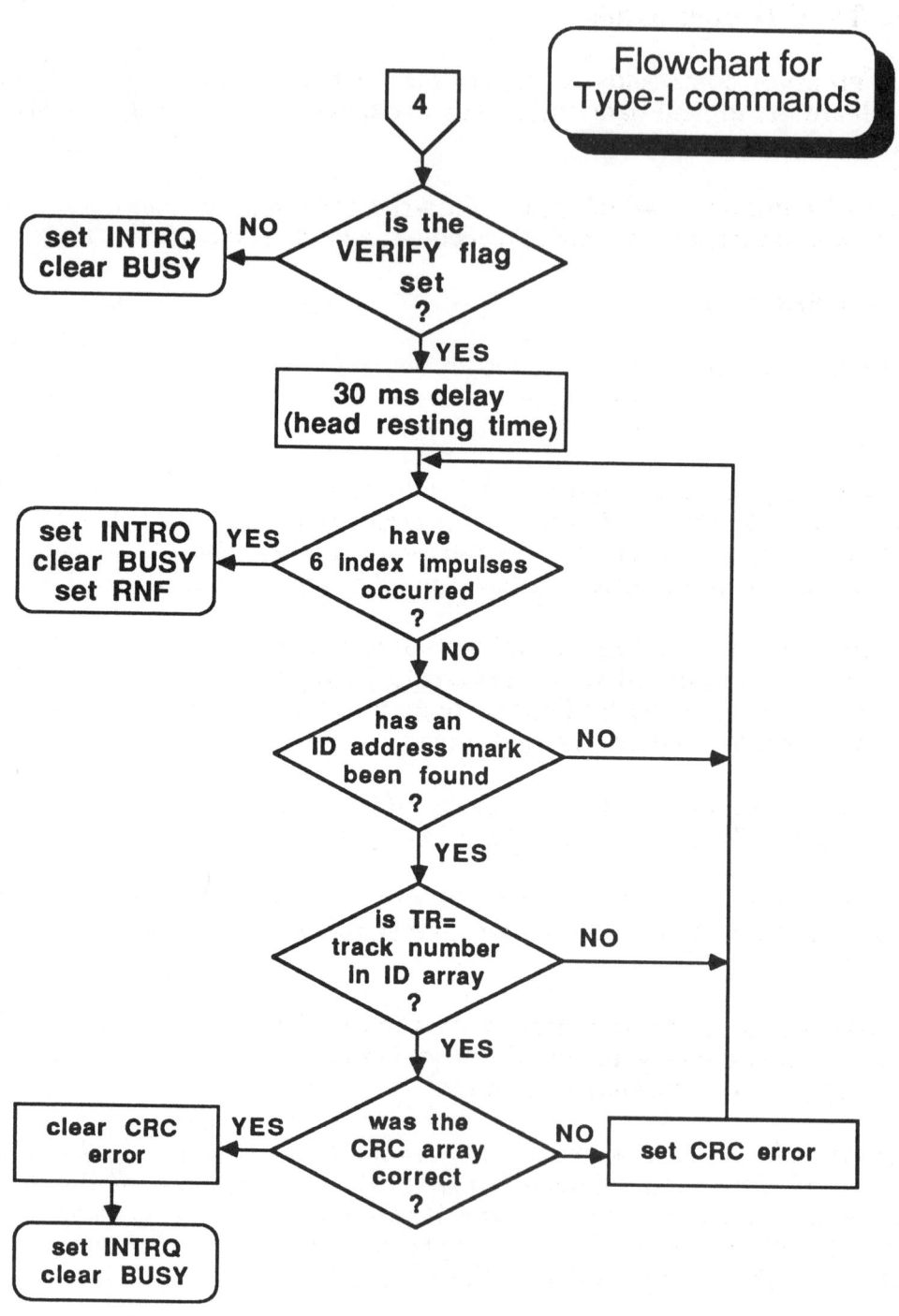

The Type II commands

This group of commands is responsible for reading and writing sectors, which are the logical data units. Data exchange is carried out exclusively with these commands.

Like all commands which read and write information, these also work relative to the track over which the read/write head is currently located.

READ SECTOR

```
Command word:   7   6   5   4   3   2   1   0
                ---------------------------------
                1   0   0   m   h   E   0   0
```

The FDC is given the number of the sector to be read in the sector register. When a READ SECTOR command is then started, the controller reads an ID field and tests to see if its track and sector numbers match the contents of the track and sector registers. If this is not the case, the next ID field is read.

If they were the same, the sector length is saved and the CRC checksum of the ID field is compared with the one calculated from the data read. If these are the same, then the ID field belonging to the desired sector has been found. Otherwise another ID field is read.

Before the data field can be read, a *data address mark* (DAM) must be found in the next 43 bytes. If a DAM is not found, another ID field is read.

If no matching ID field is found after five revolutions, or a DAM did not follow in the 43 bytes after it, the RNF status bit is set and the command terminated.

As you can see, certain conditions must be fulfilled before the FDC reads a data field containing a sector. If everything has gone smoothly up to now, then the process continues as follows:

The type of data address mark (normal=0, erased=1) is indicated in status bit 5. The address mark detector is disabled and the appropriate number of data bytes (calculated from the specification in the sector-length field) is read. A DRQ is generated for each byte read. If no reaction is made to this DRQ, the FDC sets the LOST DATA status bit.

After all of the data bytes have been read, a CRC checksum is tested again. This is located in the two bytes following the sector and is compared with the checksum calculated from the sector data. If the two do not match, the CRC error status bit is set.

The end of the operation is indicated by setting the DRQ output and clearing the BUSY status bit.

READ SECTOR (with m-bit set)

If the m-bit is set in the command word of the READ SECTOR command, the FDC tries to read multiple sectors (up to one track). The number of the first sector to be read is passed to the controller in the sector register. The operation of the command is first identical to the one described above. After the sector has been read, however, the controller automatically increments the sector register and starts another READ SECTOR.

This continues until no more sectors are found. In other words, this command is always terminated with a RECORD NOT FOUND error.

Since we can't tell the controller how many sectors to read, there has to be some other way to read multiple sectors. This is where the FORCE INTERRUPT command comes in. We don't wait until the FDC finishes the command itself, but instead we determine when we're done.

Here is an example of how we might do this:

Let's assume the following: The read/write head is positioned over an Atari-formatted track. The sectors of this track are numbered 1-9. We want to read the five sectors from 3-7. The sector number is passed to the sector register, and the read operation is started by passing the command word.

If nothing else happens, seven sectors are read (3-9) and the command is terminated after five rotations with an RNF error (because sector 10 could not be found).

But we want to read just sectors 3-7 (and we don't want an error message). This is how we do it:

Since the data transfer is handled by the DMA controller, it is initialized with a DMA start address before the FDC command is started. This address is continually incremented as the FDC passes the data to the DMA controller. Therefore the current DMA address can be determined by reading the DMA address register. This register is continually read until its contents are incremented beyond $A00 (5*$200), the start address. When this is the case, the READ SECTOR command is terminated with a FORCE INTERRUPT command.

WRITE SECTOR

```
Command word:   7   6   5   4   3   2   1   0
                ----------------------------
                1   0   1   m   h   E   P   a0
```

Here we'll just explain the differences from the READ SECTOR command, since much of the operation is the same.

At the beginning of the command, the FDC checks to see if the WRITE PROTECT input is low. If this is the case (write-protected diskette), the WPRT status bit is set and the command is terminated. If the disk is not write-protected, the ID field search starts.

If the matching ID field is found, a delay corresponding to 23 bytes is made. After this, 12 *zero bytes* and a data address mark are written (type depending on a0). Following this is the actual sector information, followed by the CRC checksum. Finally, an $FF byte is written.

Whether the sector was written correctly or not can only be determined by a READ SECTOR command.

WRITE SECTOR (with m-bit set)

See the discussion of the READ SECTOR command with m-bit set.

Flowcharts of the Type II commands

We also have flowcharts for the Type II commands.

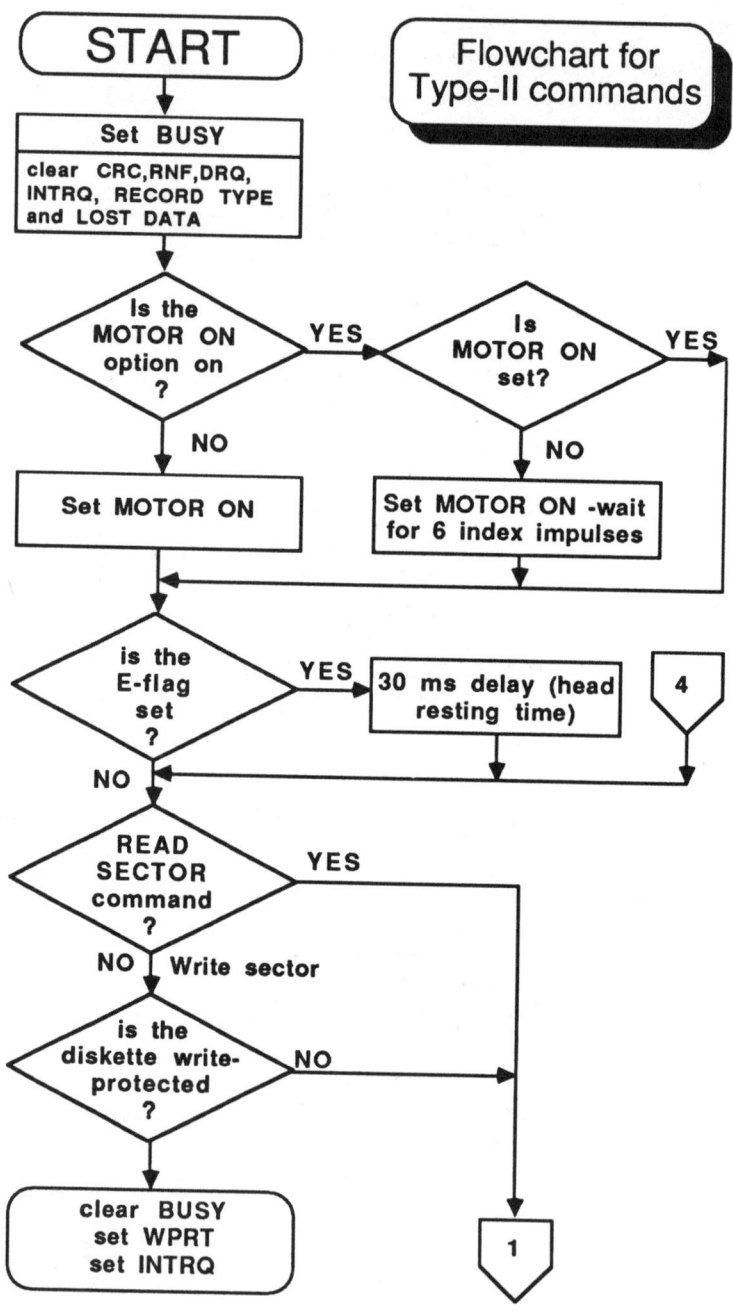

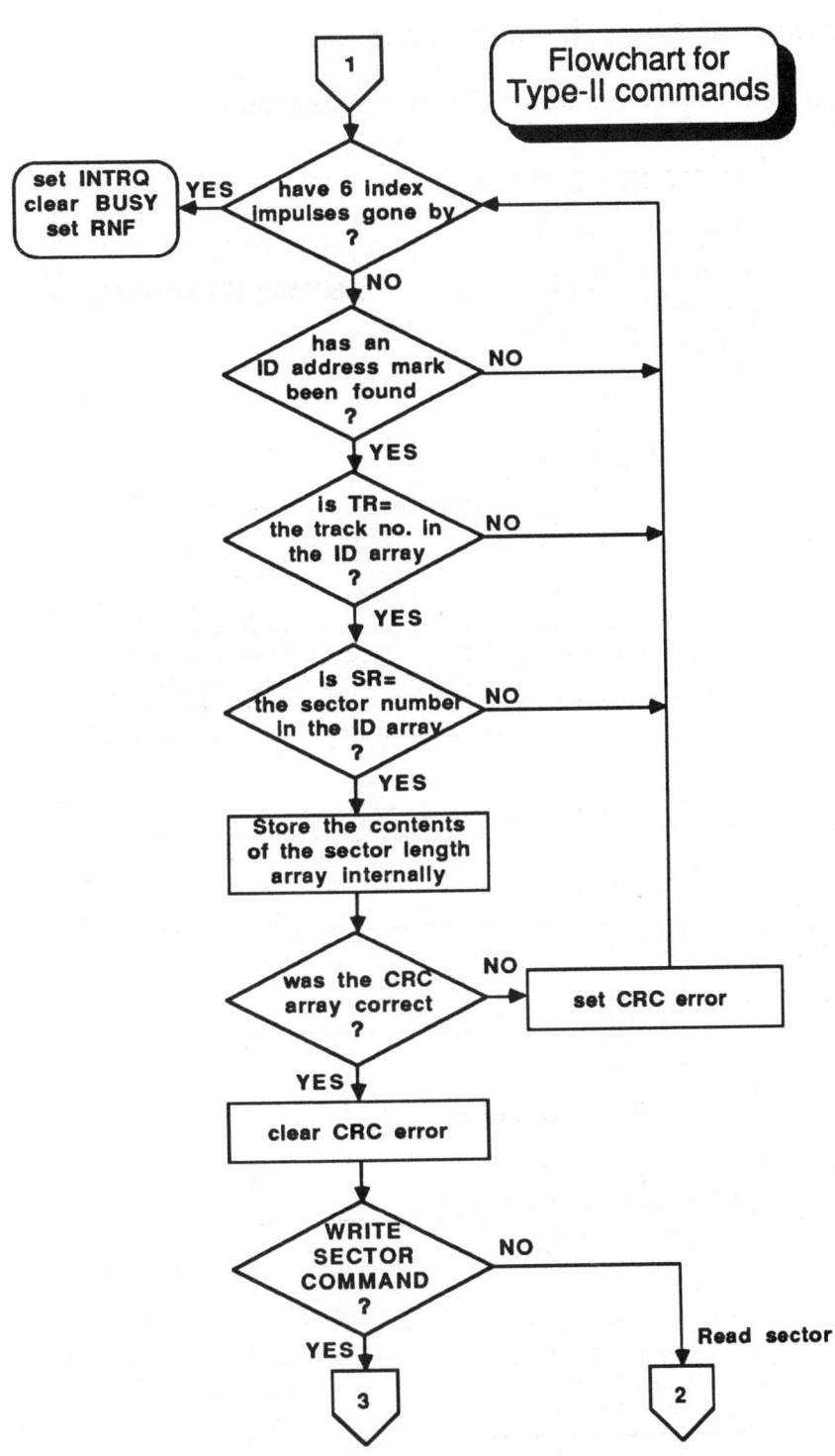

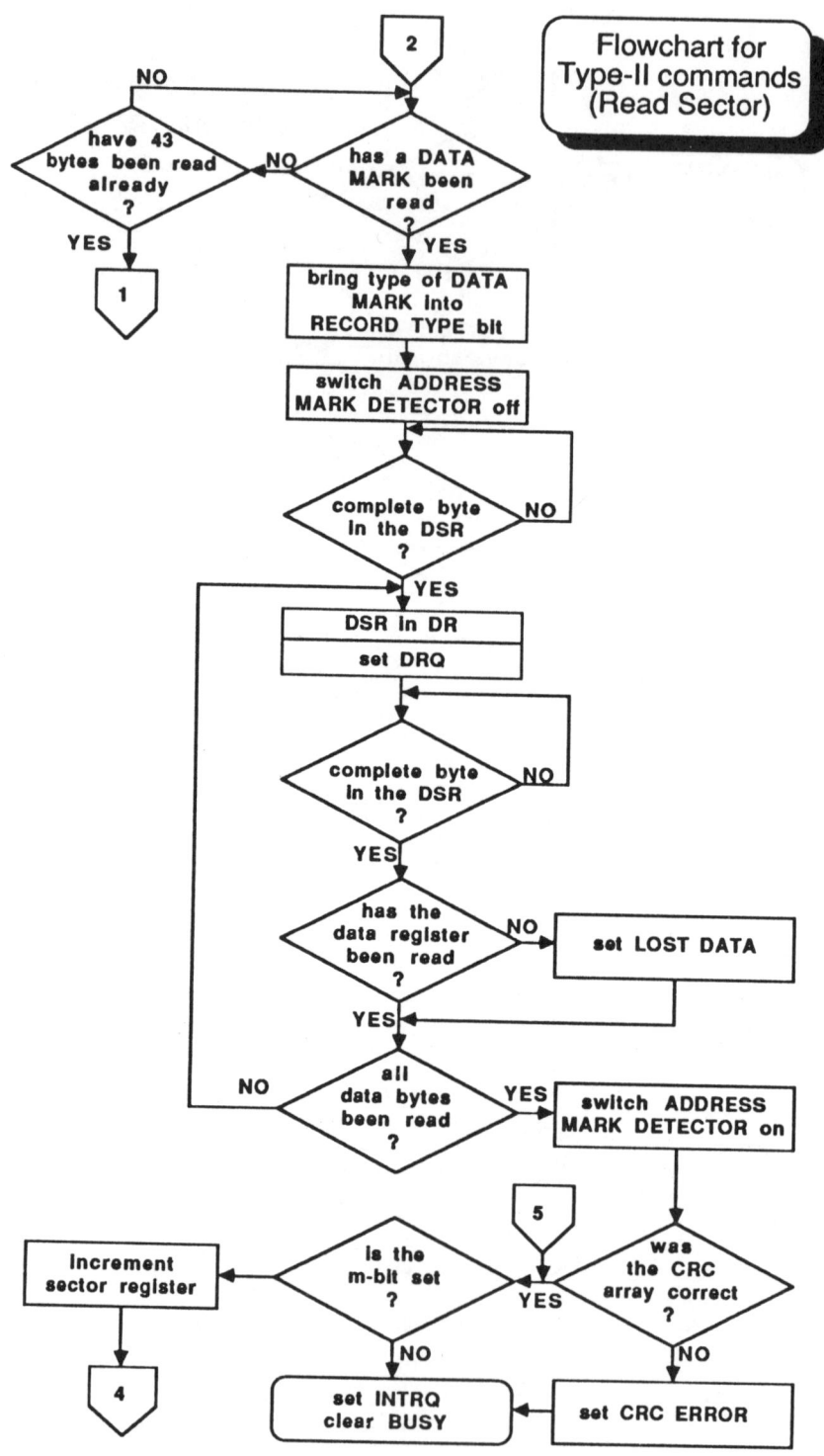

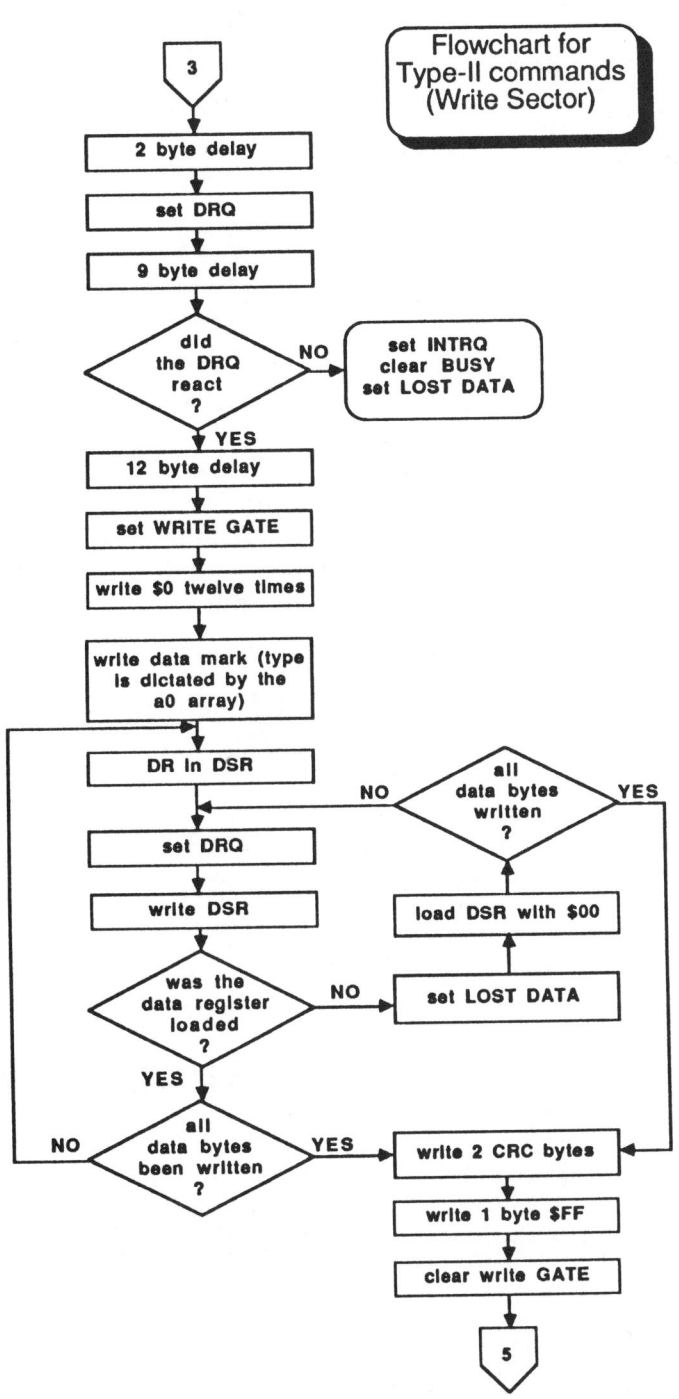

The Type III commands

The WRITE TRACK command is used for formatting a track. The READ TRACK and READ ADDRESS commands are used to analyze track format.

READ ADDRESS

```
Command word:   7   6   5   4   3   2   1   0
                ---------------------------------
                1   1   0   0   h   E   0   0
```

Here we give you a few warnings about the DMA controller. Programming the READ ADDRESS command can easily drive a person crazy!

After the READ ADDRESS command is started and executed, you might be surprised to discover that the ID field is not in RAM. A test of the status registers (DMA and FDC) show that no errors occurred. If you subtract the start DMA address from the end DMA address, the difference is zero. As a result, zero bytes were transferred—fewer than we had hoped. What happened to the six-byte ID field? That's easy—it's in the DMA controller!

The DMA controller does not transfer bytes individually. It waits until it has received 16. Not until then does it request the bus from the 68000 processor to transfer these 16 bytes into RAM.

Now, you might ask, how do we get the ID field out of the DMA controller? There's only one way to do it: read more data. This is done by reading several ID fields in succession. After three READ ADDRESS commands (18 bytes), we get 16 bytes in RAM and two in the DMA controller. To get all of the bytes transferred from the DMA controller to RAM, we have to read a number of byte which is evenly divisible by 16.

But there's another problem. This results from clearing the DMA status register, which is done by toggling the read/write line. If we reset this register before each DMA transfer, "just to be safe," we get the second surprise. This erases not only the status register, but all of the bytes still in the controller. In this case we can read ID fields until the disk falls apart, and the DMA controller wouldn't transfer a single byte into memory.

The moral of the story is that **the DMA status register may be cleared only before the first READ ADDRESS command.**

Now on to the READ ADDRESS command itself.

The READ ADDRESS command causes the next ID field which the read/write head encounters to be read. It can be used in connection with the READ TRACK command to analyze the format of a disk. Moreover, it is also possible to verify a track without leaving it.

The READ ADDRESS command reads an ID field without testing to see if a matching data field exists. Six bytes are read. They have the following meanings:

Byte #	Meaning
1	Track number
2	Side number
3	Sector number
4	Sector size
5	CRC byte 1
6	CRC byte 2

The track number (byte 1) is also written in the sector register. This can be used to do a track verify without using the data read. At first, this may seem unnecessary, because it doesn't matter if (for a track verify) we compare the contents of the sector register, or the first byte to the contents of the track register. In addition, it is simpler to use the transferred byte because we don't have to select the sector register first to use it.

As we said before, no information is transferred to RAM until the DMA controller has accrued 16 bytes. But since the FDC also writes the first byte of the ID field in the sector register, it is still possible to execute a track verify with a single READ ADDRESS command.

If no ID field is found within six index pulses (which corresponds to at least five rotations), the RNF status bit is set (RECORD NOT FOUND). Once the FDC has finished the command, it sets the INTRQ output and clears the BUSY status bit.

READ TRACK

Command word:	7	6	5	4	3	2	1	0
	1	1	1	0	h	E	0	0

The READ TRACK command is also used only for track diagnosis. It reads a complete track, including all GAP, SYNC, and data bytes. The reading begins on the rising edge of the next index pulse which the controller receives from the drive. Data is read until another index pulse reaches the controller. As usual, the end of the operation is indicated by setting the INTRQ output and clearing the BUSY status bit.

A DRQ is created for each byte read. As with all commands, the LOST DATA status bit is set if there is no reaction to the DRQ. Regarding the LOST DATA bit, we found that it would sometimes be set for no apparent reason. The reason is that this bit doesn't really give information about whether data was lost or not after a READ TRACK command. Curiously, these cases never occurred for READ TRACK attempts on an unformatted disk.

The "collection" of data bits is synchronized with each received address mark. The address mark detector, which is responsible for this, is not turned off (as it is for a READ SECTOR command, for instance) but remains active during the entire reading process. It is constantly on the lookout for an address mark, and therefore creates read errors.

According to manufacturer specifications, all information can be read correctly (with the exception of the GAP bytes). Our attempts had different results. In practice, it seems that only the ID fields can be read properly. But read errors can even occur at the checksum of the ID field.

You may wonder where the READ TRACK command can actually be used. The data themselves are of dubious value because of possible read errors; the READ ADDRESS command is much easier to use for reading ID fields, because the ID field search in the track information raises another problem. If we have a byte sequence of FE-01-00-01-02-BC-DB, for instance, we can't tell whether it is actually an ID field or not. This byte sequence could also occur in a data field. A "real" ID field is simply an ID field that the controller <u>recognizes</u> as an ID field.

Used by itself, the READ TRACK command is not very useful. However, when used in conjunction with the READ ADDRESS command, a track may be analyzed fairly precisely. Even if the data themselves don't say much, the number of data present is of great importance. The distances between given points can be measured, which is very important for track analysis. This makes up for a disadvantage of READ ADDRESS, which reads only ID fields and doesn't test whether a corresponding data field exists.

As an example, we'll describe how a track analysis would work:

1) All ID fields on the track are read with READ ADDRESS commands.

2) All track information is read with a READ TRACK command.

3) All sectors on the track (track and sector numbers are obtained from the ID fields) are read with READ SECTOR commands.

Our analysis is complete if there are no ID fields in the track, because the format is unreadable.

We search for the first ID field in the track information. Here we have to orient ourselves by "landmark" points. The first of these points is the byte sequence $A1, $FE (or $C2, $FE), which is made up of the SYNC byte and the ID address mark. An ID field can follow only a byte sequence like this. Once it is found, the second landmark becomes interesting. This is located a maximum of 42 bytes behind the ID field. We must find a SYNC byte followed by a data address mark. If we don't find a SYNC byte, then there is no valid data field for the ID field.

Another test checks the plausibility of the ID field. For example, if this indicates a sector size of 512 bytes, and the next ID field follows at a distance of 200 bytes, then something is wrong.

We read the sectors for two reasons. First, the sector information cannot be taken from the data obtained from READ TRACK. Second, the only way to check the CRC checksum of a data field is with READ SECTOR.

WRITE TRACK (FORMAT TRACK)

```
Command word:   7   6   5   4   3   2   1   0
                ---------------------------------
                1   0   0   m   h   E   0   0
```

A diskette must be formatted before it can be used for data storage. But what actually happens when we format a disk?

The sector is the logical data unit used for data transfer between the drive and controller is. Since a fresh blank diskette contains no information about the start of a sector, it must be assigned starting points before it can be used.

Every sector has a field that contains information about the sector. A checksum for the data must be also written to a blank disk. Synchronization bytes are also missing. These are very important for finding the start of a byte which is hidden somewhere in the serial bit stream from a later read operation.

The purpose of formatting is to write all of this information or marks on the diskette. This must be done according to certain rules, however, or sector transfer is impossible later. If one stays within these rules, a number of nonstandard but usable formats can be created.

The FDC is passed a data byte, a value between $00 and $FF. But to write the marks, which differ from the "normal" data, on the disk, it must be possible to operate the controller so that a mark is written to the disk instead of a data byte.

First we'll look at the control bytes, which are represented by values $F5 and $FF. In contrast to the READ SECTOR and WRITE SECTOR commands, which write these values as "normal" data bytes, the controller can be used to write special marks to the disk with a WRITE TRACK command. The common bond for all of these is that they are written without clock pulses and can thereby be distinguished from data bytes which the same values (see address mark detector). The following table shows what effect these control bytes have when they are encountered by later read operations:

Byte given to the FDC	Byte written from the FDC	Meaning
$F5	$A1	Sync-byte, CRC-reg. cleared
$F6	$C2	Sync-byte
$f7	$XX,$XX	2 CRC-bytes
$F8	$F8	'cleared' data address mark
$F9	$F9	Data mark
$FA	$FA	Data mark
$FB	$FB	'normal' data address mark
$FC	$FC	Data mark
$FD	$FD	Data mark
$FE	$FE	Index address mark
$FF	$FF	

These control bytes can be used to create different formats. We use some examples for creating the ST disk format to help explain how this is done. At the appropriate places we'll point out which elements can be changed.

Let's start with a buffer that can hold all of the information which is written to the diskette by the WRITE TRACK command. This buffer must be at least 6250 bytes long. Now we have to fill the buffer so it will correspond to a format that can store nine sectors of 512 bytes each.

If we divide our buffer into two components, we get the following setup, which is valid for all formats. Differences in the number of records are possible, of course.

```
GAP 1      RECORD 1     RECORD 2          RECORD 9      GAP 5
```

A track starts and ends with a block called a GAP. As we'll see later, these GAPs are also present in the RECORDs. A GAP is a blank space that separates the individual components in the track. It contains no useful information, just fill bytes or, if the GAP comes before an ID field or a data field, SYNC bytes as well. The FDC is given a length of time corresponding to the length of the GAP to prepare itself for the requirements of the next component.

Identifer	Value	Gap length ATARI format	Gap length Foreign format
GAP1 (track leader)	$4E	60 bytes	min. 32 bytes
GAP5 (track end)	$4E	ca. 664 bytes	min. 16 bytes

The length of GAP5 is irrelevant at the moment. Simply put, GAP5 is just what is left over on the disk. For calculations of the buffer length, we have to leave at least 16 bytes for GAP5.

If we subtract the number of bytes we reserve for GAP1 from our buffer, we have 6190 bytes available to divided up among the records. But we can't do this yet—we don't know the length of a record.

As you probably guessed by now, each record contains one of our nine sectors. So we know one thing for certain: the record length must be larger than the sector length. If we take a closer look at a record, we get the following picture:

```
GAP 2     INDEX-FIELD       GAP 3        DATA-FIELD   GAP 4
```

First we see the GAPs. In the order they are given above, these GAPs are called *pre-record*, *inter-record*, and *post-record gaps*.

Identifer		Value	Gap length ATARI format		Gap length Foreign format
GAP2		$00	12 bytes	min.	8 bytes
	SYNC	$F5	3 bytes		3 bytes
GAP3		$4E	22 bytes		22 bytes
		$00	12 bytes		12 bytes
	SYNC	$F5	3 bytes		3 bytes
GAP4		$4E	40 byte	min.	24 bytes
Total of GAP-bytes per RECORD			92 byte min.		72 bytes

The synchronization bytes ($F5) in GAP2 and GAP3 ensure that the reading of the serial data bytes is synchronized with the start of the byte. Also, they alert the FDC to look for a following address mark and initialize the CRC logic. To write a SYNC, the FDC is passed the value $F5, which writes an $A1 byte without clock pulses.

The data field

Now that we know about the GAPs found within a RECORD, let's take a closer look at the data field in which our sector is found.

DAM	Sector	CRD
$FB	512 data bytes	$F7

The data field starts with the data address mark, which designates the start of the sector. The value $FB is interpreted as a "normal" data address mark by a later READ SECTOR command, while the value $F8, which can be used instead of $FB, is viewed as an "erased" DAM.

The sector field is filled with "dummy bytes" when formatting. The values can be almost anything, but they should never be larger than $F4. There can be 128, 256, 512, or 1024 bytes. The FDC uses the index field to determine the number of bytes in the sector.

Passing the value $F7 to the FDC causes it to write the contents of its 16-bit CRC register, which contains a checksum, to the disk. Although only one byte is passed, the controller still writes two bytes.

The total length of the data field for a sector length of 512 bytes, in our example, is 515 bytes.

The index field

The index field, also called the ID field, contains information about the data field which follows it.

ID-AM	Track	Side	Sector	Length	CRC
$FE	00-79	00-01	00-09	00-03	$F7

The index address mark (ID-AM) is the start mark of the ID field. If the controller encounters an ID-AM during a later read operation, it reads the next six bytes with its address mark detector turned off. The ID-AM is written without clock pulses.

The three bytes which follow the ID-AM describe the RECORDs. The first specification is the track number on which the ID field is located. In our case this is a value between 0 and 79, depending on which track is being formatted. The side field specifies whether the record is on the front or back of the diskette. The byte is not used by the controller for any operations. The sector field contains the number of the sector (1-9).

Since the FDC distinguishes between different sector sizes, it must be told how many data bytes are contained in the following sector. This is done by the length field.

Table of sector lengths

Length field	Bytes per sector
00	128
01	256
02	512
03	1024

For a sector size of 512 bytes, this field contains "02".

All that's missing is the checksum. As in the data field, this sum is written by passing the value $F7. Adding the lengths of all these values gives a total length of seven bytes for an ID field.

Now that we have looked at all of the components in the track an their order, we can calculate the length of a record.

Data field	515 bytes
ID field	+ 7 bytes
GAP2-GAP4	+ 92 bytes
Record length	= 614 bytes

This is the actual size of the record. In our buffer a record is only 612 bytes long because only one byte is passed to the FDC to write each of the two checksums. If one record requires 614 bytes, then we for a track we need 9 * 614 bytes = 5526 bytes. If we subtract this from the 6190 available bytes, we have 644 bytes left over for the track trailer (GAP5). This is more than enough since only 16 bytes are actually required here. Even a format which uses ten sectors at 512 bytes each would leave 50 bytes for GAP5.

Let's look at the data with which we'll prepare our buffer. The following explanations apply to the table which follows:

The data for GAP2 through GAP4 inclusive (one complete record) repeat for each sector. For example, a format with 29 sectors would have the corresponding block repeated 29 times in the buffer. You have to determining the values specified with $XX yourself, although this isn't very complicated. If you are formatting track 54, for example, the value for the track number would be 54.

The value for the side number is generally 0 for the front side and 1 for the back.

The sector numbers form a sequence, usually starting with 1. The order is variable and might be 3, 6, 9, 1, 4, 7, 2, 5, 8 for a format with 9 sectors. The only important thing is that the sequence is complete. If the sectors are designated with 1, 2, 3, 5, 6, 7, 8, 9, 10, a later READ SECTOR or WRITE SECTOR command with the m-bit set terminates after the third sector with a RECORD NOT FOUND error because the FDC couldn't find a sector number 4.

Atari format is listed in the first column. Our table differs from the one found in *A Hitchhiker's Guide to the BIOS*. The length of the track trailer (GAP5) is listed there as 1401 bytes instead of 644 bytes. If you add the values given in the *Hitchhiker's Guide*, it would appear that the track length is about 7000 bytes, which is not the case in reality. A buffer is prepared that is somewhat larger than what the track can actually hold, but no more than about 6250 bytes fits in one track.

Number of sectors/sector size

	9 / 512	18 / 256	29 / 128	5 / 1024
GAP 1	60 * $4E	42 * $4E	40 * $4e	60 * $4E
GAP 2	12 * $00	11 * $00	10 * $00	40 * $00
SYNC	3 * $F5	3 * $F5	3 * $F5	3 * $F5
ID-AM	1 $FE	1 * $FE	1 * $FE	1 * $FE
TRACK NUMBER	1 * $XX	1 * $XX	1 * $XX	1 * $XX
SIDE NUMBER	1 * $XX	1 * $XX	1 * $XX	1 * $XX
SECTOR NYMBER	1 * $XX	1 * $XX	1 * $XX	1 * $XX
SECTOR LENGTH	1 * $02	1 * $01	1 * $00	1 * $03
ID-CRC	1 * $F7	1 * $F7	1 * $F7	1 * $F7
GAP 3	22 * $4E	22 * $4E	22 * $4E	22 * $4E
	12 * $00	12 * $00	12 * $00	12 * $00
SYNC	3 * $F5	3 * $F5	3 * $F5	3 * $F5
DAM	1 * $FB	1 * $FB	1 * $FB	1 * $FB
DATA	512 * $E5	512 * $E5	512 * $E5	512 * $E5
GAP 4	40 * $4E	26 * $4E	25 * $4E	40 * $4E
GAP 5	664 * $4E	34 * $4E	33 * $4E	420 * $4E

Flowcharts of the Type III commands

We have also prepared flowcharts for the Type III commands. These flowcharts are illustrated starting on the next page.

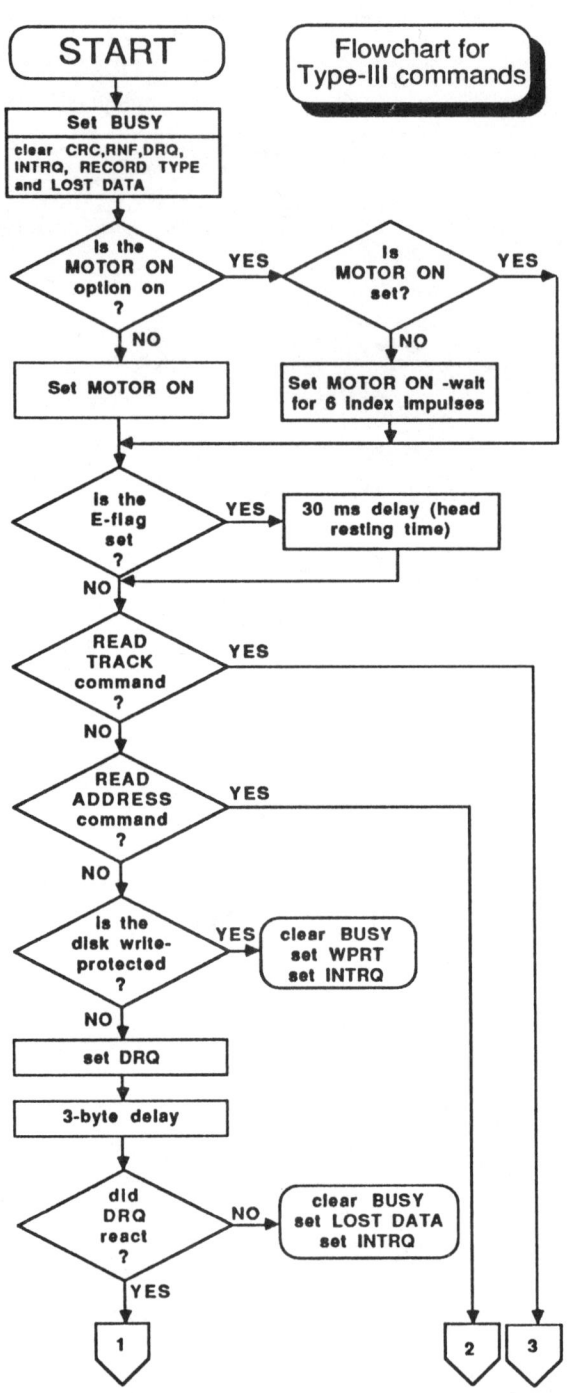

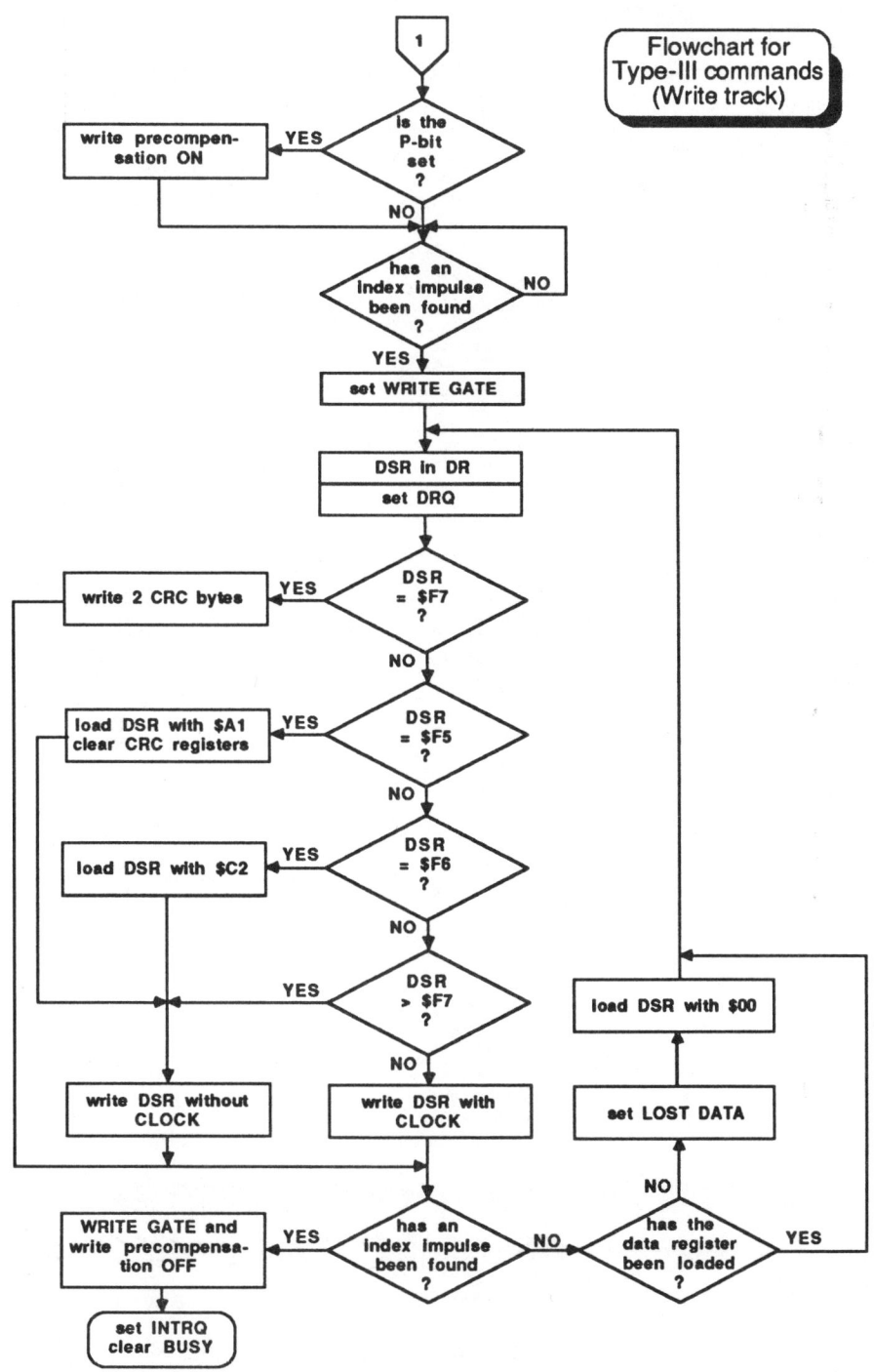

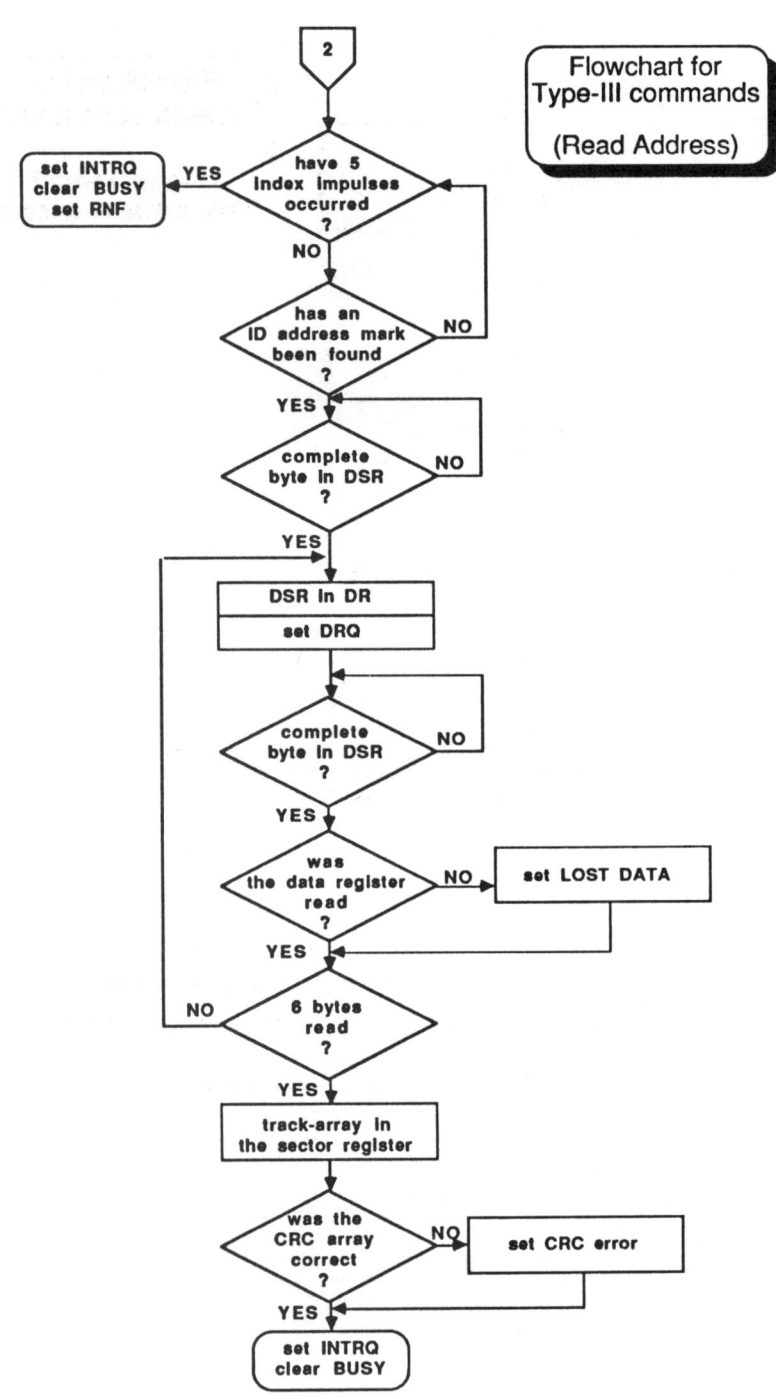

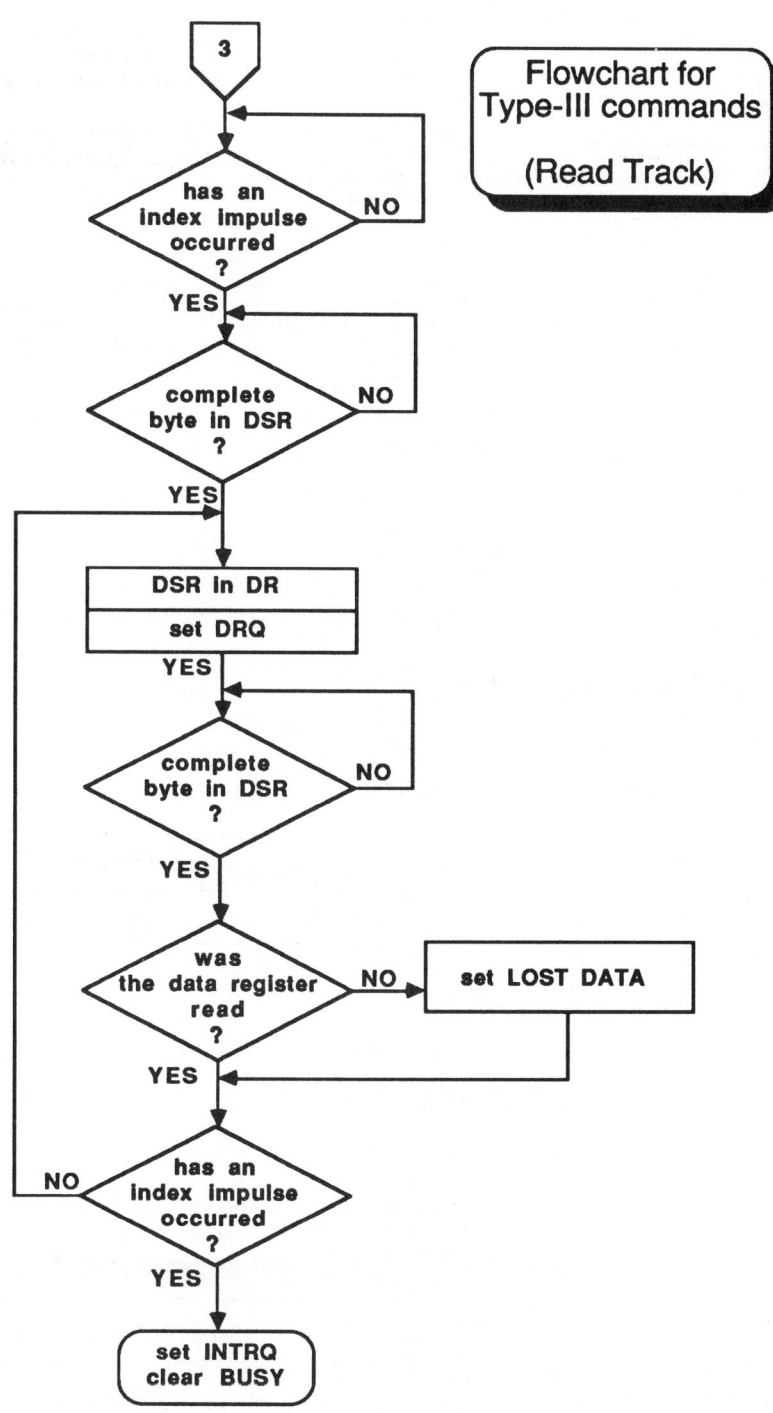

The Type IV command

FORCE INTERRUPT

```
Command word:   7   6   5   4   3   2   1   0
              ----------------------------------
                1   1   0   1   I3  I2  I1  I0
```

This command is the only one that may be passed to the controller while it is executing another command. It is used to stop the execution of a READ SECTOR command or WRITE SECTOR command with the m-bit set.

There are three types of interrupts. These are determined by the status bits (I0-I3) in the command word. I0 and I1 have no meaning and should be cleared. Bits I2 and I3 select the type of interrupt as follows:

    ($D4)   I2   = 1, interrupt on every index pulse
    ($D8)   I3   = 1, end current command with interrupt
    ($D0)   I2-I3 = 0, end current command without interrupt

The interrupt on every index pulse ($D4) can be used to determine the speed of the drive. Another use is the synchronization of the READ ADDRESS command with the start of the track. It is not necessary to start with the index pulse for the READ TRACK and WRITE TRACK commands.

A command currently being executed can be terminated by the interrupts $D8 and $D0. It should be noted that the INTRQ output is not reset by reading or writing the command register after a $D8 interrupt as it usually is. This line can be reset only by following a $D8 interrupt with $D0 interrupt and then reading the status register.

If a FORCE INTERRUPT is sent to the FDC, a delay time of 16µs must be inserted before the next command or the interrupt won't be executed.

4.2.2.4 Status interpretation

We said that the programming of the peripheral components responsible for data transfer is handled almost exclusively by the operating system. In most cases, these components offer more features than are necessary for normal system operation. This is the reason that the less-frequently-used capabilities cannot be accessed through the operating system.

In certain cases, however, these "sleeping" talents of the peripheral chips can make a programming problem much easier or even solve it. Why don't many programmers have enough confidence to wake these "talents"? Just because there's no operating system call to do it? No, the most common reason is "fear of status."

This says that a programmer knows how a chip can accomplish a given task, but he doesn't know how to interpret the status which the chip returns. Often he doesn't know what status is returned after error-free execution because certain bits in the status register are almost always set. An OK status can therefore vary. Not knowing how to interpret the status results can stop a programming project dead in its tracks. It's a waste of time to try out all of the possibilities and determine the status returned in each case experimentally. But this isn't the only way to do it either. We have taken care of this for you with the floppy disk controller.

Here again we have a table of the meanings of the individual status bits, which were previously described in section 4.2.2.2:

FDC status register

Bit	**Command**	**Bit=1 means**
7	Motor On (MO)	Drive motor
6	Write Protect (WPRT)	Disk write protected
5	Record Type or	DATA MARK cleared
	Spin Up	Turn number reached
4	Record not found	Sector not found
3	CRC-Error	Checksum error
2	Track 0	Head at track 0
	lost data	Data loss
1	Index inpulse or	Index pulse status
	Data Request	Ready to transfer
0	Busy	Command active

It is of interest that we can determine whether or not the disk in the drive is write-protected, or even whether there is a disk in the drive at all, after the read/write head is positioned.

All the commands from Type I to Type III have the following in common: Bit 7 is set (the motor is not turned off immediately) and bit 0 is cleared (the FDC has completed the command) in the status word, which is read immediately after a command. In addition, bit 5 (spin up) is set after a Type I command.

The status after a Type I command

Let's start with the status after a Type I command. In the command words used, the stepping-rate bits for 3ms track to track time are set (r0=1, r1=0).

RESTORE command	normal	write protected
01 (with MO option, no verify)	A6	E4
01 (note (1))	A6	E6
05 (with MO option, with verify)	A4	E4
09 (no MO option, no verify)	A4	E4
0D (no MO option, with verify)	A4	E4

SEEK command	normal	write protected
11 (with MO option, no verify)	A0	E0
11 (note (3))	A2	E2
11 (note (2))	A4	E4
11 (note (1))	A6	E6
15 (with MO option, with verify)	A0	E0
15 (note (2))	A4	E4
19 (no MO option, no verify)	A0	E0
19 (note (2))	A4	E4
1D (no MO option, with verify)	A0	E0
1D (note (2))	A4	E4

STEP, STEP IN, STEP OUT	normal	write protected
x1 (with MO option, no verify)	A)	E0
x1 (note (2))	A4	E4
x5 (with MO option, with verify)	A0	E0
x5 (note (2))	A4	E4
x9 (no MO option, no verify)	A0	E0
x9 (note (2))	A4	E4
xD (no MO option, with verify)	A0	E0
xD (note (2))	A4	E4

(1) This value is valid if the read/write head is already over track 0 before a RESTORE or SEEK command to track 0. In addition to the track-0 bit, the IP bit is also set. This is because six index pulses are counted if the motor-on option is enabled. This means that the FDC determines that the desired track is reached during an index impulse and ends the command.

(2) This status is encountered after a SEEK, STEP IN, or STEP OUT command when the read/write head is moved over track 0.

(3) If the read/write head is already over the desired track (except for track 0) for a SEEK command, the IP bit is set in the status word. The same relationship applies here as in (1).

In general, an error status can only be received after a Type I command if the verify bit is set in the command word. In addition:

(a) If no ID field was found, the RNF bit is set.
and
(b) If no correct ID field was found, the RNF and CRC bits is set.

The status is $B2 or $BA, or $F2 or $FA for a write-protected disk.

If the whole thing happens on track 0, the track 0 is also set, of course. The status word then has the value $B6 or $BE, or $F6 or $FE for a write-protected disk.

It occurs that the IP bit is always set in case of error. This has nothing to do with the motor-on option, however, but results because the fruitless search for an ID field is ended on the sixth index pulse.

The status after a Type II command

The status interpretation is somewhat simpler for Type II commands. After a successful WRITE SECTOR command the status register always contains the value $80. After a READ SECTOR command, the status word can also be $A0 if a sector with an "erased" data mark was read. Otherwise the value will also be $80 here.

If the command was not successful, the status after a WRITE SECTOR command is one of the following:

(a) $C0 after an attempt to write to a write-protected disk

(b) $90 if the ID belonging to the desired sector was not found

(c) $88 if the checksum (CRC) of the ID field was not correct

(d) $84 if no reaction was made to a DATA REQUEST by the FDC

After an error occurred during a READ SECTOR command:

   (a) $90 if the ID field belonging to the desired sector or the data mark was not found

   (b) $98 if the checksum (CRC) of the ID field was wrong

   (c) $88 if the checksum (CRC) in the data field indicated an error

   (d) $84 if no reaction was made to a DATA REQUEST by the FDC

The status after a Type III command

The status after a Type III command is even simpler to evaluate. The value $80 indicates successful execution. In case of an error during a WRITE TRACK command, one of the following holds:

   (a) $C0 for a write-protected disk

   (b) $84 if no reaction was made to an FDC DRQ

There is no such thing as improper execution of the READ TRACK command. The FDC simply reads the RD input between two index pulses, and it doesn't even matter if there's a disk in the drive or not.

The only imaginable error, LOST DATA (status $84), cannot be evaluated because of a software error in a subprogram in the FDC. The LOST DATA is also set depending on the format read in addition to actual loss of data.

For the READ ADDRESS command, a status value of $80 also means that no errors occurred. Otherwise, one of the following can result:

   (a) $90 if no ID field was found

   (b) $88 if the FDC found a checksum error in the ID field

   (c) $84 if no reaction was made to a DRQ

4.2.3 The floppy interface

The floppy disk connector on the back of the ST is a rather unusual 14-pin socket. Complete control of the drive and the data transfer takes place over these fourteen lines. This control is fairly easy to describe because the drive doesn't possess any intelligence of its own.

This has one big advantage. The interface to such drives is standardized and is called the Shugart interface, and is found on many drives. This is the reason that it is so easy to connect foreign drives to the Atari ST.

The Shugart interface has a 34-pin connector which is usually equipped with a ribbon connector. Half of these 34 pins are tied together and grounded. On a ribbon cable every other wire is a ground, so all of the odd pins are grounded. This results in some shielding between the signal lines, which is important given the high clock rates of the signals.

Fourteen of the remaining eighteen lines are connected to the Atari. Let's look at these signals on the Shugart connector:

Pin 2: Head Load
A low signal on this line sets the read/write head on the diskette. This feature is designed to protect the disk because the head rubs on the disk only when it is actually going to access it. Unfortunately, this signal is not available on the ST because the WD1772 controller does not have this connection available. This line is often connected to "Motor on" however.

Pin 3: Ground
All odd-numbered lines through 33 are tied to ground. This ground connection is used for operation as well as shielding.

Pin 4: In Use
This signal tells the drive that it is connected and is used. It is not available on the Atari.

Pin 6: Drive Select 3
A low level on this line means that drive three is being selected. Only the drive which is assigned as drive three by a wire jumper in the drive reacts to commands, and all others remain neutral. This signal is not used on the Atari because a maximum of two floppies can be connected (0 and 1, or A and B).

Pin 8: **Index**
The drive uses this line to send a low pulse upon each rotation of the disk. This signal tells the controller that the data which follow are at the very start of the current track. This can be used to synchronize the controller.

Pin 10: **DriveSelect 0**
This signal corresponds to the one on Pin 6, except that it concerns drive 0 (Drive A).

Pin 12: **Drive Select 1**
As above, except for drive 2 (Drive B).

Pin 14: **Drive Select 2**
As above, except for drive 2. Not connected on the ST because only two drives are possible.

Pin 16: **Motor on**
A high level on this connection starts the motors of all drives and a low stops them.

Pin 18: **Direction**
This signal indicates the direction of the next step of the read/write head. If this pin is zero, the direction is in, toward track 79, while a 1 means out, toward track 0.

Pin 20: **Step**
A low pulse causes the step motor in the drive to move the read/write head one step in the direction specified.

Pin 22: **Write Data**
This line carries the serial data which are to be written to the disk.

Pin 24: **Write Gate**
This signal selects the data direction. If it is low, the disk is written, while a high signal indicates read. If the disk is write-protected, no write access is allowed by the drive.

Pin 26: **Track 0**
If the read/write head is over track 0, this pin is low.

Pin 28: **Write Protect**
A low on this line means that the diskette is write-protected.

Pin 30: Read Data
　　　　　The data read from the disk are sent to the computer via this line.

Pin 32: Side Select
　　　　　This line selects the desired side of the disk. A low level selects side 1 and a high selects side 0. This line is unused for single-sided drives.

Pin 34: Ready
　　　　　A low level on this line indicates that a disk is inserted in the drive and that it is rotating normally. The computer can use this line to determine if the disk has been changed. This line is not connected to the Atari ST.

All of these signals are TTL-compatible, meaning that 0-0.4 volts indicates a LO (zero) and 2.5-5.25 volts means HI (one). To ensure these signals, most drives have a set of pull-up resistors built into them.

If several drives are connected in parallel, it is advisable to remove the resistors from all drives except the last one or the outputs on the Atari may be overloaded. On some drives (such as the Epson) the resistors are in a single package so that they can be removed easily. For the original Atari drives, which are Epson drives, by the way, this is not necessary.

4.3 Connecting the disk drives

The floppy disk drives which Atari sells for the ST are very easy to connect: Plug the cable into the computer and drive and you're done.

It becomes more complicated if you want to connect a different drive. The first problem which we encounter is the connector, which at the time of this writing (5/86) is difficult or impossible to find. Solder pins soldered to a suitable circuit board or held in position by some other means can be used as a substitute.

Once you have devised a suitable connector, you have to wire it. A shielded cable is highly recommended if the length exceeds about one meter. The high transfer rates lead to electrical effects like inductance and capacitance, which can have unfavorable effects on data transfer. The best way to avoid this is to use a cable in which the lines are individually shielded.

After the connection between the Atari and the drive has been made, the cable must be connected. Here is the wiring table:

Atari ST	Line	Shugart connector
1	Read Data	30
2	Side 0 select	32
3	Ground	all odd lines
4	Index Pulse	8
5	Drive 0 select	10
6	Drive 1 select	12
7	Ground	see above
8	Motor on	16
9	Direction in	18
10	Step	20
11	Write Data	22
12	Write Gate	24
13	Track 00	26
14	Write Protect	28

When these lines are connected to the two drives, all connections are in parallel. The selection between drives A and B is made directly in the drive. The jumpers in the drives must be set properly for this selection. Information on how to set the jumpers is found in the documentation for a given drive.

Chapter Five

The SH204 hard disk

The SH204 hard disk

A hard disk is a significantly faster—and significantly more expensive—method of data storage. But the SH204 hard disk that Atari sells for use with the ST is available for a very reasonable price.

What are the advantages and disadvantages of a hard disk? The first disadvantage is obviously the hard disk's high cost. In addition, you can't exchange media for copying files and programs, or for backups and archival storage—all of which are possible with floppy diskettes.

But if we look at the advantages which a hard disk has to offer, the investment becomes more appealing. A hard disk's first advantage is the speed at which it transfers data between the ST and the hard disk itself, approximately 10 times faster than floppy diskette operations.

Another advantage is the capacity of a hard disk. The currently available device has a capacity of twenty megabytes. This can hold, for example, all of the programs and files for an extensive compiler together with the source files for your C or Pascal programs. Since these compilers are usually disk-oriented (i.e., they constantly access information on the disk), both the speed and large capacity of the hard disk represent significant advantages for working with compilers.

A popular use of hard disks is in electronic data processing, where large quantities of data must be managed. Having to change disks all of the time in such applications simply wouldn't work. Imagine a bank teller having to insert the correct disk into the bank computer for every withdrawal!

An Atari ST with a twenty megabyte hard disk probably isn't sufficient for the data processing needs of a bank. But it would work for managing a small business in which inventory, accounting, and payroll were done on a computer. This is the principle application of a hard disk.

We will now look at how such a data set is managed by the hard disk and also by the computer connected to it.

5.1 Function and design

The function of a hard disk is very similar to that of a floppy disk drive. In both cases, one or more disks (just one in the Atari hard disk) rotate at a constant speed and a read/write head moves over it. There are some important differences from a floppy drive, however. The rotation speed of the hard disk is significantly higher than that of a floppy diskette, which makes possible the high access and transfer speeds.

In order to protect the read/write head, which flies over a disk that rotates about ten times faster than a floppy diskette, it does not contact the disk at all. The head floats over the disk on a cushion of air that is so thin that the head would collide with a dust particle on the disk surface.

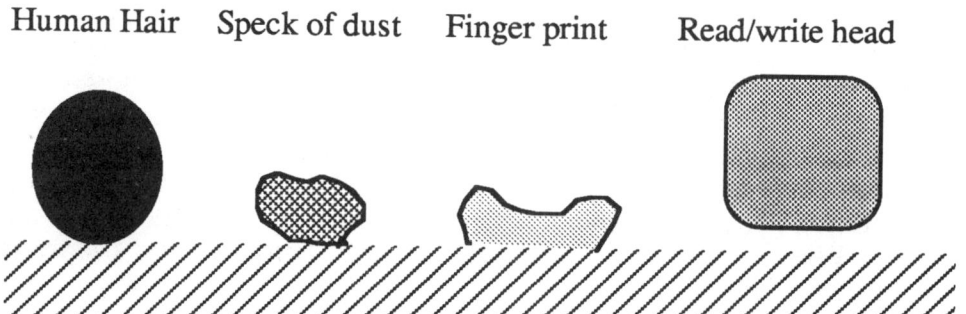

With the high tangential speed of the disk, if the head contacts such a dust particle, it can lead to severe damage to the disk and/or the read/write head. This is called a "head crash," and it can have very expensive consequences in terms of lost data and actual physical damage to the drive.

To minimize the chances of a head crash, the disk and the head are sealed in an airtight enclosure. This is why the media in hard disks are usually not exchangeable like diskettes. There are exchangeable-media hard drives available on the market, but they are quite expensive. Also, no such drive is currently available for the ST, so we will not explore this any further.

Another difference between a diskette drive and the hard disk on the Atari ST shows up in the controller. The floppy disk controller built into the Atari ST is, as the name indicates, only responsible for the floppy drives. The hard disk has its own controller, which is built into the drive housing. This makes it considerably harder to connect a foreign hard drive to the Atari. Let's take a closer look at this controller.

5.1.1 The hard disk controller

The controller used in the Atari ST hard disk is a very powerful device. This controller can achieve data transfer rates up to eight megabits per second, which is about one megabyte/second. This would fill the memory of a 1040ST in one second! Unfortunately, this number does not apply to actual data transfer.

One factor that dramatically slows the data transfer is the mechanism in the hard disk. This refers to the rotation speed of the disk and the step motor which moves the read/write head to the proper track on the disk. All of these points reduce the actual maximum speed of the data exchange, although it is still very high.

The controller has a very simple internal structure. Its command set is so versatile that it even supports error correction. The hardware of the controller consists mainly of a disk controller, an encoder/decoder, and a microcontroller. These components have the following tasks or functions:

The disk controller converts the data from serial into parallel and back again. In addition, it converts the data itself into a different bit pattern, which is then actually written to the disk. This different format allows simple read errors to be recognized.

The encoder/decoder converts the data sent by the disk controller into electrical signals which control the write head. It also converts the signals which arrive from the head when reading into bits, whereby it also serves as a data separator (cf. floppy disk controller).

The microcontroller works like an actual disk controller. Its tasks are:

- interpretation of the commands from the computer
- selection of the drive being accessed (usually there is only one)
- selection of the head in the drive (top or underside of the disk)
- control of the stepper motor which moves the read/write head
- status reporting

Here is a simple block diagram of the Atari hard disk controller:

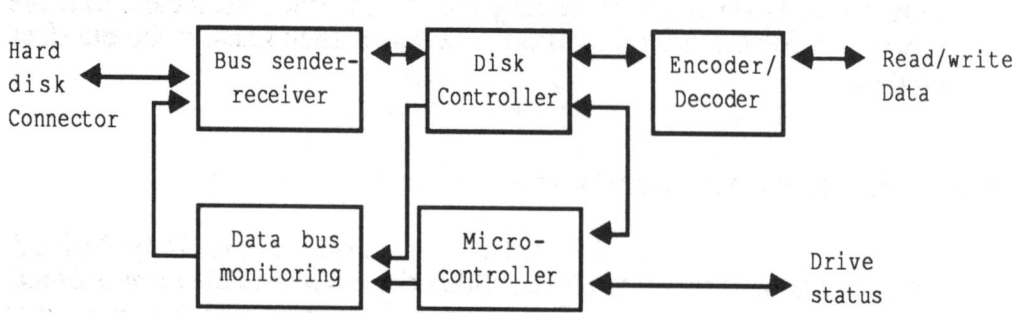

Atari Hard Disk Controller Block Diagram

The operations which can be performed with the hard disk over the DMA bus are divided into five different phases, which are defined as follows:

Reset phase
   Occurs when either the RESET button on the ST is pressed, the computer is turned on, or the RESET command is executed by the 68000 processor. The bus and the HDC are reset to their initial states.

Bus-free phase
   Occurs when no device is accessing the bus.

Destination-selection phase
   Starts with calling a device by reseting the SEL line. The desired device is addressed through a set data bit on the 8-bit parallel bus. The addressed device (here: HDC) answers with a BUSY signal, upon which the SEL line is set again. Then starts the

Information-transfer phase
   During this phase the following data are transferred:

   • the command block, 6 bytes from the ST to the HDC
   • the data block(s), if the command requires it
   • the status byte from the HDC to the ST, which indicates whether the operation was successful or whether an error occurred. This byte is always zero, however, so status transmission is possible through the recognition of a timeout
   • the completion byte from the HDC to the ST, a zero byte which signals the end of the entire operation

Bus-release phase

This phase is initiated by setting the BUSY line and means that the bus is free for the next operation. The bus is then back in the bus-free phase.

5.1.1.1 Command structure

The transfer of commands to the hard disk controller is precisely defined. Each command is sent a 6-byte block, called the *command descriptor block*. When the controller receives such a command, it acknowledges receipt to the initiator, the ST, through an interrupt. If the block contains a command to find a specific track (verify, format track, read, write), this will be performed automatically. The specified logical data block is converted by the controller to physical quantities like disk side and track number.

The following diagram shows the structure of a command block:

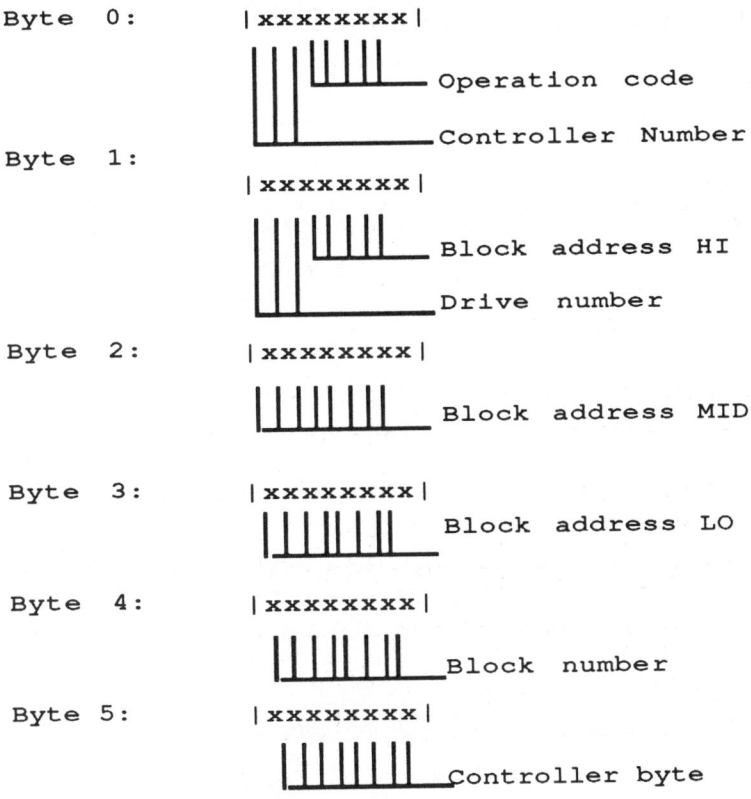

Controller number

This is a 3-bit value (0-7) which represents the number of the selected controller. This allows up to eight different controllers to be connected and served. The number which addresses each individual controller is set with the help of three switches on the controller board. When a command arrives at the controllers over the common bus line, each one tests to see if it is the one being accessed. If not, it behaves as if it didn't exist. If so, communication between the computer (initiator) and the addressed controller (target) begins. If no controller answers the command within four seconds, the computer gives up: time out.

Operation code:

This code, also called the *opcode*, contains the command to be executed in five bits. This means that only commands from 0 to 31 are possible.

Drive number:

Similar to the controller number, this is a 3-bit number which designates the selected drive. Each of the eight controllers can control up to eight drives, which means that 64 drives can be theoretically connected to the Atari.

Block address:

This 21-bit number designates the selected logical sector. The conversion of this number (up to 2097151) into the physical values is accomplished by the controller. The Atari hard disk contains 41616 sectors, so the block addresses may not exceed this value and, since the block numbers start at zero, may not reach it either.

Block counter:

This counter determines the number of sectors to read or write. The counter must have a non-zero value (1-255).

Control byte:

This byte contains various specifications, depending on the given command.

The following procedure must be executed in order to send such a command to the HDC:

First, the processor is placed in the supervisor mode through the SUPER function ($20) of GEMDOS (TRAP #1), because some privileged accesses must be made to hardware registers.

After this, the floppy-processing routines are disabled by setting the system variable FLOCK ($43E). This is necessary because both the FDC and the HDC are controlled via the same hardware registers. To make sure that there are no crossed signals, such as an OK from one controller when we are waiting for the OK from the other one, the FDC is essentially removed from the system so that it doesn't interfere.

In the hardware register $FF8606, called WDL, bits 7 and 3 are set and all others cleared by writing the value $88. This selects the HDC and places the line A1, which is addressed through bit 1, to zero.

Line A1 is used to signal the HDC that a command byte (the first byte of a command block) will be transferred.

Following this, the command byte is placed in register $FF8604, called WDC. The HDC accepts this byte and acknowledges reception with a 0-signal on the HDC interrupt line. This line lies on bit 5 of the I/O port on the Multi-Function Peripheral chip (MFP), and can be found at address $FFFA01.

This interrupt also occurs after each additional byte is transmitted. If it does not occur, the byte was either not recognized or the HDC is not ready to receive data.

During the transmission of the command bytes, there is a maximum wait of 100 milliseconds for the interrupt, and up to three seconds after the complete transmission of the command block, because the command must be completely executed before the HDC can respond OK. If no interrupt occurs within this time, the transmission of the command bytes is terminated and a timeout is indicated.

If the command byte is transferred and acknowledged on time through the interrupt, an $8A is written in the WDL, which sets the A1 line to 1 again.

The remaining five bytes of the command block are now transferred according to the same scheme, except with bit 1 (A1) set. The byte is written to WDC together with an $8A in WDL, the computer waits 100 ms for an interrupt (else timeout) and the next byte is transferred.

After transmission of the last byte (byte 5) of the command block, the computer waits a maximum of three seconds for the interrupt, so that the HDC has enough time to execute the command.

Finally, the system variable FLOCK ($43E) is again set to 0 in order to permit floppy operations again, and last of all, the computer can be switched back into the user mode.

Here is a small program which performs the steps listed above and sends a command block to the HDC. Please note that this works completely only if the command does not cause data transfer via DMA (such as READ and WRITE), because the DMA controller must then be programmed. We will come to this later.

```
; ** Hard disk access S.D. **
; ** Send command-bytes from COM-field to HDC **


wdc        = $ff8604
wdl        = $ff8606
wdcwdl     = wdc
port       = $fffa01
flock      = $43e

run:
           move.b      #'0',num        ;Timeout-report preparation
           clr.l       -(sp)
           move        #$20,-(sp)
           trap        #1              ;Switch to Supervisor-Mode
           addq.l      #6,sp
           move.l      d0,spsave       ;Alter stack pointer--save

           lea         com,a0          ;pointer to command-block
           bsr         send            ;Send command-block on HDC
           bra         exit            ;Ready

send:                                  ;* Send command-Block on HDC *
           st          flock           ;Floppy block
           move        #$88,wdl        ;Select HDC, A1=0
           clr.l       d0
           moveq       #5,d2           ;Number: 6 Bytes
```

```
loop:
        clr.l       d0
        move.b      (a0)+,d0        ;Greatest byte
        bsr         send_byte       ;Send byte to HDC
        bmi         error           ;Timeout !
        dbra        d2,loop         ;Loop

cont:
        move        #$8a,wdl
        bsr         wait1           ;Wait a max. of 3 seconds for
                                    ;interrupt
        bmi         error           ;Timeout !
        move        #$8a,wdl
        move        wdc,d0          ;Get status-byte
        move        #$80,wdl        ;Deselect HDC
        move        wdc,d1          ;Get completion-byte
        clr         flock           ;Stop floppy disk access
        rts                         ;Ready

exit:
        move.l      spsave,-(sp)
        move        #$20,-(sp)
        trap        #1              ;Switch to User-Mode
        addq.l      #6,sp
;       rts                         ;End as subroutine

        clr.w       -(sp)
        trap        #1              ;Return to desktop

error:                              ;Show error
        clr         flock           ;Stop floppy disk access
        move.l      #senderr,d0
        bsr         pline           ;Display error message
        bra         exit            ;and end

send_byte:                          ;* Semd a byte to the HDC *
        swap        d0              ;Byte in HIGH-value
        move        #$8a,d0         ;$8A in LOW-value
        move.l      d0,wdcwdl       ;Set WDC and WDL
        bra         wait            ;Wait for OK (Interrupt)

wait1:
        add.b       #1,num          ;Running number+1
        move.l      #450000,d3      ;Timeout for 3 seconds
        bra         wait1           ;Wait...
wait:
        add.b       #1,num          ;Running number+1
```

```
                move.l      #15000,d3       ;Timeout for 100 ms
wait1:
                subq.l      #1,d3           ;Timeout counter-1
                bmi         timeout         ;Timeout !
                move.b      port,d0         ;Load I/O-Port
                and.b       #$20,d0         ;Combine bit 5
                bne         wait1           ;If it's still set,
                                            ;continue waiting
                moveq       #0,d3           ;Display OK
                rts                         ;Ready
timeout:
                moveq       #-1,d3          ;Don't display OK
                rts

pline:                                      ;* Print a line on the screen *
                move.l      d0,-(sp)
                move        #9,-(sp)
                trap        #1
                addq.l      #6,sp
                rts

spsave:         dc.l 1
senderr:        dc.b "ERROR in send_byte "
num:            dc.b "1. time!",10,13,0
com:            dc.b $b,$0,$0,0,0,$0
  align
  end
```

The command block bytes which this program transmits cause the read/write head of the hard disk to move to track 0 ($B=Seek). The program contains an error output for testing purposes which displays a timeout on the screen. This section can be omitted, of course, since it only checks to see that the command block was properly transmitted.

The transmission of a read or write command to the HDC is somewhat more complicated. In addition to transferring the command block, the DMA (Direct Memory Access) controller, which is responsible for the transfer of data between the hard disk and computer memory, must be programmed.

The DMA controller requires the following information:

- the memory address from which the data will be read or to which they will be written. This address is written in the hardware registers $FF8609, $FF860B, and $FF860D—first the low byte, then the middle byte, and last the high byte of the address. Since this represents a 24-bit address instead of a full 32 bits, the address can "only" be between 0 and $FFFFFF (also used for FDC programming).

- the direction in which the data are to be transferred (read or written). The DMA controller gets this information from bit eight of the WDL word, whereby 0 means read and 1 means write outside of memory.

- the status of the DMA controller, on or off. The DMAC gets this information from bit six of the WDL register $FF8606. Normally the DMA controller is always on, meaning bit 6 = 0.

The exact moment at which the DMAC is given this information is also important so that any operations in progress are not disturbed. If we want to read from the hard disk, the command byte is first sent to the HDC and then the DMA address is set. This prevents the DMAC from loading undesirable information into memory because the HDC first waits for the additional bytes of the command block after receiving the command block.

To write to the hard disk, the DMA address is set first, and then the command byte is transferred. You can see how this is done in the program `HDC tools` in section 5.1.1.3. First, however, we stick to theory and take a look at the HDC commands.

5.1.1.2 List of commands

The command set used for the ST hard disk contains only nine different commands. Other commands are listed in the various manuals for the hard disk, but either they don't work as indicated, or they don't work at all. Here is an overview of the working commands and their hexadecimal opcodes:

Opcode	Command
00	Test Unit Ready
01	Restore
03	Request Sense
04	Format Drive
08	Read
0A	Write
0B	Seek
15	Mode Select
1B	Seek to shipping position

The following is an explanation of the individual commands, together with their parameter bytes. The "-" character indicates that a byte has no meaning, and should be cleared.

Test Unit Ready (00)

With this command the computer can address the bus and determine which devices are connected.

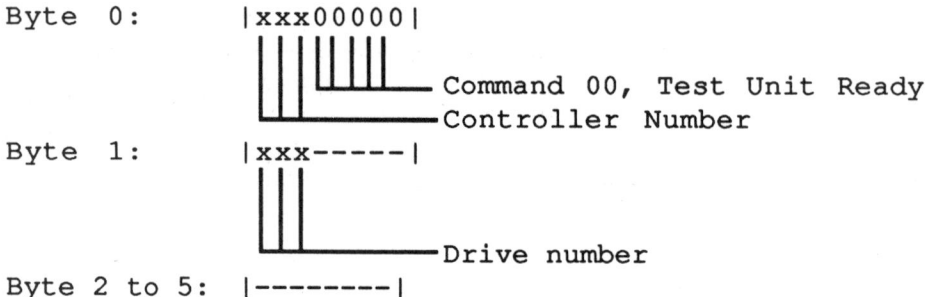

If the specified drive is turned on and ready, a zero will be returned in the status byte, else the Check Condition bit will be set.

Restore (01)

This command resets the HDC to its initial state and causes the drive read/write head to move to track 0.

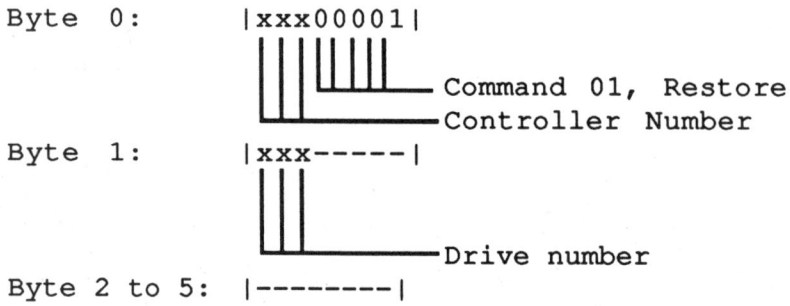

Request Sense (03)

This command returns four bytes (read the WDC four times), of which only the first byte has any meaning. It contains the error code of the last command to be executed. If no error occurred, this will contain a zero.

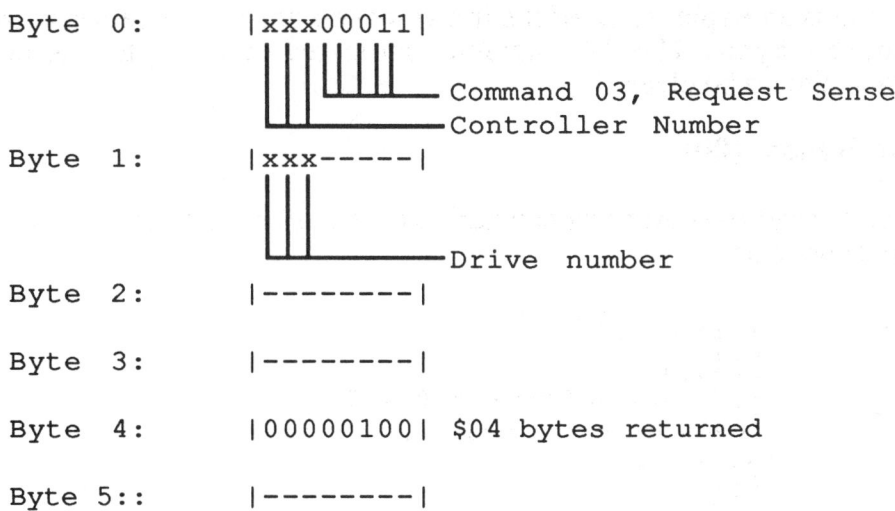

```
Byte 0:      |xxx00011|
                 ||||||
                 |||||└── Command 03, Request Sense
                 ||└───── Controller Number
Byte 1:      |xxx-----|
                 |||
                 |||
                 ||└───── Drive number

Byte 2:      |--------|

Byte 3:      |--------|

Byte 4:      |00000100|  $04 bytes returned

Byte 5::     |--------|
```

Format Drive (04)

This command instructs the HDC to format the entire disk. It should go without saying that you shouldn't experiment with this command!

Some parameters are included with the command:

- the Data Pattern flag, which consists of two bits and determines what data will be written to the empty sectors. If the bits are not set (0), all sectors will be written with $6C. If the bits are set, the byte passed in command byte 2 will be written.

- Data Pattern. Here is the byte with which the formatted sectors will be filled if the Data Pattern flag is set. If the flag is not set, this byte has no meaning.

- Interleave factor. This value specifies the distance between two consecutively numbered sectors on the disk. If the factor is 1, the sectors will be written on the track in order. If, for example, it is 2, another sectors is placed between sectors 1 and 2. The order of the seventeen sectors on the track would be as follows:

```
Floating number
    1   2   3   4   5   6   7   8   9  10  11  12  13  14  15  16  17
    ┼───┼───┼───┼───┼───┼───┼───┼───┼───┼───┼───┼───┼───┼───┼───┼───┼
    1  10   2  11   3  12   4  13   5  14   6  15   7  16   8  17   9
Sector number
```

This means that two revolutions of the disk are necessary in order to read all of the sectors in a track. This makes reading a track longer, but also more reliable because there is a small pause after reading each sector. Normally this factor is set to 1.

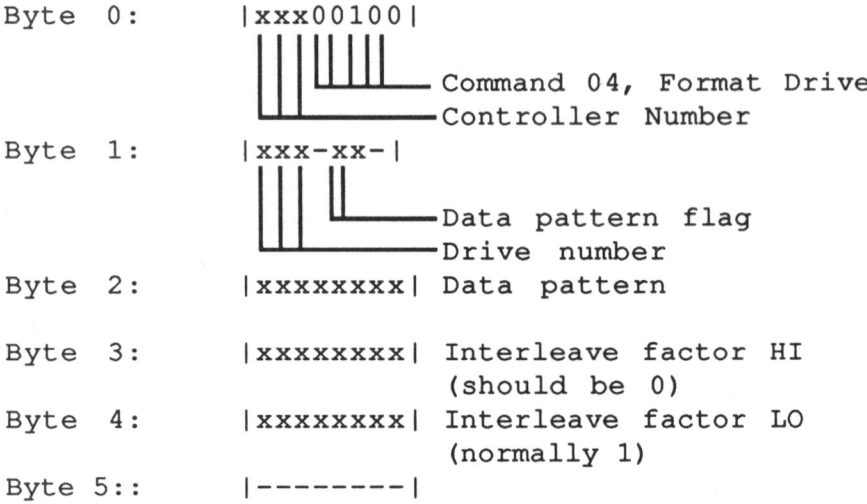

```
Byte 0:      |xxx00100|
                        Command 04, Format Drive
                        Controller Number

Byte 1:      |xxx-xx-|
                        Data pattern flag
                        Drive number

Byte 2:      |xxxxxxxx| Data pattern

Byte 3:      |xxxxxxxx| Interleave factor HI
                        (should be 0)

Byte 4:      |xxxxxxxx| Interleave factor LO
                        (normally 1)

Byte 5::     |--------|
```

Read sector (08)

This command instructs the controller to move the read/write head to the track which contains the desired start sector, to read the specified number of sectors, and to transmit them to the computer. In addition to the transfer of the command block to the HDC, the DMAC must be programmed so that the arriving data are written into the appropriate area of memory.

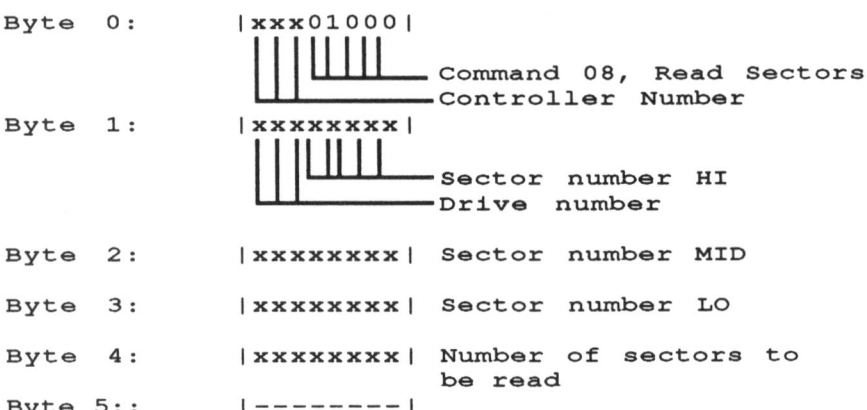

```
Byte 0:      |xxx01000|
                        Command 08, Read Sectors
                        Controller Number

Byte 1:      |xxxxxxxx|
                        Sector number HI
                        Drive number

Byte 2:      |xxxxxxxx| Sector number MID

Byte 3:      |xxxxxxxx| Sector number LO

Byte 4:      |xxxxxxxx| Number of sectors to
                        be read

Byte 5::     |--------|
```

Write Sectors (0A)

This command writes sectors on the disk. The head is moved to the corresponding track and the data sent via the DMA channel are received and written to the sectors. The DMAC must again be programmed in addition to sending the command block.

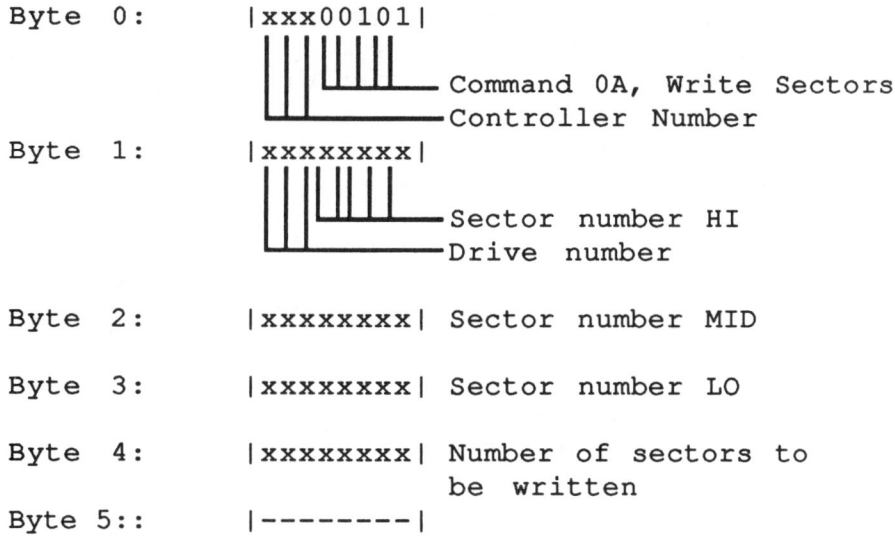

```
Byte 0:    |xxx00101|
                     Command 0A, Write Sectors
                     Controller Number

Byte 1:    |xxxxxxxx|
                     Sector number HI
                     Drive number

Byte 2:    |xxxxxxxx| Sector number MID

Byte 3:    |xxxxxxxx| Sector number LO

Byte 4:    |xxxxxxxx| Number of sectors to
                            be written
Byte 5::   |--------|
```

Seek (0B)

The read/write head in the drive is moved by this command. The controller calculates the corresponding track from the sector number passed with the command and moves the head there.

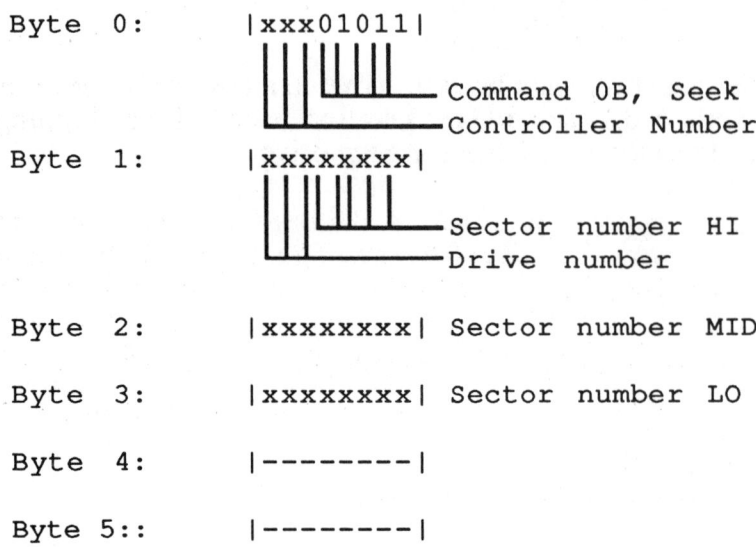

Mode Select (15)

This command is used for setting the parameters for formatting the hard disk. A 16-byte clock is sent to the HDC after passing the command (and programming the DMAC).

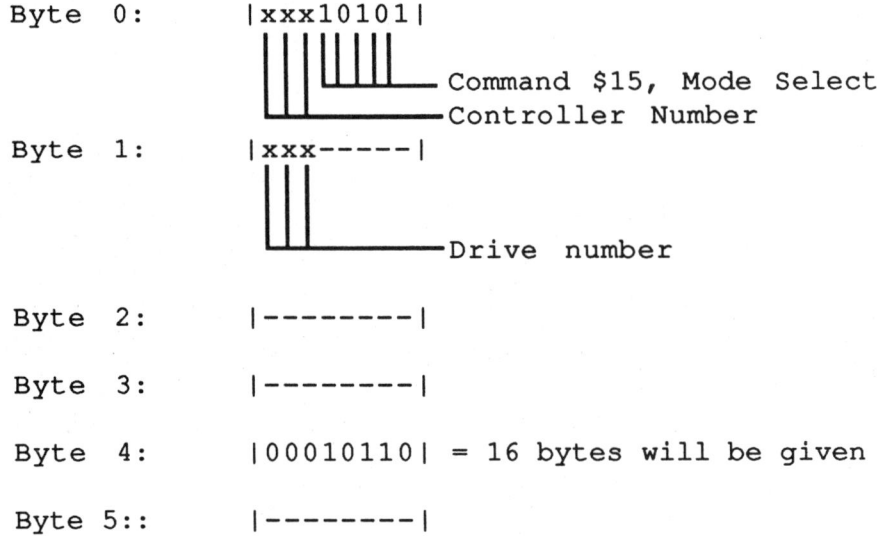

Seek to shipping position (1B)

This command causes the read/write head to move to a position where it is safe against movements of the drive. This position is called the shipping position because it is provided for transporting the drive.

The program SHIP.PRG moves the heads in all connected hard drives to this position. It should always be run before moving a hard disk. It should be noted that the screen should be free of all hard disk directory windows when calling this program, otherwise the hard disk directory will be read when the program is done, moving the head out of its safe position.

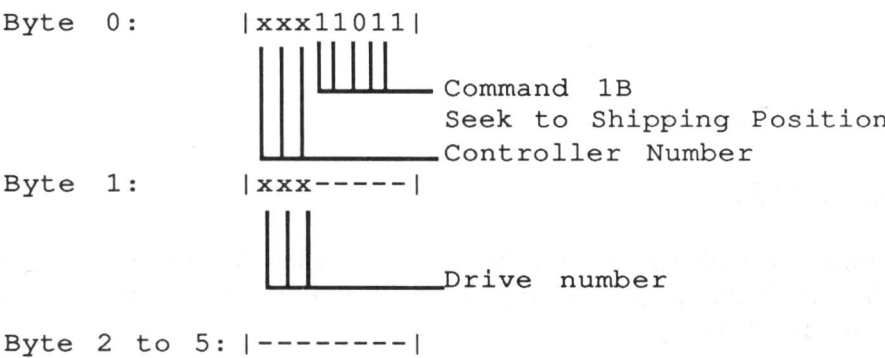

5.1.1.3 HDC tools

To demonstrate read and write accesses to the hard disk, here is a program which reads one or more sectors and transfers them to memory, or writes data to sectors from memory. In the example, eight sectors from sector 132 on are loaded into memory. This is where the directory of the first hard disk partition is stored.

This program also contains a simple method of transmitting the command block, similar to the example in section 5.1.1.1.

```
;** Read/write hard disk sector, send command **

wdc       = $ff8604 ;FDC/HDC access, DMA-sector count
wdl       = wdc+2   ;DMA-Mode/Status
dma       = $ff8609 ;DMA-address HI
flock     = $43e    ;Floppy-VBL-Flag
port      = $fffa01 ;Parallel port, bit 5=HDC-IRQ
```

```
run:
            clr.l        -(sp)
            move         #$20,-(sp)
            trap         #1              ;Switch to Supervisor-Mode
            addq.l       #6,sp
            move.l       d0,spsave       ;Store user stack pointer
bp1:
            bra          put             ;for transfer only
            pea          BUFFER          ;Buffer address
            move         #8,-(sp)        ;8 sectors
            move.l       #132,-(sp)      ;Up to sector 132
            bsr          read            ;Read sector(s) in buffer
            bra          bp2
put:
            bsr          send            ;Transfer command block
bp2:
            move.l       spsave,-(sp)
            move         #$20,-(sp)
            trap         #1              ;Switch to User-Mode
            addq.l       #6,sp

;           rts                          ;Return for subroutine
                                         ;or
            clr          -(sp)
            trap         #1              ;Return to Desktop

send:       ;* Transfer command block *
            lea          wdc,a0
            lea          com,a1          ;Pointer to command block
            st           flock           ;Save floppy
            move         #$88,wdl        ;Select HDC, A1=0
            clr.l        d0
            moveq        #5,d1
loop:
            clr.l        d0
            move.b       (a1)+,d0
            bsr          send_byte       ;Send byte on HDC
            bmi          tout            ;Timeout!
            dbra         d1,loop         ;Otherwise keep looping

            bsr          waitl           ;Wait a max. of 3 seconds
            bmi          tout            ;Timeout!
            move         wdc,d6
            move         #$80,wdl        ;Else
            clr          flock           ;stop disk access
            rts                          ;Ready
```

```
read:       ; * Sector(s) read *
            lea         wdc,a0
            st          flock               ;Save Floppy-VBL routine
            move        #$88,2(a0)          ;HDC-access, A1=0
            nop
            move.l      #$08008a,(a0)       ;READ command

            move.l      10(sp),-(sp)        ;Buffer address
            bsr         setdma              ;Set DMA
            addq.l      #4,sp

            bsr         set_parameters      ;Amount and number of sectors
            bmi         tout                ;Timeout !

            move        #$190,2(a0)
            nop
            move        #$90,2(a0)          ;Switch to READ
            nop
            move        8(sp),(a0)          ;Send sector count to DMA
            nop
            move        #$8a,2(a0)
            nop
            move.l      #0,(a0)             ;Start transfer
            bsr         wait1               ;Wait a max. of 3 seconds
            bmi         tout                ;Timeout !
            move        #$8a,2(a0)
            bra         exec

write:      ; * Sector(s) write *
            lea         wdc,a0
            st          flock               ;Save Floppy-VBL
            move.l      10(sp),-(sp)
            bsr         setdma              ;Set DMA address
            addq.l      #4,sp

            move        #$88,2(a0)          ;HDC access, A1=0
            nop
            move.l      #$0a008a,(a0)       ;WRITE command

            bsr         set_parameters      ;Amount and number of sectors
            bmi         tout                ;Timeout !

            move        #$90,2(a0)
            nop
            move        #$190,2(a0)         ;Switch to WRITE
            nop
            move        8(sp),(a0)          ;Send sector count to DMA
```

```
                nop
                move        #$18a,2(a0)
                nop
                move.l      #$100,(a0)          ;Begin transfer
                bsr         wait1               ;Wait a max. of 3 seconds
                bmi         tout                ;Timeout !
                move        #$18a,2(a0)

exec:
                nop
                move.l      (a0),d6             ;Get HDC/DMA status in D6
                and.l       #$ff00ff,d6         ;HI=HDC, LO=DMA
tout:
                move        #$80,2(a0)          ;Switch to FDC
                nop
                move.l      (a0),d7             ;Get completion byte
                and.l       #$ff00ff,d7         ;HI=HDC (0), LO=DMA
                clr         flock               ;Stop Floppy-VBL routine
                rts                             ;Ready

set_parameters:             ;Set sector number and sector count
                move        #$8a,2(a0)
                bsr         wait                ;Wait for HDC-OK
                bmi         setpx               ;Timeout !

                clr         d0
                move.b      4+5(sp),d0
                bsr         send_byte           ;Sector no. HI
                bmi         setpx

                move.b      4+6(sp),d0
                bsr         send_byte           ;Sector no. MID
                bmi         setpx

                move.b      4+7(sp),d0
                bsr         send_byte           ;Sector no. LO
                bmi         setpx

                move        4+8(sp),d0          ;Number of sectors
                bsr         send_byte
setpx:
                rts                             ;Ready

send_byte: ;  * Send 1 byte to HDC *
                swap        d0
                move        #$8a,d0
                move.l      d0,(a0)
```

```
                    bra             wait
waitl:  ;Wait a max. of 3 seconds for OK
                    move.l          #450000,count
                    bra             wait1
wait:   ;Wait a max. of 100 ms for OK
                    move.l          #15000,count
wait1:
                    subq.l          #1,count
                    bmi             timeout
                    move.b          port,d0
                    and.b           #$20,d0         ;HDC-Interrupt ?
                    bne             wait1           ;no
                    moveq           #0,d0           ;Yes => OK
                    rts
timeout:
                    move.l          #errline,d0
                    bsr             pline           ;Send 'Timeout'
                    moveq           #-1,d0          ;Display Timeout
                    rts

setdma:  ; * Set DMA-address *
                    move.b          7(sp),dma+4     ;LO
                    move.b          6(sp),dma+2     ;MID
                    move.b          5(sp),dma       ;HI
                    rts
pline:   ; * Print line on screen *
                    move.l          d0,-(sp)
                    move            #9,-(sp)
                    trap            #1
                    addq.l          #6,sp
                    rts

errline:            dc.b            "Timeout encountered!",10,13,0
com:                dc.b            $b,0,0,132,0,0
  ALIGN.L
count:              dc.l            1               ;Timeout counter
spsave:             dc.l            0               ;User stack pointer
BUFFER:             ds.B            512*8,$FF       ;BUFFER FOR 8 SECTORS

    end
```

This program gives you the ability to load sectors directly from the hard disk or write information to them. The status information is written in register D6, which can be displayed using a machine-language monitor or debugger such as SID or the *AssemPro* debugger.

The difference between this program and the functions available in the operating system for reading and writing sectors is that the operating system functions can access only the selected partition on the disk. If you want to read sector 0 from the hard disk, for example, you must do it with the program above.

5.1.1.4 Partition analyzer

Sector zero of the hard disk is very interesting because it contains information about the hard disk and its partitions. The following program can be used to read and evaluate this information. Among other things, it contains parts of the previous program (read), which can be taken directly from the previous source code.

The program reads sector 0 of the hard disk and interprets the data it contains. These are then displayed on the screen in hexadecimal.

```
;** Partition Analyzer S.D. HD 3**

wdc     = $ff8604                ;FDC/HDC-Access, DMA sector count
wdl     = wdc+2                  ;DMA-Mode/Status
dma     = $ff8609                ;DMA-address HI
flock   = $43e                   ;Floppy-VBL flag
port    = $fffa01                ;Parallel port, bit 5=HDC-IRQ

run:
            lea         stp,sp
            clr.l       -(sp)
            move        #$20,-(sp)
            trap        #1              ;Switch to Supervisor-Mode
            addq.l      #6,sp
            move.l      d0,spsave       ;Store user stack pointer

            pea         buf             ;Buffer address
            move        #1,-(sp)        ;1st sector
            move.l      #0,-(sp)        ;from sector 0
            bsr         read            ;Read sector(s) in buffer

            move.l      spsave,-(sp)
            move        #$20,-(sp)
            trap        #1              ;Switch to User-Mode
            addq.l      #6,sp
```

```
        move.l      #head,d0
        bsr         pline               ;Print amount

        move.l      #hi_cc,d0
        bsr         pmsg
        move        buf+$1b6,d0
        bsr         pword               ;Print cylinder number
        bsr         pcrlf

        move.l      #hi_dhc,d0
        bsr         pmsg
        move.b      buf+$1b8,d0
        bsr         pbyt                ;Display number of heads
        bsr         pcrlf

        move.l      #hi_lz,d0
        bsr         pmsg
        move.b      buf+$1be,d0
        bsr         pbyt                ;Display park position
        bsr         pcrlf

        move.l      #hi_rt,d0
        bsr         pmsg
        move.b      buf+$1bf,d0
        bsr         pbyt                ;Output seek rate
        bsr         pcrlf

        move.l      #hi_in,d0
        bsr         pmsg
        move.b      buf+$1c0,d0
        bsr         pbyt                ;Output interleave factor
        bsr         pcrlf

        move.l      #hi_spt,d0
        bsr         pmsg
        move.b      buf+$1c1,d0
        bsr         pbyt                ;Display sectors/track
        bsr         pcrlf

        move.l      #hd_size,d0
        bsr         pmsg
        move.l      buf+$1c2,d0
        bsr         plong               ;Display sectors
                                        ;of hard disk
        bsr         pcrlf

        move.l      #bsl_count,d0
```

```
        bsr         pmsg
        move.l      buf+$1fa,d0
        bsr         plong               ;Display number of dead
                                        ;sectors
        bsr         pcrlf

        clr         d5
        clr.l       d6
        lea         buf+$1c6,a6         ;Partition field 0

        bsr         key
loop:
        bsr         pcrlf
        move.b      d5,px_on
        add.b       #'0',px_on
        cmp.b       #0,0(a6,d6)         ;Partition active?
        bne         pon                 ;Yes
        move.l      #' out',px_on+14    ;Else display 'Out'
        move.l      #px_on,d0
        bsr         pline
        bra         nextp
pon:
        move.l      #' on ',px_on+14
        move.l      #px_on,d0
        bsr         pline               ;Display 'Partition on'
        and.b       #$80,0(a6,d6)       ;Bootable?
        beq         noboot              ;No
        move.l      #boot,d0
        bsr         pline               ;Else display 'Bootable'
noboot:
        move.b      1(a6,d6),px_id+18
        move.w      2(a6,d6),px_id+19
        move.l      #px_id,d0
        bsr         pline

        move.l      #px_start,d0
        bsr         pmsg
        move.l      4(a6,d6),d0
        bsr         plong               ;Display start sector
        bsr         pcrlf

        move.l      #px_size,d0
        bsr         pmsg
        move.l      8(a6,d6),d0
        bsr         plong               ;Display sectors/track
        bsr         pcrlf
```

```
nextp:
                addq        #1,d5
                add         #12,d6
                cmp         #4*12,d6
                blt         loop

                bsr         key             ;wait for keypress
                clr         -(sp)
                trap        #1              ;Return to Desktop

read:       ;Read sector(s) (as above)
                lea         wdc,a0
                st          flock           ;Save floppy-VBL routine
                move        #$88,2(a0)      ;HDC access, A1=0
                nop
                move.l      #$8008a,(a0)    ;READ command

                move.l      10(sp),-(sp)    ;Buffer address
                bsr         setdma          ;Set DMA
                addq.l       #4,sp

                bsr         set_parameters  ;Set amount and
                                            ;number of sectors

                bmi         tout            ;Timeout encountered!

                move        #$190,2(a0)
                nop
                move        #$90,2(a0)      ;Switch to READ
                nop
                move        8(sp),(a0)      ;Send sector count to DMA
                nop
                move        #$8a,2(a0)
                nop
                move.l      #0,(a0)         ;Start transfer
                bsr         wait1
                bmi         tout
                move        #$8a,2(a0)
                move.l      (a0),d6         ;Get HDC/DMA status
                and.l       #$ff00ff,d6     ;HI=HDC, LO=DMA
tout:
                move        #$80,2(a0)      ;Switch to FDC
                nop
                move.l      (a0),d7         ;Get completion byte
                and.l       #$ff00ff,d7     ;HI=FDC, LO=DMA
                clr         flock           ;Release floppy-VBL-routine
                rts                         ;Ready
```

```
set_parameters:   ;Set sector numbers and sector count
            move          #$8a,2(a0)
            bsr           wait              ;Wait for HDC-OK
            bmi           setpx             ;Timeout !

            clr           d0
            move.b        4+5(sp),d0        ;Sector no. HI
            bsr           send_byte
            bmi           setpx
            move.b        4+6(sp),d0        ;Sector no. MID
            bsr           send_byte
            bmi           setpx
            move.b        4+7(sp),d0        ;Sector no. LO
            bsr           send_byte
            bmi           setpx
            move          4+8(sp),d0        ;Number of sectors
            bsr           send_byte
setpx:
            rts

send_byte:    ;Send 1 byte to HDC
            swap          d0
            move          #$8a,d0
            move.l        d0,(a0)
            bra           wait

wait1:     ;Wait a max. of 3 seconds for OK
            move.l        #450000,count
            bra           wait1
wait:      ;Wait a max. of 100 ms for OK
            move.l        #15000,count
wait1:
            subq.l        #1,count
            bmi           timeout
            move.b        port,d0
            and.b         #$20,d0           ;HDC-Interrupt ?
            bne           wait1             ;No
            moveq         #0,d0             ;Yes => OK
            rts
timeout:
            move.l        #errline,d0
            bsr           pline
            moveq         #-1,d0            ;Display timeout
            rts

setdma:    ;Set DMA-addresse
            move.b        7(sp),dma+4       ;LO
```

```
                move.b      6(sp),dma+2     ;MID
                move.b      5(sp),dma       ;HI
                rts

                                            ; ** other subroutines **

pline:      ;Print Line/CR
                bsr         pmsg
pcrlf:      ;Print CR,LF
                move        #10,d0
                bsr         pchar
                move        #13,d0
pchar:      ;Print Character D0
                move        d0,-(sp)
                move        #2,-(sp)
                trap        #1
                addq.l      #4,sp
                rts
pmsg:       ;Print Line (D0)
                move.l      d0,-(sp)
                move        #9,-(sp)
                trap        #1
                addq        #6,sp
                rts

plong:      ;Display D0 as an 8-digit hex number
                moveq       #7,d1
                bra         phexwll
pword:      ;Print hex-word D0
                swap        d0
                moveq       #3,d1
                bra         phexwll
pbyt:       ; Print hex-byte D0
                moveq       #1,d1
                ror.l       #8,d0
phexwll:
                rol.l       #4,d0
                move.l      d0,-(sp)
                move.l      d1,-(sp)
                bsr         phexnib
                move.l      (sp)+,d1
                move.l      (sp)+,d0
                dbra        d1,phexwll
                rts
phexnib:
                and.l       #$0f,d0
                add.b       #$30,d0
```

```
                cmp.b       #$3a,d0
                bcs         phexn1
                add.b       #7,d0
phexn1:
                bra         pchar                   ;Print character

key:
                bsr         pcrlf
                move.l      #keymsg,d0
                bsr         pmsg
                move        #1,-(sp)
                trap        #1                      ;Wait for keypress
                addq        #2,sp
                rts

head:           dc.b        "** Hard disk-Analysis 8/86 S.D. **",0
hi_cc:          dc.b        "Cylinder          : ",0
hi_dhc:         dc.b        "Head              : ",0
hi_lz:          dc.b        "Park Position     : ",0
hi_rt:          dc.b        "Seek Rate         : ",0
hi_in:          dc.b        "Interleave        : ",0
hi_spt:         dc.b        "Sectors/Track     : ",0
hd_size:        dc.b        "Complete sectors: ",0
bsl_count:      dc.b        "Dead sectors      : ",0
   align
px_on:          dc.b        "1st partition:      ",0
boot:           dc.b        "Bootable            ",0
px_id:          dc.b        "Partition ID      : ",0
px_start:       dc.b        "Start sector      : ",0
px_size:        dc.b        "No. of sectors    : ",0

errline:        dc.b        "Timeout encountered!",10,13,0
keymsg:         dc.b        "Press any key to continue",10,13,0
   align
   bss                                              ;DATA
count:          dc.l        1                       ;Timeout counter
spsave:         dc.l        0                       ;User stackpointer
                ds.l        200
STP:            ds.l        1
BUF:            ds.b        512                     ;BUFFER FOR A SECTOR

    end
```

And here is the BASIC loader, which creates the program ANAPART.TOS on the disk:

```
10   '*********    Analyze partition loader      A.S.      *********
15   '
20   ?:fullw 2:clearw 2:gotoxy 0,0
25   ? "File >> anapart.tos << now being created":?:?:?
30   dim c%( 634):cs#=0
35   for i=0 to   634
40   read a$:c%(i)=val("&H"+a$)
45   check#=check#+(c%(i))
50   next i
55   if check#= 6754423.04 then   70
60   ?"Can't go any farther;something wrong with the DATA."
65   goto 80
70   bsave"anapart.tos",varptr(c%(0)), 1270
75   ? "The program >> anapart.tos << is now written."
80   ?:?"Please press a key";:a=inp(2):end
85   '
90   '*********  DATA for anapart.tos *********
95   '
100  DATA 601A,0000,04AE,0000,0000,0000,052C,0000
101  DATA 0000,0000,0000,0000,0000,0000,4FF9,0000
102  DATA 07D6,42A7,3F3C,0020,4E41,5C8F,23C0,0000
103  DATA 04B2,4879,0000,07DA,3F3C,0001,2F3C,0000
104  DATA 0000,6100,01A0,2F39,0000,04B2,3F3C,0020
105  DATA 4E41,5C8F,203C,0000,0364,6100,02AA,203C
106  DATA 0000,0387,6100,02BC,3039,0000,0990,6100
107  DATA 02C4,6100,0296,203C,0000,039A,6100,02A4
108  DATA 1039,0000,0992,6100,02B4,6100,027E,203C
109  DATA 0000,03AD,6100,028C,1039,0000,0998,6100
110  DATA 029C,6100,0266,203C,0000,03C0,6100,0274
111  DATA 1039,0000,0999,6100,0284,6100,024E,203C
112  DATA 0000,03D3,6100,025C,1039,0000,099A,6100
113  DATA 026C,6100,0236,203C,0000,03E6,6100,0244
114  DATA 1039,0000,099B,6100,0254,6100,021E,203C
115  DATA 0000,03F9,6100,022C,2039,0000,099C,6100
116  DATA 022E,6100,0206,203C,0000,040C,6100,0214
117  DATA 2039,0000,09D4,6100,0216,6100,01EE,4245
118  DATA 4286,4DF9,0000,09A0,6100,0242,6100,01DC
119  DATA 13C5,0000,0420,0639,0030,0000,0420,0C36
120  DATA 0000,6000,6600,001A,23FC,206F,7574,0000
121  DATA 042E,203C,0000,0420,6100,01AC,6000,0070
122  DATA 23FC,206F,6E20,0000,042E,203C,0000,0420
123  DATA 6100,0194,0236,0080,6000,6700,000C,203C
124  DATA 0000,0433,6100,0180,13F6,6001,0000,044F
125  DATA 33F6,6002,0000,0450,203C,0000,043D,6100
126  DATA 0166,203C,0000,0454,6100,0178,2036,6004
127  DATA 6100,017C,6100,0154,203C,0000,0467,6100
128  DATA 0162,2036,6008,6100,0166,6100,013E,5245
```

```
129     DATA DC7C,000C,BC7C,0030,6D00,FF52,6100,018E
130     DATA 4267,4E41,41F9,00FF,8604,50F9,0000,043E
131     DATA 317C,0088,0002,4E71,20BC,0008,008A,2F2F
132     DATA 000A,6100,00E8,588F,6100,0058,6B00,003C
133     DATA 317C,0190,0002,4E71,317C,0090,0002,4E71
134     DATA 30AF,0008,4E71,317C,008A,0002,4E71,20BC
135     DATA 0000,0000,6100,0076,6B00,0010,317C,008A
136     DATA 0002,2C10,CCBC,00FF,00FF,317C,0080,0002
137     DATA 4E71,2E10,CEBC,00FF,00FF,4279,0000,043E
138     DATA 4E75,317C,008A,0002,6100,0050,6B00,0030
139     DATA 4240,102F,0009,6100,0028,6B00,0022,102F
140     DATA 000A,6100,001C,6B00,0016,102F,000B,6100
141     DATA 0010,6B00,000A,302F,000C,6100,0004,4E75
142     DATA 4840,303C,008A,2080,6000,0010,23FC,0006
143     DATA DDD0,0000,04AE,6000,000C,23FC,0000,3A98
144     DATA 0000,04AE,53B9,0000,04AE,6B00,0012,1039
145     DATA 00FF,FA01,C03C,0020,66EA,7000,4E75,203C
146     DATA 0000,047A,6100,0020,70FF,4E75,13EF,0007
147     DATA 00FF,860D,13EF,0006,00FF,860B,13EF,0005
148     DATA 00FF,8609,4E75,6100,001A,303C,000A,6100
149     DATA 0006,303C,000D,3F00,3F3C,0002,4E41,588F
150     DATA 4E75,2F00,3F3C,0009,4E41,5C4F,4E75,7207
151     DATA 6000,000E,4840,7203,6000,0006,7201,E098
152     DATA E998,2F00,2F01,6100,000C,221F,201F,51C9
153     DATA FFF0,4E75,C0BC,0000,000F,D03C,0030,B03C
154     DATA 003A,6500,0006,D03C,0007,60AA,619C,203C
155     DATA 0000,0491,61AC,3F3C,0001,4E41,544F,4E75
156     DATA 2A2A,2048,6172,6420,6469,736B,2D41,6E61
157     DATA 6C79,7369,7320,382F,3836,2053,2E44,2E20
158     DATA 2A2A,0043,796C,696E,6465,7220,2020,2020
159     DATA 2020,203A,2000,4865,6164,2020,2020,2020
160     DATA 2020,2020,2020,3A20,0050,6172,6B20,506F
161     DATA 7369,7469,6F6E,2020,203A,2000,5365,656B
162     DATA 2052,6174,6520,2020,2020,2020,3A20,0049
163     DATA 6E74,6572,6C65,6176,6520,2020,2020,203A
164     DATA 2000,5365,6374,6F72,732F,5472,6163,6B20
165     DATA 2020,3A20,0043,6F6D,706C,6574,6520,7365
166     DATA 6374,6F72,733A,2000,4465,6164,2073,6563
167     DATA 746F,7273,2020,2020,3A20,0000,3173,7420
168     DATA 7061,7274,6974,696F,6E3A,2020,2020,0042
169     DATA 6F6F,7461,626C,6520,0050,6172,7469,7469
170     DATA 6F6E,2049,4420,2020,203A,2020,2020,2000
171     DATA 5374,6172,7420,7365,6374,6F72,2020,2020
172     DATA 3A20,004E,6F2E,206F,6620,7365,6374,6F72
173     DATA 7320,203A,2000,5469,6D65,6F75,7420,656E
174     DATA 636F,756E,7465,7265,6421,0A0D,0050,7265
175     DATA 7373,2061,6E79,206B,6579,2074,6F20,636F
```

```
176     DATA 6E74,696E,7565,0A0D,0000,0000,0002,1006
177     DATA 140E,0A0A,0E0A,0E0A,0E0A,0E0A,0E0A,0E0A
178     DATA 0E0A,120E,0814,0612,0614,0C08,060A,16F8
179     DATA 0E06,1A90,0000
```

As we mentioned in the section on boot sectors, the `px_flag` for each partition (maximum of four) indicates whether it is active and bootable. The Atari ST hard disk usually contains no bootable sectors because the ST cannot boot from the hard disk without the hard disk driver `AHDI.PRG`.

The `Seek Rate` is usually given as 2, which corresponds to 3 ms per step. `Interleave` can be from 1 to 16 (sectors/track - 1), but it is usually 1. This represents the distance between two consecutively-numbered sectors on the track.

The value behind `Dead sectors` indicates the number of defective sectors on the entire hard disk. These sectors are recognized and marked by the `HDX.PRG` program. A zero here means that the hard disk is perfect. Otherwise, one defective sector per megabyte is quite normal.

5.2 Connecting the hard disk

The 19-pin jack on the back of the ST is the DMA interface. The hard disk is connected to this jack by the included (short) cable and thereby has direct access to the memory in ST via the DMA controller. The reason for the short cable lies in the high data transfer rate. Wires tend to act as antennae, so that signals from one wire can find their way into another and disturb the data exchange if the wires are too long.

The data are transferred in parallel over eight data lines (pins 1-8), so that an entire byte can be transferred at one time. In addition, this interface has various service lines like Reset (pin 12), which the ST can use to reset the hard disk, or an interrupt line (pin 10), which the hard disk uses to signal the ST and acknowledge the reception of data.

You can theoretically connect up to eight controllers with up to eight hard drives each to the Atari ST, but since there is no second connector on the hard disk, this would require some homebrew modifications.

To communicate with the hard disk, the computer must send its commands in the form of command blocks over the data lines. These command blocks have already been described. In the HDC program this was accomplished by simply selecting the appropriate register and writing the command byte. The byte is then on the data lines and can be accepted by the hard disk, which then acknowledges it over the interrupt line.

In order to permit any data exchange at all, the drive program AHDI.PRG (Atari Hard Disk Interface) must be loaded. This and the HDX program run only if TOS is built into the computer; the driver works, but the HDX program does not, which makes it impossible to use the hard disk. The hard disk must be formatted before it can be used and also partitioned, because the controller can process a maximum of 16 megabytes per partition.

5.3 Print the complete directory

Folders are used heavily to organize the large number of files which the hard disk can store, and folders can even be nested within each other. This makes things much neater, but it can also make it harder to find a given file on the disk.

To find the file, you must keep opening and closing folders in order to view their contents. It would be much more practical if we could just print out the entire contents of the hard disk or diskette. This is not directly possible with the Atari operating system, however.

We will now present a program that does this. After it is loaded it asks for the drive designation (a-f) and then outputs the names of all the files on the selected disk to the printer, together with their folders. Folder contents are always indented two spaces to the right so that the nesting can be seen.

In addition to the names, the length of each file is also given in decimal next to the name. An output like this can be quite long if the hard disk contains a lot of data, but it can be very useful for finding files and for checking to see if more than one copy of a file exists on the disk.

Here is the program, written entirely in assembly language for the *AssemPro* assembler. If you use a different assembler, you may have to use an asterisk (*) instead of the semicolon for comments and replace the ds.x instruction with blk.x.

```
;** Display complete disk directory 8/86 S.D. **

run:
            lea         stp,sp
            move.l      #menu,d0
            bsr         pmsg
            bsr         getkey          ;Input drive
            cmp         #'a',d0
            blt         run             ;False drive
            cmp         #'f',d0
            bgt         run             ;False drive

            move.b      d0,fname
            bsr         pcrlf
            lea         fname+7,a6      ;Pointer to end of filename+1
            pea         dta
            move        #$1a,-(sp)
            trap        #1              ;SETDTA
            addq.l       #6,sp

            clr         d4              ;Depth=0
            lea         DEPTH,a4        ;Pointer to counter()-array
            move.b      #0,(a4)         ;Counter=0
            bsr         sfirst
            bra         test

sfirst:
            move        #$10,-(sp)      ;subdirectory
            pea         fname
            move        #$4e,-(sp)
            trap        #1              ;SFIRST
            addq.l      #8,sp
sea:
            cmp.b       #'.',dta+30     ;Subdirectory?
            bne         seax
            bsr         snext1
            tst         d0
            bne         seax
            bra         sea
seax:
            rts

snext:
            add.b       #1,(a4,d4)
snext1:
            move        #$4f,-(sp)
            trap        #1              ;SNEXT
```

```
                addq.l      #2,sp
                rts

next:
                bsr         snext
test:
                tst         d0
                bne         up              ;Go one level higher
                cmp.b       #$10,dta+21     ;Subdirectory ?
                bne         output          ;No: Display entry
                bra         down

up:
                subq        #1,d4           ;Depth=-1
                bmi         ready           ;Ready!
                sub         #6,a6
mlop:
                cmp.b       #'\',-(a6)
                bne         mlop
                bsr         addwc           ;"*.*",0 added
                bsr         sfirst
                clr         d7
                move.b      (a4,d4),d7      ;Counter(depth) in D7
                addq        #1,d7           ;Counter+1
                move.b      #0,(a4,d4)
selop:
                subq        #1,d7
                beq         next            ;Ready for this level
                bsr         snext           ;Look for counter(depth) entry

                bra         selop

down:
                move.l      #sub1,a5
                bsr         prtline
                move.l      #dta+30,a5
                bsr         prtline
                bsr         prtcr           ;Print CR
                addq        #1,d4           ;Depth+1
                move.b      #0,(a4,d4)
                subq.l      #4,a6
                move        #13,d7
                lea         dta+30,a3
flop:
                move.b      (a3)+,d0
                beq         flopx
                move.b      d0,(a6)+        ;Transfer filename as path
```

```
                dbra        d7,flop
flopx:
                bsr         addwc           ;"\*.*",0 added
bp:
                bsr         sfirst
                bra         test            ;Look for next depth

addwc:
                move.b      #'\',(a6)+
                move.b      #'*',(a6)+
                move.b      #'.',(a6)+
                move.b      #'*',(a6)+
                move.b      #0,(a6)+
                rts

output:     ;Output entry
                cmp.b       #8,$e1b         ;Alternate-key pressed?
                bne         out1            ;No
                bra         ready           ;Else stop
out1:
                lea         dta+30,a0
                lea         OUTLN,a5        ;Line output
                move        d4,d5
blop:
                move        #' ',(a5)+      ;Two spaces will assemble to
;                                            move.w $#2020,(a5)+
                dbra        d5,blop
blop1:
                move.b      (a0)+,d0
                beq         blop1x
                move.b      d0,(a5)+
                bra         blop1
blop1x:
                move.b      #' ',(a5)+      ; single space only
                cmp.l       #outln+26,a5
                blt         blop1x
                move.l      dta+26,d0
                bsr         pdec8
                move.b      #0,(a5)
                move.l      #outln,a5
                bsr         prtline
                bsr         prtcr
                bra         next

ready:      ;All done
                clr         -(sp)
                trap        #1              ;Exit => Desktop
```

```
menu:           dc.b    "**        Directory Output      S.D.       **",10,13
                dc.b    "Please input drive letter(a-f):",0
sub1:           dc.b    "Sub-Directory : ",0
fname:          dc.b    "a:\*.*",0,"                                        ",0
ALIGN.W

; ** Subroutines **

getkey:         ;Get Key -> D0
                move            #1,-(sp)
                trap            #1
                and.l           #$ff,d0
                addq.l          #2,sp
                rts

pline:          ;Print Line/CR
                bsr             pmsg
PCRLF:          ;PRINT CR,LF
                move            #10,d0
                bsr             pchar
                move            #13,d0
pchar:          ;Print Character D0
                move            d0,-(sp)
                move            #2,-(sp)
                trap            #1
                addq.l          #4,sp
                rts

prtline:        ;Print line from (a5)
                move.b          (a5)+,d0
                beq             prtx
                bsr             prtchr          ;Print character
                bra             prtline
prtx:
                rts

prtcr:                                          ;Print CR/LF
                move            #10,d0
                bsr             prtchr
                move            #13,d0
prtchr:
                move            d0,-(sp)
                move            #5,-(sp)        ;#2 for screen output
                trap            #1              ;Print character
                addq.l          #4,sp
                rts
```

```
pmsg:                                           ;Print Line (D0)
        move.l      d0,-(sp)
        move        #9,-(sp)
        trap        #1
        addq        #6,sp
        rts

pdec8:                                          ;Display D0 as 8-digit decimal
number
        divu        #10000,d0
        swap        d0
        move        d0,-(sp)        ;Remainder
        swap        d0
        and.l       #$ffff,d0
        move.l      #1000,d1
        bsr         dec1
        move        (sp)+,d0
pdec4:                                          ;Display D0 as 4-digit decimal
        move.l      #1000,d1
dec1:
        divu        d1,d0
        move.l      d0,-(sp)
        add         #'0',d0
        move.b      d0,(a5)+        ;Characters in output line
        move.l      (sp)+,d0
        swap        d0
        and.l       #$ffff,d0
        divu        #10,d1
        bne         dec1
        rts


        bss                                     ; data
dta:    ds.b        44
temp:   ds.l        0
depth:  ds.b        10
ouTln:  ds.b        80
        ds.l        200
stp:    ds.l        1

        end
```

Here is a BASIC loader that creates the program ALLDIR.TOS on the disk:

```
10 '********    ALLDIR loader       A.S.     ********
15 '
20 ?:fullw 2:clearw 2:gotoxy 0,0
```

```
25 ? "File >> alldir.tos << now being created":?:?:?
30 dim c%( 364):cs#=0
35 for i=0 to  364
40 read a$:c%(i)=val("&H"+a$)
45 check#=check#+(c%(i))
50 next i
55 if check#= 3584742.08 then  70
60 ?"Can't go any farther;something wrong with the DATA."
65 goto 80
70 bsave"alldir.tos",varptr(c%(0)), 730
75 ? "The program >> alldir.tos << is now written."
80 ?:?"Please press a key";:a=inp(2):end
85 '
90 '********* DATA for alldir.tos **********
100 DATA 601A,0000,02A8,0000,0000,0000,03AA,0000
101 DATA 0000,0000,0000,0000,0000,0000,4FF9,0000
102 DATA 064E,203C,0000,018C,6100,0250,6100,01FA
103 DATA B07C,0061,6DE6,B07C,0066,6EE0,13C0,0000
104 DATA 01E4,6100,01F8,4DF9,0000,01EB,4879,0000
105 DATA 02A8,3F3C,001A,4E41,5C8F,4244,49F9,0000
106 DATA 02D4,18BC,0000,6100,0006,6000,0040,3F3C
107 DATA 0010,4879,0000,01E4,3F3C,004E,4E41,508F
108 DATA 0C39,002E,0000,02C6,6600,000E,6100,0012
109 DATA 4A40,6600,0004,60E8,4E75,0634,0001,4000
110 DATA 3F3C,004F,4E41,548F,4E75,61EE,4A40,6600
111 DATA 0012,0C39,0010,0000,02BD,6600,008C,6000
112 DATA 002E,5344,6B00,00DE,9CFC,0006,0C26,005C
113 DATA 66FA,6100,005E,6196,4247,1E34,4000,5247
114 DATA 19BC,0000,4000,5347,67C0,61AE,60F8,2A7C
115 DATA 0000,01D3,6100,015E,2A7C,0000,02C6,6100
116 DATA 0154,6100,015E,5244,19BC,0000,4000,598E
117 DATA 3E3C,000D,47F9,0000,02C6,101B,6700,0008
118 DATA 1CC0,51CF,FFF6,6100,000A,6100,FF42,6000
119 DATA FF7C,1CFC,005C,1CFC,002A,1CFC,002E,1CFC
120 DATA 002A,1CFC,0000,4E75,0C39,0008,0000,0E1B
121 DATA 6600,0006,6000,004E,41F9,0000,02C6,4BF9
122 DATA 0000,02DE,3A04,3AFC,2020,51CD,FFFA,1018
123 DATA 6700,0006,1AC0,60F6,1AFC,0020,BBFC,0000
124 DATA 02F8,6DF4,2039,0000,02C2,6100,00FA,1ABC
125 DATA 0000,2A7C,0000,02DE,6100,00BA,6100,00C4
126 DATA 6000,FF08,4267,4E41,2A2A,2020,2020,2044
127 DATA 6972,6563,746F,7279,204F,7574,7075,7420
128 DATA 2020,2053,2E44,2E20,2020,202A,2A0A,0D50
129 DATA 6C65,6173,6520,696E,7075,7420,6472,6976
130 DATA 6520,6C65,7474,6572,2861,2D66,293A,0053
131 DATA 7562,2D44,6972,6563,746F,7279,203A,2000
132 DATA 613A,5C2A,2E2A,0020,2020,2020,2020,2020
```

```
133 DATA 2020,2020,2020,2020,2020,2020,2020,2020
134 DATA 2020,2020,2020,0000,3F3C,0001,4E41,C0BC
135 DATA 0000,00FF,548F,4E75,6100,0040,303C,000A
136 DATA 6100,0006,303C,000D,3F00,3F3C,0002,4E41
137 DATA 588F,4E75,101D,6700,0008,6100,0012,60F4
138 DATA 4E75,303C,000A,6100,0006,303C,000D,3F00
139 DATA 3F3C,0005,4E41,588F,4E75,2F00,3F3C,0009
140 DATA 4E41,5C4F,4E75,80FC,2710,4840,3F00,4840
141 DATA C0BC,0000,FFFF,223C,0000,03E8,6100,000A
142 DATA 301F,223C,0000,03E8,80C1,2F00,D07C,0030
143 DATA 1AC0,201F,4840,C0BC,0000,FFFF,82FC,000A
144 DATA 66E6,4E75,0000,0002,061A,0A06,1016,1032
145 DATA 3A0A,1C44,061E,080E,0000
```

Chapter Six

The RAM disk

The RAM disk

The third member of the storage media family for the Atari ST which we will look at is the RAM disk. Using memory to imitate the actions of a disk drive is an interesting, and above all, very fast method of data storage. How does it work?

First, we need an area of memory that cannot be used by any other application running on the computer. We will put data here instead of writing it to a diskette. The advantage is obvious: moving data in and out of memory can be done very quickly and easily by the 68000 processor in the ST. In addition, all of the mechanical operations that slow a disk drive (head positioning, spin up, etc.) are avoided. The result: a RAM disk is very fast.

What we need now is a program to manage RAM disk memory and move the data into memory as required. There are such programs on the market, and some can be found in various books on the ST (such as *Atari ST Tricks & Tips*). They all follow the same principle, which we will now examine.

First, the memory used by the RAM disk must be initialized. A boot sector must be created which contains all of the information about the type, partitioning, and size of the RAM disk. On real disks this sector is the first sector on the disk, so these parameters must be written at the start of the RAM disk memory.

Next, the program must install itself so that it knows whether a data transfer is to take place, and if so, in what direction the transfer is to go. This is accomplished by changing three operating system pointers to point to our routine. These pointers are memory locations which contain the addresses of programs. If the operating system wants to call such a program, it reads the appropriate pointer and branches to the address indicated.

The pointers which are used for installing the RAM disk are intended for servicing the hard disk. They lie at memory addresses $472 to $47E and point to routines which have the following significance:

Address	Name	Significance
$472	hdv_bpb	Determine and return the parameter block, which contains specifications about the diskette or hard disk.
$476	hdv_rw	Read/write routine for the hard disk. Data transfer takes place via this vector.

Address	Name	Significance
$47A	hdv_boot	Boot routine for the hard disk. Not required by the RAM disk because it cannot be booted.
$47E	hdv_mediach	Determine if the medium (disk) was changed.

Once the pointers have been changed and their old contents saved, the program can be exited. A special BIOS call is used to do this which allows a given area of memory to be reserved. The RAM disk is now installed.

Now we have to prepare a Desktop disk icon for the RAM disk. To do this we click on one of the disk icons, select the menu option `Install disk drive...` and change the name and designator of the drive. After selecting OK, another icon appears on the screen. This can then be used in the usual manner for loading and storing data and programs. Only the functions `Format...` and `diskcopy` do not work, so only individual files can be copied or deleted.

Now when the operating system wants to access the hard disk or RAM disk, it always jumps to the RAM disk program, which is still in memory, via the pointers mentioned above. The RAM disk program checks to see if the RAM disk is being accessed or not. If not, a branch is made to the actual routine, whose address was saved.

If the RAM disk is accessed, the program starts to work. For a read/write access, the parameters like sector, number of sectors to read, and data transfer direction are read from the stack and the appropriate data are copied into memory. If the operating system performs a "media changed" test (mediach), the RAM disk program returns a 0, which means that the medium was not changed, which of course is impossible with a RAM disk.

The third type of call means that the operating system wants the memory address of the parameter block. The address is returned in register D0.

This is all a RAM disk program does. What it can't do is retain data after the computer is turned off. This is the main disadvantage of this program: The data are not really saved, just temporarily stored. For this reason, files and programs that you create or modify on the RAM disk must be copied to a real diskette or hard disk before you turn the computer off.

But enough of theory. Let's take a look at a RAM disk program which contains all of these elements.

6.1 An easy-to-use RAM disk program

The program listed in this chapter contains some features which really aren't required for the normal use of a RAM disk. But they are quite useful, and although they make the program somewhat longer, they also make the program easier to use. The program is designed for use of the RAM disk as drive C, but it can be easily adapted for a different drive letter.

The program is a desk accessory, which appears in the **Desk** menu under the name RAMDISK.ACC after booting. If this menu option is selected, a small dialog box appears which contains three options.

The first option, which is outlined, is EXIT. If you click this button or press <Return>, the box will disappear and nothing will happen. This button is provided in case you accidentally select the menu entry RAMDISK.ACC.

The second button is labeled MORE. Clicking this button changes the number in the selection box on the right. This number indicates the size of the RAM disk to be installed. Clicking MORE will cause this number to increase in steps of 100 up to 800, whereupon another click will return it to zero.

Once the desired RAM disk capacity has been set, click on the button with the number. Since the old contents of the RAM disk will be erased when a new memory area is installed, another dialog box appears. This contains the question, Erase old contents of the RAM disk? which must be answered with Yes, or the RAM disk's old capacity and contents will remain intact.

After all of the settings have been made by selecting Yes, the program goes to work. It first releases the memory area which the RAM disk has previously occupied back to the operating system. Then the program attempts to reserve the desired memory area for itself. If there is not enough memory available, you get the message Not enough RAM. After this message is acknowledged, both the message and the RAM disk disappear. You must call the RAMDISK.ACC accessory again and choose a smaller RAM disk size.

If you select zero as the capacity of the RAM disk, it will be completely removed and will not occupy any memory. The program can thus change the size of its RAM disk and install and remove it as often as desired. Most of the RAM disk programs on the market do not have this capability, and if you use RAM disks a lot you will appreciate these advantages.

One more thing should be mentioned before we look at the program itself. Since a RAM disk cannot be formatted (please don't try it, because it may address the disk drives and accidentally format a real diskette instead), each file must be deleted individually in order to delete such a "disk." With this program, you just select the same capacity in the dialog box, and the whole RAM disk will be erased.

Here is the program:

```
;*****   RAM-Disk with comfort S.D.   *****

hdv_bpb       = $472
hdv_rw        = $476
hdv_mediach   = $47e

drvbits       = $4c2

start:
        move.l  #nstack,a7   ;set new stack

        move    #10,opcode   ;appl_init
        move    #0,sintin
        move    #1,sintout
        move    #0,saddrin
        move    #0,saddrout
        bsr     aes
        move    intout,appid ;Application ID

        move    #77,opcode   ;graf_handle
        move    #5,sintout
        move    #0,saddrin
        move    #0,saddrout
        bsr     aes
        move    intout,grhandle ;Graphic handle

        move    #35,opcode   ;Menu_Register
        move    #1,sintin
        move    #1,sintout
        move    #1,saddrin
        move    appid,intin
        move.l  #accname,addrin
        bsr     aes
```

```
            move    intout,accid    ;Accessory number

;** Here is the preparation loop **

loop:   bsr     event           ;Event_Multi
        cmp     #40,msgbuff     ;Acc_open ?
        bne     loop            ;no
        move    msgbuff+8,d0
        cmp     accid,d0        ;our accessory number ?
        bne     loop            ;no
        bsr     run             ;display menu
        bra     loop            ;and again

; ** Selection **

run:
        move.l  #howmuch,addrin
        bsr     formalert       ;display selection
        move    intout,choice
        cmp     #1,choice       ;Exit?
        beq     ende            ;yes => end
        cmp     #3,choice       ;OK ?
        beq     ok              ;yes
        addq    #2,size         ;display different size
        cmp     #18,size        ;over 800 KByte?
        blt     more            ;no
        clr     size            ;no, back to 0 KByte
more:
        lea     sizes,a0
        clr.l   d0
        move    size,d0
        move    0(a0,d0),capacit ;set new size
        lsl     #1,d0
        lea     deci,a0
        move.l  0(a0,d0),offer  ;display new size
        bra     run             ;repeat

; * Reserve memory *

ok:
        move.l  #clear,addrin
        bsr     formalert       ;really erase it?
        cmp     #2,intout
        beq     okx             ;no => end
        bsr     mfree           ;release memory
        tst     size            ;0 KByte ?
        bne     ok1             ;no
```

```
okx:
        rts                     ;0 Kbyte: done
ok1:
        move    #2,changed      ;'Disk changed'
        clr.l   d7
        move    capacit,d7      ;capacity in Kbyte
        add.l   #9,d7           ;plus 9K for management
        asl.l   #5,d7
        asl.l   #5,d7           ;times 1024: capacity in bytes
        move.l  d7,-(sp)        ;RAM area to install
        move    #$48,-(sp)      ;MALLOC function
        trap    #1
        addq.l  #6,sp
        tst.l   d0              ;error occurred ?
        beq     ferror          ;yes => error message
        move.l  d0,buffer       ;save start address of the RAM disk

        move.l  #init,-(sp)
        move    #38,-(sp)       ;Initialization in Supervisor
        trap    #14
        addq.l  #6,sp
        rts

ferror:
        move.l  #error,addrin
        bsr     formalert       ;'Not enough RAM !'
        bra     ende            ;terminate

init:
        move.l  hdv_bpb,bpbsave ;save old vectors
        move.l  #bpb,hdv_bpb
        move.l  hdv_rw,rwsave   ;set vectors to new routines
        move.l  #rw,hdv_rw
        move.l  hdv_mediach,mediasave
        move.l  #media,hdv_mediach

        move.l  buffer,a0
        move.l  #10240/4,d0
iloop1:
        clr.l   (a0)+           ;clear boot sector and FATs
        dbra    d0,iloop1

; * Generate boot sector *
        move.l  buffer,a0
        add.l   #11,a0          ;at buffer+11
        lea     boottab,a1
        moveq   #tabend-boottab-1,d0
```

```
bloop:
        move.b  (a1)+,(a0)+     ;copy data in boot sector
        dbra    d0,bloop

        move    capacit,d7
        move    d7,numcl        ;capacity in KByte in BPB

        lsl     #1,d7           ;capacity in sectors
        add     #18,d7          ;plus 18 sectors
        move.l  buffer,a0
        add.l   #19,a0          ;in buffer+19 and +20
        move.b  d7,(a0)+        ;LO
        lsr     #8,d7
        move.b  d7,(a0)         ;HI

        bset    #2,drvbits+3    ;install drive C
        rts                     ;done

;* Function: Get BPB *

bpb:    cmp     #2,4(sp)        ;Drive C ?
        beq     bpb1            ;yes
        move.l  bpbsave,a0      ;old routine
        jmp     (a0)            ;call

bpb1:   move.l  #bpbtab,d0      ;Pointer to BIOS parameter block
        rts

;* Function: Read/Write *

rw:     cmp     #2,14(sp)       ;Drive C ?
        beq     rw1             ;yes
        move.l  rwsave,a0       ;old routine
        jmp     (a0)            ;call

rw1:    move    12(sp),d0       ;recno, logical sector number
        ext.l   d0
        lsl.l   #8,d0
        lsl.l   #1,d0           ;times 512

        move.l  6(sp),a0        ;buffer address
        move    10(sp),d1       ;number of sectors
        subq    #1,d1
        move.l  buffer,a1       ;base address
        add.l   d0,a1           ;plus relative address in RAM-Disk

        move    4(sp),d0        ;rwflag
```

```
        btst    #0,d0           ;read ?
        beq     rloop0          ;yes
        exg     a0,a1           ;exchange destination and source

rloop0: move.l  #511,d0         ;one sector
rloop:  move.b  (a1)+,(a0)+     ;copy buffer
        dbra    d0,rloop
        dbra    d1,rloop0       ;next sector
        clr     d0              ;OK
        rts

;* Function: Media-Change *

media:  cmp     #2,4(sp)        ;Drive C ?
        beq     media1          ;yes
        move.l  mediasave,a0    ;old routine
        jmp     (a0)            ;call

media1: move    changed,d0      ;Diskette changed
        clr     changed         ;but just once
        rts

event:
        move    #25,opcode      ;Event_Multi, determine GEM event
        move    #16,sintin
        move    #7,sintout
        move    #1,saddrin
        move.l  #msgbuff,addrin
        lea     table,a1
        lea     intin,a2
        moveq   #15,d0
lop1:
        move    (a1)+,(a2)+     ;set parameters
        dbra    d0,lop1
        bsr     aes
        rts

aes:                            ; AES call
        move.l  #aespb,d1
        move    #$c8,d0
        trap    #2
        rts

mfree:                          ;release memory
        tst.l   buffer
        beq     ende            ;is already removed
```

```
        move.l  #reinit,-(sp)
        move    #38,-(sp)       ;reinitialization
        trap    #14             ;in supervisor mode
        addq.l  #6,sp

        move.l  buffer,-(sp)
        move    #$49,-(sp)      ;MFREE function, release memory
        trap    #1
        addq.l  #6,sp
        tst.l   d0              ;error?
        beq     ende            ;no
        move.l  #error1,addrin
        bsr     formalert       ;error message
ende:
        clr.l   buffer          ;no more memory reserved
        rts

reinit:
        move.l  bpbsave,hdv_bpb
        move.l  rwsave,hdv_rw   ;set vectors to old routine
        move.l  mediasave,hdv_mediach
        bclr    #2,drvbits+3    ;remove old routine
        rts

formalert:
        move    #52,contrl      ;form_alert, display alarm window
        move    #1,contrl+2
        move    #1,contrl+4
        move    #1,contrl+6
        move    #0,contrl+8
        move    #1,intin
        bsr     aes
        rts

table:      dc.w $13,1,1,1,0,0,0,0,0,0,0,0,0,0,0,0
accname:    dc.b "  RAM-Disk  C ",0
 align
howmuch:    dc.b "[1][Size of RAM disk in Kbytes? ]"
            dc.b "[Exit| more  |"
offer:      dc.b " 100 ]",0,0
clear:      dc.b "[1][Erase old contents| of the RAM disk?]"
            dc.b "[ Yes! | No ]",0,0
error:      dc.b "[2][Not enough RAM !]"
            dc.b "[OK]",0,0
error1:     dc.b "[2][Error during MFREE !]"
            dc.b "[OK]",0,0
 align.l
```

```
capacit:    dc.w 100
size:       dc.w 2
sizes:      dc.w 0,100,200,300,400,500,600,700,800
deci:       dc.b ' 0 100 200 300 400 500 600 700 800'

buffer:     dc.l 0              ;RAM disk buffer address
changed:    dc.w 0              ;Flag for "disk changed"

bpbtab:
recsiz:     dc.w $200           ;Sector size
clsiz:      dc.w 2              ;Cluster size in sectors
clsizb:     dc.w $400           ;Cluster size in bytes
rdlen:      dc.w 7              ;Directory length in sectors
fsiz:       dc.w 5              ;FAT size
fatrec:     dc.w 6              ;FAT sectors
datrec:     dc.w 18             ;Sectors for management
numcl:      dc.w 1              ;capacity in Kbytes
flags:      dc.l 0,0,0,0

boottab:    ; data in 8086 format
            dc.b 0,2             ;bytes per sector
            dc.b 2               ;sectors per cluster
            dc.b 1,0             ;reserved sectors
            dc.b 2               ;FATs
            dc.b 112,0           ;directory entries
            dc.b 2               ;sectors on media
            dc.b 0               ;media descriptor
            dc.b 5,0             ;sectors per FAT
            dc.b 9,0             ;sectors per track
            dc.b 1,0             ;sides
            dc.b 0               ;hidden
tabend:

    align

bpbsave:    ds.l 1              ;Space for old vectors
rwsave:     ds.l 1
mediasave:  ds.l 1

aespb:      dc.l contrl,global,intin,intout,addrin,addrout


    bss                         ;data

choice:     ds.w 1
grhandle:   ds.w 1
appid:      ds.w 1              ;Application ID
```

```
accid:      ds.w 1          ;Accessory unit
msgbuff:    ds.w 16
            ds.l 128        ;NEW STACK
nstack:     ds.l 1

contrl:                     ;GEM parameter block
opcode:     ds.w 1
sintin:     ds.w 1
sintout:    ds.w 1
saddrin:    ds.w 1
saddrout:   ds.l 1
            ds.w 5

global:     ds.l 8

intin:      ds.w 80
ptsin:      ds.w 80
intout:     ds.w 80
ptsout:     ds.w 80
addrin:     ds.w 80
addrout:    ds.w 80

            end
```

This program was created with the *AssemPro* macro-assembler, which differs in certain respects from the DRI assembler included in the Atari Developer's Package. The comment lines need to be changed, which for the DRI assembler must start with an asterisk (*), the `align` instruction which must be `even`, and the `bss` instruction must be `data` for DRI.

The program is divided into a number of parts:

1. Installation of the accessory.
2. Preparation loop, which in normal operation of the Atari ST runs constantly in the background and may therefore never end.
3. Display and service dialog box, whereby the selected capacity is placed in CAPACIT.
4. Display dialog prompt
5. Release previously used memory (MFREE).
6. Reserve new memory, output error message if not enough.
7. Save BIOS vectors for the disk routines and set new vectors.
8. GETBPB function.
9. Read/write function.
10. Media change function.
11. Data fields for parameter blocks.

Points 7 to 10 were already discussed in the previous section. A complete description of points 1 though 6 would be too comprehensive to take up here. Information on the functions used can be found in the books *Atari ST Internals* and *Atari ST GEM Programmer's Reference* by Abacus Software.

Here is a BASIC loader program which creates the accessory program RAMDISK.ACC on the disk:

```
10      '********   ramdisk.acc loader      A.S.    *********
15      '
20      ?:fullw 2:clearw 2:gotoxy 0,0
25      ? "File >> a:ramdisk.acc << now being created":?:?:?
30      dim c%( 735):cs#=0
35      for i=0 to   735
40      read a$:c%(i)=val("&H"+a$)
45      check#=check#+(c%(i))
50      next i
55      if check#= 4997481.92 then   70
60      ?"Can't go any farther;something wrong with the DATA."
65      goto 80
70      bsave"a:ramdisk.acc",varptr(c%(0)), 1472
75      ? "The program >> a:ramdisk.acc << is now written."
80      ?:?:?:?"Please press a key":a=inp(2):end
85      '
90      '********* DATA for a:ramdisk.acc **********
95      '
100     DATA 601A,0000,053A,0000,0000,0000,0622,0000
101     DATA 0000,0000,0000,0000,0000,0000,2E7C,0000
102     DATA 0762,33FC,000A,0000,0766,33FC,0000,0000
103     DATA 0768,33FC,0001,0000,076A,33FC,0000,0000
104     DATA 076C,33FC,0000,0000,076E,6100,02EE,33F9
105     DATA 0000,08DC,0000,053E,33FC,004D,0000,0766
106     DATA 33FC,0005,0000,076A,33FC,0000,0000,076C
107     DATA 33FC,0000,0000,076E,6100,02C0,33F9,0000
108     DATA 08DC,0000,053C,33FC,0023,0000,0766,33FC
109     DATA 0001,0000,0768,33FC,0001,0000,076A,33FC
110     DATA 0001,0000,076C,33F9,0000,053E,0000,079C
111     DATA 23FC,0000,03EC,0000,0A1C,6100,027E,33F9
112     DATA 0000,08DC,0000,0540,6100,022C,0C79,0028
113     DATA 0000,0542,66F2,3039,0000,054A,B079,0000
114     DATA 0540,66E4,6100,0004,60DE,23FC,0000,03FC
115     DATA 0000,0A1C,6100,02BC,33F9,0000,08DC,0000
116     DATA 053A,0C79,0001,0000,053A,6700,0276,0C79
117     DATA 0003,0000,053A,6700,0042,5479,0000,04A6
```

```
118    DATA 0C79,0012,0000,04A6,6D00,0008,4279,0000
119    DATA 04A6,41F9,0000,04A8,4280,3039,0000,04A6
120    DATA 33F0,0000,0000,04A4,E348,41F9,0000,04BA
121    DATA 23F0,0000,0000,042A,6090,23FC,0000,0432
122    DATA 0000,0A1C,6100,024C,0C79,0002,0000,08DC
123    DATA 6700,0010,6100,01D2,4A79,0000,04A6,6600
124    DATA 0004,4E75,33FC,0002,0000,04E2,4287,3E39
125    DATA 0000,04A4,DEBC,0000,0009,EB87,EB87,2F07
126    DATA 3F3C,0048,4E41,5C8F,4A80,6700,0018,23C0
127    DATA 0000,04DE,2F3C,0000,01BA,3F3C,0026,4E4E
128    DATA 5C8F,4E75,23FC,0000,046A,0000,0A1C,6100
129    DATA 01E2,6000,01AE,23F9,0000,0472,0000,0516
130    DATA 23FC,0000,0250,0000,0472,23F9,0000,0476
131    DATA 0000,051A,23FC,0000,026A,0000,0476,23F9
132    DATA 0000,047E,0000,051E,23FC,0000,02BA,0000
133    DATA 047E,2079,0000,04DE,203C,0000,0A00,4298
134    DATA 51C8,FFFC,2079,0000,04DE,D1FC,0000,000B
135    DATA 43F9,0000,0504,7010,10D9,51C8,FFFC,3E39
136    DATA 0000,04A4,33C7,0000,04F2,E34F,DE7C,0012
137    DATA 2079,0000,04DE,D1FC,0000,0013,10C7,E04F
138    DATA 1087,08F9,0002,0000,04C5,4E75,0C6F,0002
139    DATA 0004,6700,000A,2079,0000,0516,4ED0,203C
140    DATA 0000,04E4,4E75,0C6F,0002,000E,6700,000A
141    DATA 2079,0000,051A,4ED0,302F,000C,48C0,E188
142    DATA E388,206F,0006,322F,000A,5341,2279,0000
143    DATA 04DE,D3C0,302F,0004,0800,0000,6700,0004
144    DATA C348,203C,0000,01FF,10D9,51C8,FFFC,51C9
145    DATA FFF2,4240,4E75,0C6F,0002,0004,6700,000A
146    DATA 2079,0000,051E,4ED0,3039,0000,04E2,4279
147    DATA 0000,04E2,4E75,33FC,0019,0000,0766,33FC
148    DATA 0010,0000,0768,33FC,0007,0000,076A,33FC
149    DATA 0001,0000,076C,23FC,0000,0542,0000,0A1C
150    DATA 43F9,0000,03CC,45F9,0000,079C,700F,34D9
151    DATA 51C8,FFFC,6100,0004,4E75,223C,0000,0522
152    DATA 303C,00C8,4E42,4E75,4AB9,0000,04DE,6700
153    DATA 0032,2F3C,0000,036E,3F3C,0026,4E4E,5C8F
154    DATA 2F39,0000,04DE,3F3C,0049,4E41,5C8F,4A80
155    DATA 6700,0010,23FC,0000,0485,0000,0A1C,6100
156    DATA 0032,42B9,0000,04DE,4E75,23F9,0000,0516
157    DATA 0000,0472,23F9,0000,051A,0000,0476,23F9
158    DATA 0000,051E,0000,047E,08B9,0002,0000,04C5
159    DATA 4E75,33FC,0034,0000,0766,33FC,0001,0000
160    DATA 0768,33FC,0001,0000,076A,33FC,0001,0000
161    DATA 076C,33FC,0000,0000,076E,33FC,0001,0000
162    DATA 079C,6100,FF56,4E75,0013,0001,0001,0001
```

```
163  DATA 0000,0000,0000,0000,0000,0000,0000,0000
164  DATA 0000,0000,0000,0000,2020,5241,4D2D,4469
165  DATA 736B,2020,4320,0000,5B31,5D5B,5369,7A65
166  DATA 206F,6620,5241,4D20,6469,736B,2069,6E20
167  DATA 4B62,7974,6573,3F20,5D5B,4578,6974,7C20
168  DATA 6D6F,7265,207C,2031,3030,205D,0000,5B31
169  DATA 5D5B,4572,6173,6520,6F6C,6420,636F,6E74
170  DATA 656E,7473,7C20,6F66,2074,6865,2052,414D
171  DATA 2064,6973,6B3F,5D5B,2059,6573,2120,7C20
172  DATA 4E6F,205D,0000,5B32,5D5B,4E6F,7420,656E
173  DATA 6F75,6768,2052,414D,2021,5D5B,4F4B,5D00
174  DATA 005B,325D,5B45,7272,6F72,2064,7572,696E
175  DATA 6720,4D46,5245,4520,215D,5B4F,4B5D,0000
176  DATA 0064,0002,0000,0064,00C8,012C,0190,01F4
177  DATA 0258,02BC,0320,2020,3020,2031,3030,2032
178  DATA 3030,2033,3030,2034,3030,2035,3030,2036
179  DATA 3030,2037,3030,2038,3030,0000,0000,0000
180  DATA 0200,0002,0400,0007,0005,0006,0012,0001
181  DATA 0000,0000,0000,0000,0000,0000,0000,0000
182  DATA 0002,0201,0002,7000,0200,0500,0900,0100
183  DATA 0000,0000,0000,0000,0000,0000,0000,0000
184  DATA 0766,0000,077C,0000,079C,0000,08DC,0000
185  DATA 0A1C,0000,0ABC,0000,0002,0808,0808,080A
186  DATA 0408,0808,080A,0408,0808,0806,0406,040A
187  DATA 040C,0806,0E04,0A04,080C,0A08,0A06,0808
188  DATA 0808,0804,0C0E,0E08,2006,1004,1206,0E06
189  DATA 0E06,0A12,0C0E,060C,2608,121C,3408,060A
190  DATA 0808,0806,0406,0614,0E0A,0E14,040A,080A
191  DATA 0A16,0808,0808,0801,6204,0404,0404,0000
```

When you turn your computer on and install the RAM disk, you often have to copy certain files to the RAM disk before you can start working. To save you time and effort in doing this, we have written a program that takes care of this for you.

6.2 Disk to RAM disk copy

The following program simply copies the entire contents of a single-sided disk to the RAM disk C. All sectors from 0 (logical sector number) to 9*80-1 (719) are read from the selected drive and copied to the "sectors" of the RAM disk. You **must** make sure that the RAM disk has a capacity of at least **400K** so that sector 719 also exists.

In order to make the program as fast as possible, we read or write nine sectors at a time each time we call the routine FLOPRW. This speed advantage over copying sectors individually is supplied by the DMA chip, which can be programmed to read nine sectors (an entire track) at once and send then to the computer. The speed advantage is not tremendous, but every little bit helps. Naturally, it would go even faster if all of the sectors on the disk were read with one call, but this would produce certain memory size problems.

If you use this program with a double-sided disk, all of the filenames from the diskette will naturally appear in the directory of the RAM disk. The directory is copied in its entirety, but not the other side of the disk. If the original disk is more than half full, the programs and files on the other side cannot be loaded into the RAM disk. Otherwise this program also works with double-sided disks.

Let's look at the program:

```
;*** Disk - to - RAM-Disk - Copy   S.D. ***

run:
      clr.l     ap1rsv
      clr.l     ap2rsv
      clr.l     ap3rsv
      clr.l     ap4rsv
      move      #10,opcode      ;appl_init
      move      #0,sintin
      move      #1,sintout
      move      #0,saddrin
      move      #0,sintin
      jsr       aes
      move      #77,opcode      ;graf_handle
      move      #5,sintout
      move      #0,saddrin
      move      #0,saddrout
```

```
        jsr     aes
        move    intout,grhandle

        move.l  #alarm,d0
        bsr     formalert       ;output selection window
        subq    #2,d0           ;correct drive number
        tst     d0
        bmi     quit            ;terminate

        move    d0,drive        ;save drive number
        clr     sector          ;start with sector 0
loop:
        move    drive,d1        ;selected diskette
        move    #2,d0           ;read
        bsr     floprw          ;read 9 sectors
        bne     readerr         ;error during read!
        move    #2,d1           ;drive C = RAM disk
        move    #1,d0           ;write
        bsr     floprw          ;write 9 sectors
        bne     wrerr           ;error during write!
        add     #9,sector       ;sector number + 9
        cmp     #9*80,sector    ;end ?
        blt     loop            ;no

quit:
        clr     -(sp)
        trap    #1              ;exit => desktop

floprw:                         ;read/write diskette
        move    d1,-(sp)        ;drive
        move    sector,-(sp)    ;start sector
        move    #9,-(sp)        ;read/write 9 sectors
        pea     buffer          ;buffer
        move    d0,-(sp)        ;read/write
        move    #4,-(sp)
        trap    #13             ;rwabs function
        add.l   #14,sp
        tst     d0              ;test for error
        rts

readerr:
        move.l  #reer,d0
        bsr     formalert       ;"Error during read!"
        bra     quit
```

```
wrerr:
        move.l    #wrer,d0
        bsr       formalert       ;"Error during write"
        bra       quit

aes:                              ;AES call
        move.l    #aespb,d1
        move      #$c8,d0
        trap      #2
        rts

formalert:
        move      #52,contrl      ;form_alert
        move      #1,contrl+2
        move      #1,contrl+4
        move      #1,contrl+6
        move      #0,contrl+8
        move      #1,intin
        move.l    d0,addrin
        jsr       aes
        move      intout,d0
        rts

alarm:  dc.b "[1][Source drive to | copy from ?]"
        dc.b "[Exit| A | B ]",0,0
reer:   dc.b "[2][Error during read!][Quit]",0,0
wrer:   dc.b "[2][Error during write!][Quit]",0,0

  ALIGN.L
aespb:    dc.l  contrl,global,intin,intout,addrin,addrout

  bss                             ;DATA
contrl:                           ;various fields for the AES
opcode:    dc.w 1
sintin:    dc.w 1
sintout:   dc.w 1
saddrin:   dc.w 1
saddrout:  dc.l 1
           dc.w 5

global:    dc.w 7
ap1rsv:    dc.l 1
ap2rsv:    dc.l 1
ap3rsv:    dc.l 1
ap4rsv:    dc.l 1

intin:     dc.w 128
```

```
ptsin:      dc.w 128
intout:     dc.w 128
ptsout:     dc.w 128
addrin:     dc.w 128
addrout:    dc.w 128

grhandle:   dc.w 1
drive:      dc.w 1          ;drive number
sector:     dc.w 1          ;sector counter
buffer:     dc.w 9*512      ;buffer for 9 sectors

    end
```

The rather simple construction of this program makes some variations easily possible. For example, you can copy double-sided disks to an 800K RAM disk by changing the end condition in CMP #9*80, SECTOR command by simply inserting #9*80*2.

Another variation would be to make the copy direction selectable. This would make it possible to copy the RAM disk contents back to the diskette when you are done working.

It would also be interesting to convert the program into a desk accessory. Equipped with various additional functions, it could be a very useful tool.

Here is the BASIC loader for the program. It creates the program DSKTORAM.PRG on the diskette:

```
10      '********* dsktoram loader      A.S.    *********
15      '
20      ?:fullw 2:clearw 2:gotoxy 0,0
25      ? "File >> a:dsktoram.prg << now being created":?:?:?
30      dim c%( 279):cs#=0
35      for i=0 to  279
40      read a$:c%(i)=val("&H"+a$)
45      check#=check#+(c%(i))
50      next i
55      if check#= 2432944.96 then   70
60      ?"Can't go any farther;something wrong with the DATA."
65      goto 80
70      bsave"a:dsktoram.prg",varptr(c%(0)), 560
75      ? "The program >> a:dsktoram.prg << is now written."
80      ?:?"Please press a key":a=inp(2):end
85      '
```

```
90   '********* DATA for a:dsktoram.prg **********
95   '
100  DATA 601A,0000,01E4,0000,0000,0000,0034,0000
101  DATA 0000,0000,0000,0000,0000,0000,42B9,0000
102  DATA 01F4,42B9,0000,01F8,42B9,0000,01FC,42B9
103  DATA 0000,0200,33FC,000A,0000,01E4,33FC,0000
104  DATA 0000,01E6,33FC,0001,0000,01E8,33FC,0000
105  DATA 0000,01EA,33FC,0000,0000,01E6,4EB9,0000
106  DATA 0108,33FC,004D,0000,01E4,33FC,0005,0000
107  DATA 01E8,33FC,0000,0000,01EA,33FC,0000,0000
108  DATA 01EC,4EB9,0000,0108,33F9,0000,0208,0000
109  DATA 0210,203C,0000,015A,6100,0098,5540,4A40
110  DATA 6B00,0042,33C0,0000,0212,4279,0000,0214
111  DATA 3239,0000,0212,303C,0002,6100,002C,6600
112  DATA 004C,323C,0002,303C,0001,6100,001C,6600
113  DATA 0048,0679,0009,0000,0214,0C79,02D0,0000
114  DATA 0214,6DCC,4267,4E41,3F01,3F39,0000,0214
115  DATA 3F3C,0009,4879,0000,0216,3F00,3F3C,0004
116  DATA 4E4D,DFFC,0000,000E,4A40,4E75,203C,0000
117  DATA 018C,6100,001E,60CC,203C,0000,01AB,6100
118  DATA 0012,60C0,223C,0000,01CC,303C,00C8,4E42
119  DATA 4E75,33FC,0034,0000,01E4,33FC,0001,0000
120  DATA 01E6,33FC,0001,0000,01E8,33FC,0001,0000
121  DATA 01EA,33FC,0000,0000,01EC,33FC,0001,0000
122  DATA 0204,23C0,0000,020C,4EB9,0000,0108,3039
123  DATA 0000,0208,4E75,5B31,5D5B,536F,7572,6365
124  DATA 2064,7269,7665,2074,6F20,7C20,636F,7079
125  DATA 2066,726F,6D20,3F5D,5B45,7869,747C,2041
126  DATA 207C,2042,205D,0000,5B32,5D5B,4572,726F
127  DATA 7220,6475,7269,6E67,2072,6561,6421,5D5B
128  DATA 5175,6974,5D00,005B,325D,5B45,7272,6F72
129  DATA 2064,7572,696E,6720,7772,6974,6521,5D5B
130  DATA 5175,6974,5D00,00EA,0000,01E4,0000,01F2
131  DATA 0000,0204,0000,0208,0000,020C,0000,020E
132  DATA 0000,0002,0606,0608,0808,0808,0608,0808
133  DATA 0806,0604,0612,0606,2408,0E0A,180C,0C10
134  DATA 0808,0808,0806,0606,7804,0404,0404,0001
```

Chapter Seven

Programming a disk monitor

Programming a disk monitor

The programs presented thus far in this book allow you to view and modify some data on the diskette, but what is a disk book without a disk editor which you can use to view and change all of the data on the disk? Since I've had seven years of experience in typing in programs from magazines and books, I'd like to try to save you some frustration and present a quasi-modular construction of the program. We'll look at the program section by section, and this will hopefully lead to a complete program with relatively little typing effort.

This listing `edit.s` contains all of the menu options and all of the data and subroutines of the entire disk editor, but only the subroutines of the sector menu are listed and all others routines contain just an RTS. The listing `subrout.s` contains the subroutines which are called by the main program, which you can insert at the locations of the place holders in the program `edit.s` as required, and thereby gradually build the program up to its full power and size.

When entering the program, your biggest problem in producing the editor will be the naming of labels and variables. Eight significant characters are simply too few for such a comprehensive assembly language project in order to formulate suggestive and logical names for subroutines and variables.

If you want to use the editor right away, or you don't wish to type it in, it is also possible to order the optional diskette from Abacus which contains many of the programs and sources in this book (see the back of this book for ordering information).

7.1 The TOS functions for disk access

The editor functions are largely built on operating system functions (TOS or GEMDOS), and only a few directly access the disk controller and DMA chip of the Atari ST. It is possible to access these chips from various levels of the hierarchically-organized TOS.

The high-level languages like Pascal, C, FORTRAN, and BASIC make it possible to work with sequential and random-access files, which means that a high-level language does not divide the disk into tracks and sectors, but that the disk access is file-oriented and moves only within the limits of these files.

If we go one step deeper in the hierarchy of the operating system, we see that high-level languages use the GEMDOS functions. These GEMDOS functions are offered to the languages by operating-system routines, meaning that these GEMDOS functions are still file-oriented and offer only random and sequential access to files on the disk.

At the next level we encounter the BIOS functions, which make the first real physical contact with the diskette possible, in which the disk is divided into logical sectors from 0 to the maximum possible number (1440 for double-sided disks, 720 for single-sided disks). The BIOS functions thus allow access to all sectors on the disk, but we still don't know which track and side the given logical sector is on. This information can be computed with the help of the specifications in the BIOS parameter block. If we use the XBIOS functions, it is possible to access tracks, sides, and physical sectors. The user must know how many sectors there are on a track, etc. The XBIOS functions offer ways of determining such disk-specific properties. For example, you can format individual tracks and specify the desired number of sector per track.

The center of all routines are the WD1772 disk controller and the DMA chip, which occupy I/O addresses in the range $FF800 to $FFFFF.

For example: The BASIC command WRITE#, which writes data to a sequential file, uses the GEMDOS function WRITE, which in turn calls the BIOS function RWABS, which makes use of the XBIOS function FLOPWR, which finally tells the DMA and controller chips where and what to write on the disk.

All operating system functions (GEMDOS, BIOS, XBIOS) are described in detail in the Abacus book *Atari ST Internals*, so we will discuss only the eight BIOS and XBIOS calls which directly communicate with the disk. All of the calls expect their parameters on the stack, and return results or a negative error code in the case of an error in the register D0. Registers D0-D2 and A0-A2 are often changed after a call, and so must be saved if their contents are required. The two BIOS functions RWABS and GETBPB are called via the BIOS specific TRAP #13 and perform the following:

RWABS: BIOS function number 4

This very flexible function is used to both read from and write to one or more logical sectors. These sectors can be on a physical diskette, the hard disk, or even a RAM disk. The following parameters are passed to it:

device: determines the drive which will be accessed. The numbering starts with 0 for drive A and has no upper limit. The RAM disk presented in section 6.1 of this book is addressed as drive C, so it would have device number 2.

recnr: specifies the logical number of sector to be processed. Numbering again starts at 0. The maximum number of sectors varies depending on the device: 720 logical sectors fit on a single-sided 80 track diskette in Atari format (double density), of which "only" 702 are available for user data. TOS uses the remaining 18 sectors to manage the user data with the directory and FAT (File Allocation Table).

number: the number of logical sectors to be processed.

buffer: an address from which or to which the data is to be written. If you want to read 4 logical sectors of the Atari-specific format (512 bytes/sector), there must be 4*512=2048 bytes available at this address.

rwflag: determines whether the function will write to or read from the disk. Four possible values are possible:

rwflag:	Meaning:
0	Read sectors
1	Write sectors
2	Forced read sectors (even if disk changed)
3	Forced write sectors (even if disk changed)

A possible call in machine language could look like this:

```
move.w  #0,-(a7)        * drive A (device)
move.w  #11,-(a7)       * recnr start at logical sector 11
move.w  #5,-(a7)        * number, all 5 directory sectors
move.l  #buffer,-(a7)   * address of free space
move.w  #2,-(a7)        * rwflag, forced read
move.w  #4,-(a7)        * BIOS function number
trap    #13             * BIOS call
add.l   #14,a7          * restore stack
tst.w   d0              * check if error occurred
bmi     error           * negative value means error
...
...                     * continue here for no error
...                     * the data read is now in
...                     * RAM at the address "buffer"
```

GETBPB: BIOS function number 7

The BIOS parameter block contains the data about the current disk. These data are found in the boot sector of the diskette and are placed into the BPB (BIOS Parameter Block) in RAM by this function. Assembly language call:

```
move.w  device,-(a7)    * drive 0 = A
move.w  #7,-(a7)        * BIOS number
trap    #13
addq.l  #4,a7           * clean up stack
tst.w   d0
bmi     error           * d0 negative if error
...
...
...                     * else D0 contains the addr of the BPB
...                     * Normally this is $4DCE for drive A
...                     * and $4DEE for drive B
```

At the address returned in D0 you will find the data in word (2-byte) quantities:

Drive A

Address:	Name:	Meaning:	SS	DS
$4DCE	recsiz	sector size in bytes	512	512
$4DD0	clsiz	cluster size in sectors	2	2
$4DD2	clsizb	cluster size in bytes	1024	1024
$4DD4	rdlen	directory length in sectors	7	7

Address:	Name:	Meaning:	SS	DS
$4DD6	fsiz	FAT size in sectors	5	5
$4DD8	fatrec	sector number in the second FAT	6	6
$4DDA	datrec	sector number of the first data cluster	18	18
$4DDC	numcl	number of clusters on the disk	351	711
$4DDE	bflags	various flags		
$4DE0		unknown		
$4DE2	nside	number of sides on disk	1	2

The data shown apply for the Atari-specific recording format with 80 tracks (SS = single-sided, DS = double-sided).

MEDIACH: BIOS function number 9

This function uses the disk name to see if the disk has been changed. The drive number is passed as the parameter.

```
move.w  device,-(a7)   * drive number
move.w  #9,-(a7)       * BIOS function number
trap    #13            * call
addq.l  #4,a7          * restore stack
...
```

The value passed back in D0 is between 0 and 2 and has the following meaning:

Number:	Meaning:
0	Disk was not changed
1	Disk might have been changed
2	Disk was changed

Here are the four XBIOS functions which are important for our purposes.

FLOPRD: XBIOS function number 8

With this function you can read one or more consecutive sectors on a track. The parameters to be passed are:

number: determines how many sectors are to be read. The possible values for the Atari format vary from one to ten. Ten sectors can be read only if a special program is used to format the disk, because the Atari format program writes only nine sectors per track on the disk.

side: specifies the side of the disk, 0 or 1.

track: determines the track on which the sectors are located.

sector: the physical sector itself.

device: the drive parameter (0=A).

filler: a meaningless longword, probably intended for later expansion.

buffer: the address to which the data are to be transferred.

```
            move.w   #1,-(a7)         * number, one sector
            move.w   #0,-(a7)         * side
            move.w   #0,-(a7)         * track zero
            move.w   #1,-(a7)         * sector one = boot sector
            move.w   #0,-(a7)         * drive A
            move.l   #0,-(a7)         * filler, dummy long word
            move.l   #buffer,-(a7)    * address of the data destination
            move.w   #8,-(a7)         * XBIOS function number
            trap     #14
            add.l    #20,a7
            tst.w    d0
            bmi      error
            ...
buffer:     ds.b     512
```

FLOPWR: XBIOS function number 9

The counterpart of the previous function, FLOPWR is used to write sectors to the disk. The parameters to be passed are the same as for FLOPRD.

```
            move.w   #4,-(a7)         * number, four sectors
            move.w   #0,-(a7)         * side
            move.w   #5,-(a7)         * track five
            move.w   #1,-(a7)         * sector one = start sector for write
            move.w   #0,-(a7)         * drive A
            move.l   #0,-(a7)         * filler, dummy long word
            move.l   #buffer,-(a7)    * address of the data to be written
            move.w   #9,-(a7)         * XBIOS function number
            trap     #14
            add.l    #20,a7
            tst.w    d0
            bmi      error
            ...
buffer:     ds.b     4*512
```

This call writes the 2048 bytes which are located in memory at address `buffer` to the sectors 1, 2, 3, and 4 of track 5 on side 0 of the disk.

FLOPFMT: XBIOS function number 10

This routine makes it possible to format a track with 1-10 sectors per track. The parameters are:

virgin: determines the contents of new sectors; this data will be placed in the individual sectors. The same value that TOS uses ($E5E5) should be used. Byte values greater than $EF should not be used under any circumstances because these represent special functions and will cause things like address marks or checksums of the previous data to be written.

magic: the magic constant $87654321.

interleave: determines the sector interval on the disk. Computers with disk controllers without DMA must evaluate data read from disk, which takes some time. This can cause the next sector to rotate past the read/write head before the CPU is done. If the sectors are written in some order other than 1 2 3 4 5 6 7 8 9 (interleave = 1), line 1 6 2 7 3 8 4 9 5 (interleave = 2), the time between the current and next sectors is sufficient for the data evaluation. This can speed the transfer quite a bit because otherwise the disk would have to turn one complete revolution in order to find the next sector. On the ST the data evaluation is handled by the controller, so sectors can be written without an interleave. A value of one should be passed here.

side: the disk side

track: the destination track

spt: number of sectors per track. The disk can have ten sectors per track, TOS works with nine.

device: drive number

filler: another dummy longword for later expansion

buffer: determines the address at which the XBIOS constructs the complete track. About 8K of memory is required.

```
            move.w   #$e5e5,-(a7)        * virgin
            move.w   #$87654321,-(a7)    * magic
            move.w   #1,-(a7)            * interleave equals 1
            move.w   #0,-(a7)            * side 0
            move.w   #5,-(a7)            * track 5
            move.w   #9,-(a7)            * spt, 9 sectors per track
            move.w   #0,-(a7)            * device 0 equals drive A
            move.l   #0,-(a7)            * filler, dummy long word
            move.l   #buffer,-(a7)       * address of the free space
            move.w   #10,-(a7)           * XBIOS function number
            trap     #14
            add.l    #26,a7
            tst.w    d0                  * error occurred?
            bmi      error               * yes
            ...
            ...
buffer:     ds.b     8*1024              * space for track
```

PROTOBT: XBIOS function number 18

This function makes it easier to create a boot sector for various disk formats. First you read sector 1 of track 0, side 0 of a arbitrarily formatted disk, call PROTOBT, and then write the boot sector with PROTOBT modified back to sector 1, track 0, side 0 of the disk on which the boot sector is to be created. The parameters to be passed:

execflag: indicates whether the boot sector is executable, that is whether there is an executable boot program at byte 30 relative to the start of the sector. Possible values are:

Value:	Meaning:
0	not executable
1	executable
-1	buffer stays the way it was

disktype:

0	40 track, single-sided (SS, SD 180K)
1	40 track, double-sided (DS, SD 360)
2	80 track, single-sided (SS, DD 360)
3	80 track, double-sided (DS, DD 720)
-1	Disk type remains unchanged

The Atari formats, as we have already mentioned, are the double-density formats 2 and 3.

serialnr: the serial number is a 24-bit number which is written in the boot sector and is used by the operating system to detect when the disk has been changed. If the serial number passed is greater than 24 bits (such as $01000000), the operating system will write a random number. If it is -1, the buffer serial number will not be changed.

buffer: the address at which the boot sector is located (512 bytes).

```
        move.w  #-1,-(a7)      * execflag, don't change executability
        move.w  #3,-(a7)       * disk type, 80 track, double-sided
        move.l  #buffer,-(a7)  * location of sector
        move.w  #18            * XBIOS function number
        trap    #14
        add.l   #14,a7
        tst.w   d0
        bmi     error          * didn't work
        ...
        ...
buffer: ds.b    512
```

This program fragment converts a boot sector from a single-sided disk to one for a double-sided disk, which can then be written on the second formatted side of the disk.

Now let's take a look at the information found in the boot sector.

The 16-bit data are stored in Intel format (first low byte, then high byte) on the disk, and an executable boot sector is indicated by a checksum of $1234.

Byte		40 track SS	40 tr DS	80 tr SS	80 tr DS
0,1	bra 30	Jump to $30 if the boot sector is executable			
2-7	Text: 'Loader'				
8-10	serialnr				
11-12	bps	512	512	512	512
13	spc	2	2	2	2
14-15	res	1	1	1	1
16	fat	2	2	2	2
17-18	dir	64	112	112	112
19-20	sec	360	720	720	1440
21	media	252	253	248	249

Byte		40 track SS	40 tr DS	80 tr SS	80 tr DS
22-23	spf	2	2	5	5
24-25	spt	9	9	9	9
26-27	side	1	2	1	2
28-29	hide	0	0	0	0
30	bootcode: boot code for an executable sector				

...
...

510-511   checksum of the entire boot sector from bytes 0 to 509

7.2 Listing and operation of the disk editor

As mentioned before, here is the first part of the disk editor. This listing is written for the Abacus *AssemPro* assembler package. After you have typed in the listing correctly and assembled the program, only the sector menu works in the program `edit.tos`. To complete the program, you must replace the "dummy subroutines" with the working versions of the routines, which we shall introduce later on in this chapter.

```
;****************************************************************
;*                                                              *
;*        The little disk editor, U. Braun , August 1986        *
;*                                                              *
;*              ATARI ST DISK DRIVES INSIDE AND OUT             *
;*                                                              *
;****************************************************************

        text

;****************************************************************
;*                                                              *
;*  Entry after loading, calculate length, and reserve space    *
;*                                                              *
;****************************************************************
sstart: move.l   a7,a5       ;* base address on the stack
    move.l   4(a5),a5        ;* basepage address = start of program - $100
    move.l   $c(a5),d0       ;* program length
    add.l    $14(a5),d0      ;* length of the initialized data area
    add.l    $1c(a5),d0      ;* length of the uninitialized data area
    add.l    #$1100,d0       ;* 4 K userstack=sufficient space
    move.l   a5,d1           ;* start address of the program
```

```
        add.l   d0,d1           ;* plus number of occupied bytes =
                                ;* space requirement
        and.l   #-2,d1          ;* even address for stack
        move.l  d1,a7           ;* user stack pointer to last 4K
        move.l  d0,-(sp)        ;* length of reserved area
        move.l  a5,-(sp)        ;* start address of the reserved area
        move.w  d0,-(sp)        ;* dummy word
        move.w  #$4a,-(sp)      ;* GEMDOS function SETBLOCK
        trap    #1
        add.l   #12,sp          ;* restore old stack address again
        jsr     main            ;* jump to main program. ( user-created )
        move.l  #0,-(a7)        ;* ends the current program
        trap    #1              ;* back to GEM desktop

;******************************************************************
;*                                                                *
;*   This is the start of the actual program                      *
;*                                                                *
;******************************************************************

main:   jsr     start1          ;* initialize line-A
        jsr     emptybuf        ;* empty keyboard buffer
        jsr     clear           ;* clear screen
        jsr     init            ;* set default parameters
        jsr     gomain          ;* go to main menu
        jsr     menu11          ;* pass control to menu handler
mainend: rts                    ;* return to desktop

;******************************************************************

init:   jsr     cursoff         ;* turn cursor off
        jsr     clear           ;* clear screen
        move.w  #0,wtrack       ;* track zero, side zero
        move.w  #0,wside
        move.w  #0,wdrive       ;* drive zero, sector one
        move.w  #1,wsector      ;* set
        move.w  #0,d0
        move.w  #6,maxdriv      ;* max number of drives
        move.w  #1,maxside      ;* max number of sides-1
        move.w  #79,maxtrack    ;* default max number of tracks
        move.w  #9,maxsect      ;* default max sectors
        move.w  #9,asector      ;* max number of sec/track
        move.b  #'0',setrack    ;* put correct values in
        move.b  #'9',setrack+1  ;* menus
        move.w  #1500,maxclust  ;* max number of clusters
        MOVE.L  #spacetr,EDITPTR ;* BUFFER
        jsr     prmessag        ;* output message
```

```
                rts                     ;* and return

;*******************************************************************
;*   Output message with copyright                                 *
;*******************************************************************

prmessag:   jsr     emptybuf            ;* empty keyboard buffer
            move.w  #20,column          ;* position cursor
            move.w  #10,line
            jsr     loccurs
            move.l  #hafrag1,a0         ;* message part 1
            jsr     printf              ;* output
            move.w  #20,column
            move.w  #12,line
            jsr     loccurs             ;* position cursor
            move.l  #hafrag2,a0         ;* message part 2
            jsr     printf              ;* output
            move.w  #20,column
            move.w  #14,line
            jsr     loccurs             ;* position cursor
            move.l  #hafrag3,a0         ;* message part 3
            jsr     printf              ;* output
            jsr     wkey                ;* wait for a key
            jsr     clear               ;* clear screen
            jsr     emptybuf            ;* empty keyboard buffer
            rts                         ;* and return

;*******************************************************************
;*    This is the menu loop, the part of the program that controls *
;*    the whole program.  Here we check to see if a different menu *
;*    option was selected by cursor right or left, or a menu option*
;*    is selected with cursor up and down. If so, control is passed*
;*    to these menu options by means of meselct.                   *
;*******************************************************************

menul1:     jsr     key                 ;* read keyboard
            tst.l   d0                  ;* no input, keep waiting
            beq     menul1
            swap    d0                  ;* else check for various keys
            cmp.b   #$44,d0             ;* F-10 key = end, NOTSTOP, for Debug
            beq     menend

menul2:     cmp.b   #$4b,d0             ;* cursor left
            bne     menul3
            jsr     curleft
            bra     menul1
```

```
menu13: cmp.b      #$4d,d0       ;* cursor right
        bne        menu14
        jsr        curright
        bra        menu11

menu14: cmp.b      #$50,d0       ;* cursor down
        bne        menu15
        jsr        cursdown
        bra        menu11

menu15: cmp.b      #$48,d0       ;* cursor up
        bne        menu16
        jsr        cursup

menu16: bra        menu11
mainend2: add.l    #8,a7         ;* two return addresses still on the stack
menend: rts                      ;* (remove)


;***************************************************************
;*   A menu option is selected with cursor up, the corresponding   *
;*   jump address block is loaded from jmptable, and control branches *
;*   to mselect.                                                   *
;***************************************************************


cursup:   move.l   incvar,jmptable  ;* jump table for selection by
          jsr      meselect         ;* cursor up, execute routine
          rts                       ;* and back to menu loop


;***************************************************************
;*   A menu option was selected with cursor down, in some menus the *
;*   subroutine to be executed is determined by the selecting key   *
;*   (up or down), such as inctrack and dectrack on the sector menu. *
;***************************************************************


cursdown: move.l   decvar,jmptable  ;* jump table for selection
          jsr      meselect         ;* by cursor down
          rts


;***************************************************************
;*   The user "travels" through the individual menu options with the *
;*   cursor left key and they are displayed in reverse.              *
;***************************************************************
```

```
curleft:  move.l    revnum,d0        ;* selection of menu options
          sub.l     #1,d0
          beq       laround          ;* write in reverse
          move.l    d0,revnum
          bra       curlend
laround:  move.l    ganz,revnum      ;* swap around
curlend:  jsr       dispmen          ;* display the menu
          rts

;************************************************************************
;*   as curleft, except for cursor right                                *
;************************************************************************

curright: move.l    revnum,d0        ;* as for curleft
          add.l     #1,d0
          cmp.l     ganz,d0
          bgt       raround
          move.l    d0,revnum
          bra       currend
raround:  move.l    #1,revnum
currend:  jsr       dispmen
          rts

;************************************************************************
;*   Execute the appropriate subroutine                                 *
;************************************************************************

meselect: jsr       emptybuf         ;* Call the selected routine
          move.l    jmptable,a0      ;* the jump table contains
          move.l    revnum,d0        ;* the start address of the
          subq.l    #1,d0            ;* jump address block
          lsl.l     #2,d0            ;* times four, one address
          move.l    (a0,d0.l),a1     ;* occupies four bytes, load
          jmp       (a1)             ;* and execute the routine

;************************************************************************
;*   Error handler: an error string is obtained from the negative       *
;*   error number passed on the stack, and this error string is then    *
;*   displayed.                                                         *
;************************************************************************

errhand:  move.w    #10,column       ;* the error number is passed
          move.w    #2,line          ;* on the stack (word)
          jsr       loccurs          ;* position cursor in line 2
          jsr       delline          ;* delete line
          move.w    4(a7),d0         ;* get error number
```

```
            neg.w     d0                    ;* make positive
            cmp.w     #29,d0                ;* compare with max error
            blt       errhand1
            move.w    #29,d0                ;* default error number

errhand1:   lsl.w     #2,d0                 ;* use as pointer in
            move.l    #errtab,a1            ;* the error table
            move.l    0(a1,d0.w),a0         ;* get error string
            jsr       printf                ;* print it
            jsr       wkey                  ;* wait for keypress
            jsr       delline               ;* delete line again
            jsr       cursbuf               ;* cursor back to line 4
            move.l    (a7)+,a0              ;* get return address
            addq.l    #2,a7                 ;* correct stack (error #)
            jmp       (a0)                  ;* back to caller

;*********************************************************************
;*   Passes the parameters for the main menu to the various variables *
;*   menuadr, incvar, decvar, ganz, revnum                            *
;*********************************************************************

gomain:     jsr       clear                 ;* clear the screen
            move.l    #7,ganz               ;* seven options in mani menu
            move.l    #1,revnum             ;* invert first option
            move.l    #menmain,menuadr      ;* addresses of the menu strings
            move.l    #haincjmp,incvar      ;* address of the menu routines
            move.l    #haincjmp,decvar      ;* same for cursor up and down
            jsr       dispmen               ;* display menu
            rts                             ;* and return


;*********************************************************************
;*   Here are the main menu routines                                  *
;*********************************************************************

;*********************************************************************
;*   supplies the variables of the menu-select system with the        *
;*   addresses for the TRACK menu point                               *
;*********************************************************************

gotrack:    jsr       clear                 ;* clear screen
            move.l    #mentrack,menuadr     ;* addresses of the menu strings
            move.l    #8,ganz               ;* the track menu has 8 options
            move.l    #5,revnum             ;* invert 5th option
            move.l    #trincjmp,incvar      ;* Cursor-up jump table
            move.l    #trdecjmp,decvar      ;* Cursor-down jump table
            jsr       dispmen               ;* display menu
```

```
            jsr        cursmess              ;* and output a message
            move.l     #trfrag1,a0           ;* "TRACK MODE"
            jsr        printf
            rts                              ;* Return to menu

;**********************************************************************
;*  supplies the variables of the menu-select system with the         *
;*  addresses for the TRACK with SYNC menu point                      *
;**********************************************************************

gosync: move.l         #6,ganz               ;* Track with SYNC menu
            move.l     #4,revnum             ;* has six menu options
            move.l     #syincjmp,incvar      ;* up jump table
            move.l     #sydecjmp,decvar      ;* down jump table
            move.l     #mensync,menuadr      ;* addresses of the menu strings
            jsr        dispmen               ;* display the menu
            jsr        cursmess              ;* position cursor
            move.l     #trfrag2,a0           ;* "Track with Syncs"
            jsr        printf                ;* print
            rts

;**********************************************************************
;*  supplies the variables of the menu-select system with the         *
;*  addresses for the SECTOR menu point                               *
;**********************************************************************

gosector:   jsr        clear
            move.l     #mensect,menuadr      ;* sector menu options
            move.l     #seincjmp,incvar
            move.l     #sedecjmp,decvar
            move.l     #spacetr,editptr
            move.l     #8,ganz               ;* 8 options
            move.l     #5,revnum             ;* display 5th in reverse
            jsr        dispmen
            jsr        cursmess
            move.l     #sefrag1,a0
            jsr        printf
            rts

;**********************************************************************
;*  supplies the variables of the menu-select system with the         *
;*  addresses for the CLUSTER menu option                             *
;**********************************************************************

goclust:    jsr        initdriv              ;* cluster menu, initialize
            jsr        rdfat                 ;* first drive, then read FAT
```

```
            move.l    #8,ganz              ;* menu has 8 subpoints
            move.l    #3,revnum            ;* read = reverse
            move.l    #menclust,menuadr    ;* address of the menu string
            move.l    #clincjmp,incvar     ;* jump table
            move.l    #cldecjmp,decvar
            jsr       cursmess
            move.l    #clfrag1,a0          ;* "cluster mode"
            jsr       printf               ;* write
            jsr       dispmen              ;* display menu and
            rts                            ;* return

;************************************************************************
;*   supplies the variables of the menu-select system with the          *
;*   addresses for the FORMAT menu option                               *
;************************************************************************

goformat:   jsr       clear                ;* format menu
            move.l    #formmen,menuadr     ;* address of the menu string
            move.l    #8,ganz              ;* eight menu options
            move.l    #3,revnum            ;* third in reverse
            move.l    #foincjmp,incvar
            move.l    #fodecjmp,decvar
            jsr       dispmen
            jsr       cursmess
            move.l    #drfrag1,a0
            jsr       printf
            rts

;************************************************************************
;*   Submenu for the FORMAT menu, supplies the variables with the       *
;*   addresses of the GAP menu                                          *
;************************************************************************

gogaps:     jsr       clear
            move.l    #mengap,menuadr
            move.l    #7,ganz              ;* seven menu options
            move.l    #1,revnum
            move.l    #gpincjmp,incvar
            move.l    #gpdecjmp,decvar
            jsr       dispmen
            jsr       cursmess
            move.l    #gpfrag1,a0
            jsr       printf
            rts
```

```
;************************************************************************
;*   supplies the variables of the menu-select system with the          *
;*   for the OPTION menu option                                         *
;************************************************************************

goinit:     move.l      #6,ganz             ;* init menu has six
            move.l      #4,revnum           ;* options
            move.l      #inincjmp,incvar
            move.l      #indecjmp,decvar
            move.l      #meninit,menuadr
            jsr         dispmen
            jsr         cursmess
            move.l      #drifrag1,a0
            jsr         printf
            rts

;************************************************************************
;*   Here follow the first routines of the SECTOR menu                  *
;************************************************************************
;************************************************************************
;*   Increments the drive number within the menu option                 *
;************************************************************************

incdrive:   move.w      wdrive,d0           ;* compare active drive
            cmp.w       maxdriv,d0          ;* with maxdrive
            blt         incdr1              ;* if smaller, then increment
            move.w      #0,d0               ;* else active drive to zero
            bra         incdr2
incdr1:     addq.w      #1,d0
incdr2:     move.w      d0,wdrive           ;* store again
            add.b       #'0',d0             ;* and enter in menu
            move.b      d0,mdrive           ;*
            jsr         dispmen             ;* display it
            rts                             ;* and return

;************************************************************************
;*   Decrements the drive number within the menu option, the following  *
;*   subroutines work like inctrack, incside                            *
;************************************************************************

decdrive:   move.w      wdrive,d0           ;* decrement current drive
            cmp.w       #0,d0
            ble         decdr1
            subq.w      #1,d0
            bra         decdr2
decdr1:     move.w      maxdriv,d0
decdr2:     move.w      d0,wdrive
```

```
            add.b       #'0',d0
            move.b      d0,mdrive
            jsr         dispmen
            rts

;*****************************************************************

incside:    move.w      wside,d0        ;* current side
            cmp.w       #1,d0           ;* equal to one?
            blt         incsi1          ;* if so, then
            move.w      #0,d0           ;* set side zero
            bra         incsi2
incsi1:     move.w      #1,d0           ;* else side one
incsi2:     move.w      d0,wside        ;* and store
            add.b       #'0',d0         ;* and enter in menu string
            move.b      d0,mside
            jsr         dispmen         ;* display menu
            rts                         ;* and return

decside:    move.w      wside,d0        ;* decrement side
            cmp.w       #0,d0
            ble         decsi1
            move.w      #0,d0
            bra         decsi2
decsi1:     move.w      #1,d0
decsi2:     move.w      d0,wside
            add.b       #'0',d0
            move.b      d0,mside
            jsr         dispmen
            rts

;*****************************************************************

inctrack:   move.w      wtrack,d0       ;* increment track, compare
            cmp.w       maxtrack,d0     ;* current with maxtrack
            blt         inctr1          ;* if smaller, then continue
            move.w      #0,d0           ;* else current track to zero
            bra         inctr2
inctr1:     addq.w      #1,d0           ;* add one
inctr2:     move.w      d0,wtrack       ;* and store
            ext.l       d0
            divu        #10,d0          ;* enter in menu
            add.b       #'0',d0         ;* binary -> ASCII
            move.b      d0,mtrack       ;* high byte
            swap        d0
            add.b       #'0',d0
            move.b      d0,mtrack+1     ;* low byte
```

219

```
            jsr     dispmen         ;* display menu
            rts

dectrack:   move.w  wtrack,d0       ;* decrement track
            cmp.w   #0,d0           ;* current track equals zero
            ble     dectr1
            subq.w  #1,d0
            bra     dectr2
dectr1:     move.w  maxtrack,d0     ;* then current track = maxtrack
dectr2:     move.w  d0,wtrack
            ext.l   d0
            divu    #10,d0
            add.b   #'0',d0
            move.b  d0,mtrack
            swap    d0
            add.b   #'0',d0
            move.b  d0,mtrack+1     ;* enter in menu string
            jsr     dispmen         ;* display and back
            rts

;****************************************************************

incsect:    move.w  wsector,d0      ;* increment current sector
            cmp.w   maxsect,d0      ;* see inctrack
            blt     incse1
            move.w  #0,d0
            bra     incse2
incse1:     addq.w  #1,d0
incse2:     move.w  d0,wsector
            ext.l   d0
            divu    #10,d0
            add.b   #'0',d0
            move.b  d0,msector
            swap    d0
            add.b   #'0',d0
            move.b  d0,msector+1
            jsr     dispmen
            rts

decsect:    move.w  wsector,d0      ;* decrement current sector
            cmp.w   #0,d0
            ble     decse1
            subq.w  #1,d0
            bra     decse2
decse1:     move.w  maxsect,d0
decse2:     move.w  d0,wsector
            ext.l   d0
```

```
            divu       #10,d0
            add.b      #'0',d0
            move.b     d0,msector
            swap       d0
            add.b      #'0',d0
            move.b     d0,msector+1
            jsr        dispmen
            rts

;**********************************************************************
;*  Reads the current sector, in wsector, if drbyte = 1024 then 1024  *
;*  bytes will be read, because the operating system calculates the   *
;*  bytes to be read from the number of sectors by multiplying the    *
;*  number of sectors by 512. If you pass 2 sectors, then 1024 bytes  *
;*  will be read, regardless of whether they are organized as one     *
;*  sector of 1024 bytes, or 2 of 512 bytes, or 4 of 256 bytes.       *
;**********************************************************************

readsec:    move.w     drbyte,d0         ;* number of bytes/sector
            move.w     #1,d1             ;* default equals 1 sector
            cmp.w      #1024,d0          ;* if drbyte = 1024, then
            bne        readweit          ;* read one sector of 1024 bytes
            move.w     #2,d1
readweit:   move.w     d1,-(a7)          ;* number of sectors
            move.w     wside,-(a7)       ;* side
            move.w     wtrack,-(a7)      ;* track
            move.w     wsector,-(a7)     ;* sector, or start sector
            move.w     wdrive,-(a7)      ;* drive
            clr.l      -(a7)             ;* dummy long word
            move.l     #spacetr,-(a7)    ;* buffer address
            move.w     #8,-(a7)          ;* floprd
            trap       #14               ;* XBIOS call
            add.l      #20,a7            ;* restore stack
            tst.w      d0                ;* did an error occur?
            bmi        readser           ;* if so, then print message
            jsr        showsec           ;* else display sector read
            rts                          ;* and return

readser:    move.w     d0,-(a7)          ;* error number on stack
            jsr        errhand           ;* handle error
            jsr        cursmess          ;*
            move.l     #sefrag1,a0
            jsr        printf
            rts                          ;* and return
```

```
;******************************************************************
;*   Show the sector on the screen; the showit subroutine is used,  *
;*   which displays everything passed to it; see also editsec       *
;******************************************************************

showsec:    move.w    #0,head2            ;* pointer in sector
            move.l    editptr,topptr      ;* pointer to start of sector
            move.w    #31,prcount         ;* counter for printing
            move.w    #18,lincount        ;* number of displayed lines
            move.w    #0,maxdown          ;* scroll-down flag
            move.w    #208,maxup          ;* scroll-up flag
            move.w    drbyte,d0           ;* bytes in sector/ from GAP menu
            cmp.w     #1024,d0            ;* if 1024, then
            bne       showse2
            move.w    #512,maxdown        ;* set scroll-up and scroll-down
            move.w    #720,maxup          ;* flags accordingly
            move.w    #63,prcount         ;* and print-line counter
showse2:    jsr       showit
            rts


;******************************************************************
;*   Universal display routine, which handles keyboard input, scrolls *
;*   up and down and checks for the 'p' key for printer output. A    *
;*   pointer to the start of the memory area to be displayed is passed *
;*     as well as the upper and lower boundaries.                    *
;******************************************************************

showit:     jsr       cursbuf
            jsr       emptybuf            ;* empty keyboard buffer
            move.w    #0,head2            ;* pointer in sector
showit3:    move.w    head2,head1         ;* to pointer for dispbuf routine
            jsr       dispbuf             ;* write this buffer
            jsr       emptybuf            ;* empty keyboard buffer
            jsr       cursbuf
showit4:    jsr       key                 ;* read keyboard
            swap      d0
            cmp.b     #$19,d0             ;* test if 'p'-key pressed
            beq       printit             ;* if so, output to printer
            cmp.b     #$48,d0             ;* test for cursor up
            beq       upper               ;* if so, handle it
            cmp.b     #$50,d0             ;* test for cursor down
            beq       lower               ;* if so, handle it
            cmp.b     #$1c,d0             ;* test for 'RETURN' key
            beq       shsecli
            cmp.b     #$4b,d0             ;* test for cursor left
            beq       shsecli             ;* if so
```

```
              cmp.b    #$4d,d0             ;* test for cursor right
              bne      showit4             ;* if not, then back to loop
              jsr      curright            ;* else cursor right
              bra      showiten            ;* to calling program section
shsecli:      jsr      curleft             ;* call cursor left and back
showiten:     rts                          ;* to calling program section

upper:        move.w   head2,d0            ;* handle cursor up
              cmp.w    #0,d0               ;* if the pointer points to the start
              beq      uppend              ;* of the sector, then do nothing
              cmp.w    maxup,d0            ;* if it points to the upper limit,
              beq      upper1              ;* then subtract 208
              sub.w    #256,head2          ;* else subtract 256
              sub.l    #256,topptr         ;* from pointer in sector,
              bra      uppend              ;* and counter and return
upper1:       sub.w    #208,head2          ;* subtract 208 from pointer in
              sub.l    #208,topptr         ;* sector
uppend:       bra      showit3             ;* and back to display

lower:        move.w   head2,d0            ;* handling cursor down
              cmp.w    maxup,d0            ;* as upper, except add to
              beq      lowend              ;* pointer and counter
              cmp.w    maxdown,d0
              bne      lower1
              add.w    #208,head2
              add.l    #208,topptr
              bra      lowend
lower1:       add.w    #256,head2
              add.l    #256,topptr
lowend:       bra      showit3             ;* keep displaying

;*********************************************************************
;* Print the contents of the buffer to which topptr points as 16     *
;* 2-digit hex numbers and 16 ASCII characters on the printer. The   *
;* number of lines to be printed is passed in prcount.               *
;*********************************************************************

printit:      move.w   #0,device           ;* conout to printer
              movem.l  a3-a5/d3-d7,savereg ;* save the registers
              move.l   #m1secta,a5         ;* print current
              move.w   #45,d7              ;* track, sector, and side
printit0:     move.b   (a5)+,d0
              move.w   d0,-(a7)
              jsr      conout              ;* print
              dbra     d7,printit0
              move.l   #m1clusa,a5         ;* print cluster number
              move.w   #13,d7
```

```
printit1: move.b    (a5)+,d0
          move.w    d0,-(a7)
          jsr       conout
          dbra      d7,printit1
          jsr       crlinef         ;* Carriage return + line feed
          jsr       crlinef         ;* 2 times
          move.l    topptr,a4       ;* pointer in sector
          move.l    a4,a5           ;* store
          move.w    head2,head1     ;* current counter
          move.w    #15,d3          ;* column ctr corresponds to 16 cols
          move.w    d3,d4           ;* store
          move.w    prcount,d5      ;* number of lines to print
printit2: move.w    d4,d3           ;* number of lines
          jsr       header          ;* output the count byte
          jsr       hex16           ;* output 16 hex bytes
          move.w    d4,d3           ;* restore counter
          move.l    a5,a4           ;* pointer back to start of sector
          move.w    #5,d7           ;* insert five spaces
printit3: move.w    #$20,-(a7)
          jsr       conout          ;* output
          dbra      d7,printit3
          jsr       char16          ;* output 16 ASCII characters
          add.l     #16,a5
          add.w     #16,head1
          jsr       crlinef         ;* start new line
          dbra      d5,printit2     ;* until all lines
          jsr       emptybuf        ;* have been printed
          movem.l   savereg,a3-a5/d3-d7   ;* restore registers
          move.w    #2,device       ;* output back to screen
          bra       showit4         ;* and display the sector

printerr: rts

;*******************************************************************
;*  Switch to edit mode in the sector mode; a very flexible editit *
;*  routine is called, which is passed only a pointer to the start of *
;*  the memory area to be edited and two limit variables.           *
;*******************************************************************

editsec:  jsr       cursmess
          move.l    #edfrag1,a0     ;* display edit message
          jsr       printf
          move.w    #0,column
          move.w    #4,line
          jsr       loccurs
          jsr       clrest          ;* clear rest of screen
          move.w    drbyte,d0
```

```
            cmp.w       #1024,d0            ;* if 1024 bytes/sector then
            bne         edsewei1
            move.w      #512,maxdown        ;* select higher limit so that
            move.w      #720,maxup          ;* all 1024 can be edited
            bra         edsewei2

edsewei1:   move.w      #0,maxdown          ;* else choose appropriately
            move.w      #208,maxup          ;* smaller limits
edsewei2:   move.w      #18,lincount        ;* display 19 lines
            move.l      #spacetr,editptr    ;* buffer address
            jsr         editit              ;* and edit
            jsr         curleft             ;* set sector menu
            jsr         curleft             ;* back to read
            move.w      #2,line
            jsr         loccurs
            jsr         delline             ;* delete line
            jsr         cursmess
            move.l      #sefrag1,a0         ;* display message
            jsr         printf
            jsr         cursoff             ;* disable cursor
            jsr         showsec             ;* and display sector again
            jsr         emptybuf            ;* empty keyboard buffer
            rts                             ;* and return

;**********************************************************************
;*    This is the flexible edit routine, which can edit an arbitrary  *
;*    number of 16-byte lines and which displays these as 16 hex      *
;*    numbers and 16 ASCII characters.                                *
;**********************************************************************

editit:     movem.l     a3-a6/d3-d7,-(a7)   ;* save registers
            move.l      editptr,topptr      ;* buffer address
            move.w      #0,head2            ;* initialize counter for buffer
            move.w      #0,head1
            jsr         dispbuf             ;* display first buffer side
            jsr         emptybuf            ;* empty keyboard buffer
            move.w      #7,column           ;* edit starts in column 7
            move.w      #4,line
            jsr         loccurs             ;* position cursor
edits0:     jsr         curson              ;* turn cursor on
            move.l      #retw1,-(a7)        ;* pass address of variable
            jsr         hexin               ;* to hexin, this address
            jsr         cursoff             ;* contains the number
            tst.w       retw1               ;* entered, if the number was
            bmi         otherkey            ;* negative, then other key pressed
            move.w      line,d0             ;* current line
            subq.w      #4,d0               ;* start offset of the first line
```

```
              lsl.w     #4,d0              ;* times 16 characters/line
              move.w    column,d2          ;* plus column - start offset
              sub.w     #7,d2
              ext.l     d2                 ;* divided by 3 characters per
              divu      #3,d2              ;* byte (1 space + 2 digits)
              add.w     d2,d0              ;* plus line offset
              move.w    retw1,d1           ;* hex digit entered
              move.l    topptr,a3          ;* start address of the buffer
              move.b    d1,0(a3,d0.w)      ;* enter digit in buffer, with
              jsr       dispzeil           ;* offset as pointer, display line
              cmp.w     #52,column         ;* was it the last edit byte
              blt       edits1             ;* in the line?
              move.w    #4,column          ;* if so, then back to start of line
edits1:       addq.w    #3,column          ;* else add 3 char/byte
              jsr       loccurs            ;* position cursor
              bra       edits0             ;* and continue editing

otherkey:     move.l    var11,d0           ;* branch here if invalid
              swap      d0                 ;* digit is entered
              cmp.b     #$4b,d0            ;* cursor left?
              beq       oleft              ;* yes, handle it
              cmp.b     #$4d,d0            ;* cursor right
              beq       oright
              cmp.b     #$50,d0            ;* cursor down
              beq       odown
              cmp.b     #$48,d0            ;* cursor up
              beq       oup
              cmp.b     #$52,d0            ;* insert key
              beq       edend1
              cmp.b     #$72,d0            ;* enter key
              beq       edend1             ;* end edit mode
              cmp.b     #$1c,d0            ;* Return key ends
              beq       edend1             ;* the edit mode
              jsr       dispzeil           ;* else display line
              jsr       loccurs            ;* position cursor
              bra       edits0             ;* and continue editing
oleft:        move.w    column,d0          ;* cursor left
              cmp.w     #7,d0              ;* cursor already at left edge
              bgt       oleft1             ;* if not, then continue
              move.w    #55,column         ;* if so, wrap around
oleft1:       subq.w    #3,column          ;* if not, subtract 3 char/byte
              jsr       loccurs            ;* position cursor
              jsr       emptybuf           ;* empty keyboard buffer
              bra       edits0             ;* and continue editing

oright:       move.w    column,d0          ;* the same in green for cursor
              cmp.w     #52,d0             ;* right
```

```
            blt       oright1
            move.w    #4,column
oright1:    addq.w    #3,column
            jsr       loccurs
            jsr       emptybuf
            bra       edits0

odown:      jsr       cursoff          ;* cursor down pressed
            move.w    line,d0          ;* current line
            cmp.w     #22,d0           ;* less than 22
            blt       odown2           ;* if so, continue
            move.w    head2,d0         ;* else compare counter
            cmp.w     maxdown,d0       ;* with limit
            bne       odown1           ;* if not equal, continue
            add.w     #208,head2       ;* if equal, process rest of
            add.l     #208,topptr      ;* buffer, adding
            move.w    column,oldspa1   ;* 208 instead of 256
            jsr       dispbuf          ;* first display buffer
            move.w    oldspa1,column   ;* cursor in old column
            move.w    #5,line          ;* offset in buffer
            jsr       loccurs          ;* position cursor
            bra       odownend         ;* and back
odown1:     cmp.w     maxup,d0         ;* if equal to upper limit
            beq       odownend         ;* then do nothing
            add.w     #256,head2       ;* else add 256 to the
            add.l     #256,topptr      ;* pointers
            move.w    column,oldspa1
            jsr       dispbuf          ;* and display the buffer
            move.w    oldspa1,column
            move.w    #6,line
            jsr       loccurs
            bra       odownend         ;* and return
odown2:     addq.w    #1,line          ;* if not in line 22, then
            jsr       loccurs          ;* increment current line by one
odownend:   jsr       emptybuf         ;* empty keyboard buffer and
            bra       edits0           ;* continue editing

oup:        jsr       cursoff          ;* same as for cursor down
            move.w    line,d0          ;* except for cursor up
            cmp.w     #4,d0            ;* current line = line 4
            bne       oup2             ;* if not, then continue
            move.w    head2,d0         ;* if so, load counter
            cmp.w     #0,d0            ;* at top of edit buffer?
            beq       oupend           ;* yes, do nothing
            cmp.w     maxup,d0         ;* no, compare with limit
            beq       oup1             ;* if equal, subtract only 208
            sub.w     #256,head2       ;* else subtract 256 from the
```

```
                sub.l       #256,topptr
                move.w      column,oldspa1   ;* pointers,
                jsr         dispbuf          ;* load old column
                move.w      oldspa1,column   ;* display buffer
                move.w      #19,line         ;* cursor in old column
                jsr         loccurs          ;* offset in line
                bra         oupend           ;* position cursor
                                             ;* and to end
oup1:           sub.w       #208,head2       ;* display top of buffer
                sub.l       #208,topptr
                move.w      column,oldspa1
                jsr         dispbuf
                move.w      oldspa1,column
                move.w      #19,line
                jsr         loccurs
oup2:           subq.w      #1,line          ;* if not in top line,
                jsr         loccurs          ;* simply decrement line
oupend:         jsr         emptybuf         ;* empty keyboard buffer
                bra         edits0           ;* and continue editing
edend1:         move.w      #0,column        ;* terminate edit, position
                move.w      #4,line          ;* cursor in line 4
                jsr         loccurs
                movem.l     (a7)+,a3-a6/d3-d7 ;* restore registers
                rts                          ;* and return

;****************************************************************

writsec: movem.l a3-a6/d3-d7,-(a7) ;* write a sector to the disk
                move.w      #0,column        ;* first ask if we should
                move.w      #2,line          ;* really write it
                jsr         loccurs
                move.l      #wrfrag1,a0
                jsr         printf
                move.l      #m1secta,a3      ;* current track, sector, etc.
                move.w      #45,d3           ;* output to screen
writ11:         move.b      (a3)+,d0
                move.w      d0,-(a7)
                jsr         conout
                dbra        d3,writ11
                move.l      #wrfrag2,a0
                jsr         printf
                jsr         emptybuf         ;* empty keyboard, and
                jsr         wkey             ;* wait for keypress
                cmp.b       #'y',d0          ;* if neither 'y' nor 'Y'
                beq         writit           ;* was pressed, then don't write
                cmp.b       #'Y',d0
                bne         wrend1           ;* jump to end
```

```
writit:   move.w    drbyte,d0         ;* if drbyte = 1024, then use
          cmp.w     #1024,d0          ;* custom write-sector
          BEQ       SELFSECT          ;* routine
          move.w    #1,d1             ;* else write a sector
writil:   move.w    d1,-(a7)          ;* number
          move.w    wside,-(a7)       ;* side
          move.w    wtrack,-(a7)      ;* track
          move.w    wsector,-(a7)     ;* sector
          move.w    wdrive,-(a7)      ;* drive
          clr.l     -(a7)             ;* dummy long word
          move.l    #spacetr,-(a7)    ;* buffer address
          move.w    #9,-(a7)          ;* flopwr
          trap      #14               ;* XBIOS call
          add.l     #20,a7
          tst.w     d0                ;* test for error
          bmi       writerr           ;* handle error

wrend2:   jsr       delline
          jsr       emptybuf
          jsr       cursmess          ;* display mode
          move.l    #sefrag1,a0
          jsr       printf
          movem.l   (a7)+,a3-a6/d3-d7
          rts                         ;* and return

wrend1:   jsr       delline
          move.l    #wrfrag3,a0       ;* message = "not written"
          jsr       printf
          jsr       emptybuf
          jsr       wkey
          bra       wrend2

writerr:  move.w    d0,-(a7)          ;* handle error
          jsr       errhand
          bra       wrend2


;****************************************************************
;*   Here we start with the modular assembly language routines.   *
;*   Routines here are simply the routine name and an RTS. Only the *
;*   sector menu is operational, meaning that you can only read and *
;*   and write sectors. Provided this shell program works properly, *
;*   you can add the complete subroutines from the other listings   *
;*   here. The best thing to do is enter the entire block that belongs*
;*   to a menu option, because most menu options access routines in  *
;*   other menu options. You should pay some attention to the order  *
;*   of the implementation. Recommended: first OPTION, then TRACK,   *
```

```
;*      followed by TRACK with SYNCS, FORMAT, and CLUSTER.           *
;*********************************************************************

;*********************************************************************
;*   Subroutines of the menu option OPTION should be implemented first *
;*   because this makes it possible to read the 10th sector, access    *
;*   track 82, etc. In addition, some routines are called by other     *
;*   program parts.                                                    *
;*********************************************************************

;Include OPTIONS.S   * See page 256 *
incmaxtr:  rts
decmaxtr:  rts
incmaxse:  rts
decmaxse:  rts
dodrivin:  rts
showbpb:   rts
initdriv:  rts
rdfat:     rts


;*********************************************************************
;*   Subroutines of the menu option TRACK of the main menu plus       *
;*   a custom write-sector routine                                    *
;*********************************************************************


;*********************************************************************
;*   custom sector-write routine, directly accesses the controller and *
;*   DMA chip. The XBIOS routinefor writing sectors, in contrast to the*
;*   sector-read routine, cannot write sectors of 1024 bytes, so we    *
;*   our own routine. It is not possible to write 1024-byte sectors    *
;*   with the initial version of the program (sector menu only).      *
;*********************************************************************


;INCLUDE SELFSECT.S      * See page 262 *
selfsect:  rts


;*********************************************************************
;*   Subroutines of the option TRACK from the main menu               *
;*********************************************************************

;include "track.s"   * See page 263 *
readltr:  rts
incstra:  rts
decstra:  rts
edittr:   rts
showtr:   rts
```

```
writ1tr:    rts

;******************************************************************
;*   Subroutines of the menu option TRACK with SYNCS, the routines  *
;*   don't access any other routines, so this option can be         *
;*   implemented as desired.                                        *
;******************************************************************

    ;include "tracksync.s"    * See page 269 *
rdtracks:   rts
shtracks:   rts
readadr:    rts
showadr:    rts

;******************************************************************
;*   Subroutines of the menu option CLUSTER of the main menu, the   *
;*   routines access routines from OPTION, so you must implement OPTION *
;*   first.                                                         *
;******************************************************************

    ;INCLUDE  "cluster.s"    * See page 278 *
edclust:    rts
decclust:   rts
incclust:   rts
nextclst:   rts
wrclust:    rts
rdclust:    rts
stclust:    rts

;******************************************************************
;*   Format subroutines from the main menu                          *
;*   These routines access subroutines from the menu option         *
;*   TRACK with SYNCS, so TRACK with SYNCS must be implemented first *
;******************************************************************

    ;include "format.s"      * See page 293 *
format1:    rts
xformat:    rts
incgap1:    rts
incgap2:    rts
incgap3:    rts
incgap4:    rts
incgap5:    rts
decgap1:    rts
decgap2:    rts
decgap3:    rts
decgap4:    rts
```

```
decgap5:    rts
incbyte:    rts
decbyte:    rts

;****************************************************************
;*                                                              *
;*   Here are some often-needed subroutines                     *
;*                                                              *
;****************************************************************

;****************************************************************
;*  draws a horizontal line from 0,10 to 639,10 (color)         *
;****************************************************************

hline:      move.l    lineavar,a0      ;* pointer to line-A variables
            move.w    #0,38(a0)        ;* X1
            move.w    #10,40(a0)       ;* Y1     20 for mono
            move.w    #639,42(a0)
            move.w    #1,24(a0)        ;* color
            move.w    #0,36(a0)        ;* write mode
            move.l    #pattern,46(a0)  ;* pattern + number of pattern words
            move.w    #0,50(a0)        ;* horizontal line
            dc.w      $a004
            rts

;****************************************************************
;*  Write a string to the screen                                *
;****************************************************************

printf:     move.l    a0,-(a7)         ;* write the string pointed to
            move.w    #9,-(a7)         ;* by address register A0
            trap      #1               ;* to the screen
            addq.l    #6,a7            ;* string must be terminated
            rts                        ;* with zero

;****************************************************************
;*  Initialize the line-A variables, and store the address of the *
;*  variable block in "lineavar".                                *
;****************************************************************

inlinea:    dc.w      $a000            ;* initializes the line-A variables
            move.l    a0,lineavar      ;* store address
            move.w    #0,32(a0)
            move.w    #$ffff,34(a0)    ;* line pattern
            move.w    #0,36(a0)        ;* Writing mode = replace
            move.w    #1,24(a0)        ;* character color
            rts
```

```
;************************************************************
;*  Initialize line-A                                        *
;************************************************************

start1:   jsr      inlinea           ;* Initialize line-A
          rts

;************************************************************
;*  Writes a word passed on the stack to the screen as a 2-digit  *
;*  hexadecimal number, or to the device determined by device    *
;************************************************************

hexpr:    move.w   4(a7),d1          ;* get argument from stack
          and.w    #$00ff,d1         ;* mask out high word
          move.w   d1,varw1          ;* store byte
          lsr.w    #4,d1             ;* shift lower nibble out
          ext.w    d1                ;* expand to word
          and.w    #$00ff,d1         ;* mask out high byte
          cmp.w    #9,d1             ;* greate than nine, then
          bgt      ischar1           ;* print a char from 'A'-'F'
          jsr      hexdig            ;* else a digit '0'-'9'
          bra      secdig1
ischar1:  jsr      hexchar
secdig1:  move.w   varw1,d1          ;* convert lower nibble of low byte
          and.w    #$000f,d1         ;* mask out upper
          cmp.w    #9,d1             ;* greater than nine, see above
          bgt      ischar2
          jsr      hexdig
          bra      hexpren           ;* to end

ischar2:  jsr      hexchar
hexpren:  move.l   (a7)+,a0          ;* return address still on the stack
          add.l    #2,a7
          jmp      (a0)              ;* back to caller, like rts

hexdig:   add.w    #48,d1            ;* add ASCII value of '0'
          MOVE.W   D1,-(A7)
          move.w   device,-(a7)      ;* and print
          move.w   #3,-(a7)          ;* conout
          trap     #13               ;* BIOS-TRAP
          addq.l   #6,a7
          rts

hexchar:  sub.w    #10,d1            ;* subtract ten and add ASCII
          add.w    #65,d1            ;* value of 'A'
          move.w   d1,-(a7)
          move.w   device,-(a7)      ;* and print
```

```
              move.w    #3,-(a7)
              trap      #13
              addq.l    #6,a7
              rts

;******************************************************************
;*      Output a 2-byte integer in decimal                        *
;******************************************************************

dezpr:        move.w    #0,dflag        ;* print a 2-byte integer in decimal
              move.w    4(a7),d3        ;* suppress leading zeros
              ext.l     d3              ;* and output as spaces
              divs      #10000,d3
              beq       dezpr1          ;*
              move.w    #-1,dflag       ;* flag for requested output, don't
dezpr1:       jsr       deznum          ;* print
              swap      d3              ;* rem of 1st division by 1000
              ext.l     d3              ;* divide
              divs      #1000,d3        ;* and print as 1000's place
              beq       dezpr3
dezpr2:       move.w    #-1,dflag       ;* not zero, set flag
dezpr3:       jsr       deznum
              swap      d3
              ext.l     d3              ;* divide rem by 100
              divs      #100,d3
              beq       dezpr4
              move.w    #-1,dflag
dezpr4:       jsr       deznum          ;* and print
dezpr5:       swap      d3
              ext.l     d3
              divs      #10,d3          ;* divide rem by 10 and
              beq       dezpr7
              move.w    #-1,dflag
dezpr7:       jsr       deznum          ;* print as ten's place of number
              swap      d3              ;* print rem of last division
              move.w    #-1,dflag       ;* in any event because zero
              jsr       deznum          ;* should be displayed if
              move.l    (a7)+,a0        ;* the result is zero.
              addq.l    #2,a7           ;* get return address in A0, restore
              jmp       (a0)            ;* stack, and return to caller

deznum:       tst.w     dflag           ;* print a digit from '0'-'9'
              bne       deznum1         ;* but only if dflag is not null
              move.b    #' ',d0
              move.w    d0,-(a7)
              bra       deznum2
```

```
deznum1: add.b    #'0',d3         ;* add ASCII value of '0'
         move.w   d3,-(a7)
deznum2: jsr      conout          ;* print
         rts

dezlpr:  move.w   #0,dflag        ;* prints a 4-byte integer, which
         move.l   4(a7),d3        ;* is passed on the stack as a long word,
         move.l   d3,d4           ;* in decimal
         divs     #10000,d3       ;* leading zeros
         ext.l    d3              ;* will be printed as
         divs     #10,d3          ;* spaces
         move.w   d3,d5           ;* first divide by 100000
         tst.w    d3              ;* if zero, then no 100000's place
         beq      dezlpr1
         move.w   #-1,dflag
dezlpr1: jsr      deznum          ;* else print the 100000's place
         move.w   d5,d3           ;* multiply result of division
         muls     #10,d3          ;* by 100000, handle result
         muls     #10000,d3       ;* as for dezpr
         sub.l    d3,d4
         move.l   d4,d3
         divs     #10000,d3
         beq      dezlpr3
dezlpr2: move.w   #-1,dflag
dezlpr3: jsr      deznum
         swap     d3
         ext.l    d3
         divs     #1000,d3
         beq      dezlpr4
         move.w   #-1,dflag
dezlpr4: jsr      deznum
         swap     d3
         ext.l    d3
         divs     #100,d3
         beq      dezlpr5
         move.w   #-1,dflag
dezlpr5: jsr      deznum
         swap     d3
         ext.l    d3
         divs     #10,d3
         beq      dezlpr6
         move.w   #-1,dflag
dezlpr6: jsr      deznum
         swap     d3
         move.w   #-1,dflag
         jsr      deznum
```

```
              move.l    (a7)+,a0
              addq.l    #4,a7
              jmp       (a0)

;*******************************************************************
;*      Display the menu                                           *
;*******************************************************************

dispmen:   move.w    #0,column        ;* cursor to top line
           move.w    #0,line
           jsr       loccurs          ;* position
           move.l    menuadr,a6       ;* here is a pointer to the
           move.l    revnum,d6        ;* addresses of the mnu strings
           subq.l    #1,d6            ;* revnum contains the number
           beq       dispweil         ;* of the menu option displayed
           subq.l    #1,d6            ;* in reverse
dispmen1:  move.l    (a6)+,a0         ;* get the individual addresses,
           jsr       printf           ;* and print with printf, until all
           dbra      d6,dispmen1      ;* strings up to the reverse are
                                      ;* printed
dispweil:  jsr       revon            ;* then display the reverse
           move.l    (a6)+,a0         ;* string
           jsr       printf
           jsr       revout           ;* turn reverse off again
           move.l    ganz,d7          ;* total number of menu options
           sub.l     revnum,d7        ;* minus the reverse number
           beq       dispmen3         ;* if zero, then it was the last
           subq.l    #1,d7            ;* else display the remaining
dispmen2:  move.l    (a6)+,a0         ;* options in normal
           jsr       printf
           dbra      d7,dispmen2      ;* until all have been printed
dispmen3:  jsr       hline            ;* then draw a horizontal line
           jsr       delrest          ;* and return
           rts

;*******************************************************************
;*    Write the contents of a memory range, whose start address is *
;*    passed in topptr, as 16 2-digit hex numbers, as well as 16 ASCII *
;*    characters, on the screen.                                   *
;*******************************************************************

dispbuf:   movem.l   a3-a5/d3-d7,savereg   ;* store registers
           move.l    topptr,a4        ;* start address of memory range
           move.l    a4,a5            ;* store
           move.w    head2,head1      ;* counter for offset in block
           move.w    #15,d3           ;* column counter = 16 columns
           move.w    d3,d4            ;* store
```

```
            move.w      lincount,d5         ;* number of lines passed
            move.w      #4,line             ;* in lincount
            move.w      #4,curzeil          ;* cursor to line 4 column 0
            move.w      #0,column
            jsr         loccurs             ;* position

dispbl:     move.w      #0,column           ;* position cursor
            move.w      curzeil,line        ;* to current line
            move.w      d4,d3               ;* column counter
            jsr         loccurs
            jsr         header              ;* print counter in block
            jsr         hex16               ;* print 16 hex numbers
            move.w      d4,d3               ;* column counter
            move.l      a5,a4               ;* topptr
            move.w      #59,column          ;* ASCII characters in column 59
            move.w      curzeil,line
            jsr         loccurs
            jsr         char16              ;* print 16 ASCII characters
            add.l       #16,a5              ;* add 16 to pointer in memory
            add.w       #1,curzeil          ;* continue with next line
            add.w       #16,head1           ;* add 16 to counter
            dbra        d5,dispbl           ;* until all lines displayed
            jsr         emptybuf            ;* empty keyboard buffer
            movem.l     savereg,a3-a5/d3-d7 ;* and restore registers
            rts

;*****************************************************************************
;*   write a header before each line                                         *
;*****************************************************************************

header:     move.w      head1,d6            ;* counter
            lsr.w       #8,d6               ;* divide by 256 (high byte)
            move.w      d6,-(a7)            ;* print as hex number
            jsr         hexpr
            move.w      head1,-(a7)         ;* print low byte
            jsr         hexpr
            move.b      #':',d6             ;* print colon
            move.w      d6,-(a7)
            jsr         conout
            rts

;*****************************************************************************
;*   write 16 hex numbers                                                    *
;*****************************************************************************

hex16:      move.w      #$20,-(a7)          ;* print two spaces
            jsr         conout
```

```
            move.w    #$20,-(a7)
            jsr       conout
hex161:     move.b    (a4)+,d7        ;* print the contents of 16 memory
            move.w    d7,-(a7)        ;* locations as hex numbers
            jsr       hexpr           ;* a space after each one
            move.w    #$20,-(a7)
            jsr       conout          ;* pass counter in d3
            dbra      d3,hex161
            rts

;*******************************************************************
;*      write 16 ASCII characters to the screen                    *
;*******************************************************************

char16:     move.b    #':',d7         ;* first a colon and
            move.w    d7,-(a7)
            jsr       conout
            move.w    #$20,-(a7)      ;* two spaces; then
            jsr       conout
char161:    move.b    (a4)+,d7        ;* print 16 ASCII characters
            cmp.b     #$20,d7         ;* print everything less than $20
            bgt       char162         ;* as a period
            move.b    #'.',d7
char162:    ext.w     d7              ;* else mask out high byte
            and.w     #$00ff,d7
            move.w    d7,-(a7)
            jsr       conout          ;* and print
            dbra      d3,char161      ;* 16 times, pass in d3
            rts

;*******************************************************************
;*      write an entire line on the screen                         *
;*******************************************************************

dispzeil:   move.w    column,oldspa1  ;* print a line in 16/16 format
            move.w    #0,column
            jsr       loccurs         ;* position cursor
            move.w    oldspa1,column
            move.w    #15,d3          ;* 16 columns
            move.w    d3,d4
            move.l    topptr,a4       ;* pointer to start of memory
            clr.l     d0              ;* range, calculate with help
            move.w    line,d0         ;* of current line, the position
            subq.w    #4,d0           ;* relative to the start of the
                                      ;* range
            lsl.w     #4,d0           ;* times 16
            move.w    d0,d1           ;* store
```

```
        add.w    head2,d0          ;* add counter offset
        move.w   d0,head1          ;* place in current counter
        ext.l    d1
        add.l    d1,a4             ;* add to pointer in memory range
        move.l   a4,a5             ;* equal to pointer
        jsr      header            ;* to the line being edited
        jsr      hex16             ;* print 16 numbers
        move.w   column,oldspa1
        move.w   #59,column
        jsr      loccurs
        move.w   d4,d3
        move.l   a5,a4             ;* and 16 ASCII characters
        jsr      char16
        move.w   oldspa1,column    ;* restore old column and
        jsr      loccurs           ;* position cursor
        rts


;*******************************************************************
;*      Routines for terminal emulation                            *
;*******************************************************************

revon:   move.l  #revers1,a0       ;* Turn reverse print on
         jsr     printf
         rts

revout:  move.l  #revers2,a0       ;* turn reverse off
         jsr     printf
         rts

delrest: move.l  #clrest2,a0       ;* delete rest of line
         jsr     printf
         rts

delline: move.l  #delline1,a0      ;* delete entire line
         jsr     printf
         rts

clear:   move.l  #clear1,a0        ;* clear entire screen
         jsr     printf            ;* and position cursor in
         rts                       ;* upper left corner

home:    move.l  #home1,a0         ;* position cursor in upper
         jsr     printf            ;* left corner
         rts
```

```
crlinef: move.w    #$1c,-(a7)      ;* output carriage return with
         jsr       conout          ;* linefeed on output device
         move.w    #$0a,-(a7)
         jsr       conout
         rts

clrest:  move.l    #clrest1,a0     ;* clear rest of screen
         jsr       printf
         rts

curson:  move.l    #curon1,a0      ;* turn cursor on
         jsr       printf
         rts

cursoff: move.l    #curout1,a0     ;* turn cursor off
         jsr       printf
         rts

cursmess: move.w   #30,column      ;* position cursor
          move.w   #2,line         ;* for printing messages
          jsr      loccurs
          rts

cursbuf: move.w    #0,column       ;* position cursor
         move.w    #4,line         ;* for printing sector buffer
         jsr       loccurs
         rts

;*******************************************************************
;*      Cursor positioning                                         *
;*******************************************************************

loccurs: move.l    #loccurs1,a0    ;* position the cursor to the
         addq.l    #2,a0           ;* coordinates passed in line
         move.w    line,d0         ;* and column, (0-79),(0-24)
         add.w     #32,d0          ;* add internal offset
         move.b    d0,(a0)+        ;* store
         move.w    column,d0
         add.w     #32,d0          ;* add internal offset
         move.b    d0,(a0)+        ;* and store
         move.l    #loccurs1,a0    ;* print modified
         jsr       printf          ;* position command
         rts

curstab: move.w    tab1,column     ;* positions the cursor in
         jsr       loccurs         ;* column tab1 of the current line
         rts
```

```
;***************************************************************
;*    Read keyboard, does not wait and returns scan code as well as  *
;*    ASCII in D0. If no key was pressed, D0=0.                      *
;***************************************************************

key:       move.w    #2,-(a7)        ;* read keyboard
           move.w    #1,-(a7)        ;* output the ASCII code of
           trap      #13             ;* the pressed key in the low byte
           addq.l    #4,a7           ;* of the lower word of D0
           tst.w     d0              ;* return scan code in low byte
           bpl       endtast2        ;* of upper word of D0.
           move.w    #2,-(a7)        ;* if key was pressed
           move.w    #2,-(a7)        ;* get key from buffer and
           trap      #13             ;* return
           addq.l    #4,a7
           rts

endtast2:  move.l    #0,d0           ;* else return zero
           rts

emptybuf:  move.w    #$b,-(a7)       ;* empty keyboard buffer
           trap      #1
           addq.l    #2,a7
           tst.w     d0
           beq       empty1
           move.w    #7,-(a7)
           trap      #1
           addq.l    #2,a7           ;* repeat until no more
           bra       emptybuf        ;* characters in buffer
empty1:    rts

conout:    move.w    4(a7),d0        ;* display a character on the
           move.w    d0,-(a7)        ;* specified device
           move.w    device,-(a7)    ;* see ATARI ST INTERNALS
           move.w    #3,-(a7)
           trap      #13
           addq.l    #6,a7
           move.l    (a7)+,a0        ;* get return address
           addq.l    #2,a7
           jmp       (a0)

wkey:      move.w    #1,-(a7)        ;* keyboard input
           trap      #1              ;* wait for input and
           addq.l    #2,a7           ;* display flashing cursor
           rts
```

```
;*******************************************************************
;*     Read a 1-byte hex number and store it in the address passed *
;*     on the stack.                                                *
;*******************************************************************

hexin:     jsr       wkey              ;* assign hex number (2 digits)
           move.l    d0,varl1          ;* to the variable passed
           cmp.b     #'f',d0           ;* on the stack
           bgt       hexeierr          ;* if an illegal key was pressed
           cmp.b     #'a',d0           ;* return -1
           blt       hexin1
           sub.b     #'a',d0           ;* test if between 'a' and 'f'
           add.b     #10,d0            ;* if so, subtract 'a', and add 10
           bra       hexin2
hexin1:    cmp.b     #'0',d0           ;* if not, then test if between
           blt       hexeierr          ;* zero and nine
           cmp.b     #'9',d0
           bgt       bstest1           ;* if not, then test if ('A'-'F')
           sub.b     #'0',d0           ;* else subtract '0'
hexin2:    lsl.w     #4,d0             ;* times 16 = high nibble
           move.w    d0,varw1          ;* store
           jsr       wkey              ;* get next nibble
           move.l    d0,varl1          ;* store
           cmp.b     #'f',d0           ;* same test as for first nibble
           bgt       hexeierr
           cmp.b     #'a',d0
           blt       hexin3
           sub.b     #'a',d0
           add.b     #10,d0
           bra       hexin4
hexin3:    cmp.b     #'0',d0
           blt       hexeierr
           cmp.b     #'9',d0
           bgt       bstest2           ;* test for uppercase
           sub.b     #'0',d0
hexin4:    move.w    varw1,d1
           or.w      d1,d0
           ext.w     d0
           and.w     #$00ff,d0
           move.w    d0,varw2          ;* return without error
hexin5:    move.l    4(a7),a0
           move.w    d0,(a0)
           move.l    (a7)+,a0
           addq.l    #4,a7
           jmp       (a0)              ;* back to caller
```

```
hexeierr: move.w   #-1,d0
          bra      hexin5           ;* return with error code

bstest1:  cmp.b    #'F',d0          ;* test if between 'A' and 'F'
          bgt      hexeierr         ;* if not, then return with
          cmp.b    #'A',d0          ;* error code
          blt      hexeierr         ;* else subtract ASCII 'A'
          sub.b    #'A',d0          ;* add ten
          add.b    #10,d0
          bra      hexin2           ;* get next nibble

bstest2:  cmp.b    #'F',d0          ;* same as bstest1 for the
          bgt      hexeierr         ;* second nibble
          cmp.b    #'A',d0
          blt      hexeierr
          sub.b    #'A',d0
          add.b    #10,d0
          bra      hexin4

;*******************************************************************
;* Variables for the basic program                                 *
;*******************************************************************


;*******************************************************************
;*  Menu data for the main menu, addresses of the menu strings,    *
;*  addresses of the subroutines (haincjmp)                        *
;*******************************************************************

          data

haincjmp: dc.l     gotrack
          dc.l     gosync
          dc.l     gosector
          dc.l     goclust
          dc.l     goformat
          dc.l     goinit
          dc.l     mainend2

menmain:  dc.l     m1hau1a
          dc.l     m1hau1a1
          dc.l     m1hau1b
          dc.l     m1hau1b1
          dc.l     m1hau1c
          dc.l     m1hau1d1
          dc.l     m1hau1e
```

```
m1hau1a:    dc.b      ' TRACK    ',0
m1hau1a1:   dc.b      ' TRACK/SYNCS ',0
m1hau1b:    dc.b      ' SECTOR   ',0
m1hau1b1:   dc.b      ' CLUSTER  ',0
m1hau1c:    dc.b      ' FORMAT   ',0
m1hau1d:    dc.b      ' FATS    ',0
m1hau1d1:   dc.b      ' OPTIONS  ',0
m1hau1e:    dc.b      ' END    ',0

hafrag1:    dc.b      27,'p  A LITTLE DISK UTILITY    (C) U. Braun 1986 '
            dc.b      27,'q',0
hafrag2:    dc.b      27,'p     ATARI ST DISK DRIVES INSIDE AND OUT    '
            dc.b      27,'q',0
hafrag3:    dc.b      27,'p    Select menu items with cursor keys       '
            dc.b      27,'q',0

;*********************************************************************
;*  Addresses of sector menu strings (mensect) and the sector menu   *
;*  routines                                                         *
;*********************************************************************
 align
seincjmp:   dc.l      incdrive
            dc.l      incside
            dc.l      inctrack
            dc.l      incsect
            dc.l      readsec
            dc.l      writsec
            dc.l      editsec
            dc.l      gomain

sedecjmp:   dc.l      decdrive
            dc.l      decside
            dc.l      dectrack
            dc.l      decsect
            dc.l      readsec
            dc.l      writsec
            dc.l      editsec
            dc.l      gomain

mensect:    dc.l      m1secta
            dc.l      m1sectb
            dc.l      m1sectc
            dc.l      m1sectd
            dc.l      m1secte
            dc.l      m1sectf
            dc.l      m1sectg
            dc.l      m1secth
```

```
m1secta:  dc.b      ' drive: '
mdrive:   dc.b      '0',' ',0
m1sectb:  dc.b      ' side: '
mside:    dc.b      '0',' ',0
m1sectc:  dc.b      ' track: '
mtrack:   dc.b      '0','0',' ',0
m1sectd:  dc.b      ' sector: '
msector:  dc.b      '0','1',' ',0
m1secte:  dc.b      '  READ  ',0
m1sectf:  dc.b      '  WRITE ',0
m1sectg:  dc.b      '  EDIT  ',0
m1secth:  dc.b      '  BACK  ',0

wrfrag1:  dc.b      27,'p',' Write this sector to: ',27,'q',0
wrfrag2:  dc.b      27,'p  <yes,no> ? ',27,'q',0
wrfrag3:  dc.b      27,'p Not written.  <press key> ',27,'q',0
sefrag1:  dc.b      27,'p  SECTOR MODE  ',27,'q',0
edfrag1:  dc.b      27,'p  EDIT MODE:  < return > := END ',27,'q',0

;******************************************************************
;*    Addresses for the TRACK menu                                *
;******************************************************************

trincjmp: dc.l      incdrive
          dc.l      incside
          dc.l      inctrack
          dc.l      incstra
          dc.l      read1tr
          dc.l      writ1tr
          dc.l      edittr
          dc.l      gomain

trdecjmp: dc.l      decdrive
          dc.l      decside
          dc.l      dectrack
          dc.l      decstra
          dc.l      read1tr
          dc.l      writ1tr
          dc.l      edittr
          dc.l      gomain

mentrack: dc.l      m1secta
          dc.l      m1sectb
          dc.l      m1sectc
          dc.l      m1traca1
          dc.l      m1tracka
          dc.l      m1trackb
```

```
                dc.l       mltrackc
                dc.l       mltrackd

mltracal:  dc.b       ' Sec/Trk : '
setrack:   dc.b       '0','9',' ',0
mltracka:  dc.b       ' READ ',0
mltrackb:  dc.b       ' WRITE ',0
mltrackc:  dc.b       ' EDIT Tr. ',0
mltrackd:  dc.b       ' BACK ',0

trfrag1:   dc.b       27,'p  TRACK MODE ',27,'q',0
trfrag2:   dc.b       27,'p  TRACK WITH SYNCS MODE ',27,'q',0
trfrag3:   dc.b       27,'p  Sector: ',0
trfrag4:   dc.b       ' ',27,'q',0
trfrag5:   dc.b       27,'p Write this track to ',27,'q',0
trfrag6:   dc.b       27,'p < yes/no > ',27,'q',0


;**********************************************************************
;*     Addresses for the TRACK with SYNCS menu                        *
;**********************************************************************
        align
syincjmp: dc.l       incdrive
          dc.l       incside
          dc.l       inctrack
          dc.l       rdtracks
          dc.l       readadr
          dc.l       gomain

sydecjmp: dc.l       decdrive
          dc.l       decside
          dc.l       dectrack
          dc.l       rdtracks
          dc.l       readadr
          dc.l       gomain

mensync:  dc.l       mlsecta
          dc.l       mlsectb
          dc.l       mlsectc
          dc.l       mlsynca
          dc.l       mlsyncb
          dc.l       mltrackd

mlsynca:  dc.b       ' READ WITH SYNCS ',0
mlsyncb:  dc.b       ' ADDR. FIELD ',0
```

```
;****************************************************************
;*   Cluster                                                    *
;****************************************************************

clincjmp: dc.l      incdrive
          dc.l      incclust
          dc.l      rdclust
          dc.l      nextclst
          dc.l      wrclust
          dc.l      edclust
          dc.l      stclust
          dc.l      gomain

cldecjmp: dc.l      decdrive
          dc.l      decclust
          dc.l      rdclust
          dc.l      nextclst
          dc.l      wrclust
          dc.l      edclust
          dc.l      stclust
          dc.l      gomain

menclust: dc.l      m1secta
          dc.l      m1clusa
          dc.l      m1secte
          dc.l      m1clusb
          dc.l      m1sectf
          dc.l      m1clusd
          dc.l      m1clusc
          dc.l      m1secth

m1clusa:  dc.b      ' CLUST: '
m1clusa1: dc.b      '0','0','0','0',' ',' ',0
m1clusb:  dc.b      ' NEXT ',0
m1clusc:  dc.b      ' STARTofFILE ',0
m1clusd:  dc.b      ' EDIT ',0

clfrag1:  dc.b      27,'p CLUSTER MODE  ',27,'q',0
clfrag2:  dc.b      27,'p When leaving CLUSTER MODE, last read '
          dc.b      'Cluster is updated in SECTOR Menu ',27,'q',0
clfrag4:  dc.b      27,'p This was the last cluster ',27,'q',0
sclfrag1: dc.b      27,'p Filename:           File attribute: '
          dc.b      '   Start cluster:     Number of bytes: ',27,'q',0
sclfrag2: dc.b      27,'p Put start cluster in menu with <RETURN>'
          dc.b      ' read with <up>, <down>. ',27,'q',0
clfrag5:  dc.b      27,'p Write this cluster to: ',27,'q',0
```

```
trecsiz: dc.b      ' Bytes per sector: ',0
tclsiz:  dc.b      ' Sectors per cluster: ',0
tclsizb: dc.b      ' Bytes per cluster: ',0
trdlen:  dc.b      ' Sectors per directory: ',0
tfsiz:   dc.b      ' Sector per FAT: ',0
tfatrec: dc.b      ' Sector number of second FAT:',0
tdatrec: dc.b      ' Sector of first data cluster:',0
tnumcl:  dc.b      ' Number of clusters: ',0
tnumsides: dc.b    ' Number of sides: ',0
tdir1:   dc.b      27,'p First directory sector on Side: 0  Track: 1 '
         dc.b      ' Sector: 3 ',27,'q',0
tdir2:   dc.b      27,'p First directory sector on Side: 1  Track: 0 '
         dc.b      ' Sector: 3 ',27,'q',0

tfolder: dc.b      ' Subdirectory ',0
treadwr: dc.b      ' Read/Write   ',0
treadon: dc.b      ' Read only    ',0
thidden: dc.b      ' HIDDEN File  ',0
tdelet:  dc.b      ' Deleted      ',0
tdisname: dc.b     ' Diskette name ',0

;*******************************************************************
;*  Format menu                                                    *
;*******************************************************************
         align
foincjmp: dc.l     incdrive
          dc.l     incside
          dc.l     inctrack
          dc.l     incstra
          dc.l     format1
          dc.l     xformat
          dc.l     gogaps
          dc.l     gomain

fodecjmp: dc.l     decdrive
          dc.l     decside
          dc.l     dectrack
          dc.l     decstra
          dc.l     format1
          dc.l     xformat
          dc.l     gogaps
          dc.l     gomain

formmen: dc.l      m1secta
         dc.l      m1sectb
         dc.l      m1sectc
         dc.l      m1traca1
```

```
              dc.l       m1formd
              dc.l       m1forme
              dc.l       m1formf
              dc.l       m1formg

m1formd:  dc.b       ' FORMAT ',0
m1forme:  dc.b       ' XFORMAT ',0
m1formf:  dc.b       '  GAPS  ',0
m1formg:  dc.b       '  BACK  ',0

fofrag1:  dc.b       27,'p  Format track mode  ',27,'q',0
fofrag2:  dc.b       27,'p  Track:',0
fofrag3:  dc.b       ' format ?   <yes/no>  ',27,'q',0
fofrag4:  dc.b       27,'p  Not formatted       <key> ',27,'q',0
fofrag5:  dc.b       '   on side :',0
fofrag6:  dc.b       '   of drive:',0
xffrag1:  dc.b       27,'p Really format with new GAPs '
          dc.b       'between the sectors? <yes/no> ',27,'q',0
xffrag2:  dc.b       27,'p Wait a second, then press key ',27,'q',0
M1FORM1:  DC.b       '  Format track  ',0

;******************************************************************
;*      Init menu                                                 *
;******************************************************************

inincjmp: dc.l       incdrive
          dc.l       incmaxtr
          dc.l       incmaxse
          dc.l       dodrivin
          dc.l       showbpb
          dc.l       gomain

indecjmp: dc.l       decdrive
          dc.l       decmaxtr
          dc.l       decmaxse
          dc.l       dodrivin
          dc.l       showbpb
          dc.l       gomain

meninit:  dc.l       m1secta
          dc.l       m1drina
          dc.l       m1drinb
          dc.l       m1drinc
          dc.l       m1drinc1
          dc.l       m1drind
```

```
m1drina: dc.b       '  MAXTRACK: '
max1tr:  dc.b       '7','9',' ',0
m1drinb: dc.b       '  MAXSECTOR: '
max1se:  dc.b       '0','9',' ',0
m1drinc: dc.b       '  INIT DRIVE  ',0
m1drinc1: dc.b      '  SHOW BPB   ',0
m1drind: dc.b       '  BACK       ',0

drifrag1: dc.b      27,'p   INIT DRIVE MENU  ',27,'q',0
drifrag2: dc.b      27,'p  Bios Parameter Block of active drive  '
          dc.b      ' < press key > ',27,'q',0
catfra1:  dc.b      27,'p   Directory starts at Side: 0 Track: 1 Sector: 3 '
          dc.b      27,'q',0
catfra2:  dc.b      27,'p   Directory starts at Side: 1 Track: 0 Sector: 3 '
          dc.b      27,'q',0

device:   dc.w      2
drive:    dc.w      0
side:     dc.w      0
track:    dc.w      0
sektor:   dc.w      0

seek:     dc.w      3
savesr:   dc.w      0
flstatus: dc.w      0

;****************************************************************
;*    Gap menu                                                  *
;****************************************************************

gpincjmp: dc.l      incgap1
          dc.l      incgap2
          dc.l      incgap3
          dc.l      incgap4
          dc.l      incgap5
          dc.l      incbyte
          dc.l      goformat

gpdecjmp: dc.l      decgap1
          dc.l      decgap2
          dc.l      decgap3
          dc.l      decgap4
          dc.l      decgap5
          dc.l      decbyte
          dc.l      goformat
```

```
mengap:    dc.l      m1gapa
           dc.l      m1gapb
           dc.l      m1gapc
           dc.l      m1gapd
           dc.l      m1gape
           dc.l      m1gapf
           dc.l      m1gapg

m1gapa:    dc.b      ' GAP1: '
mgap1:     dc.b      '60 ',0
m1gapb:    dc.b      ' GAP2: '
mgap2:     dc.b      '12 ',0
m1gapc:    dc.b      ' GAP3: '
mgap3:     dc.b      '22 ',0
m1gapd:    dc.b      ' GAP4: '
mgap4:     dc.b      '40 ',0
m1gape:    dc.b      ' GAP5: '
mgap5:     dc.b      '664 ',0
m1gapf: dc.b         ' Bytes/ec: '
mdrisect: dc.b       '0512 ',0
m1gapg:    dc.b      ' BACK ',0

drfrag1:   dc.b      27,'p Drive format mode   ',27,'q',0
gpfrag1:   dc.b      27,'p Change gaps between sectors   ',27,'q',0
slfrag1:   dc.b      27,'p Please wait a second, then press a key
',27,'q',0
slfrag3:   dc.b      27,'p SECTOR MODE   ',27,'q',0

drbyte:    dc.w      512
gap1:      dc.w      60
gap2:      dc.w      12
gap3:      dc.w      22
gap4:      dc.w      40
gap5:      dc.w      664

sadfrag1:  dc.b      27,'p Track: Side: Sector: Bytes: Checksum(hex) '
           dc.b      27,'q',0

;********************************************************************
;*  Here are the escape sequences for the terminal emulation, such as  *
;*  reverse on and off, cursor positioning, etc.                       *
;********************************************************************

clrest1:   dc.b      27,'J',0
clrest2:   dc.b      27,'K',0
revers1:   dc.b      27,'p',0
revers2:   dc.b      27,'q',0
```

```
loccurs1:  dc.b        27,'Y',33,33,0
home1:     dc.b        27,'H',0
clear1:    dc.b        27,'E',0
curup1:    dc.b        27,'A',0
curdown1:  dc.b        27,'B',0
insline1:  dc.b        27,'L',0
delline1:  dc.b        27,'l',0
overout1:  dc.b        27,'w',0
curout1:   dc.b        27,'f',0
curon1:    dc.b        27,'e',0
spaces:    dc.b        '            ',0
hilcurs:   dc.b        27,'J',0

;*****************************************************************
;*     Addresses of error strings                                *
;*****************************************************************
    align
errtab:    dc.l        error1
           dc.l        error2
           dc.l        error3
           dc.l        error4
           dc.l        error5
           dc.l        error6
           dc.l        error7
           dc.l        error8
           dc.l        error9
           dc.l        error10
           dc.l        error11
           dc.l        error12
           dc.l        error13
           dc.l        error14
           dc.l        error15
           dc.l        error16
           dc.l        error17
           dc.l        error18
           dc.l        error19
           dc.l        error20
           dc.l        error21
           dc.l        error22
           dc.l        error23
           dc.l        error24
           dc.l        error25
           dc.l        error26
           dc.l        error27
           dc.l        error28
           dc.l        error29
```

```
;**********************************************************************
;*   Here are the actual error strings                                 *
;**********************************************************************

        error1:    dc.b      27,'p',' NO BOOTSECTOR ',27,'q',0
        error2:    dc.b      27,'p Directory sector defective   <key> ',27,'q',0
        error3:    dc.b      ' error3',0
        error4:    dc.b      ' error4',0
        error5:    dc.b      ' error5 ',0
        error6:    dc.b      ' error6 ',0
        error7:    dc.b      27,'p',' Insert disk / track not present ',27,'q',0
        error8:    dc.b      ' error8 ',0
        error9:    dc.b      27,'p',' Sector does not exist!',27,'q',0
        error10:   dc.b      ' error10',0
        error11:   dc.b      ' error11',0
        error12:   dc.b      ' error12',0
        error13:   dc.b      ' error13 ',0
        error14:   dc.b      27,'p  Please remove write protect.  ',27,'q',0
        error15:   dc.b      ' error15 ',0
        error16:   dc.b      ' error16 ',0
        error17:   dc.b      ' error17',0
        error18:   dc.b      ' error18 ',0
        error19:   dc.b      ' error19 ',0
        error20:   dc.b      27,'p No more clusters ',27,'q',0
        error21:   dc.b      ' error21 ',0
        error22:   dc.b      ' error22 ',0
        error23:   dc.b      ' error23 ',0
        error24:   dc.b      ' error24 ',0
        error25:   dc.b      ' error25 ',0
        error26:   dc.b      ' error26 ',0
        error27:   dc.b      ' error27 ',0
        error28:   dc.b      ' error28 ',0
        error29:   dc.b      ' error29 ',0

        pattern:   dc.w      $ffff

                   bss

menuadr:   ds.l    1
ganz:      ds.l    1
revnum:    ds.l    1
jmptable:  ds.l    1

wtrack:    ds.w    1
wsector:   ds.w    1
wside:     ds.w    1
wdrive:    ds.w    1
```

```
wclust:    ds.w    1

maxtrack:  ds.w    1
maxsect:   ds.w    1
maxdriv:   ds.w    1
maxside:   ds.w    1
maxclust:  ds.w    1

topptr:    ds.l    1
oldtop:    ds.l    1
botptr:    ds.l    1

column:    ds.w    1
line:      ds.w    1
head1:     ds.w    1
head2:     ds.w    1

curzei1:   ds.w    1
curspa1:   ds.w    1
oldzei1:   ds.w    1
oldspa1:   ds.w    1

lincount:  ds.w    1
prcount:   ds.w    1

retw1:     ds.w    1
incvar:    ds.l    1
decvar:    ds.l    1
usstack:   ds.l    1
sustack:   ds.l    1

dmastat:   ds.w    1

currdma:   ds.b    1
highdma:   ds.b    1
middma:    ds.b    1
lowdma:    ds.b    1

maxhead:   ds.w    1

savebpb:   ds.l    1
recsiz:    ds.w    1
clsiz:     ds.w    1
clsizb:    ds.w    1
rdlen:     ds.w    1
fsiz:      ds.w    1
fatrec:    ds.w    1
```

```
datrec:    ds.w     1
numcl:     ds.w     1
bflags:    ds.w     1

oldsec:    ds.w     1

dflag:     ds.w     1
eflag:     ds.w     1
edflag:    ds.w     1

numsides:  ds.w     1
tabl:      ds.w     1

oldclst:   ds.w     1
newclst:   ds.w     1
clstnum:   ds.w     1
logsect:   ds.w     1

asector:   ds.w     1

topdma:    ds.l     1
editptr:   ds.l     1

savereg:   ds.l     16

maxdown:   ds.w     1
maxup:     ds.w     1

lineavar:  ds.l     1

varl1:     ds.l     1
varw1:     ds.w     1
varw2:     ds.w     1
varw3:     ds.w     1

dirptr:    ds.l     1

dirbuf:    ds.w     4000
fatbuf:    ds.w     4000
formbuf:   ds.w     6000
spacetr:   ds.w     6000
 end
```

Next are the complete subroutines for the individual menu options, which end in rts in the above listing of edit.s.

You should stick to the suggested order of implementation because some menu options access subroutines from other menus. If you complete the program in the manner suggested, you will not run into problems of this type.

First is the subroutine for the Options menu, which allows you to set the maximum track and sector and view the BIOS parameter block.

```
;*******************************************************************
;*   OPTION.S subroutines should be implemented first because they allow*
;*   access to the 10th sector, 82nd track, etc, and some routines are  *
;*   called by other parts of the program.                              *
;*******************************************************************


;*******************************************************************
;*   initialize current drive (from the menu) and store the variables *
;*   of the BIOS parameter block.                                     *
;*******************************************************************
initdriv: move.w  wdrive,d0        ;* current drive
          move.w  wdrive,-(a7)     ;* on the stack
          move.w  #7,-(a7)         ;* Getbpb function
          trap    #13              ;* BIOS trap
          addq.l  #4,a7            ;* restore stack
          tst.l   d0               ;* error occurred?
          bne     doinit1
          move.w  d0,-(a7)         ;* if so than pass it
          jsr     errhand          ;* and return
          bra     doiniten
doinit1:  move.l  d0,a0            ;* else d0 = base address of the BPB
          move.w  (a0)+,recsiz     ;* bytes per sector
          move.w  (a0)+,clsiz      ;* sectors/cluster
          move.w  (a0)+,clsizb     ;* bytes/cluster
          move.w  (a0)+,rdlen      ;* sectors/directory
          move.w  (a0)+,fsiz       ;* sectors/FAT
          move.w  (a0)+,fatrec     ;* sec. # of second FAT
          move.w  (a0)+,datrec     ;* sec. # of first data cluster
          move.w  (a0)+,numcl      ;* number of data clusters
          move.w  (a0)+,bflags     ;* flags
          move.w  (a0)+,numsides   ;* still dummy
          move.w  (a0)+,numsides   ;* number of sides
doiniten: rts                      ;* and return

;*******************************************************************
;*  Read the FAT sectors from the disk into the FAT buffer            *
;*******************************************************************
```

```
rdfat:      move.w      wdrive,-(a7)    ;* current drive
            move.w      fatrec,-(a7)    ;* sector # of the second FAT
            move.w      fsiz,-(a7)      ;* # of sectors per FAT
            move.l      #fatbuf,-(a7)   ;* buffer address on the stack
            move.w      #2,-(a7)        ;* read
            move.w      #4,-(a7)        ;* Rwabs function
            trap        #13             ;* BIOS trap
            add.l       #14,a7          ;* restore stack
            tst.w       d0              ;* error occurred?
            bmi         rdfater         ;* if so, then handle
rdfatend:   rts                         ;* else return

rdfater:    move.w      d0,-(a7)        ;* error number on the stack
            jsr         errhand         ;* handle
            bra         rdfatend        ;* and return

;****************************************************************
;*  Read the directory sectors from the disk into a buffer      *
;****************************************************************

rddir:      move.w      wdrive,-(a7)    ;* current drive
            move.w      fsiz,d0         ;* number of FAT sectors
            lsl.w       #1,d0           ;* times two (FAT's) plus one
            addq.w      #1,d0           ;* equals logical sector number of the
            move.w      d0,-(a7)        ;* first directory sector
            move.w      rdlen,-(a7)     ;* number of directory sectors
            move.l      #dirbuf,-(a7)   ;* address of the buffer
            move.w      #2,-(a7)        ;* read
            move.w      #4,-(a7)        ;* Rwabs function
            trap        #13             ;* BIOS
            add.l       #14,a7
            tst.w       d0              ;* error?
            bmi         rddirer         ;* yes
rddirend:   rts                         ;* if not, then return immediately

rddirer:    move.w      d0,-(a7)        ;* error number
            jsr         errhand
            bra         rddirend

;****************************************************************
;* Increments the maximum track number that can be set in the Init  *
;* drive menu. This also becomes the maximum track number for all   *
;* other menues.                                                    *
;****************************************************************

incmaxtr:   move.w      maxtrack,d0
            cmp.w       #99,d0          ;* 99 is the maximum
```

```
            blt       incma1            ;* else same procedure as for
            move.w    #0,d0             ;* previous menu changes
            bra       incma2

incma1:     addq.w    #1,d0
incma2:     move.w    d0,maxtrack
            ext.l     d0
            divu      #10,d0
            add.b     #'0',d0
            move.b    d0,max1tr         ;* also change in menu text
            swap      d0
            add.b     #'0',d0
            move.b    d0,max1tr+1
            jsr       dispmen           ;* display menu
            rts                         ;* and return

decmaxtr:   move.w    maxtrack,d0       ;* decrements the maximum
            cmp.w     #0,d0             ;* track number
            ble       decma1
            subq.w    #1,d0
            bra       decma2

decma1:     move.w    #99,d0
decma2:     move.w    d0,maxtrack
            ext.l     d0
            divu      #10,d0
            add.b     #'0',d0
            move.b    d0,max1tr         ;* change in menu string
            swap      d0
            add.b     #'0',d0
            move.b    d0,max1tr+1
            jsr       dispmen           ;* display menu
            rts                         ;* and return

incmaxse:   move.w    maxsect,d0        ;* same thing with maximum
            cmp.w     #99,d0            ;* sector number
            blt       incmas1
            move.w    #0,d0
            bra       incmas2

incmas1:    addq.w    #1,d0
incmas2:    move.w    d0,maxsect
            ext.l     d0
            divu      #10,d0
            add.b     #'0',d0
            move.b    d0,max1se         ;* put in menu text
            swap      d0
```

```
                add.b       #'0',d0
                move.b      d0,max1se+1
                jsr         dispmen         ;* display menu
                rts                         ;* and return

decmaxse:       move.w      maxsect,d0      ;* decrement maximum
                cmp.w       #0,d0           ;* sector number
                ble         decmas1
                subq.w      #1,d0
                bra         decmas2

decmas1:        move.w      #99,d0
decmas2:        move.w      d0,maxsect
                ext.l       d0
                divu        #10,d0
                add.b       #'0',d0
                move.b      d0,max1se       ;* change in menu text
                swap        d0
                add.b       #'0',d0
                move.b      d0,max1se+1
                jsr         dispmen         ;* display menu
                rts                         ;* and return

;************************************************************************
;* This is the actual drive init routine, which initializes the         *
;* current drive (in wdrive) and reads the  Bios Parameter Block as     *
;* well as reading the FAT  und directory sectors into the given        *
;* buffer.                                                              *
;************************************************************************

dodrivin:       jsr         initdriv        ;* initialize drive
                jsr         rdfat           ;* read FAT sectors
                jsr         rddir           ;* read directory sectors
                jsr         showbpb         ;* display BIOS parameter block
                jsr         curleft
dodriven:       rts                         ;* and return

;************************************************************************
;* Display the BIOS parameter block                                     *
;************************************************************************

showbpb:        move.w      #4,line         ;* cursor in line 4, column 10
                move.w      #10,column
                jsr         loccurs         ;* position
                move.l      #drifrag2,a0    ;* output message
                jsr         printf
                move.w      #42,tab1        ;* tab on screen for
```

```
        move.w     #6,line          ;* outputting numbers
        move.w     #12,column
        jsr        loccurs
        move.l     #trecsiz,a0      ;* bytes per cluster
        jsr        printf
        jsr        curstab          ;* write text
        move.w     recsiz,-(a7)     ;* write bytes/cluster as decimal
                                    ;* number
        jsr        dezpr
        addq.w     #1,line          ;* move down one line
        move.w     #12,column
        jsr        loccurs
        move.l     #tclsiz,a0       ;* sectors per cluster
        jsr        printf
        jsr        curstab
        move.w     clsiz,-(a7)
        jsr        dezpr
        addq.w     #1,line
        move.w     #12,column
        jsr        loccurs
        move.l     #tclsizb,a0      ;* bytes per cluster
        jsr        printf
        jsr        curstab
        move.w     clsizb,-(a7)
        jsr        dezpr
        addq.w     #1,line
        move.w     #12,column
        jsr        loccurs
        move.l     #trdlen,a0       ;* sectors per directory
        jsr        printf
        jsr        curstab
        move.w     rdlen,-(a7)
        jsr        dezpr
        addq.w     #1,line
        move.w     #12,column
        jsr        loccurs
        move.l     #tfsiz,a0        ;* sectors per FAT
        jsr        printf
        jsr        curstab
        move.w     fsiz,-(a7)
        jsr        dezpr
        addq.w     #1,line
        move.w     #12,column
        jsr        loccurs
        move.l     #tfatrec,a0      ;* sector number of the 2nd FAT
        jsr        printf
        jsr        curstab
```

```
            move.w    fatrec,-(a7)      ;*
            jsr       dezpr
            addq.w    #1,line
            move.w    #12,column
            jsr       loccurs
            move.l    #tdatrec,a0       ;* sector number of the first data
            jsr       printf            ;* cluster
            jsr       curstab
            move.w    datrec,-(a7)
            jsr       dezpr
            addq.w    #1,line
            move.w    #12,column
            jsr       loccurs
            move.l    #tnumcl,a0        ;* number of data clusters
            jsr       printf
            jsr       curstab
            move.w    numcl,-(a7)
            jsr       dezpr
            addq.w    #1,line
            move.w    #12,column
            jsr       loccurs
            move.l    #tnumsides,a0     ;* number of disk sides
            jsr       printf
            jsr       curstab
            move.w    numsides,-(a7)
            jsr       dezpr
            addq.w    #2,line
            move.w    #10,column
            jsr       loccurs
            move.l    #tdir1,a0         ;* location of first directory
            move.w    numsides,d0       ;* sector, differentiated fpr
            cmp.w     #2,d0             ;* single and double-sided disks
            bne       showbpb1
            move.l    #tdir2,a0
showbpb1:   jsr       printf
            jsr       emptybuf          ;* empty keyboard buffer
            jsr       wkey              ;* wait for key
            jsr       cursmess
            jsr       delline
            jsr       cursmess
            move.l    #drifrag1,a0      ;* display message
            jsr       printf
            rts                         ;* and return

            end
```

Here are the subroutines for the Track menu:

```
;*****************************************************************
;*   TRACK menu subroutines plus custom sector-write routine     *
;*****************************************************************

;*****************************************************************
;*  Custom sector-write routine, accesses controller and DMA chip *
;*  directly. The XBIOS write-sector routine does not work for    *
;*  1024-byte sectors, so this routine is called. The rdstrack menu *
;*  must be implemented before this function can be inserted because *
;*  some routines from this menu are called (super, seldrive, etc.). *
;*  It is not possible to write 1024-byte sectors with the basic *
;*  version of the program (with sector menu only).              *
;*****************************************************************

selfsect: jsr     super           ;* enable supervisor mode
          st      flock           ;* disable floppy interrupt
          jsr     seldrive        ;* select drive and side
          jsr     flreset         ;* reset the controller
          jsr     searcht         ;* seek track in wtrack
          jsr     selwrite        ;* write sector
          sf      flock           ;* enable floppy interrupt
          jsr     emptybuf        ;* empty keyboard buffer
          jsr     cursmess        ;* position cursor
          jsr     delline         ;* delete line
          jsr     flreset         ;* controller reset
          jsr     user            ;* enter user mode
          move.l  #slfrag1,a0     ;* output message
          jsr     printf
          jsr     wkey            ;* wait for keypress
          jsr     super           ;* enter supervisor mode
          jsr     deselect        ;* deselect floppy
          jsr     user            ;* enter user mode
          jsr     cursmess        ;* position cursor
          jsr     delline         ;* delete line
          jsr     cursmess        ;* position again
          move.l  #slfrag3,a0     ;* output message
          jsr     printf
          movem.l (a7)+,a3-a6/d3-d7 ;* restore registers
          rts                     ;* and return

;*****************************************************************
;*  Here the sector is written to the disk                       *
;*****************************************************************
```

```
selwrite: jsr      setspace            ;* set address of the buffer
          move.w   #$190,dmamode       ;* switch to write
          move.w   #$90,dmamode        ;* by "toggling" the read/write
          move.w   #$190,dmamode       ;* line
          move.w   #4,d6               ;* write 4 to sector count
          jsr      wrcontr             ;* register
          move.w   #$184,dmamode       ;* select FDC sector register
          move.w   wsector,d6          ;* pass current sector to FDC
          jsr      wrcontr
          move.w   #$180,dmamode       ;* select controller
          move.w   #$a0,d6             ;* sector-write command to
                                       ;* controller
          jsr      wrcontr             ;* pass
          move.l   #$50000,d7          ;* timeout counter
selwrit1: btst     #5,mfp              ;* interrupt input of FDC to MFP
          beq      selwrend            ;* if 1 then done
          subq.l   #1,d7               ;* decrement timeout counter, if
          bne      selwrit1            ;* not timed-out, keep waiting
          move.w   #-9,-(a7)           ;* else error number 9 on the stack
          jsr      errhand             ;* pass to error handler
          jsr      cursmess            ;* output line
          jsr      delline             ;* delete
          rts

selwrend: jsr      rdstatus            ;* branch here if no error
          move.w   flstatus,d0
          btst     #6,d0               ;* write protect
          bne      selwerr1            ;* yes
          rts                          ;* if not, then return
selwerr1: move.w   #-8,-(a7)           ;* error message # 8 (write protect)
          jsr      errhand             ;* output and clear
          jsr      cursmess            ;* output line
          jsr      delline
          rts

;**************************************************************
;*    TRACK subroutines                                       *
;**************************************************************

;**************************************************************
;*    This routine reads an entire track or the number of sectors passed *
;*    in asector. Standard sectors of 512 bytes are assumed, so any      *
;*    deviations must be taken into account by modifying the variable    *
;*    asector.                                                           *
;**************************************************************
```

```
readltr:  move.w   #512,d0          ;* standard sector size
          mulu     asector,d0       ;* number of sectors per track
          move.w   d0,maxhead       ;* max. number of bytes as counter
          move.w   asector,-(a7)    ;* number of sectors/track from menu
          move.w   wside,-(a7)      ;* current side
          move.w   wtrack,-(a7)     ;* current track
          move.w   #1,-(a7)         ;* at sector 1
          move.w   wdrive,-(a7)     ;* current drive
          clr.l    -(a7)            ;* dummy long word
          move.l   #spacetr,-(a7)   ;* buffer address
          move.w   #8,-(a7)         ;* call XBios function 8
          trap     #14              ;* clean up stack and
          add.l    #20,a7           ;* check for errors
          tst.w    d0
          bmi      readt1er         ;* if error then output
          jsr      showtr           ;* else display track
readt12:  rts                       ;* and return

readt1er: move.w   d0,-(a7)         ;* pass error number on stack to the
          jsr      errhand          ;* error handler, then
          jsr      emptybuf         ;* empty keyboard buffer
          jsr      wkey             ;* and wait for keypress
          jsr      cursmess         ;* output message
          move.l   #trfrag1,a0
          jsr      printf
          jsr      delrest
          bra      readt12          ;* and return

;*****************************************************************
;* Increases number of sectors per track in menu when cursor up is  *
;* pressed                                                          *
;*****************************************************************

incstra:  move.w   asector,d0       ;* number of sectors per track
          cmp.w    maxsect,d0       ;* compare with max number of sectors
          blt      incst1           ;* if greater or equal, then set
          move.w   #0,d0            ;* # sectors/track to zero
          bra      incst2           ;* and return
incst1:   addq.w   #1,d0            ;* else add one to sectors/track
incst2:   move.w   d0,asector
          ext.l    d0               ;* make change in menu text
          divu     #10,d0           ;* split into ASCII bytes by
          add.b    #'0',d0          ;* dividing by 10
          move.b   d0,setrack       ;* and enter in menu
          swap     d0               ;* do low byte
          add.b    #'0',d0          ;* convert into ASCII
          move.b   d0,setrack+1     ;* and put in menu
```

```
            jsr       dispmen           ;* display menu
            rts                         ;* and return

;*****************************************************************
;*  decrement sectors per track in menu                          *
;*****************************************************************

decstra:    move.w    asector,d0        ;* sectors/track
            cmp.w     #0,d0
            ble       decst1            ;* if greater than zero, then
            subq.w    #1,d0             ;* subtract one, else
            bra       decst2
decst1:     move.w    maxsect,d0        ;* set maximum number
decst2:     move.w    d0,asector
            ext.l     d0
            divu      #10,d0
            add.b     #'0',d0
            move.b    d0,setrack        ;* enter in menu
            swap      d0
            add.b     #'0',d0
            move.b    d0,setrack+1
            jsr       dispmen           ;* display menu and return
            rts

;*****************************************************************
;*  Supplies variables in general edit routine with values (maxdown, *
;*  maxup, etc.) and then calls the edit routine                 *
;*****************************************************************

edittr:     move.w    #0,maxdown        ;* only 512 bytes will be edited
            move.w    #208,maxup
            move.w    #18,lincount      ;* and 19 lines will be displayed
            move.l    topptr,d0         ;* pointer in the track buffer
            sub.l     #spacetr,d0       ;* minus start address of the buffer
            divu      #512,d0           ;* divide by number of bytes per
            swap      d0                ;* sector. if remainder,
            tst.w     d0                ;* then it was not the start of
            beq       edittr1           ;* of a sector and we must
            sub.l     #256,topptr       ;* subtract 256
edittr1:    move.l    topptr,editptr    ;* pass this pointer
            move.w    #0,head2          ;* in track buffer to editit
            move.w    #20,column        ;* output message in column 20 of
            move.w    #2,line           ;* line 2
            jsr       loccurs
            move.l    #edfrag1,a0
            jsr       printf
            jsr       editit            ;* and call edit
```

```
            jsr         cursmess            ;* message line
            jsr         delline             ;* delete
            jsr         cursmess
            move.l      #trfrag1,a0         ;*
            jsr         printf
            jsr         curleft             ;* set menu back to read
            jsr         curleft
            jsr         cursbuf             ;*
            jsr         clrest              ;* clear rest of screen
            rts                             ;* and return

;*********************************************************************
;* Allows the tracks read into the buffer to be viewed               *
;*********************************************************************

showtr:     move.w      #0,head2            ;* byte counter
            move.l      #spacetr,topptr     ;* start of buffer
            move.w      #0,edflag           ;* flag
            move.w      #15,lincount        ;* 16 lines will be displayed
            move.w      #2,line             ;* the current sector in column 59
            move.w      #59,column          ;* of the second line
            jsr         loccurs
            move.l      #trfrag3,a0         ;* display
            jsr         printf
            clr.w       d0
            move.w      #1,d0
            move.w      d0,-(a7)
            jsr         dezpr               ;* Print sector
            move.l      #trfrag4,a0
            jsr         printf

showt1:     move.w      #4,line             ;* position cursor
            move.w      #0,column
            jsr         loccurs
            jsr         clrest              ;* clear rest of screen
            jsr         emptybuf
showt2:     jsr         dispbuf             ;* display first page and
showt3:     jsr         key                 ;* read keyboard
            swap        d0
            cmp.b       #$48,d0             ;* cursor up ?
            beq         showtup
            cmp.b       #$50,d0             ;* cursor down ?
            beq         showtdo
            cmp.b       #$1c,d0             ;* Return ?
            beq         showten1
            cmp.b       #$4b,d0             ;* cursor left ?
            beq         showtli
```

```
            cmp.b       #$4d,d0         ;* cursor right ?
            beq         showtre
            bra         showt3          ;* none of the above, keep reading
showtre:    jsr         curright        ;* cursor on right menu option
            bra         showten1        ;* and return

showtli:    jsr         curleft         ;* display left menu option in
                                        ;* reverse
            bra         showten1        ;* and return

showtup:    move.w      head2,d0        ;* compare byte counter
            cmp.w       #0,d0           ;* with zero
            beq         showtuen        ;* if not equal to zero,
            sub.w       #256,head2      ;* then subtract 256, corresponds to
            sub.l       #256,topptr     ;* half a sector
showtuen:   move.w      head2,d0        ;* byte counter
            lsr.w       #8,d0           ;* divide by 512
            lsr.w       #1,d0
            add.w       #1,d0           ;* plus one equals sector number
            move.w      d0,varw3
            move.w      #59,column
            move.w      #2,line
            jsr         loccurs
            move.l      #trfrag3,a0     ;* output current sector number
            jsr         printf          ;* in line 2
            move.w      varw3,-(a7)
            jsr         dezpr
            move.l      #trfrag4,a0
            jsr         printf
            jsr         delrest         ;* clear rest of line

showtue1:   bra         showt2          ;* an back to loop
showtdo:    move.w      head2,d0        ;* cursor down handling
            move.w      maxhead,d1
            sub.w       #256,d1
            cmp.w       d1,d0
            beq         shwtrden
            add.w       #256,head2      ;* add 256 buffer pointer and
            add.l       #256,topptr     ;* byte counter
shwtrden:   move.w      head2,d0
            lsr.w       #8,d0
            lsr.w       #1,d0           ;* divide byte counter by 512
            add.w       #1,d0           ;* and add one
            move.w      d0,varw3        ;* yields current sector number
            move.w      #59,column
            move.w      #2,line
            jsr         loccurs
```

```
          move.l    #trfrag3,a0
          jsr       printf
          move.w    varw3,-(a7)        ;* display sector number
          jsr       dezpr
          move.l    #trfrag4,a0
          jsr       printf
          jsr       delrest            ;* clear rest of line
shwtrd1:  bra       showt2
showten1: jsr       emptybuf           ;* empty keyboard buffer
          rts                          ;* and return

writ1tr:  move.l    a4,-(a7)           ;* write track back to disk
          move.w    #2,line
          jsr       loccurs
          jsr       delline
          move.l    #trfrag5,a0
          jsr       printf
          move.w    #33,d2             ;* output 34 bytes at m1secta
          move.l    #m1secta,a4        ;* on the screen
writ1t1:  move.b    (a4)+,d0
          move.w    d0,-(a7)
          jsr       conout
          dbra      d2,writ1t1
          move.l    #trfrag6,a0        ;* ask for confirmation to
          jsr       printf             ;* write to disk
          jsr       emptybuf           ;* empty keyboard buffer
          jsr       wkey               ;* read keyboard and check for
          cmp.b     #'Y',d0            ;* upper and lowercase y
          beq       writ1t2
          cmp.b     #'y',d0
          bne       writ1ten           ;* if other key, then don't write
writ1t2:  move.w    asector,-(a7)      ;* number of sectors on stack
          move.w    wside,-(a7)        ;* current side
          move.w    wtrack,-(a7)       ;* current track
          move.w    #1,-(a7)           ;* start sector equals one
          move.w    wdrive,-(a7)       ;* current drive
          clr.l     -(a7)              ;* dummy long word
          move.l    #spacetr,-(a7)     ;* buffer address
          move.w    #9,-(a7)           ;* Flopwr command on stack
          trap      #14                ;* XBIOS trap
          add.l     #20,a7             ;* restore stack
          tst.w     d0                 ;* did an error occur?
          bmi       writ1er1           ;* yes
writ1ten: jsr       cursmess           ;* no error, then clear status line
          jsr       delline            ;* and output message
writ1te1: jsr       cursmess
          move.l    #trfrag1,a0
```

```
            jsr       printf
            move.l    (a7)+,a4           ;* get a4 back
            rts

writ1er1:   move.w    d0,-(a7)           ;* error number on stack
            jsr       errhand            ;* handle error
            bra       writ1te1           ;* and done

            end
```

Now for the Track with Sync menu routine.

```
;*********************************************************************
;*  Subroutines for option TRACK with SYNCS. Routines do not access  *
;*  any other routines, so this option can be implemented as desired. *
;*********************************************************************


;*********************************************************************
;*  first some often-used variables                                   *
;*********************************************************************

dmamode:    equ       $ff8606
dmadat:     equ       $ff8604

dmahigh:    equ       $ff8609
dmamid:     equ       $ff860b
dmalow:     equ       $ff860d

mfp:        equ       $fffa01

flselec:    equ       $ff8800
flwrite:    equ       $ff8802

flock:      equ       $43e

;*********************************************************************
;*  switch the processor into the supervisor mode. If the processor is *
;*  already in the supervisor mode, nothing happens.                 *
;*********************************************************************

super:      move.l    #1,-(a7)           ;*
            move.w    #$20,-(a7)         ;* GEMDOS function super
            trap      #1                 ;* test if already in super mode
            add.l     #6,a7
            tst.w     d0
```

```
                bne     super1          ;* processor already in super mode
                clr.l   -(a7)           ;* if not, then swtich to
                move.w  #$20,-(a7)      ;* supervisor mode
                trap    #1
                add.l   #6,a7
                move.l  d0,usstack      ;* store user stack
super1:         rts                     ;* now in supervisor mode

;****************************************************************
;*      switch back to user mode.                               *
;****************************************************************

user:           move.l  #1,-(a7)
                move.w  #$20,-(a7)      ;* GEMDOS function super
                trap    #1
                add.l   #6,a7
                tst.w   d0
                beq     user1           ;* already in user mode
                move.l  usstack,-(a7)
                move.w  #$20,-(a7)
                trap    #1
                add.l   #6,a7
user1:          rts


fwait:          dbra    d7,fwait
                rts


;****************************************************************
;*  Reset the floppy disk controller (FDC)                      *
;****************************************************************

flreset:        jsr     super           ;* switch to supervisor mode
                move.w  #$80,dmamode    ;* access the FDC register
                move.w  #$d0,d6         ;* reset through interrupt command
                jsr     wrcontr         ;* command to controller
                move.w  #40,d7          ;* wait a bit
                jsr     fwait
                rts                     ;* and return

;****************************************************************
;*   read the controller status register and store it           *
;****************************************************************

rdcontr:        jsr     super           ;* enable supervisor mode
                move.w  dmadat,d3       ;* status register to D3
                jsr     readco1         ;* wait a bit
```

```
readco1: move.w    sr,-(a7)
         move.w    d7,-(a7)       ;* save timeout counter
         move.w    #40,d7
readco2: dbra      d7,readco2
         move.w    (a7)+,d7       ;* back again
         move.w    (a7)+,sr
         rts

;****************************************************************
;*  pass the number in D6 to the floppy disk controller         *
;****************************************************************

wrcontr: jsr       super          ;* supervisor on
         jsr       readco1
         move.w    d6,dmadat
         jsr       readco1        ;* wait a bit
         rts

;****************************************************************
;*  read the FDC status register and store it in flstatus       *
;****************************************************************

rdstatus: jsr      super          ;* supervisor on
          jsr      readco1
          move.w   dmadat,flstatus ;* status in flstatus
          jsr      readco1        ;* wait a bit and
          rts                     ;* then return

;****************************************************************
;*  select the current drive (red light on)                     *
;****************************************************************

seldrive: jsr      super          ;* supervisor on
          move.w   wdrive,d0      ;* current drive
          cmp.w    #1,d0          ;* greate than 1
          bgt      seldrend       ;* if yes, then return
          addq.b   #1,d0          ;* else combine with current side
          lsl.b    #1,d0
          or.w     wside,d0
          eor.b    #7,d0
          and.b    #7,d0
select:   move.w   sr,-(a7)
          or.w     #$700,sr       ;* disable interrupt, because
          move.b   #$e,flselec    ;* the interrupt deselects
          move.b   flselec,d1     ;* the drives
          and.b    #$f8,d1
          or.b     d0,d1
```

```
              move.b      d1,flwrite       ;* pass to ACIA
              move.w      (a7)+,sr         ;* get status register back
seldrend: rts                              ;* and return

;*********************************************************************
;*   deselect current drive (red light off)                          *
;*   the timing between floppy reset and deselecting must be right or *
;*   the disk motor will still run.                                  *
;*********************************************************************

deselect: jsr      super            ;* supervisor on
          move.w   #$80,dmamode     ;* select FDC register
          move.b   #7,d0
          jsr      select           ;* deselect
          rts                       ;* and return

;*********************************************************************
;*   read an entire track with all syncs into the buffer that starts *
;*   at the address spacetr                                          *
;*********************************************************************


rdstrack: jsr      super            ;* supervisor on
          clr.l    currdma
          move.w   sr,varw3         ;* save old status register
          move.w   #$2700,sr        ;* disable interrupts; not actually
          move.w   #$90,dmamode     ;* necessary, switch sector count
register
          move.w   #$190,dmamode    ;* toggle DMAMODE to read
          move.w   #$90,dmamode     ;* and clear the DMA register
          move.w   #$16,d6          ;* 22*512 bytes will be read
          move.w   #512,d2          ;* (although there aren't that
          mulu     d6,d2            ;* many on the diskette)
          move.w   d2,maxhead
          add.l    #spacetr,d2      ;* calculate the DMA end address
          move.l   d2,topdma        ;* store it
          jsr      wrcontr          ;* d6 (number of sectors) to FDC
          move.l   #spacetr,d0      ;* pass address of the DMA buffer
          move.b   d0,dmalow        ;* to the DMAC
          lsr.l    #8,d0
          move.b   d0,dmamid
          lsr.l    #8,d0
          move.b   d0,dmahigh
          move.w   #$80,dmamode     ;* select FDC register
          move.w   #$e8,d6          ;* read-track command to the FDC
          jsr      wrcontr          ;* pass it
          move.l   #$50000,d7       ;* timeout counter
```

```
                move.l      topdma,a5       ;* DMA end address
                move.w      #$200,d0        ;* wait a bit
rd1:            dbra        d0,rd1

rdstrl1:        btst        #5,mfp          ;* command already processed?
                beq         rdtrend1        ;* if so, then end
                subq.l      #1,d7           ;* else decrement timeout counter
                beq         rdtrerr1        ;* if counter run out, then error
                move.b      dmahigh,highdma ;* test if end DMA address already
                move.b      dmamid,middma   ;* reached; is unnecessary because the
                move.b      dmalow,lowdma   ;* controller stopped earlier (fewer
                cmp.l       currdma,a5      ;* bytes on the disk)
                bgt         rdstrl1

rdtrend1:       move.w      #$90,dmamode    ;* switch to sector count register
                move.w      dmamode,d5      ;* read status of the DMA chip
                move.w      d5,dmastat      ;* and store
                btst        #0,d5
                beq         rdtrerr2
                move.w      #$80,dmamode    ;* switch to FDC register
                jsr         rdstatus        ;* read FDC status

rdtend:         move.w      varw3,sr        ;* get status register back
                rts                         ;* and return

rdtrerr2:       bra         rdtend

rdtrerr1:       bra         rdtend

;****************************************************************
;*      Place the read/write head on the track passed in wtrack *
;****************************************************************

searcht:        jsr         super           ;* supervisor on
                jsr         track0          ;* seek track zero
                move.w      #$86,dmamode    ;* select track register
                move.w      wtrack,d6       ;* current track to track register
                jsr         wrcontr
                move.w      #$80,dmamode    ;* select FDC register
                move.w      #$1b,d6         ;* search track command
                jsr         wrcontr         ;* pass to controller
                move.l      #$60000,d7      ;* timeout counter
search1:        subq.l      #1,d7
                beq         searend1
                btst        #5,mfp          ;* command aleady processed?
                bne         search1         ;* no, keep waiting
                rts
```

```
searend1:  move.w    #-7,-(a7)        ;* error = no disk
           jsr       errhand
           rts

;******************************************************************
;*   Seek track zero                                              *
;******************************************************************

track0:    move.w    seek,d6          ;* seek rate
           and.w     #3,d6            ;* combine with track-zero command
           move.l    #$50000,d7       ;* timeout counter
           move.w    #$80,dmamode     ;* access FDC register
           jsr       wrcontr          ;* pass command

track0ll:  subq.l    #1,d7            ;* decrement counter
           beq       track0er         ;* timeout
           btst      #5,mfp           ;* FDC ready?
           bne       track0ll         ;* no, keep waiting
           rts                        ;* and return


track0er:  move.w    #-7,-(a7)        ;* pass error number to
           jsr       errhand          ;* error handler
           rts                        ;* and return

;******************************************************************
;*   Pass the address of the buffer spacetr to the DMA controller *
;******************************************************************

setspace:  move.l    #spacetr,d0
           move.b    d0,dmalow
           lsr.l     #8,d0
           move.b    d0,dmamid
           lsr.l     #8,d0
           move.b    d0,dmahigh
           rts

;******************************************************************
;*   Read track with all syncs control routine, calls all necessary *
;*   subroutines                                                  *
;******************************************************************

rdtracks:  movem.l   a3-a6/d3-d7,-(a7)   ;* save registers
           jsr       cursmess
           jsr       delline
           jsr       cursmess
           move.l    #trfrag2,a0         ;* output message
```

```
        jsr     printf
        move.w  #18,lincount    ;* for subroutine Dispbuf = 19 lines
        jsr     super           ;* supervisor on
        st      flock           ;* floppy interrupt off
        jsr     seldrive        ;* select drive
        jsr     flreset         ;* reset controller
        jsr     searcht         ;* seek current track
        jsr     rdstrack        ;* read track twice
        jsr     rdstrack
        jsr     flreset         ;* reset FDC
        jsr     user            ;* user mode on
        jsr     shtracks        ;* display this track
        jsr     super           ;* supervisor on
        jsr     deselect        ;* deselect floppy
        sf      flock           ;* release floppy interrupt
        jsr     user            ;* enable user mode
        movem.l (a7)+,a3-a6/d3-d7  ;* get registers back
        rts                     ;* and return

;*********************************************************************
;* Pass the parameters for displaying the track to the general showit *
;* routine                                                            *
;*********************************************************************

shtracks: move.w #0,head2
        move.l  #spacetr,topptr
        move.w  #18,lincount    ;* 19 lines on the screen
        move.w  #100,prcount    ;* 101 lines to print
        move.w  #7680,maxdown
        move.w  #7888,maxup
        jsr     cursbuf
        jsr     clrest          ;* clear rest of screen
        jsr     showit          ;* display buffer, with handle
        jsr     emptybuf        ;* cursor keys, etc.
        rts

;*********************************************************************
;* read address fields on the disk                                   *
;*********************************************************************

readadr: jsr    cursmess        ;* position cursor
        jsr     delline         ;* delete line
        move.l  #hilcurs,a0     ;* output message
        jsr     printf
        move.w  wdrive,d0
        cmp.w   #2,d0
        bgt     rdaderr
```

```
            jsr     super           ;* supervisor on
            jsr     seldrive        ;* select current drive
            jsr     flreset         ;* FDC reset
            jsr     searcht         ;* seek current track twice
            jsr     searcht         ;* so the drive is ready
            jsr     setspace        ;* set DMA transfer address
readad1:    jsr     rdadr           ;* read address fields
            jsr     flreset         ;* FDC reset
            jsr     user            ;* user mode on
            jsr     showadr         ;* display address fields
            jsr     super           ;* supervisor on
            jsr     deselect        ;* deselect current drive
            jsr     user            ;* user mode on
            rts                     ;* and return

;*******************************************************************
;*   Read 25 address fields from the disk                          *
;*******************************************************************

rdadr:      jsr     super           ;* enable supervisor mode
            move.w  #$90,dmamode    ;* toggle the read/write line
            move.w  #$190,dmamode   ;* clear the DMA status, reset DMA
            move.w  #$90,dmamode    ;* switch to read and sector count
            move.w  #1,d6           ;* register, read 1 sector
            jsr     wrcontr         ;* to FDC controller
            move.w  #$80,dmamode    ;* switch to FDC register
            move.w  #24,d4          ;* read 24+1 address fields
rdadr1:     move.w  #$c8,d6         ;* read-address command
            move.l  #$40000,d7      ;* timeout counter
            jsr     wrcontr         ;* command to FDC
rdadr2:     btst    #5,mfp          ;* command already processed?
            beq     rdadren1        ;* yes
            subq.l  #1,d7           ;* else decrement timeout
            beq     rdaderr         ;* timeout?, then error
            bra     rdadr2          ;* else keep waiting
rdadren1:   dbra    d4,rdadr1       ;* repeat 25 times
            rts                     ;* and return

rdaderr:    move.w  #-6,-(a7)       ;* error message
            jsr     errhand         ;* output, and terminate
            rts

;*******************************************************************
;* Display the address fields read. More address fields are read than *
;* are displayed because the DMA controller transfers the bytes in    *
;* groups of 16, whereas an address field contains only 6 bytes.      *
;*******************************************************************
```

```
showadr:   jsr      cursmess         ;* position cursor and delete and
           jsr      delline          ;* output message
           move.l   #sadfrag1,a0
           jsr      printf
           jsr      cursbuf          ;* position cursor
           move.w   #17,d5           ;* display 18 address fields
           move.l   #spacetr,a3      ;* buffer address of the address fields
showadr1:  move.w   #2,d4            ;* output 3 data (track, side,
           move.w   #$20,-(a7)       ;* sector), first output a space
           jsr      conout
showadr2:  move.b   (a3)+,d0         ;* get byte from buffer
           move.w   d0,-(a7)         ;* move to stack as word
           jsr      dezpr            ;* and output in decimal
           move.w   #$20,-(a7)       ;* two spaces after it
           jsr      conout
           move.w   #$20,-(a7)
           jsr      conout
           dbra     d4,showadr2      ;* repeat three times
           move.w   #$20,-(a7)       ;* then write 2 spaces
           jsr      conout
           move.w   #$20,-(a7)
           jsr      conout
           move.b   (a3)+,d0         ;* next byte from buffer (contains
           ext.w    d0               ;* the sector size)
           move.w   #128,d1          ;* a 0 means 128 bytes/sector
           cmp.w    #0,d0
           beq      showadr7
           move.w   #256,d1
           cmp.w    #1,d0            ;* 1 means 256 bytes/sector
           beq      showadr7
           move.w   #512,d1
           cmp.w    #2,d0            ;* 2 means 512 bytes/sector
           beq      showadr7
           move.w   #1024,d1         ;* else 1024 bytes/sector as default
showadr7:  move.w   d1,-(a7)         ;* output number of bytes/sector
           jsr      dezpr            ;* in decimal
           move.w   #$20,-(a7)       ;* output spaces
           jsr      conout
           move.l   #spaces,a0
           jsr      printf
           move.b   (a3)+,d0         ;* next byte in buffer is the checksum
           move.w   d0,-(a7)         ;* of the address field, which is
           jsr      hexpr            ;* printed as a hex number
           move.b   (a3)+,d0         ;* next byte from buffer
           move.w   d0,-(a7)
           jsr      hexpr            ;* as hex number
```

```
            move.w    #13,-(a7)        ;* carriage return plus linefeed
            jsr       conout
            move.w    #10,-(a7)
            jsr       conout
            dbra      d5,showadr1      ;* repeat 18 times
            jsr       wkey             ;* and wait for keypress
            rts                        ;* and back

            end
```

Next is the Cluster menu subroutine.

```
;******************************************************************
;*   Subroutines for the option CLUSTER. The routines access routines   *
;*   from the OPTION menu, so OPTION must be implemented first.         *
;******************************************************************

edclust:    jsr       cursmess         ;* cursor pos., etc.
            jsr       delline
            move.w    #20,column
            move.w    #2,line
            jsr       loccurs
            move.l    #edfrag1,a0      ;* message
            jsr       printf
            move.w    #512,maxdown     ;* scroll up and down variables
            move.w    #720,maxup
            move.l    #spacetr,editptr ;* buffer address
            jsr       editit           ;* edit cluster
            jsr       cursmess         ;* delete message line
            jsr       delline
            jsr       cursmess
            move.l    #clfrag1,a0      ;* output message
            jsr       printf
            jsr       curleft          ;* left three times
            jsr       curleft          ;* to jump into read
            jsr       curleft          ;* submenu
            jsr       shclust          ;* display the cluster
            rts                        ;* and return

;******************************************************************
;*   decrement the cluster number in the cluster menu                   *
;******************************************************************

decclust:   move.w    #-1,-(a7)
            move.w    #11,-(a7)        ;* test keyboard shift
            trap      #13              ;* if shift pressed
            addq.l    #4,a7            ;* then decrement is 10
```

```
            btst        #0,d0               ;* else decrement by one
            bne         decclshi
            btst        #1,d0
            bne         decclshi            ;* shift pressed
            move.w      #1,d2               ;* else not pressed,
            bra         declst0             ;* so decrement by one
decclshi:   move.w      #10,d2              ;* decrement by 10
declst0:    move.w      wclust,d0           ;* current cluster number
            sub.w       d2,d0               ;* subtract decrement
            cmp.w       #0,d0               ;* less than 0
            blt         declst1             ;* yes
            bra         declst2             ;* no
declst1:    move.w      maxclust,d0         ;* max cluster number as new current
declst2:    move.w      d0,wclust           ;* cluster number
            ext.l       d0                  ;* the new cluster number must also be
            divu        #1000,d0            ;* entered in the menu
            add.b       #'0',d0             ;* se we split it into powers of ten
            move.b      d0,m1clusa1         ;* and put it in the cluster menu
            swap        d0
            ext.l       d0
            divu        #100,d0
            add.b       #'0',d0
            move.b      d0,m1clusa1+1       ;* enter 100's
            swap        d0
            ext.l       d0
            divu        #10,d0
            add.b       #'0',d0
            move.b      d0,m1clusa1+2       ;* enter 10's
            swap        d0
            add.b       #'0',d0
            move.b      d0,m1clusa1+3       ;* and finally the 1'2 in the menu
            jsr         dispmen             ;* display menu and
            rts                             ;* return

;*******************************************************************
;*     increment the current cluster number                        *
;*******************************************************************

incclust:   move.w      #-1,-(a7)
            move.w      #11,-(a7)           ;* test keyboard shift
            trap        #13                 ;* as for decclust
            addq.l      #4,a7
            btst        #0,d0
            bne         incclshi
            btst        #1,d0
            bne         incclshi
            move.w      #1,d2               ;* no shift key, then 1 as
```

```
            bra       inclst0         ;* increment
incclshi:   move.w    #10,d2          ;* else increment equals 10
inclst0:    move.w    wclust,d0       ;* add increment to current cluster
            add.w     d2,d0           ;* number and compare with maximum
            cmp.w     maxclust,d0     ;* number
            blt       inclst1         ;* less than maximum number
            move.w    #0,d0
inclst1:    move.w    d0,wclust       ;* store new current number
            ext.l     d0              ;* and enter current number in menu
            divu      #1000,d0        ;* 1000's place
            add.b     #'0',d0
            move.b    d0,m1clusa1     ;* enter 1000's place
            swap      d0
            ext.l     d0
            divu      #100,d0
            add.b     #'0',d0
            move.b    d0,m1clusa1+1   ;* enter 100's place
            swap      d0
            ext.l     d0
            divu      #10,d0
            add.b     #'0',d0
            move.b    d0,m1clusa1+2   ;* enter 10's place
            swap      d0
            add.b     #'0',d0
            move.b    d0,m1clusa1+3   ;* 1's place
            jsr       dispmen         ;* display menu and
            rts                       ;* return

;*****************************************************************
;*  Find the next cluster following the current cluster. If this is   *
;*  the last cluster, this is indicated.                              *
;*****************************************************************

nextclst:   move.w    wclust,d0       ;* current cluster number
            move.w    d0,oldclst      ;* store
            jsr       findclst        ;* find next cluster
            move.w    newclst,d0      ;* here is next cluster
            tst.w     d0              ;* or a 0, which signals an error
            beq       neclerr1
            cmp.w     #$ff8,d0        ;* or an end marker, which
            bge       neclerr1        ;* indicates the last cluster
            subq.w    #1,d0           ;* subtract one for better handling
            move.w    d0,wclust       ;* of the menu display
            move.l    #3,revnum       ;* the incclust routine can be called
            jsr       incclust        ;* which displays the incremented
                                      ;* cluster
            jsr       rdclust         ;* and then reads this cluster
```

```
neclend: rts

neclerr1: jsr     cursmess
          move.w  #-19,-(a7)      ;* announce last cluster as such
          jsr     errhand
          jsr     cursmess
          move.l  #clfrag1,a0
          jsr     printf
          bra     neclend         ;* and return

findclst: move.l  #fatbuf,a0      ;* address of the FAT buffer
          move.w  oldclst,d0      ;* old cluster number
          move.w  #3,d1           ;* times 3, and
          mulu    d0,d1
          lsr.w   #1,d1           ;* divide by 2, equals times 1.5
          btst    #0,d0           ;* was old cluster # even or odd
          bne     codd            ;* (divisible by 2 or not)
ceven:    move.b  1(a0,d1.w),d0   ;* if even, the get most significant
          lsl.w   #8,d0           ;* nibble, shift 8 bits to the left
          or.b    0(a0,d1.w),d0   ;* and OR the two remaining nibbles
          and.w   #$0fff,d0       ;* to it
          move.w  d0,newclst      ;* store as new cluster number
          bra     ficlend         ;* and return
codd:     move.b  1(a0,d1.w),d0   ;* else: get most significant nibble and
          lsl.w   #8,d0           ;* shift 8 bits to the left
          move.b  0(a0,d1.w),d0   ;* least significant nibble
          lsr.w   #4,d0           ;* the upper 12 bits contain the
          and.w   #$0fff,d0       ;* cluster number, so mask out
          move.w  d0,newclst      ;* 4 bits on the right, store
ficlend:  rts                     ;* and return

;*******************************************************************
;* write the current cluster to disk after confirmation            *
;*******************************************************************

wrclust:  movem.l a3-a5/d3-d5,-(a7) ;* save registers
          move.w  #0,column
          move.w  #2,line         ;* output message
          jsr     loccurs
          move.l  #clfrag5,a0
          jsr     printf
          move.l  #m1secta,a3     ;* current track
          move.w  #9,d3
wrcl1:    move.b  (a3)+,d0
          move.w  d0,-(a7)
          jsr     conout
          dbra    d3,wrcl1
```

```
            move.l    #m1clusa,a3      ;* output cluster as question
            move.w    #12,d3
wrcl2:      move.b    (a3)+,d0
            move.w    d0,-(a7)
            jsr       conout
            dbra      d3,wrcl2
            move.l    #wrfrag2,a0
            jsr       printf
            jsr       emptybuf
            jsr       wkey             ;* really write
            cmp.b     #'y',d0          ;* yes
            beq       writclst
            cmp.b     #'Y',d0          ;* yes
            bne       wrclend1         ;* else don't write
writclst:   move.w    wdrive,-(a7)     ;* pass current drive
            move.w    wclust,d0        ;* current cluster number
            sub.w     #2,d0            ;* number 2 is first data cluster
            muls      clsiz,d0         ;* calculate logical sector number
            add.w     datrec,d0
            move.w    d0,-(a7)         ;* logical sector number on ST
            move.w    clsiz,-(a7)      ;* number of sectors per cluster
            move.l    #spacetr,-(a7)   ;* start address of the cluster
            move.w    #3,-(a7)         ;* write, ignore disk change
            move.w    #4,-(a7)         ;* Rwabs
            trap      #13              ;* BIOS trap
            add.l     #14,a7           ;* restore stack
            tst.w     d0               ;* error occurred
            bmi       wrclster         ;* yes, then handle
wrclend:    jsr       cursmess
            jsr       delline          ;* else output message
            jsr       cursmess
            move.l    #clfrag1,a0
            jsr       printf
            movem.l   (a7)+,a3-a5/d3-d5  ;* restore registers
            rts                        ;* and return

wrclster:   move.w    d0,-(a7)         ;* error number to
            jsr       errhand          ;* error handler and display
            bra       wrclend          ;* and return

wrclend1:   jsr       cursmess
            jsr       delline
            jsr       cursmess
            move.l    #wrfrag3,a0
            jsr       printf
            jsr       emptybuf
            jsr       wkey
```

```
                jsr     delline
                bra     wrclend
                rts

;***********************************************************************
;*  Read the current cluster into memory, also works with RAM disk.    *
;***********************************************************************

rdclust:        movem.l a3-a6/d3-d7,-(a7)    ;* save registers
rdcl0:          move.w  wdrive,-(a7)    ;* current drive
                move.w  wclust,d0       ;* current cluster
                subq.w  #2,d0           ;* calculate logical sector number
                muls    clsiz,d0
                add.w   datrec,d0
                tst.w   d0
                bpl     rdcl2           ;* greater than zero
                move.w  #0,d0           ;* if not, then zero
rdcl2:          move.w  d0,logsect      ;* store logical sector
                move.w  d0,-(a7)        ;* and on stack
                move.w  #2,-(a7)        ;* read 2 sectors
                move.l  #spacetr,-(a7)  ;* buffer address
                move.w  #0,-(a7)        ;*
                move.w  #4,-(a7)        ;* Rwabs command
                trap    #13             ;* BIOS trap
                add.l   #14,a7          ;* restore stack
                tst.w   d0              ;* did an error occur?
                bmi     rdclster        ;* if so, then display
                move.w  logsect,d0      ;* convert logical sector to physical
                divs    #9,d0
                swap    d0
                addq.w  #1,d0           ;* add one to remainder of division
                move.w  d0,wsector      ;* equals physical sector
                swap    d0
                move.w  d0,d2           ;* store result of division
                move.w  #0,wside        ;* side zero as default
                move.w  numsides,d1     ;* number of sides
                cmp.w   #2,d1           ;* if 2 sides,
                bne     rdcl3
                lsr.w   #1,d0           ;* then divide by 2
                btst    #0,d2           ;* test if result odd
                beq     rdcl4           ;*
                move.w  #1,wside
rdcl3:
rdcl4:          move.w  d0,wtrack       ;* equals physical sector
                jsr     secinmem        ;* sector into memory
                jsr     shclust         ;* display cluster
rdclend:        jsr     cursmess
```

```
            move.l      #clfrag1,a0       ;* output message
            jsr         printf
            movem.l     (a7)+,a3-a6/d3-d7 ;* restore registers
            rts                           ;* and return

rdclster:   jsr         initdriv          ;* if error occurred, then
            tst.l       d0                ;* initialize first drive
            bne         rdcl0             ;* if no error, then again
            move.w      d0,-(a7)
            jsr         errhand           ;* must be changed
            bra         rdclend

secinmem:   move.w      wside,d0          ;* transfer current sector into
            add.b       #'0',d0           ;* sector menu for later display
            move.b      d0,mside
            move.w      wsector,d0
            ext.l       d0
            divs        #10,d0
            add.b       #'0',d0
            move.b      d0,msector
            swap        d0
            add.b       #'0',d0
            move.b      d0,msector+1      ;* low byte of sector
            move.w      wtrack,d0
            ext.l       d0
            divs        #10,d0
            add.b       #'0',d0
            move.b      d0,mtrack
            swap        d0
            add.b       #'0',d0
            move.b      d0,mtrack+1       ;* low byte of track
            rts

;****************************************************************
;*    Display the cluster                                       *
;****************************************************************

shclust:    move.w      #0,head2          ;* byte counter
            move.w      #18,lincount      ;* display 19 lines
            move.w      #63,prcount       ;* 64 lines for printer output
            move.l      #spacetr,topptr   ;* buffer address
            move.w      #512,maxdown      ;* scroll limit
            move.w      #720,maxup
            jsr         cursbuf           ;* position cursor and
            jsr         clrest            ;* clear rest of screen
            move.w      #0,column         ;* cursor to last screen line
            move.w      #24,line
```

```
            jsr     loccurs         ;* position
            move.l  #clfrag2,a0
            jsr     printf
            jsr     showit          ;* display the cluster
            rts                     ;* return

;**********************************************************************
;*  Display the first cluster of the file on the disk. Start cluster  *
;*  is accepted as the cluster number in the menu by pressing <return>.*
;*  If the filename in reverse is a subdirectory, this must first be   *
;*  entered.                                                           *
;**********************************************************************

stclust:  movem.l a3-a5/d3-d7,-(a7)
          jsr     initdriv        ;* initialize drive
          jsr     rdfat           ;* read FAT and directory sectors
          jsr     rddir           ;* into the buffer
stclst0:  move.w  #0,column
          move.w  #2,line
          jsr     loccurs         ;* position cursor
          move.l  #sclfrag1,a0
          jsr     printf
          move.w  #17,lincount    ;* display 18 lines
          jsr     delrest         ;* delete rest of line
          move.l  #dirbuf,a3      ;* store address of
          move.l  a3,a4           ;* directory buffer
          move.l  a3,topptr       ;* use as pointer
          move.l  a3,oldtop       ;* store cursor
          jsr     cursbuf         ;* again
          jsr     showdir         ;* display 18 lines
          jsr     cursbuf         ;* cursor to start
          move.l  #dirbuf,topptr  ;* start of directory buffer
          jsr     revon           ;* turn on reverse
          jsr     dirline         ;* first filename (disk name)
          jsr     revout          ;* write in reverse, then reverse off
stclst1:  jsr     key             ;* and read keyboard
          swap    d0
          cmp.b   #$1c,d0         ;* Return key pressed?
          beq     dirclsel        ;* yes
          cmp.b   #$48,d0         ;* cursor up?
          beq     stclup          ;* yes
          cmp.b   #$50,d0         ;* cursor down?
          beq     stcldo          ;* yes
          cmp.b   #$4b,d0         ;* cursor left?
          beq     stclli          ;* yes
          cmp.b   #$4d,d0         ;* cursor right
          bne     stclst1
```

```
            jsr     curright        ;* yes, then call
            bra     stclend1
stclli:     jsr     curleft
            bra     stclend1

stclup:     move.w  line,d0         ;* current cursor line
            cmp.w   #4,d0           ;* line 4 equals upper border
            ble     stclup3         ;* equals 4, then scroll
            move.w  #0,column
            jsr     loccurs
            jsr     dirline         ;* else subtract one from
            subq.w  #1,line         ;* the current line, cursor
            move.w  #0,column       ;* to the new line and set
            jsr     loccurs         ;* column to zero
            jsr     revon
            jsr     dirline         ;* and display this line in reverse
            jsr     revout          ;* turn reverse off
            bra     stclupen        ;* and return

stclup3:    cmp.l   #dirbuf,topptr  ;* top line in buffer reached?
            beq     stclupen        ;* if so, then don't scroll
            move.l  topptr,d0       ;* else decrement ptr by number of lines
            move.w  lincount,d0     ;* times number of characters per line
            addq.w  #1,d0           ;* changed 8/18/86
            muls    #32,d0
            sub.l   d0,topptr       ;* decrement pointer in buffer
            jsr     showdir         ;* display 18 lines
            move.w  #21,line
            move.w  #0,column       ;* last displayed line reverse
            jsr     loccurs         ;* cursor pos.
            jsr     revon           ;* reverse on
            jsr     dirline         ;* display line
            jsr     revout          ;* reverse off again
stclupen:   bra     stclst1         ;* to loop

stcldo:     move.w  line,d0         ;* current line greater than 20
            cmp.w   #20,d0
            bgt     stcldo3         ;* yes
            move.w  line,d0         ;* if not, then add 1
            addq.w  #1,d0           ;*
            sub.w   #4,d0           ;* offset to upper screen border
            ext.l   d0
            lsl.l   #5,d0           ;* multiply by 32
            move.l  topptr,a6       ;* pointer in directory buffer
            move.b  0(a6,d0.l),d0   ;* get first byte of this entry
            beq     stcldoen        ;* if byte=0, then empty entry
            move.w  #0,column       ;* else position cursor and
```

```
          jsr     loccurs
          jsr     dirline         ;* display old line normal
          addq.w  #1,line         ;* increment line counter and
          move.w  #0,column
          jsr     loccurs
          jsr     revon           ;* display new line
          jsr     dirline         ;* in reverse
          jsr     revout          ;* turn reverse off again
          jsr     loccurs
stcldo1:  bra     stcldoen        ;* to loop

stcldo3:  move.w  line,d0         ;* get first byte of the next directory
          addq.w  #1,d0           ;* entry, add one and subtract
          sub.w   #4,d0           ;* offset to top
          ext.l   d0
          lsl.l   #5,d0           ;* times 32 (# of bytes/directory entry)
          move.l  topptr,a6       ;* pointer to start of dir buffer
          move.b  0(a6,d0.l),d0   ;* is the next entry zero?
          beq     stcldoen        ;* then back to loop
          move.w  lincount,d0     ;* number of lines to display
          addq.w  #1,d0           ;* plus one times
          muls    #32,d0          ;* 32 equals offset from start of buf
          add.l   topptr,d0       ;* add offset to topptr
          move.l  d0,topptr
          jsr     cursbuf         ;* pos. cursor
          jsr     showdir         ;* display directory
          jsr     cursbuf         ;* first entry in reverse
          jsr     revon
          jsr     dirline         ;* display
          jsr     revout
stcldoen: bra     stclst1         ;* back to loop

stclend1: jsr     cursmess        ;* delete message line
          jsr     delline
          jsr     cursmess
          move.l  #clfrag1,a0     ;* display mode
          jsr     printf
          movem.l (a7)+,a3-a5/d3-d7  ;* restore registers
          rts                     ;* and return

;****************************************************************
;* reacts to pressing of Return key, accepts it or displays a   *
;* subdirectory.                                                *
;****************************************************************

dirclsel: move.l  topptr,a0       ;* ptr to current start of buffer
          move.w  line,d0
```

```
            sub.w       #4,d0             ;*
            ext.l       d0
            lsl.l       #5,d0             ;* times 32
            move.b      11(a0,d0.l),d1    ;* get file type byte
            cmp.b       #$10,d1           ;* is it a subdirectory?
            beq         subdir            ;* yes

dirsel1:    move.w      clstnum,d0        ;* else current cluster number
            subq.w      #1,d0             ;* subtract 1 for incclust
            move.w      d0,wclust
            move.l      #3,revnum         ;* 3rd menu option in reverse
            jsr         incclust          ;* increment cluster number and display
            bra         stclend1          ;* menu, then back to loop

dirsel2:    jsr         rddir             ;* read directory sectors
            bra         subdiren

subdir:     tst.w       clstnum           ;* if cluster number is zero then just
            beq         dirsel2           ;* reread directory sectors
            move.w      clstnum,d0        ;* else read at the initial cluster
number
            move.l      #dirbuf,dirptr
            clr.w       d3
subdir1:    move.w      clstnum,d0
            move.w      wdrive,-(a7)      ;* current drive
            subq.w      #2,d0             ;* convert cluster number to
            muls        clsiz,d0          ;* logical sector number
            add.w       datrec,d0
            move.w      d0,-(a7)
            move.w      #2,-(a7)          ;* read 2 logical sectors
            move.l      dirptr,-(a7)      ;* buffer address
            move.w      #2,-(a7)          ;* read
            move.w      #4,-(a7)          ;* BIOS Rwabs
            trap        #13               ;* BIOS Trap
            add.l       #14,a7
            tst.w       d0                ;* error occurred?
            bmi         subdierr          ;* yes, then handle
            add.l       #1024,dirptr      ;* else add 1024 bytes per cluster
            move.w      clstnum,oldclst   ;* store cluster number
            jsr         findclst          ;* and find next cluster
            move.w      newclst,d0
            move.w      d0,clstnum
            tst.w       d0                ;* next cluster found?
            beq         subdiren          ;* if not, then end
            cmp.w       #$ff8,d0          ;* was it an end marker?
            bge         subdiren          ;* if so, then end
            bra         subdir1           ;* else read second
```

```
subdiren: bra       stclst0           ;* to loop

subdierr: move.w   d0,-(a7)           ;* handle error, error number
          jsr      errhand
          bra      stclend1

;**********************************************************************
;* Display a page of directory entries                                *
;**********************************************************************

showdir:  move.w   #0,eflag
          jsr      cursbuf            ;* pos. cursos
          jsr      clrest             ;* clear rest of screen
          move.l   topptr,a5          ;* pointer in dir buffer
          move.w   lincount,d7        ;* number of lines per page
showd1:   move.b   #' ',d0            ;* first output spaces
          move.w   d0,-(a7)
          jsr      conout
          move.b   #' ',d0
          move.w   d0,-(a7)
          jsr      conout
          clr.l    d4
          move.w   #9,d6              ;* length of filename with extension
          move.b   0(a5,d4.l),d0      ;* test if empty dir entry
          beq      showdien           ;* if so, then end
          addq.l   #1,d4              ;* if not, then
          move.w   d0,-(a7)
          jsr      conout
showd2:   move.b   0(a5,d4.l),d0      ;* output filename with ext.
          addq.l   #1,d4
          move.w   d0,-(a7)
          jsr      conout
          dbra     d6,showd2
          move.w   #20,tab1
          jsr      curstab            ;* output file attribute
          jsr      disattr
          move.w   #40,tab1
          jsr      curstab
          jsr      disclus            ;* output start cluster
          move.w   #55,tab1
          jsr      curstab
          jsr      dissize            ;* and file size in bytes
          move.w   #0,column
          addq.w   #1,line
          jsr      loccurs
          add.l    #32,a5             ;* 32 bytes per dir entry
          dbra     d7,showd1
```

```
showd8:    move.w    #0,column       ;* output message in last line
           move.w    #24,line        ;* and
           jsr       loccurs
           move.l    #sclfrag2,a0
           jsr       printf
           rts                       ;* return

showdien:  move.w    #1,eflag
           bra       showd8

;**********************************************************************
;* Output a directory line on the screen                              *
;**********************************************************************

dirline:   move.l    topptr,a3       ;* pointer in dir buffer
           move.w    #0,eflag
           move.w    line,d3
           sub.w     #4,d3           ;* offset from top of screen
           ext.l     d3
           lsl.l     #5,d3           ;* times 32, corresponds to 1 dir entry
           move.b    #' ',d4
           move.w    d4,-(a7)        ;* two spaces
           jsr       conout
           move.w    d4,-(a7)
           jsr       conout
           move.b    0(a3,d3.l),d0   ;* first byte of the entry, if
           beq       dirlend1        ;* zero, then empty entry
           move.w    d0,-(a7)        ;* else output byte
           jsr       conout
           addq.l    #1,d3
           move.w    #9,d6           ;* remaining length of entry
dirlin1:   move.b    0(a3,d3.l),d0   ;* get remaining bytes of entry
           addq.l    #1,d3
           move.w    d0,-(a7)
           jsr       conout          ;* and output
           dbra      d6,dirlin1
           move.w    #20,tab1
           jsr       curstab
           jsr       disattr         ;* output file attribute
           move.w    #40,tab1
           jsr       curstab
           jsr       disclus         ;* and the start cluster
           move.w    #55,tab1
           jsr       curstab
           jsr       dissize         ;* finally file size in bytes
dirlend:   rts                       ;* and return
```

```
dirlend1: move.w    #1,eflag
          bra       dirlend

;**********************************************************************
;*  Output the number of the first cluster of the current dir entry.  *
;**********************************************************************

disclus:  move.b    #' ',d0
          move.w    d0,-(a7)
          jsr       conout           ;* output space
          move.w    line,d0
          sub.w     #4,d0
          ext.l     d0
          lsl.l     #5,d0            ;* times 32
          move.b    27(a3,d0.l),d1   ;* access start cluster in entry
          lsl.w     #8,d1            ;* times 256 because high byte
          move.b    26(a3,d0.l),d1   ;* load low byte
          move.w    d1,clstnum       ;* store as cluster number
          move.w    d1,-(a7)
          jsr       dezpr            ;* output as decimal number
          move.b    #' ',d0          ;* another space and
          move.w    d0,-(a7)
          jsr       conout
          rts                        ;* return

;**********************************************************************
;*  Output the file size of the current dir entry in bytes            *
;**********************************************************************

dissize:  move.w    line,d3
          sub.w     #4,d3            ;* subtract offset from
          ext.l     d3               ;* top of screen
          lsl.l     #5,d3            ;* times 32
          clr.l     d1
          move.l    topptr,a3
          move.b    31(a3,d3.l),d1   ;* most significant byte first (Intel)
          lsl.l     #8,d1            ;* shift byte to next byte pos
          move.b    30(a3,d3.l),d1   ;* load next signif. byte
          lsl.l     #8,d1            ;* and shift another byte pos
          move.b    29(a3,d3.l),d1   ;* to the left
          lsl.l     #8,d1            ;* until all four bytes have been
          move.b    28(a3,d3.l),d1   ;* read and converted
          move.l    d1,-(a7)         ;* to Motorola format
          jsr       dezlpr           ;* then output size in decimal
          move.w    #$20,-(a7)       ;* followed by a space
          jsr       conout
          rts                        ;* and return
```

```
;************************************************************************
;*   Output the file attribute of the current directory entry.          *
;************************************************************************

disattr:  move.w    line,d3          ;* current line
          sub.w     #4,d3            ;* offset to top of screen
          ext.l     d3
          lsl.l     #5,d3            ;* times 32
          move.l    topptr,a3        ;* pointer in dir buffer
          move.b    0(a3,d3.l),d1    ;* get first byte of the entry
          cmp.b     #$e5,d1          ;* is it the character for a deleted
          beq       deleted          ;* file? if so, then display
          move.b    11(a3,d3.l),d1   ;* else get file attribute
          cmp.b     #$10,d1          ;* is it a subdirectory? if so,
          beq       folder           ;* then output 'Subdirectory'
          cmp.b     #$01,d1          ;* read only?
          beq       readonly
          cmp.b     #$02,d1          ;* is it a hidden
          beq       hidden           ;* file?
          cmp.b     #$08,d1          ;* is it the disk name
          beq       disname
          move.l    #treadwr,a0      ;* default: file can be read
          jsr       printf           ;* and written
disatten: rts                        ;* and return

disname:  move.l    #tdisname,a0     ;* output and
          jsr       printf
          bra       disatten         ;* return

folder:   move.l    #tfolder,a0      ;* output and
          jsr       printf
          bra       disatten         ;* return

readonly: move.l    #treadon,a0      ;* output and
          jsr       printf
          bra       disatten         ;* return

hidden:   move.l    #thidden,a0      ;* output and
          jsr       printf
          bra       disatten         ;* return

deleted:  move.l    #tdelet,a0       ;* output and
          jsr       printf
          bra       disatten         ;* return

          end
```

And finally, the listing of the Format and Gap menu subroutines.

```
;*********************************************************************
;*    Format subroutines                                             *
;*    These routines access subroutines of the TRACK with SYNCS option, *
;*    so that option must be implemented first.                      *
;*********************************************************************

format1: jsr       cursmess        ;* position cursor in message line
         jsr       delline         ;* delete line
         jsr       emptybuf        ;* and delete cursor buffer
         move.l    #fofrag2,a0     ;* ask for confirmation
         jsr       printf
         move.w    wtrack,-(a7)
         jsr       dezpr
         move.l    #fofrag5,a0
         jsr       printf
         move.w    wside,-(a7)
         jsr       dezpr
         move.l    #fofrag6,a0
         jsr       printf
         move.w    wdrive,-(a7)
         jsr       dezpr
         move.l    #fofrag3,a0
         jsr       printf
         jsr       wkey            ;* read keyboard
         cmp.b     #'y',d0
         beq       doform1
         cmp.b     #'Y',d0
         beq       doform1
         jsr       delline         ;* if neither upper nor lowercase 'y',
         jsr       emptybuf        ;* then don't format
         move.l    #fofrag4,a0
         jsr       printf
         jsr       wkey            ;* wait for key and
         bra       form1end        ;* return

doform1: move.w    #$e5e5,-(a7)    ;* else format, virgin value
         move.l    #$87654321,-(a7) ;* magic number
         move.w    #1,-(a7)        ;* sector interleave
         move.w    wside,-(a7)     ;* current side
         move.w    wtrack,-(a7)    ;* current track
         move.w    asector,-(a7)   ;* current number of sectors/track
         move.w    wdrive,-(a7)    ;* current drive
         clr.l     -(a7)           ;* dummy long word
         move.l    #formbuf,-(a7)  ;* space for creating track
         move.w    #10,-(a7)       ;* XBIOS Flopfmt
```

```
               trap      #14                  ;* XBIOS Trap
               add.l     #26,a7
               tst.w     d0
               bmi       form1err             ;* error occurred?
form1end:      jsr       cursmess
               jsr       delline
               jsr       cursmess
               move.l    #fofrag1,a0          ;* output message
               jsr       printf
               jsr       curright             ;* correct menu cursor, display
               rts                            ;* menu and return

form1err:      move.w    d0,-(a7)             ;* error number on stack, handle
               jsr       errhand
               bra       form1end             ;* and return

;*******************************************************************************
;*     Create a track at the address formbuf with all syncs, which is          *
;*     then written to the disk with the controller write-track command        *
;*     for the purpose of formatting. (xformat in menu)                        *
;*******************************************************************************

maketr:        move.w    #1,sektor            ;* first sector is number 1
               move.l    #formbuf,a2          ;* address of the track buffer
               move.w    gap1,d0              ;* first gap
               move.w    #$4e,d7              ;* header byte is $4E
               jsr       wbuff                ;* create gap1 in buffer
makt1:         move.w    gap2,d0              ;* number of bytes in 2nd gap
               move.w    #0,d7                ;* byte value is 0
               jsr       wbuff                ;* enter in buffer
               move.w    #3,d0                ;* three $F5 in buffer as sync byte
               move.b    #$f5,d7              ;* and to clear CRC register
               jsr       wbuff                ;* (checksum), enter in buffer
               move.b    #$fe,(a2)+           ;* address mark directly in buffer
               move.w    wtrack,d0
               move.b    d0,(a2)+             ;* current track
               move.w    wside,d0
               move.b    d0,(a2)+             ;* current side
               move.w    sektor,d0
               move.b    d0,(a2)+             ;* current sector
               move.w    drbyte,d0            ;* number of bytes/sector
               cmp.w     #1024,d0
               beq       makt2
               cmp.w     #512,d0              ;* compare with four possible
               beq       makt3                ;* values, and then enter
               cmp.w     #256,d0
               beq       makt4
```

```
                move.w      #0,d1
                bra         makt5
makt4:          move.w      #1,d1
                bra         makt5
makt3:          move.w      #2,d1
                bra         makt5
makt2:          move.w      #3,d1
makt5:          move.b      d1,(a2)+        ;* required value
                move.b      #$f7,(a2)+      ;* checksum of address field in buffer
                move.w      gap3,d0         ;* number of bytes in gap 3
                move.w      #$4e,d7         ;* filler byte is $4E
                jsr         wbuff           ;* write in buffer
                move.w      gap2,d0         ;* write gap2 zeros
                move.w      #0,d7           ;* in buffer again
                jsr         wbuff
                move.w      #3,d0           ;* 3 sync bytes, written as $A1
                move.w      #$f5,d7         ;* on the disk, written
                jsr         wbuff           ;* as $F5 in the buffer
                move.b      #$fb,(a2)+      ;* data address mark
                move.w      drbyte,d0       ;* number of bytes/sector as counter
                move.b      #$e5,d7         ;* for data bytes in this sector
                jsr         wbuff           ;* writre $E5 as data byte
                move.b      #$f7,(a2)+      ;* write checksum
                move.w      gap4,d0         ;* gap5-many $4Es as fill byte for gap4
                move.w      #$4e,d7
                jsr         wbuff           ;* write in buffer
                move.w      sektor,d0       ;* increment current sector by one
                addq.w      #1,d0
                move.w      d0,sektor
                cmp.w       asector,d0      ;* compare number of sectors per track
                ble         makt1           ;* with one; if greater, then
                move.w      gap5,d0         ;* last is written to buffer
                move.w      #$4e,d7         ;* and 5th gap at end of track
                jsr         wbuff           ;* can be filled with $4E
                rts                         ;* then return

;****************************************************************
;*  Write the byte value in register D7, D0-times in the buffer  *
;*  addressed by address register A2.                            *
;****************************************************************

wbuff:          subq.w      #1,d0           ;* adapt counter
wbuff1:         move.b      d7,(a2)+        ;* write in buffer
                dbra        d0,wbuff1       ;* D0 times
                rts
```

```
;***********************************************************************
;*   Pass the address of the track buffer to the DMA controller.       *
;*   Routine must be called in the supervisor mode.                    *
;***********************************************************************

setbuf:   move.l    #formbuf,d0      ;* address of the track buffer
          move.b    d0,dmalow        ;* enter low byte
          lsr.l     #8,d0            ;* shift 8 bits right
          move.b    d0,dmamid        ;* and enter next byte
          lsr.l     #8,d0            ;* shift 8 bits right
          move.b    d0,dmahigh       ;* and enter high byte
          rts

;***********************************************************************
;*   Format a track by writing contents of track buffer (in formbuf)   *
;*   directly to the disk with the write-track command.                *
;***********************************************************************

xfortrac: move.w    #$190,dmamode    ;* clear DMA and set to write
          move.w    #$90,dmamode     ;* switch
          move.w    #$190,dmamode
          move.w    #$1f,d6          ;* enter 31 in sector count register
          jsr       wrcontr
          move.w    #$180,dmamode    ;* select FDC register
          move.w    #$f8,d6          ;* write-track command
          jsr       wrcontr
          move.l    #$60000,d7       ;* timeout counter
xfort1:   subq.l    #1,d7            ;* decrement
          beq       xforterr         ;* if timeout, then error
          btst      #5,mfp           ;* FDC done?
          bne       xfort1           ;* no, keep waiting
          rts                        ;* else return
xforterr: move.w    #-24,-(a7)       ;* Put error number on stack and
          jsr       errhand          ;* handle it
          rts

;***********************************************************************
;*   Call the routine for directly formatting a track                  *
;***********************************************************************

xformat:  movem.l   a3-a6/d3-d7,-(a7)
          jsr       cursmess
          jsr       delline          ;* save registers and output
          move.l    #xffrag1,a0      ;* message
          jsr       printf
          jsr       emptybuf         ;* empty keyboard buffer
          jsr       wkey             ;* and wait for keypress
```

```
              cmp.b    #'y',d0
              beq      xformit
              cmp.b    #'Y',d0
              bne      xformend         ;* not a 'y'

xformit:  jsr    super          ;* else supervisor on
          st     flock          ;* disable floppy interrupt
          jsr    setspace       ;* read the track once,
          jsr    seldrive       ;* accelerates the disk
          jsr    flreset        ;* otherwise speed
          jsr    searcht        ;* of the inner tracks
          jsr    rdstrack       ;* is not sufficient
          jsr    setbuf         ;* send track buffer to DMAC
          jsr    maketr         ;* create current track in buffer
          jsr    searcht        ;* and find track
          jsr    xfortrac       ;* write track on disk
          jsr    emptybuf
          jsr    cursmess
          jsr    delline
          jsr    flreset        ;* reset controller
          jsr    user           ;* enable user mode again
          move.l #xffrag2,a0
          jsr    printf         ;* output message
          jsr    wkey           ;* read keyboard
          jsr    super          ;* enable supervisor
          sf     flock          ;* release floppy interrupt
          jsr    deselect       ;* deselect drive
          jsr    user           ;* switch to user mode

xformend: jsr    cursmess
          jsr    delline
          jsr    cursmess       ;* output message, restore
          move.l #drfrag1,a0    ;* registers, and
          jsr    printf
          movem.l (a7)+,a3-a6/d3-d7
          rts                   ;* return

;*****************************************************************
;* The following menu options increment and decrement the gaps in the *
;* menu. See the sector menu for details.                         *
;*****************************************************************

incgaps:  cmp.w   #99,d0        ;* maximum number of fill bytes for all
          blt     incgaps1      ;* gaps is 99, this routine is called
          move.w  #0,d0         ;* by all incgap menu options
          bra     incgaps2      ;* because the limits
incgaps1: addq.w  #1,d0         ;* are the same
```

```
incgaps2:   rts

incgap1:    move.w      gap1,d0
            jsr         incgaps
            move.w      d0,gap1
            divu        #10,d0
            add.b       #'0',d0
            move.b      d0,mgap1
            swap        d0
            add.b       #'0',d0
            move.b      d0,mgap1+1
            jsr         dispmen
            rts

incgap2:    move.w      gap2,d0
            jsr         incgaps
            move.w      d0,gap2
            divu        #10,d0
            add.b       #'0',d0
            move.b      d0,mgap2
            swap        d0
            add.b       #'0',d0
            move.b      d0,mgap2+1
            jsr         dispmen
            rts

incgap3:    move.w      gap3,d0
            jsr         incgaps
            move.w      d0,gap3
            divu        #10,d0
            add.b       #'0',d0
            move.b      d0,mgap3
            swap        d0
            add.b       #'0',d0
            move.b      d0,mgap3+1
            jsr         dispmen
            rts

incgap4:    move.w      gap4,d0
            jsr         incgaps
            move.w      d0,gap4
            divu        #10,d0
            add.b       #'0',d0
            move.b      d0,mgap4
            swap        d0
            add.b       #'0',d0
            move.b      d0,mgap4+1
```

```
          jsr        dispmen
          rts

incgap5:  move.w     #-1,-(a7)
          move.w     #11,-(a7)        ;* shift pressed?
          trap       #13
          addq.l     #4,a7
          move.w     #10,d1
          btst       #0,d0
          bne        incgap5x
          btst       #1,d0
          bne        incgap5x
          move.w     #1,d1
incgap5x: move.w     gap5,d0
          add.w      d1,d0
          cmp.w      #999,d0
          ble        incgap5a
          move.w     #0,d0
incgap5a: move.w     d0,gap5
          ext.l      d0
          divs       #100,d0
          add.b      #'0',d0
          move.b     d0,mgap5
          swap       d0
          ext.l      d0
          divs       #10,d0
          add.b      #'0',d0
          move.b     d0,mgap5+1
          swap       d0
          add.b      #'0',d0
          move.b     d0,mgap5+2
          jsr        dispmen
          rts

decgaps:  cmp.w      #0,d0            ;* called from all decgap menu options
          ble        decgaps1         ;* because max and min are the
          subq.w     #1,d0            ;* same for all gaps
          bra        decgaps2
decgaps1: move.w     #99,d0
decgaps2: rts

decgap1:  move.w     gap1,d0
          jsr        decgaps
          move.w     d0,gap1
          divu       #10,d0
          add.b      #'0',d0
          move.b     d0,mgap1
```

```
             swap      d0
             add.b     #'0',d0
             move.b    d0,mgap1+1
             jsr       dispmen
             rts

decgap2:     move.w    gap2,d0
             jsr       decgaps
             move.w    d0,gap2
             divu      #10,d0
             add.b     #'0',d0
             move.b    d0,mgap2
             swap      d0
             add.b     #'0',d0
             move.b    d0,mgap2+1
             jsr       dispmen
             rts

decgap3:     move.w    gap3,d0
             jsr       decgaps
             move.w    d0,gap3
             divu      #10,d0
             add.b     #'0',d0
             move.b    d0,mgap3
             swap      d0
             add.b     #'0',d0
             move.b    d0,mgap3+1
             jsr       dispmen
             rts

decgap4:     move.w    gap4,d0
             jsr       decgaps
             move.w    d0,gap4
             divu      #10,d0
             add.b     #'0',d0
             move.b    d0,mgap4
             swap      d0
             add.b     #'0',d0
             move.b    d0,mgap4+1
             jsr       dispmen
             rts

decgap5:     move.w    #-1,-(a7)
             move.w    #11,-(a7)
             trap      #13
             addq.l    #4,a7
             move.w    #10,d1
```

```
          btst        #0,d0
          bne         decgap5x
          btst        #1,d0           ;* right shift key
          bne         decgap5x
          move.w      #1,d1

decgap5x: move.w      gap5,d0
          sub.w       d1,d0
          bpl         decgap5a
          move.w      #999,d0

decgap5a: move.w      d0,gap5
          ext.l       d0
          divs        #100,d0
          add.b       #'0',d0
          move.b      d0,mgap5
          swap        d0
          ext.l       d0
          divs        #10,d0
          add.b       #'0',d0
          move.b      d0,mgap5+1
          swap        d0
          add.b       #'0',d0
          move.b      d0,mgap5+2
          jsr         dispmen
          rts

;**********************************************************************
;*  Change number of bytes per sector, stored in drbyte and affect    *
;*  the number of displayed and written bytes in the sector menu,     *
;*  though only if format module is included.                         *
;**********************************************************************

incbyte:  move.w      drbyte,d0       ;* possible number of bytes/sector
          cmp.w       #128,d0         ;* is 128, 256, 512, or 1024 bytes
          beq         incby1
          cmp.w       #256,d0
          beq         incby2
          cmp.w       #512,d0
          beq         incby3
          move.w      #128,d0
          move.b      #'0',mdrisect   ;* enter in menu text
          move.b      #'1',mdrisect+1
          move.b      #'2',mdrisect+2
          move.b      #'8',mdrisect+3
          bra         incbywei
```

```
incby1:   move.w    #256,d0
          move.b    #'0',mdrisect
          move.b    #'2',mdrisect+1
          move.b    #'5',mdrisect+2
          move.b    #'6',mdrisect+3
          bra       incbywei

incby2:   move.w    #512,d0
          move.b    #'0',mdrisect
          move.b    #'5',mdrisect+1
          move.b    #'1',mdrisect+2
          move.b    #'2',mdrisect+3

          bra       incbywei
incby3:   move.w    #1024,d0
          move.b    #'1',mdrisect
          move.b    #'0',mdrisect+1
          move.b    #'2',mdrisect+2
          move.b    #'4',mdrisect+3

incbywei: move.w    d0,drbyte
          jsr       dispmen
          rts

;*******************************************************************
;*  Decrements number of bytes/sector, like incbyte, only allows the  *
;*  four possible FDC values (128, 256, 512, 1024).                   *
;*******************************************************************

decbyte:  move.w    drbyte,d0
          cmp.w     #128,d0
          beq       decby1
          cmp.w     #256,d0
          beq       decby2
          cmp.w     #512,d0
          beq       decby3
          move.w    #512,d0
          move.b    #'0',mdrisect
          move.b    #'5',mdrisect+1
          move.b    #'1',mdrisect+2
          move.b    #'2',mdrisect+3
          bra       decbywei

decby1:   move.w    #1024,d0
          move.b    #'1',mdrisect
          move.b    #'0',mdrisect+1
          move.b    #'2',mdrisect+2
```

```
        move.b    #'4',mdrisect+3
        bra       decbywei

decby2: move.w    #128,d0
        move.b    #'0',mdrisect
        move.b    #'1',mdrisect+1
        move.b    #'2',mdrisect+2
        move.b    #'8',mdrisect+3
        bra       decbywei

decby3: move.w    #256,d0
        move.b    #'0',mdrisect
        move.b    #'2',mdrisect+1
        move.b    #'5',mdrisect+2
        move.b    #'6',mdrisect+3

decbywei: move.w  d0,drbyte
        jsr       dispmen
        rts

        end
```

Operating the disk editor

The disk editor is primarily controlled with the cursor keys: Cursor left and cursor right move you through the different menu selections; cursor up and cursor down select the menu point, or change the variable section of a menu point (drive, side, track, etc.). Most menu point selections will bring you into a new menu, from which you select a new menu point.

The next section lists the definition of each menu point.

7.2.1 The main menu

All points in this menu except END take you to a new menu:

TRACK: Takes you to the TRACK menu, in which entire tracks can be handled.

TRACK/SYNC: Selects the TRACK WITH SYNC BYTES menu; this mode allows you to access all information on the diskette, such as gap and synchronization bytes.

SECTOR:	Selects SECTOR mode, which allows reading, editing and writing sectors.
CLUSTER:	Selects CLUSTER mode, from which diskette clusters can be accessed.
FORMAT:	Selects FORMAT mode. From this mode you can format individual tracks with different formats (including non-Atari formats).
OPTIONS:	Selects OPTIONS menu. You can declare the current drive, and determine the maximum number of tracks and sectors.
END:	End program, return to Desktop.

7.2.2 The TRACK menu

drive:	0 is default, and the cursor up and cursor down keys let you select a new drive. All menu points followed by a colon and a number have this option of selecting another number with the cursor keys.
side 0:	Selects the disk side, either 0 or 1.
track 00:	Selects the track to be accessed. The maximum selectable number will be selected in the OPTIONS menu from the main menu.
sect/trac 00:	Sets the number of sectors per track to be read from and written to.
READ:	Selecting this point will read the presently listed track from diskette, and display it. Cursor up and cursor down scroll you through the individual sectors. It is also possible to call the EDIT function with cursor left and cursor right, which lets you change the tracks as you scroll through the text.
WRITE:	Following a confirming prompt, the entire track will be rewritten to diskette.

EDIT: Provides editing for a sector of a track. It can also be called from the READ function, but then you can only edit one sector of a track.

BACK: Exit to main menu.

7.2.3 The TRACK with SYNC menu

drive 0:   Selects the current disk drive

side 0:   Selects the current side

track 00:   Selects the current track

readwithsync: Reads the entire track with all gaps and enables scrolling through the entire track

Addrfield: Shows the address field of an entire track with byte size and checksum. Output is doubled, so that 16 address fields are always displayed

BACK: Exit to main menu

7.2.4 The SECTOR menu

drive 0:   Selects the current drive

side 0:   Selects the current side

track 00:   Selects the current track

sector 00:   Selects the current sector

READ: Reads and displays the current sector

WRITE: Writes the sector currently in memory to diskette, following a confirming prompt

EDIT: Branches to EDIT mode, which allows hexadecimal input and access to all sector bytes using the cursor keys. Pressing <Return> exits the EDIT mode.

BACK: Exit to main menu

7.2.5 The CLUSTER menu

drive 0:   Selects the current drive

clust 0000:   Selects the current cluster; increases and decreases the cluster number by pressing cursor up or cursor down (<Shift> cursor up or <Shift> cursor down increases or decreases the cluster number by 10).

READ: Reads the current cluster in memory, and computes the physical sector, next to track and side, at which this cluster begins. The information regarding the physical sector will be taken over to the sector menu, i.e., when you go to the SECTOR menu after reading a cluster, you can immediately read the start sector through READ.

WRITE: Writes the cluster found in memory to the cluster on diskette displayed on the menu, following a confirmation prompt.

EDIT: Allows cluster editing. Pressing <Return> ends EDIT mode.

Startoffile: Displays all files on the current drive with identical file attributes. Scrolling through the individual files in made possible by the cursor up and cursor down keys; pressing <Return> brings the start cluster of the currently selected file into the CLUSTER menu. If the selected file represents a subdirectory, then the system will branch and allow you to select from a subdirectory. Returning to the root directory allows selection of individual points.

BACK: Exits to main menu

7.2.6 The FORMAT menu

drive 0:   Selects the current drive

side 0:   Selects the current side

track 00:   Selects the current track

sec/tra.00:   Select sectors per track. The maximum possible number depends on the menu point MAXSECT chosen from the OPTIONS menu; i.e., if there is a 10 in MAXSECT, you may select 10 sectors per track.

FORMAT: Formats the current track with sec/track sectors, preceded by a confirmation. Formatting follows from the XBIOS function, and formats basic sectors with 512 bytes (Atari format).

XFORMAT: Formats the current track with the parameters changed in the GAP menu; you may set the number of bytes per sector as well as the number of synchronization bytes.

GAPS: Branches to its own menu, in which the parameters can be stated for XFORMAT.

BACK: Exit to main menu

7.2.7 The GAP menu

GAP1 00:   Determines the number of fill bytes at the start of track; maximum is 99.

GAP2 00:   Determines the number of null bytes

GAP3 00:   Determines the number of null byte

GAP4 00:   Determines the number of null bytes

GAP5 00:   Determines the number of fill bytes that will be inserted at the end of the track.

BYT/SEC: Here one of the four byte per sector formats supported by the disk controller can be selected (128, 256, 512, 1024). The choice influences sector reading in the SECTOR menu, so that 1024-byte sectors must also be taken on when editing, etc.

BACK: Exit to main menu

7.2.8 The OPTIONS menu

drive 0:   Selects current drive

MAXTRACK00:   Selects maximum selectable tracks for the TRACK menu

MAXSECT 00:   Selects the maximum selectable sectors for the SECTOR menu point, and states the maximum number of sectors per track

INIT DRIVE: Calls the BIOS function and displays disk parameters

SHOW BPB: Displays the BIOS parameter block of the current drive

BACK: Exit to main menu

7.3 Sample use of the disk editor

First we'll look at a disk directory, then the File Allocation Table (FAT). To do this, format a single-sided disk named `WORK.TST`, and copy the `EMULATOR.ACC` program to this disk from the system disk.

As we've seen above, GEMDOS divides diskettes into clusters (blocks) of two sectors with 512 bytes apiece, or a total of 1024 bytes. Six times 1024 is 6144, so `EMULATOR.ACC` fits into 7 clusters rather than 6. Now load the disk editor, select the SECTOR menu and select drive number 0, track 1, side 0 and sector 3. This is where the first file results on a single-sided diskette. The <p> key will print out the sector.

Now we see the results of our efforts. First you'll see the name given the disk after formatting. Every directory entry, including the disk name, takes up 32 bytes. The disk name requires bytes 0 to 31 of the sector, and the first directory entry begins at byte 32 ($20 hexadecimal). The first 11 bytes (0 to 10) or every directory entry are reserved for the filenames, and spaces (hex $20) are inserted at any of the eight filename characters that are unoccupied. The next three bytes (8-10) are set aside for the file extension.

All data which now follows will be on the diskette in Intel format, i.e., any data of more than one byte will be stored as low byte and high byte. Therefore, the data word $1234 will be stored as $34 $12.

The twelfth byte (11) of every entry functions as a data attribute, and identifies the different access options of the file. The number $08 in the data attribute field of the disk name identifies this entry as the disk name.

11 bytes follow which serve no purpose (12 to 21, $0C-$15), but in bytes 22 and 23 ($16 and $17), the time of the last write access to the file stands relative to the beginning of the entry. The time is coded in the bits of these two bytes, as you have already seen in Chapter 3.3. One item of note is that the seconds are counted in 2-second-click increments, so that the second must be multiplied by 2 to arrive at the proper time.

In conclusion, the time bytes are followed in the directory entry by the date bytes (24-25, $18 $19), which are coded in a similar manner.

The two most important bytes of any directory entry are bytes 26 and 27 ($1A, $1B) relative to the beginning of the entry; this is where the starting cluster of the file is given. As you can see for yourself, our file lists $02 $00, which gives us the start cluster of $0002. The file EMULATOR.ACC, therefore, starts at cluster number 2, which is also the first free cluster that the operating system finds on a diskette. To convert the cluster number into the logical and physical sector number, some of the parameters of the BIOS parameter blocks and of the boot sector will be given (clsize, datrec, spt, nside). The conversion appears as follows:

1. Subtraction from the cluster number by 2, as cluster number 2 is numerically the first free cluster of the operating system.

2. Multiplication of the above result by the number of sectors per cluster (clsize = 2 in Atari ST).

3. Addition of the number of the first logical data sector (datrec = 18 in Atari ST).

The resultant number represents the logical sector number of the first sector of this cluster. The second sector of the cluster directly follows (single-sided diskettes). Double-sided diskettes have the first sector of the first data cluster at side 0, track 1, sector 1; the second sector of this cluster at side 0, track 1, sector 2. The cluster in this case will have the sectors to follow set on a track. When the last sector of a track on side 0 is reached, the operating system writes the next sector on the same track, sector 1 of side 1. If Atari formatting has been done with 9 sectors, the first physical sector of the fifth data cluster will be written to side 0, track 1, sector 9, and the second sector of this fifth data cluster will be on side 1, track 1, sector 1.

But we digress—back to the logical sector of the start cluster. It's still missing the computation of the physical track and sector, on which this logical sector (which numerically starts with 0) is found. Let's take a single-sided diskette as a basis, and divide the logical sector number by the number of sectors per track (spt = 9, Atari format). The result of the division is the track, the remainder of the division the offset by sector 1 of this track.

Look at the first file again: Cluster number 2 minus 2 is 0; multiplied by 2 sectors per cluster, we still have 0; adding 18 gives us 18; divide this by 9 sectors per track—the result is 2, remainder 0. The first sector of the first cluster of the file EMULATOR.ACC is located on track 2 sector 1.

The calculations for finding the logical sector of a double-sided formatted disk are the same, only the computation of the physical track and sector must take the side into consideration. The logical sector number will again be divided by the number of sectors per track (spt), and the remainder of this division gives the offset of sector 1, only the computation of the track differs a bit. The result of the number of sectors per track will be divided by the number of sides, namely, 2 for a double-sided format diskette. If there is no remainder from the division, the track of this sector is on side 0. If there is a remainder, then the computed track is on side 1 of the diskette.

Now on to computing the physical sector for cluster 2 of a double-sided formatted diskette. There is no change in calculating the logical sector: It is also 18 here; divide by the number of sectors per track (9), which gives us 2 remainder 0. The sector number is 1 (from the null remainder). To establish track and side, divide the 2 by the number of sides on the diskette (2), which is 1 remainder 0. So, according to the above rules, the sector will be found on track 1, side 0 of the diskette.

For further testing, we will now determine the start sector of the directories for single- and double-sided format diskettes. The logical start sector is given as BPB and boot sector, in which the product of the number of File Allocation Tables (fat = 2) and the number of sectors per File Allocation Table (spf = 5) added. Therefore, logical sector = 1 + 2 * 5 = 11. The start of directory will be found on all Atari diskettes at logical sector 11.

For the physical sector of a single-sided diskette: 11 / 9 (sectors/track) = 1 remainder 2. 1 + remainder = 3; the logical sector 11 is found on track 1, sector 3 of a single-side diskette.

For a double-sided diskette: 11/9 (sectors/track) = 1 remainder 2. 1 + remainder=3 (sector). 1 / 2 = 0 remainder 1 = side 1; track = result of the first division (1). The logical sector 11 is found on side 1, track 0, sector 3 of a double-side diskette, as you can see for yourself.

In the process of cluster computation, we've neglected the completion of the directory entry for the file EMULATOR.ACC. Out of the 32 bytes per directory entry, we have skipped the last 4 bytes (28-31, $1C-$1F), which gives the file size in bytes. $32 $19 $00 $00 gives us $00001932 in Intel format, and this hexadecimal number is converted by the Desktop into a decimal format (6450). Before you can again look into a table, two bytes with other functions must be mentioned: They are the first byte of the directory entry (byte 0), as well as the twelfth byte (byte 11), the attribute byte.

The first byte of the name, which in our example is $45, means that after bytes unequal to $E5 (or $00), then $2E, the ASCII code of the first character follows ($45 = "E"). The remaining entries have the following meanings:

1st byte **Meaning**
$00   This file hasn't been used yet ($E5=this file has been used, but it was deleted)

$2E   This byte indicates a path from subdirectory to root directory. If the next byte is $2E, the cluster number array will contain the cluster number of the next directory in line; if the Second byte is $00, the next directory in line is the root directory. This will be explained in detail below.

The attribute byte (byte 11) can take on the following values:

Byte: **Meaning:**
$00   This file can be read from as well as written to.
$01   This file is read only.
$02   This file is not displayed in the directory (hidden).
$08   This identifies a diskette name; all bytes after 10 have no meaning.
$10   The filename is handled as a subdirectory (folder).

The functions of the 32 bytes of every directory entry are:

Byte: **Meaning:**
0-10   Filename with extension, first byte is status byte ($E5, $2E)
11   File attribute (read/write, read only, subdirectory)
12-21 unused
22-23 Time
24-25 Date
26-27 Start cluster of the file
28-31 File size in bytes

7.3.1 File Allocation Table

Now you know how to find the beginning of a file on diskette. Bytes number 26 and 27 of the directory entry for the file are converted to decimal, and the given cluster number is converted to the logical sector number, etc., according to the abovementioned rules. But how do we find the second cluster of a file, or the last?

The answers are in the File Allocation Table, whose beginning is always found at side 0, track 0, sector 2, of single- and double-sided format disks. To understand this better, let's look at sector 2, track 0, side 0 of a single-sided diskette (the disk you've been using so far will do) with the disk editor. The first three bytes ($F7 $FF $FF) have a structure to them.

This FAT is where we'll find information about every cluster of the diskette, and even whether the disk is readable, and if so, which is the next cluster of the file. First, though, let's get away from this odd structure (03 04 00 05) and use the numerals 3,4,5, etc. Our table looks like this:

START: 1, 2, 3, 4, 5

START should only symbolize the address at which the number 1 will be found. The entire list is linear; the null list element (relative to START) has a value of 1, the first, 2, etc. If we read the address START, we'll find a value of 1. This number 1 should indicate the information of the next list element to be read. By adding the number 1 to the address of START, and read the found address (START+1), we get the result 2.

We can say this about the 2 after START: The number of the list element to be read is at the address START+2, or the number 3. So it is possible to jump from list element to list element, by just reading the elements and looking for the result of the offset relative to the start of the list. At first glance, this looks a little bit like the method used by the operating system to find the cluster on diskette.

Let's look at the rest of our simplified FAT entries (3,4,5) and add two additional dummy values (x,x,3,4,5). Our cluster number for EMULATOR.ACC is 2, the number for the address START+0 is x, as is the reading for the address START+1. But if we read START+2, we get the number 3, and reading START+3 gives us 4. This means that on EMULATOR.ACC, the next cluster following cluster 2 is number 3, after number 3 is 4, etc.

The conversion from cluster numbers to sector numbers is already familiar to you; we still need a method of finding the end of the file. The solution lies in the operating system, with the help of the FAT: By reading a specific value in an already read address, the cluster read from it will be the last one of the file.

This may be a little complicated, since Intel format with its 12-bit representation is brought into play. A FAT entry consists of 12 bits, with 3 nibbles of 4 bits. The 12-bit format is perfect, since no more than 2^{12} = 4096 clusters are available on diskette.

To explain the strange format and recognize the cluster number, let's have another look at the FAT. First we think about 16 bits per FAT entry, which are set up in Intel format. Of these 16 bits, the most significant nibble (the first of four bits) of the high byte is unnecessary, and is marked with an X. This free nibble will now be set up as the least significant nibble (the last of the four bits) of the low byte of the next entry. The most significant nibble of the low byte and the least significant nibble of the high byte take a cross exchange together in place of the low byte. From two 16-bit entries we get two 12-bit entries, from which a nibble is reserved (the high byte of the second entry). With a byte reserved per two entries, the entire system is periodically symmetrical, i.e., for every two 12-bit entries there is a nibble shift, and the whole process begins again.

To convert 12-bit Intel format entries into readable 12-bit Motorola format entries, the number of entries are of different meanings. Begin with the number 0 and count three nibbles as one entry. As we did in the simplest example above (x,x), the first couple entries (0 and 1) in the real FAT (F7 FF FF) have no meaning, and the first valid entry to follow is the number 2. If the access number is even, as in this case (2), then you'll find the two least significant nibbles (Motorola format) in the first byte of this entry (03), and the most significant nibble (in Motorola format) of the following cluster in the second nibble of the following bytes (0), so that the follow cluster number 3 (Motorola format) is conveyed.

If you want to find the following cluster of this third data cluster, then count in groups of three from the beginning and find the bytes 40 00 in the fourth entry (number 3), whereby the beginning of the third group proper is the zero in the first byte. An odd access number (in this case 3) represents the last two nibbles of the second byte (00) of the high nibble and the first nibble of the first byte as the least significant nibble of the cluster number. In concrete examples, the cluster to follow will be conveyed as the number 4.

7.3.2 Subdirectories and folders on diskette

The file system of Atari TOS is hierarchal and recursive. That is, you can get to any subdirectory (or folder) from the root (main) directory. To get a better grasp of this, select the Desktop menu point New Folder... and create two folders with the names FOLDER1.SUB and FOLDER2.SUB.

Now start the disk editor and read the directory sector from the SECTOR menu (side 0, track 1, sector 3). At byte number 11 (see above) you'll recognize the entry FOLDER1.SUB ($10) as a subdirectory entry. The start cluster of this subdirectory is cluster number 9 (bytes 26 and 27) which starts at track 3, sector 6 of a single-sided diskette. Read this sector into memory using the SECTOR menu.

Every subdirectory has its own directory sectors through the operating system. These subdirectory sectors take up the first couple of entries, even if there are no files in the subdirectory. The first entry begins with a period ($2E) followed by spaces. A $10 stands in the attribute byte as the identifier of the subdirectory, and the start cluster is entered as its own beginning, which in this case is 9. The second directory entry of a subdirectory, set apart by two periods ($2E), has in its start cluster entry (bytes 26 and 27) the start cluster of the next deepest subdirectory. In our case, we find two null bytes (00 00), which means: The next deepest subdirectory from the subdirectory FOLDER1.SUB is the main directory (root directory).

Exit the disk editor and call a directory from the subdirectory FOLDER1.SUB by double-clicking the name. When the empty folder FOLDER1.SUB is displayed, make another folder called INFOLD1.SUB by clicking the New Folder.... menu point. Now restart the disk monitor. The main directory (track 1, sector 3) remains unchanged, so you can immediately go to the starting sector of the subdirectory FOLDER1.SUB at track 3, sector 6, with the help of the SECTOR menu.

Now we can see that there is another folder inside this subdirectory from looking at the directory sector of the subdirectory; this folder has the number 11 as the start cluster. Cluster number 11 begins on a single-sided diskette at track 4, sector 1, which we'll now read. The first entry of the subdirectory has the recursive reference to itself and in the second entry, the reference to the next deepest subdirectory, which in this case corresponds to the subdirectory FOLDER1.SUB, which begins at start cluster 9.

7.3.3 Formatting in non-Atari format

There are two types of non-Atari formats. One consists of the use of more tracks and sectors than are formatted by the Desktop (80 tracks 0-79, and 9 sectors per track 1-9); the other is made up of different numbers of bytes per sector and more or fewer synchronization bytes between the address and data fields. For example, if you'd like to format 81 tracks with 10 sectors, select the OPTIONS menu and raise the variable MAXTRACK to 81 using your cursor keys. Use the same procedure in MAXSECTOR to raise that number to 10. Now exit the OPTIONS menu by selecting BACK, and select the FORMAT menu. Raise the track number to 81 and the sector number to 10. Finally, select FORMAT, put in a blank disk, and press <y> to answer the confirmation: Then you'll get a disk with track 81 formatted to 10 sectors.

If you'd like to get away from Atari format and adjust the sectors and sector sizes to your own preferences, we must get past the TOS programming and directly access the disk controller. Naturally, we must limit ourselves by choice to the limits of the disk controller itself. In other words, you can't format sectors with 630 bytes per sector, because the disk controller can only handle four types of sector sizes (128, 256, 512, 1024). To format track 79 with 4 sectors and 1024 bytes per sector, with a track width of 32 bytes of $4E instead of 60 bytes of $4E, select the menu point FORMAT, then the submenu GAPS. You'll get a new menu where you can decrease the value of GAP1 to 32, and raise the amount of BYT/SEC to 1024. Once you return to the FORMAT menu by selecting BACK, decrease the menu point SEC/TRAC to 4 and TRACK to 79. Finally, go to XFORMAT.

Answer the confirmation with <Y>, and track 79 will be reformatted. You should wait a little longer than usual since the disk drive motor runs on. I had installed a pause, but in the testing phase a constantly spinning motor is useful, especially since different drives have different spin-up times. This means that the built-in drive in the 1040ST reaches its spin-up speed faster than, e.g., the "old" SF 354, so the program section which directly accesses the floppy controller functions differently with different drives (sometimes it works, sometimes it doesn't). These errors came up in the testing phase, though, and no longer exist. However, if you happen to be working with an exotic disk drive (like an old 5 1/4") and the menu points READ with SYNCS or XFORMAT don't work, you should get the drive motor running by leaving the READ with SYNCS menu early, then call the functions again once the motor is running.

To test the TRACK with SYNC menu in a practical fashion, take a normal formatted diskette, and select this menu point. Then read track 79 by choosing READ with SYNCS, and look at the first byte.

Track span should now be around $4E sixty times from the start of track, but it could be another value (e.g., $E4, $9C, $27). This phenomenon will be set by the controller if the read procedure isn't synchronized to the start of track, so, for example, the first bit from $4E will be read, and the controller will read the next 8 data bits as the first byte.

Example:

```
 4     E     4     E     4    ..-->  9     C     9     C     9
0100  1110  0100  1110  0100 1..-->  1001  1100  1001  1100  1001
```

After the track span of 60 bytes, 12 null bytes follow ($00); the first and last null bytes can be cut off and changed to other values. In connection with these, the first synchronization bytes appear, namely three sets of $A1, whereby the first $A1 is not read correctly. The three $A1 bytes switch on the hardware checksum communications, i.e., the disk controller places the checksum above the data bytes to follow. The next byte is $FE, which identifies the following six data bytes as an address field. The contents of these bytes are ($4F, $00, $01, $02, $70, $1D), $4F: Track 79, $00: side 0, $01: sector 1, $02: the following data sector consists of 512 bytes, $70 $1D: address field checksum. Next follows $4E twenty-two times, and $00 twelve times, then $A1 three times. The next byte ($FB) contains information about the following 512 data bytes (a freshly formatted diskette has all $E5 here), followed by two checksun bytes ($C4 $0B). The end of the data sector has $4E written forty times, and then the individual synchronization range ($00, $4E, $A1, etc.) is repeated for the eight address and data fields of this track to follow.

Exit the TRACK with SYNC menu and selet the submenu GAP from the FORMAT menu. Now increase GAP2 from 12 to 15 with the cursor keys, select XFORMAT and confirm the procedure with <Y>. Now when you look at the newly formatted track 79 with the TRACK with SYNC menu, you'll see $00 fifteen times between the individual address and data fields.

7.4 Assembling with different assemblers

Digital Research:

1. Comments must be changed to begin with *
2. Assemble with: `as68.ttp -l -u editor.s`
3. Link with: `link68.ttp [u] edit.68k=edit.o`
4. Make it loadable with: `relmod.ttp edit.68k edit.tos`

The file `edit.tos` is then loadable through clicking.

GST Assembler:

1. `opt abs` must be inserted at the beginning of the file `edit.s` and all memory directives such as `text, bss, data` must be executed through `section`. `text` should become `section text`. The program file can be saved after editing with the name `edit.gst`.

2. Create a linkfile named `asl.lnk`, which contains only one line saying `input *`.

3. Assemble `edit.gst` with `asm.prg edit.gst - errors`

4. Link with `link.prg edit -with asl.lnk -prog edit.tos`

The file `edit.tos` is then startable.

Metacomco Assembler:

The program file `edit.s` can be used without alterations.

1. Make a linkfile called `asl.lnk` which contains one line-- `input *`

2. Assemble with `assem.ttp` to `edit.s` to `edit.bin`

3. Link with `link.ttp edit.bin -with asl.`

The program `edit.prg` is startable.

Chapter Eight

Machine language utilities for BASIC

Machine language utilities for BASIC

ST BASIC is equipped with a large number of functions and is also quite fast. But problems still arise which either cannot be solved at all in BASIC or are very difficult to solve. Time problems also arise when large quantities of data must be processed.

We can get some help from a more or less small machine language program which can be incorporated into the BASIC program. Such a subroutine can be easily placed in an integer array (such as A%(n)) and called. Certain things must be taken into account when combining BASIC and machine language, and we will look at them here.

8.1 Calling and passing parameters

In almost every dialect of BASIC there are two commands which allow BASIC and machine language to work together. These commands are USR and CALL.

Unfortunately, the USR function is not implemented in ST BASIC. An older version even admitted this with the message Function not yet implemented when the function was called. We will have to use the other function.

CALL, as the name implies, calls a machine language program. The following parameters must be specified:

```
CALL A (P1, P2, P3)
```

A is the address of the machine language program. P1, P2, and P3 are parameters which are passed to the program. The number of parameters passed can be set by the user, from 0 on up.

If a specific value (such as 1) is given, it will be taken as such. If a variable is used, its contents will be taken. It should be noted that the values are passed in a longword, so that only integer values between ± 2 billion are possible.

If a string variable is passed (such as A$), the address of the string in memory will be taken. This avoids having to use VARPTR, which is required for calculating the start address of the program.

The machine language program finds the following parameters on the stack:

First, the return address, to which control of the processor will be returned when RTS is encountered. This value is usually uninteresting, but it may not be changed!

Then comes a word which contains the number of parameters passed. This word can be accessed simply with the command MOVE.W 4(SP),D0, whereby the number will be placed in D0.

The longword following contains a pointer to the parameter list itself. This pointer can be loaded into address register A0, for example, with the command MOVEA.L 6(SP),A0.

The parameter list contains the parameters in the order in which they were specified in the BASIC call. These values can be processed by the machine language program.

We encountered a peculiar effect while working with this function. Some programs ran without difficulty, while others, some of them very simple, caused the computer to crash. After a good deal of hair-pulling, we came to the solution of the puzzle: Address register A6 may never be used or changed by the machine language program! After changing all references to A6 in the programs to A4, everything worked fine.

8.2 Some example programs

In the following sections we will present some subroutines for BASIC programs. Hopefully, you will find some utilities which you can use for your own applications. In addition, the example programs show how various parameters can be used and exchanged. You can then write your own machine language programs which can improve and speed up your BASIC programs.

The examples are always given in assembly language form and as BASIC listings. The BASIC programs also contain loaders which generate the machine language programs. You can also place the data for the machine language program in a file on a disk and then read it into the array with the command BLOAD "filename",A. This requires an additional disk access, but it makes the BASIC program shorter and easier to read.

8.2.1 BASIC/TOS interface

The operating system of the Atari ST offers a large number of functions, but many of them cannot be accessed from within BASIC. This problem can be easily solved with the help of a machine language program, however. Such a program must be able to accept an arbitrary number of parameters from the calling BASIC program and pass them to the operating system on the stack.

The program below possesses this capability. It offers a universal interface between BASIC and the operating system. The program can be called with an arbitrary number of parameters. The single restriction is that only 16-bit data (words) are accepted. A longword must be broken up into two parts.

The last parameter which is specified in the CALL command has a special meaning. Because some GEMDOS functions return a value, this value will be placed in the last address specified. The example program demonstrates the function Conin, which waits for a key to be pressed and then returns the value of this key.

Let's first take a look at the machine language program itself. The parameters are placed on the stack in a loop, and then sent to the operating system with a TRAP command. The return value, which is found in data register D0, will be written into the address of the last parameter.

```
;**  BASIC-TOS interface    6/86  S.D.       **
;**  call with CALL ADR (parameter list,x)   **
;**  with x as address of the return value D0 **

run:
    move    4(sp),d0        ;number of parameters
    move.l  6(sp),a5        ;pointer to parameter block
    subq    #2,d0           ;correct number of parameters
    move.l  sp,a4           ;save old stack pointer

loop:
    move.l  (a5)+,d1        ;get parameters
    move    d1,-(sp)        ;and put on stack
    dbra    d0,loop         ;continue

    trap    #1              ;call TOS
    move.l  (a5),a5         ;return address
    move.l  d0,(a5)         ;return D0
    move.l  a4,sp           ;repair stack
    rts                     ;done!

    end
```

As you see, the program is very simple. We will therefore move right on to the BASIC program, which creates the machine language program and then tries it out. The function used is the Conin function, which waits for a keypress and returns the value of the key in D0. The lower word of D0 contains the ASCII value of the key and the upper word contains the scan code. Both values are contained in the longword D0, which is written into the string variable B$.

```
10      '** BASIC-TOS interface  S.D. **
20      defdbl s
30      dim a%(200)
40      a=varptr(a%(0))
50      s=0
60      bload "a:batosint.b",a
100     b$=space$(10)
110     b=varptr(b$)            :'address for return
120     call a (1,b)            :'call the routine
130     ?peek(b),(mid$(b$,4,1)):'output the result
1000    '** data for BASTOS **
1010    data    &H302F,4,&H2A6F,6,&H5540,&H284F,&H221D,&H3F01
1020    data    &H51C8,&HFFFA,&H4E41,&H2A55,&H2A80,&H2E4C,&H4E75
```

8.2.2 Directory reader

An annoying defect of ST BASIC is its inability to read the directory of a disk. The DIR command can be used to display the directory on the screen, but what good is that? If we want to use the directory information in a program, we have to use a machine language program again. This section contains such a program. In addition to the normal access to the filenames, it can also return all of the additional information stored in the directory (see section 6.3). It also returns the total and remaining capacity of the current disk.

Let's look at the machine language program first.

```
        ;** Directory for BASIC  S.D. **

run:
        bra     sfirst          ;entry 1

snext:                          ;entry 2
        move    #$4f,-(sp)
        trap    #1              ;SNEXT function
        addq.l  #2,sp
        tst     d0
        bne     nothing         ;no more entries
        rts

sfirst:
        cmp     #3,4(sp)
        bne     quit            ;not 3 parameters!

        move.l  6(sp),a5        ;pointer to parameter block
        lea     buffer(pc),a4
        move.l  8(a5),(a4)      ;save buffer address

        move.l  8(a5),-(sp)     ;buffer address
        move    #$1a,-(sp)
        trap    #1              ;SETDTA function
        addq.l  #6,sp

        move    6(a5),-(sp)     ;Attribute
        move.l  (a5),-(sp)      ;Filename
        move    #$4e,-(sp)
        trap    #1              ;SFIRST function
        addq.l  #8,sp
```

```
        tst     d0
        bne     nothing
quit:
        rts                     ;=> BASIC
nothing:
        move.l  buffer(pc),a4
        clr     -(sp)           ;drive
        move.l  a4,-(sp)        ;buffer address
        move    #$36,-(sp)
        trap    #1              ;GET-FREE-SPACE function
        addq.l  #8,sp

        move.l  #'Free',30(a4)  ;no filename!
        rts                     ;=> BASIC

buffer: dc.l 0

        end
```

The first things we notice about the program are the two entry points. This is because the program actually consists of two programs.

The first part is the the SFIRST function. This GEMDOS function must be given some parameters like search name, file attribute, and buffer address. The function of the other program section, SNEXT, doesn't need any parameters, because the settings made in the last SFIRST call are used again.

For the calling BASIC program this means that it must first call the program at the beginning and then continue with the address + 4. The parameters need be passed only once.

If the SFIRST or the SNEXT function does not find a file which corresponds to the search criteria, another function will be called. This function returns a parameter block which contains the information about the total size and remaining space on the disk. This information is received by the BASIC program in the same parameter block as the directory entries.

The first call to the program runs

CALL S (F$, A, B$)

The parameters:

S   specifies the starting address of the machine language program.

F$ is a string containing the pathname of the file(s) to be searched for (such as B:*.BAS). The string must be terminated by a zero byte!

A   is the attribute which the file(s) must have. A zero searches for all normal files.

B$ designates a string which serves as a buffer for the data returned by the machine language program. See section 6.3 for the layout of this buffer.

Here is a BASIC program which generates the machine language program and shows how it is used. All files on the disk in the current drive are displayed, together with their lengths. Following this is the capacity of the disk in bytes.

```
10     '** read directory  S.D. **
15     clearw 2: fullw 2: gotoxy 0,0
20     defdbl s
30     dim a%(200)
40     d=varptr(a%(0))     :'1st entry for SFIRST
50     s=0
60     for i=0 to 52 :read a%(i)
70     s=s+a%(i) :next i
80     if s<> 610895 then ?"error !":stop
130    d1=d+4              :'2nd entry for SNEXT
140    input "Disk Drive :",f$
150    f$=f$+":\*.*"+chr$(0)   :'search string
160    p$=space$(50)       :'clear buffer
170    call d (f$,0,p$)    :'SFIRST
180    goto lop1
190    loop:
200    call d1             :'SNEXT
210    lop1:
220    if mid$(p$,31,3) = "Fre" then 260  :'end
230    i=27: gosub calc    :'calculate length
235    for z=31 to 50: if asc(mid$(p$,z,1)) = 0 then x=z-31:z=51
236    next z
240    ?mid$(p$,31,x),l    :'output name and length
250    goto loop
260    end
290    calc:
300    l=asc(mid$(p$,i+3,1))+&H100*asc(mid$(p$,i+2,1))
310    l=l+&H10000*asc(mid$(p$,i+1,1))
320    return
```

```
1000 '** Data for BASDIR **
1010 data &H6000,&H12,&H3F3C,&H4F,&H4E41,&H548F,&H4A40
1020 data &H6600,&H3C,&H4E75,&HC6F,3,4,&H6600,&H2E,&H2A6F
1030 data 6,&H49FA,&H42,&H28AD,8,&H2F2D,8,&H3F3C
1040 data &H1A,&H4E41,&H5C8F,&H3F2D,6,&H2F15,&H3F3C,&H4E
1050 data &H4E41,&H508F,&H4A40,&H6600,4,&H4E75,&H287A,&H18
1060 data &H4267,&H2F0C,&H3F3C,&H36,&H4E41,&H508F,&H297C
1070 data &H4672,&H6569,&H1E,&H4E75,0,0
```

8.2.3 Read/write sectors

The data on a disk, as we have said before, are stored in sectors. These sectors cannot normally be accessed directly because the operating system loads only the sectors which the selected file occupies.

If we want to be able to access sectors at random, we need a machine language program that can read or write a single sector. We will present such a program.

Three parameters are passed to the program: the logical sector number, a read or write instruction, and the address of the buffer.

The logical sector number can be from 0 to the maximum value. This maximum depends on the disk format used. The read/write instruction can have the following values:

    0 - read a sector
    1 - write a sector
    2 - read a sector, ignore disk changes
    3 - write a sector, ignore disk changes

If command 0 or 1 is used, the program accesses only the disk currently in the drive. Changing the disk results in no access being made.

The machine language program looks like this:

```
        ;**         Read sector   S.D.                  **
        ;** CALL A (sector,rw (2=read,1=write),buffer)  **
run:
        cmp     #3,4(sp)        ;3 parameters ?
        bne     quit            ;no => terminate
```

```
        move.l  6(sp),a5        ;pointer to parameters

        clr     -(sp)           ;drive A
        move    2(a5),-(sp)
        move    #1,-(sp)        ;1 sector
        move.l  8(a5),-(sp)     ;buffer
        move    6(a5),-(sp)     ;read/write
        move    #4,-(sp)        ;RWABS function
        trap    #13             ;BIOS call
        add.l   #14,sp

quit:
        rts                     ;=> BASIC

        end
```

The program accesses drive A only. If this has to be made variable, the program can be rewritten for four parameters.

Here is the corresponding BASIC program which creates the machine language program and gives a small demonstration:

```
10      '** Read/write sector from disk drive A. S.D. **
15      clearw 2: fullw 2: gotoxy 0,0
30      dim a%(100),f%(300)
40      a=varptr(a%(0))
50      defdbl s
60      s=0
70      for i=0 to 22: read a%(i)   :'load ml program
80      s=s+a%(i) :next i
90      if s<> 165974 then ?"Error in DATA! " :stop
100     f=varptr(f%(0))
200     input "Sector, rw : ";s%,r%
210     call a (s%,r%,f)            :'Call the program
220     for i=0 to 255
230     if (i mod 16)=0 then ?
240     ?mki$(f%(i));               :'ASCII output of sectors
250     next i :?
1000    '** Machine language data **
1010    data &HC6F,3,4,&H6600,&H24,&H2A6F,6,&H4267
1020    data &H3F2D,2,&H3F3C,1,&H2F2D,8,&H3F2D,6
1030    data &H3F3C,4,&H4E4D,&HDFFC,0,&HE,&H4E75
```

8.2.4 Any disk format

As we mentioned in Chapter 6, 3 1/2" disks can use a variety of formats. The number of sides used, tracks, and sectors per track are all variable.

In order to format a disk from within a BASIC program, we need some help from a machine language subroutine, since there is no corresponding command in the BASIC instruction set. In additon, even using the Desktop limits us to two different formats. We will write a small machine language program which can be called from BASIC and supplied with some parameters. These parameters define the format which will be used to initialize the disk.

The program itself is similar to the one we saw in Chapter 6. On closer examination, we'll notice some important differences.

First of all, the menu is missing and the parameter calculation connected with it. All of the important settings are taken directly from the calling BASIC program. Second, the variables are addressed differently. This is more complicated because the program will be read into an area of memory unknown to it by a BASIC loader. All addressing must therefore be relative.

The machine language program is called by a CALL command with the following construction:

CALL A (S,T,SPT,DRV)

The variables used have the following meanings:

A   is the memory address at which the machine language program was placed. In the previous example this is the address of the integer array A% as determines by the VARPTR function.

S   stands for the number of sides which are to be formatted on the disk. The number of sides - 1 is passed, so that S=0 formats a single-sided disk and S=1 a double-side disk.

T   specified the number of tracks. Normally a disk contains 80 tracks, but it is physically possible to format up to 82 tracks (sometimes even 83).

SPT   are the sectors per track. Normally this is 9, but it is possible to format 1 to 10 sectors per track.

DRV   stands for drive. This variable determines the drive in which the disk will be formatted. 0 indicates drive A and 1 is used for drive B. Please don't try to format the RAM disk (drive C) by using a 3 here; this accesses both drives A and B at the same time, instead of the RAM disk.

Here now is the machine language program which takes the parameters from the BASIC program and formats the disk:

```
        ;** BASIC subroutine: formatting routine   S.D. **

run:
        move    4(sp),d0
        cmp     #4,d0           ;4 parameters?
        bne     quit            ;no => terminate
        move.l  6(sp),a5        ;pointer to parameter block

        lea     sides(pc),a4
        move.l  (a5)+,d1
        move    d1,(a4)         ;sides
        move.l  (a5)+,d1
        move    d1,2(a4)        ;tracks
        move.l  (a5)+,d1
        move    d1,4(a4)        ;sectors per track
        move.l  (a5)+,d1
        move    d1,6(a4)        ;drive number

        move    tracks(pc),8(a4)
        subq    #1,8(a4)

floop:
        move    sides(pc),10(a4) ;determine side
floop1:
        bsr     fmttr           ;format track
        bne     quit
        sub     #1,10(a4)       ;side -1
        bpl     floop1
        sub     #1,8(a4)
        bpl     floop           ;next track

setboot:
        clr     -(sp)           ;execute flag
        moveq   #2,d0
```

331

```
        or      sides(pc),d0
        move    d0,-(sp)            ;disk type, sides
        move.l  #$1000000,-(sp)     ;create seriual number
        pea     12(a4)              ;buffer address
        move    #$12,-(sp)
        trap    #14                 ;create boot sector
        add.l   #14,sp

        lea     12(a4),a0
        clr.l   d0
        cmp     #9,4(a4)            ;9 sectors per track?
        beq     sok                 ;yes
        move.b  #10,24(a0,d0)       ;set 10 SPT
        move    tracks(pc),d1
        tst     (a4)                ;1 side?
        beq     sd11                ;yes
        lsl     #1,d1               ;else double-sided
sd11:
        bsr     addsec              ;SEC + number of tracks

sok:
        cmp     #80,2(a4)           ;80 tracks?
        beq     trok
        move    #18,d1
        tst     (a4)                ;1 side?
        beq     sd12                ;yes
        lsl     #1,d1               ;else double-sided
sd12:
        bsr     addsec              ;SEC + 2*9 or 4*9

trok:
        move    #1,-(sp)            ;1 sector
        clr.l   -(sp)               ;side 0, track 0
        move    #1,-(sp)            ;sector 1
        move    drive(pc),-(sp)     ;drive
        clr.l   -(sp)
        pea     12(a4)              ;buffer
        move    #9,-(sp)
        trap    #14                 ;flopwr
        add.l   #20,sp

quit:   rts                         ;return to BASIC

addsec:                             ;SEC = SEC + D1
        move.b  20(a0,d0),d2        ;HI
        lsl     #8,d2
        move.b  19(a0,d0),d2        ;LO
```

```
        add     d1,d2
        move.b  d2,19(a0,d0)        ;set LO
        lsr     #8,d2
        move.b  d2,20(a0,d0)        ;set HI
        rts

fmttr:                              ;format one track
        clr     -(sp)               ;virgin data
        move.l  #$87654321,-(sp)    ;magic number
        move    #1,-(sp)            ;interleave
        move    side(pc),-(sp)      ;side
        move    tracks1(pc),-(sp)   ;track
        move    secptr(pc),-(sp)    ;sectors/track
        move    drive(pc),-(sp)     ;drive
        clr.l   -(sp)
        pea     12(a4)
        move    #10,-(sp)
        trap    #14                 ;flopfmt
        add.l   #26,sp
        tst     d0                  ;test for error
        rts

sides:   dc.w 1
tracks:  dc.w 80
secptr:  dc.w 9
drive:   dc.w 0
tracks1: dc.w 80
side:    dc.w 0
buffer:  dc.w $200

        end
```

The program is completely relocatable, meaning that it will run at any memory address. The individual components of the program have already been explained in other parts of this book.

The BASIC program below calls the formatting routine. It contains a loader which generates the machine language program from DATA statements. The machine language program can also be loaded from disk, of course.

```
10   '** Format a diskette **
15   clearw 2: fullw 2: gotoxy 0,0
17   defdbl s
20   dim a%(400)
30   a=varptr(a%(0)):s = 0
40   for i=0 to 144: read a%(i)
```

```
45      s =s +a%(i) : next i
46      if s <> 1033402 then ?"error !":stop
50      ?"Extended disk formatter":?:?
100     ?"sides   0= single 1= double":?
110     ?"tracks 79-83" :?
120     ?"sectors/track  9/10":?
130     ?"drive a=0  b=1":?
140     print "sides, tracks, sectors/track, drive "
150     input s,t,spt,dr
160     call a (s,t,spt,dr)
170     '** Data for BFORMAT.obj **
180     data &H302F,&H0004,&H0C40,&H0004,&H6600,&H00CC,&H2A6F,&H0006
190     data &H49FA,&H0110,&H221D,&H3881,&H221D,&H3941,&H0002,&H221D
200     data &H3941,&H0004,&H221D,&H3941,&H0006,&H397A,&H00F8,&H0008
210     data &H536C,&H0008,&H397A,&H00EC,&H000A,&H6100,&H00B4,&H6600
220     data &H0096,&H046C,&H0001,&H000A,&H6A00,&HFFF0,&H046C,&H0001
230     data &H0008,&H6A00,&HFFE0,&H4267,&H7002,&H807A,&H00C6,&H3F00
240     data &H2F3C,&H0100,&H0000,&H486C,&H000C,&H3F3C,&H0012,&H4E4E
250     data &HDFFC,&H0000,&H000E,&H41EC,&H000C,&H4280,&H0C6C,&H0009
260     data &H0004,&H6700,&H0018,&H11BC,&H000A,&H0818,&H323A,&H0096
270     data &H4A54,&H6700,&H0004,&HE349,&H6100,&H003E,&H0C6C,&H0050
280     data &H0002,&H6700,&H0012,&H323C,&H0012,&H4A54,&H6700,&H0004
290     data &HE349,&H6100,&H0024,&H3F3C,&H0001,&H42A7,&H3F3C,&H0001
300     data &H3F3A,&H0066,&H42A7,&H486C,&H000C,&H3F3C,&H0009,&H4E4E
310     data &HDFFC,&H0000,&H0014,&H4E75,&H1430,&H0814,&HE14A,&H1430
320     data &H0813,&HD441,&H1182,&H0813,&HE04A,&H1182,&H0814,&H4E75
330     data &H4267,&H2F3C,&H8765,&H4321,&H3F3C,&H0001,&H3F3A,&H002E
340     data &H3F3A,&H0028,&H3F3A,&H0020,&H3F3A,&H001E,&H42A7,&H486C
350     data &H000C,&H3F3C,&H000A,&H4E4E,&HDFFC,&H0000,&H001A,&H4A40
360     data &H4E75
```

8.2.5 Searching for data

One use of machine language subroutines is data searching in arrays. For long lists a search can take so long in BASIC that it's not worth doing. Just think of a database which took several minutes to find a telephone number.

A machine language program which performs this task is quite easy to write. It consists of just three parts:

1. Code to get parameters from BASIC
2. A search loop
3. Code to return the result to the BASIC program

Here is such a program:

```
;**          Search in integer array  S.D.       **
;** CALL A (start-of-array,number,search word)   **
run:
    cmp     #3,4(sp)          ;3 parameters?
    bne     quit              ;no => exit

    move.l  6(sp),a5          ;pointer to parameters
lop1:
    move.l  (a5),a4           ;pointer to parameter field
    tst     (a4)+             ;set to f%(1)
    move.l  4(a5),d1          ;number of data
    move.l  8(a5),d2          ;search word
    moveq   #1,d3             ;index=1
loop:
    cmp     (a4)+,d2          ;compare
    beq     ok1               ;found
    addq    #1,d3             ;index+1
    cmp     d3,d1             ;end?
    bne     loop              ;no

    move    #-1,d3            ;not found!
ok1:
    move.l  (a5),a5           ;address for return
    move    d3,(a5)           ;return index

quit:
    rts                       ;=> BASIC

    end
```

This small program accomplishes the search in fractions of a second and returns the number of the desired entry in the first element of the list. For this reason you should use only elements 1 to n for the list data. If an element is not found, -1 will be returned.

Since there are so many uses for this program, the following loader and example program is very simple. The principle of the routine and its use will be clear, however.

```
10      '** Search in integer array  S.D. **
30      dim a%(60),f$(1000)
40      a=varptr(a%(0))
```

```
50      defdbl s
60      s=0
70      for i=0 to 25 :read a%(i)
80      s=s+a%(i) :next i
90      if s<> 211865 then ?"error !" :stop
130     f=varptr(f%(0))
140     for i%=1 to 8
150     read f%(i%)              :'read example values
170     next i%
180     clearw 2: fullw 2: gotoxy 0,0
190     ?"Machine Language search of integer array" :?
195     ? "Array contains - 6,2,99,345,7,3,0,4":?
200     input "Integer to search for : ";s%
210     call a (f,i%,s%)
220     if f%(0)=-1 then ?"** Not found ! **" :goto 200
230     ?s%;" is entry #";f%(0) :goto 200
1000    '** Data for machine language program **
1010    data &HC6F,3,4,&H6600,&H2A,&H2A6F,6,&H2855
1020    data &H4A5C,&H222D,4,&H242D,8,&H7601,&HB45C,&H6700
1030    data &HE,&H5243,&HB243,&H6600,&HFFF4,&H363C,&HFFFF
1040    data &H2a55,&H3A83,&H4E75
1100    data 6,2,99,345,7,3,0,4
```

8.2.6 Sort data

Sorting large quantities of data is a very time-consuming process. A BASIC program to sort 1000 items would create a disturbingly long pause, which can disturb the course of the program. A machine language program to do the same thing, on the other hand, is significantly faster.

Such a program will now be presented. It is designed to sort any large integer array from a BASIC program in ascending order. The program is passed the address of the start of the array and the number of entries to be sorted as parameters. This also allows a portion of the array to be sorted.

The algorithm used in this program is very simple. It isn't the fastest algorithm available, but that doesn't matter much given the high speed of the 68000 microprocessor.

Here is the machine language routine:

```
;**        Sort integer array   S.D.        **
;**        CALL A (start-of-array,number)   **
```

```
run:
        cmp     #2,4(sp)        ;2 parameters?
        bne     quit            ;no => exit

        move.l  6(sp),a5        ;pointer to parameters
lop1:
        move.l  (a5),a4         ;pointer to parameter field
        move.l  4(a5),d1        ;number of data
        clr     d3              ;clear exchange flag
lop2:
        move    (a4),d0
        cmp     2(a4),d0        ;compare
        ble     ok1             ;OK
        move    2(a4),(a4)      ;exchange
        move    d0,2(a4)
        st      d3              ;set exchange flag
ok1:
        addq.l  #2,a4           ;next value
        subq.l  #1,d1
        bne     lop2

        tst     d3              ;done?
        bne     lop1            ;no => continue

quit:
        rts                     ;=> BASIC

        end
```

Here is a BASIC program which contains the machine language program in DATA statements and which reads it into an array. Various values are then placed into another array. The input is ended with -1. The machine language routine is then called which sorts the data in the entire array. The sorted values are then printed.

This use is only intended as an example, of course. Things become more interesting when the quantities of data are much larger and the speed advantage over a straight BASIC program becomes clear.

```
10      '** Sort an integer array    S.D. **
20      defdbl s
30      dim a%(200)
40      a=varptr(a%(0)) :s = 0
60      for i=0 to 28 :read a%(i)
70      s=s+a%(i) :next i
```

```
80      if s<> 280743 then ?"error !":stop
100     dim f%(1000)              :'prepare data field
110     defint i
120     a=varptr(a%(0))           :'address of ml program
130     f=varptr(f%(1))           :'address of data
135     clearw 2: fullw 2:gotoxy 0,0
136     ?"Sort an integer array":?
137     ?"Enter -1 to end input":?
140     for i=1 to 1000
150     input "Entry : ";f%(i)    :'enter data
160     if f%(i)=-1 then 180      :'end?
170     next i                    :'no, continue
180     call a (f,i-2)            :'sort
190     for j=1 to i
200     ?j;" : ";f%(j)            :'and output
210     next j
1000    '** Data for BASSORT **
1010    data &HC6F,2,4,&H6600,&H30,&H2A6F,6,&H2855
1020    data &H222D,4,&H4243,&H3014,&HB06C,2,&H6F00,&HC
1030    data &H38AC,2,&H3940,2,&H50C3,&H548C,&H5381,&H6600
1040    data &HFFE6,&H4A43,&H6600,&HFFD8,&H4E75
```

8.2.7 Reading the date and time

Every database program intended for use in everyday life must be able to process the current date and time. Unfortunately, ST BASIC doesn't have any functions like this, so we'll need a machine language program again.

The program presented here reads the clock time and the date from the computer and returns both of these to the BASIC program which called it. This information is also formatted so that it can be processed directly.

The call is done simply by CALL A(A$), whereby the result will be placed in the string variable A$. The format used is the following:

```
HH.MM.SS. DD.MM.YYYY
 |  |  |   |  |   |
 |  |  |   |  |   --- Year      (such as 1986)
 |  |  |   |  ------- Month     (such as 07 for July)
 |  |  |   --------- Day
 |  |  ------------- Seconds    (in two-second steps)
 |  ----------------- Minutes
 -------------------- Hours     (0 to 23)
```

July 3, 1986 at 10:16 PM and 30 seconds would appear in A$ as 22.16.30. 03.07.1986.

Here is the machine language program which reads the time and date, formats it, and returns it to the BASIC program:

```
        ;**         Read clock time    S.D.        **
        ;* Call with CALL A (A$) results in A$      *
        ;* HH.MM.SS. MM.DD.YYYY., time and date      *

run:
        cmp     #1,4(sp)        ;one parameter?
        bne     quit            ;no => terminate

        move.l  6(sp),a5        ;pointer to parameter list
        move.l  (a5),a5         ;pointer to string

go:
        move    #$2c,-(sp)
        trap    #1              ;get_time BIOS function
        addq.l  #2,sp

        and.l   #$ffff,d0       ;mask out upper word
        move.b  #':',d6         ;colon seperator

        move    d0,d1
        lsr     #8,d1
        lsr     #3,d1           ;hours
        bsr     set2b           ;set hours

        move.l  d0,d1
        lsr     #5,d1
        and     #%111111,d1
        bsr     set2b           ;set minutes

        move.l  d0,d1
        lsl     #1,d1           ;seconds *2
        and     #$3f,d1         ;and mask
        bsr     set2b           ;set seconds

        move.b  #' ',(a5)+      ;set space

        move    #$2a,-(sp)
        trap    #1              ;get_date BIOS function
        addq.l  #2,sp

        and.l   #$ffff,d0       ;mask out upper word
```

```
        move.b   #'/',d6         ; / separator

        move.l   d0,d1
        lsr      #5,d1
        and      #%1111,d1       ;mask month
        bsr      set2b           ;set month

        move.l   d0,d1
        and      #%11111,d1      ;mask day
        bsr      set2b           ;set day


        move.l   d0,d1
        lsr      #8,d1
        lsr      #1,d1
        and      #%1111111,d1    ;mask year
        add      #80,d1          ;correct
        move.b   #'1',(a5)+
        move.b   #'9',(a5)+      ;prepare 19oo
        bsr      set2b           ;set year

quit:
        rts                      ;ready !

set2b:                           ;output D1 with two characters
        divu     #10,d1
        add.l    #$300030,d1     ;correct ASCII value
        move.b   d1,(a5)+        ;HI nibble
        swap     d1
        move.b   d1,(a5)+        ;LO nibble
        move.b   d6,(a5)+        ;set back-slash
        rts

        end
```

Here again is the corresponding BASIC program which creates the machine language program and demonstrates how it is used:

```
10      '** GET_TIME in BASIC S.D. **
20      defdbl s
30      dim a%(200)
40      a=varptr(a%(0))
50      s=0
55      'bload "b:readclk.b",a
60      for i=0 to 83 :read a$:    a%(i) =val("&H"+a$)
70      s=s+a%(i) :next i
80      if int(s)<> 272454 then ?"error !":stop
```

```
90      t$=space$(20)
100     call a (t$)
110     ? "Today is "; right$(t$,10)
120     ? "The time : "; left$(t$,8)
990     '** Data for GETTIME **
2000    DATA 0C6F,0001,0004,6600,0082,2A6F,0006,2A55
2010    DATA 3F3C,002C,4E41,548F,C0BC,0000,FFFF,1C3C
2020    DATA 003A,3200,E049,E649,6100,0062,2200,EA49
2030    DATA C27C,003F,6100,0056,2200,E349,C27C,003F
2040    DATA 6100,004A,1AFC,0020,3F3C,002A,4E41,548F
2050    DATA C0BC,0000,FFFF,1C3C,002F,2200,EA49,C27C
2060    DATA 000F,6100,0028,2200,C27C,001F,6100,001E
2070    DATA 2200,E049,E249,C27C,007F,D27C,0050,1AFC
2080    DATA 0031,1AFC,0039,6100,0004,4E75,82FC,000A
2090    DATA D2BC,0030,0030,1AC1,4841,1AC1,1AC6,4E75
2100    DATA 0000,0000,0000,0000
```

8.3 Programming the FDC in BASIC

There are a fairly large number of disk monitors available for the Atari ST. Unfortunately, all of the ones which we are familiar with use only the routines which the operating system offers. This suffices for most applications, but if we want to know exactly what information is hidden on the disk, we need some functions which can be performed only by accessing the floppy disk controller directly.

Such functions include reading the ID fields on a track, reading an entire track, or custom-formatting a track.

Our suggestion: Write your own disk monitor to include functions like this. In BASIC? Sure, why not? If the floppy controller functions are available, it's quite possible to do this in BASIC. But these functions can't be accessed via the operating system. The GEMDOS, BIOS, and XBIOS can't help us any more.

To give us what we need, we wrote a collection of routines which can be bound into a BASIC program and which make all of the FDC commands available in BASIC.

The times when sectors weren't readable because the operating system insisted on the "proper" ID field will be gone. If you get a message like

`Drive A: does not respond...`, you can search the disk thoroughly and find out what's wrong.

Naturally, you have to able to interpret the results which are returned by the less-used FDC commands. You will find all the information you need in the chapter on the WD1772 floppy disk controller.

There are other advantages that make full use of the flexibility of our BASIC/FDC interface. It is always possible to change the command words. These always contain some "option bits," which can influence the execution of the commands. Moreover, a single FDC command can be used to read or write all of the sectors on a track. It is also possible to format just part of a track, something which could be useful for a copy protection scheme.

But first things first, and first we need the FDC interface. The application possibilities will be explained later.

8.3.1 The BASIC/FDC interface program

Let's start with the machine language program which represents our interface to the FDC.

There are three ways of getting this program into memory:

1. Enter the assembly language source (the version printed here was produced with the *AssemPro* macroassembler) and assemble it.

2. Enter the BASIC listing and start it with `RUN`.

3. Order the optional diskette for this book.

First comes the assembly language listing, which shows how our FDC/BASIC interface works internally. Those who know both assembly language and BASIC will find all of the routines needed to operate the FDC printed here. It shouldn't be any trouble to appropriate some of the routines here for use in your own programs.

The BASIC programmer (to whom this chapter is dedicated) must excuse this little excursion into the world of machine language programming. Since direct programming of the FDC is also of general interest, we feel required to publish the assembly language listing as well as the BASIC listing.

If you are only interested in the finished product or you only know ST BASIC, skip this section and continue with the BASIC loader FDCCREAT.BAS, which creates the machine language program.

```
;*******************************************************************
;*******              FDC/BASIC INTERFACE                   *******
;*******************************************************************

;Hardware registers

dmamode   = $ff8606
dmascnt   = $ff8604
dmalow    = $ff860d
dmamid    = $ff860b
dmahigh   = $ff8609
giselect  = $ff8800
giwrite   = $ff8802
mfp       = $fffa01

;Control words for the DMA controller (DMA data direction => READ)

srcmd = $80  ; select command register
srtrk = $82  ; select track register
srsec = $84  ; select sector register
srdat = $86  ; select data register
srcnt = $90  ; select DMA sector-count register

;control words for the DMA controller (DMA data direction => WRITE)

swcmd = $180 ; same as for => READ
swtrk = $182
swsec = $184
swdat = $186
swcnt = $190

;*******************************************************************

  align
STart:
  bra.s run     ; to start of program

;********************** Command words **********************

rest:  dc.w $01 ; Restore    M0, 3ms Step rate
see:   dc.w $11 ; Seek       M0, 3ms Step rate
stp:   dc.w $31 ; Step       M0, 3ms Step rate, update track reg.
stpi:  dc.w $51 ; Step-in    M0, 3ms Step rate, update track reg.
```

```
stpo:   dc.w $71 ; Step-out      MO, 3ms Step rate, update track reg.

rsec:   dc.w $90 ; Read-Sector   MO, multiple
wsec:   dc.w $b0 ; Write-Sector  MO, multiple, write precompensation

radr:   dc.w $c0 ; Read-Address  MO,
rtrk:   dc.w $e0 ; Read-Track    MO,
wtrk:   dc.w $f0 ; Write-Track   MO, write precompensation

forc:   dc.w $d0 ; Force-Interrupt

;*****************     Parameters     **********************

prm:    dc.w 00 ; function number
        dc.w 00 ; drive number
        dc.w 00 ; track number
        dc.w 00 ; sector number
        dc.w 00 ; number of bytes to transfer
        dc.w 00 ; number of ID fields to read
        dc.w 00 ; FDC status
        dc.w 00 ; DMA status
        dc.w 00 ; timeout? (1=timeout)
        dc.w 00 ; number of bytes to transfer
        dc.l 00 ; DMA start address
        dc.l 00 ; DMA end address
        dc.l 00 ; address of the track buffer
        dc.l 00 ; address of the sector buffer
        dc.l 00 ; address of the ID buffer
        dc.l 00 ; address of the ID status buffer

;***************     Here we go     *****************

run:

    tst.w 4(sp)              ; parameters passed?
    bne exit                 ; yes, return to BASIC

;Since the source can only be addressed PC relative, we use A3
;as the program counter.

    LEA STart(PC),A3                 ; PROGRAM START IN ADDRESS REG. 3
    MOVEM.L D0-D7/A0-A6,SAVREG-STart(A3) ; SAVE REGISTERS

;******************     Set supervisor mode     **********************

    clr.l -(sp)              ; user stack => superv. stack
    move.w #$20,-(sp)        ; command => Super
```

```
    trap #1
    addq.l #6,sp              ; correct stack
    MOVE.L D0,SAVSTACK-STart(A3) ; SAVE OLD STACK POINTER

;*** Clear some flags and calculate absolute address of the ***
;*** desired function.                                       ***

    LEA PRM-STart(A3),A5      ; pointer to parameter block

    move.w #1,$43e            ; disable floppy VBL
    move.w #0,16(a5)          ; clear timeout flag
    MOVE.W #0,DMA-STart(A3)   ; clear DMA flag
    MOVE.W #0,VBLFLAG-STart(A3) ; clear VBL reset flag

    move.w 0(a5),d0           ; get function number
    and.l #$0f,d0             ; there are only 16 functions (0-15)
    lsl.l #2,d0               ; times 4 = functab offset

    LEA FUNCTAB-STart(A3),A4  ; func. table address
    move.l 0(a4,d0),d0        ; relative start address of the routine

    jsr 0(a3,d0)              ; +program start=abs. addr. of routine

    TST.W VBLFLAG-STart(A3)   ; VBL on (after deselecting)?
    beq letoff                ; no
    move.w #0,$43e            ; turn on

letoff:

;***************** back to user mode *******************

    MOVE.L SAVSTACK-STart(A3),D0 ; GET OLD STACK POINTER BACK
    move.l d0,-(a7)           ; pass old stack pointer
    move.w #$20,-(sp)         ; command => Super
    trap #1
    addq.l #6,sp              ; correct stack

    MOVEM.L SAVREG-STart(A3),D0-D7/A0-A6 ; RETURN REGISTERS

exit:
    rts                       ; back to BASIC

; That was it!  (All) we have left are the following routines
```

;********************* Restore FDC ****************************

restore:

```
    move.w  #srcmd,dmamode       ; select command reg
    MOVE.W  REST-STart(A3),D7    ; RESTORE command
    bsr     wrt1772              ; pass command
    bsr     fdcwait              ; wait until FDC is ready
    rts
```

;********************* SEEK TRACK ****************************

seek:

```
    move.w  #srdat,dmamode       ; select data reg
    move.w  4(a5),d7             ; track number in d7
    bsr     wrt1772              ; write track number
    move.w  #srcmd,dmamode       ; select command reg
    MOVE.W  SEE-STart(A3),D7     ; SEEK command
    bsr     wrt1772              ; write command
    bsr     fdcwait              ; wait until FDC ready
    rts
```

;********************* Step ********************************

step:

```
    move.w  #srcmd,dmamode       ; select FDC command reg
    MOVE.W  STP-STart(A3),D7     ; STEP command
    bsr     wrt1772              ; write command
    bsr     fdcwait              ; wait until FDC ready
    rts
```

;********************** Step in ****************************

stepin:

```
    move.w  #srcmd,dmamode       ; select FDC command reg
    MOVE.W  STPI-STart(A3),D7    ; STEP IN command
    bsr     wrt1772              ; write command
    bsr     fdcwait              ; wait until FDC is ready
    rts
```

;********************* Step out ****************************

stepout:

```
    move.w #srcmd,dmamode     ; select FDC command reg
    MOVE.W STPO-STart(A3),D7  ; STEP OUT command
    bsr wrt1772               ; write command
    bsr fdcwait               ; wait until FDC is ready
    rts

;********************** Force Interrupt  **********************

Force:

    MOVE.W FORC-STart(A3),D7  ; FORCE INTERRUPT command
    bsr wrt1772               ; write command
    move.w #$100,d7           ; delay loop
wtfrc:
    dbra d7,wtfrc
    rts

;********************  READ SECTOR(S)  *************************

readsector:

    move.l 32(a5),d7          ; DMA address to sector buffer
    bsr setdma
    MOVE.W #1,DMA-STart(A3)   ; SET DMA G
    move.w #srcnt,dmamode     ; toggle DMA R/W
    move.w #swcnt,dmamode
    move.w #srcnt,dmamode     ; select DMA sector count
    move.w #$0c,d7            ; load with 12 (corresponds to 6kB)
    bsr wrt1772               ; load DMA scnt

    move.w #srsec,dmamode     ; select sector reg
    move.w 6(a5),d7           ; sector number in d7
    bsr wrt1772               ; write sector number

    move.w #srcmd,dmamode     ; select command reg
    MOVE.W RSEC-STart(A3),D7  ; READ MULTIPLE SECTORS command
    bsr wrt1772               ; write command

    bsr fdcwait               ; wait until FDC is ready
    bsr readstat              ; read status and number of bytes
    rts

;********************  Read Address  **************************

readaddress:

    move.l 40(a5),a4          ; load address of the status buffer
```

```
    move.l 36(a5),d7           ; DMA address to ID field buffer
    bsr setdma
    move.w #srcnt,dmamode      ; toggle DMA R/W
    move.w #swcnt,dmamode
    move.w #srcnt,dmamode      ; select DMA sector count
    move.w #$01,d7             ; load with 1 (corresponds to 512 bytes)
    bsr wrt1772
    move.w #srcmd,dmamode      ; select FDC command reg
    move.w 10(a5),d4           ; #ID fields in D4
    and.w  #$7f,d4             ; but only max. 128
idloop:
    MOVE.W RADR-STart(A3),D7   ; READ ADDRESS command
    bsr wrt1772                ; write command
    bsr fdcwait                ; wait until FDC is ready
    move.b d0,(a4)+            ; save status in buffer
    tst.w 16(a5)               ; timeout ?
    dbne d4,idloop             ; no, read next ID field
    bsr readstat               ; read status and number of bytes
    rts

;*********************  READ TRACK  ***************************

readtrack:

    move.l 28(a5),d7           ; DMA address to track buffer
    bsr setdma
    MOVE.W #1,DMA-STart(A3)    ; SET DMA G
    move.w #srcnt,dmamode      ; toggle DMA R/W
    move.w #swcnt,dmamode
    move.w #srcnt,dmamode      ; select DMA sector count
    move.w #$0e,d7             ; load with 14 (corresponds to 7kB)
    bsr wrt1772
    move.w #srcmd,dmamode      ; select command reg
    MOVE.W RTRK-STart(A3),D7   ; READ TRACK command
    bsr wrt1772                ; write command
    bsr fdcwait                ; wait until FDC is ready
    bsr readstat               ; read status and number of bytes
    rts

;*********************  WRITE SECTOR(S)  **********************

writesector:

    move.l 32(a5),d7           ; DMA address to sector buffer
    bsr setdma
    MOVE.W #1,DMA-STart(A3)    ; SET DMA G
    move.w #swcnt,dmamode      ; toggle DMA R/W
```

```
    move.w #srcnt,dmamode
    move.w #swcnt,dmamode       ; select DMA sector count
    move.w #$0c,d7              ; load with 12 (corresponds to 6kB)
    bsr wrt1772                 ; write DMA scnt
    move.w #swsec,dmamode       ; select sector reg
    move.w 6(a5),d7             ; sector number in d7
    bsr wrt1772                 ; write sector reg

    move.w #swcmd,dmamode       ; select command reg
    MOVE.W WSEC-STart(A3),D7    ; WRITE MULTIPLE SECTORS command
    bsr wrt1772                 ; write command
    bsr fdcwait                 ; wait until FDC is ready
    bsr readstat                ; read status and number of bytes
    rts

;*******************   WRITE TRACK   ***************************

writetrack:

    move.l 28(a5),d7            ; DMA address to track buffer
    bsr setdma
    MOVE.W #1,DMA-STart(A3)     ; SET DMA G
    move.w #swcnt,dmamode       ; toggle DMA R/W
    move.w #srcnt,dmamode
    move.w #swcnt,dmamode       ; select DMA sector count
    move.w #$0e,d7              ; load with 14 (corresponds to 7kB)
    bsr wrt1772                 ; write DMA scnt
    move.w #swcmd,dmamode       ; select command reg
    MOVE.W WTRK-STart(A3),D7    ; WRITE TRACK command
    bsr wrt1772                 ; write command
    bsr fdcwait                 ; wait until FDC is ready
    bsr readstat                ; read status and number of bytes
    rts

;****************************************************************
;****************************************************************

;Those were the routines that access the WD1772 commands
;We now have more subroutines, which are called partially from the
;main routines and partially directly from BASIC (such as setdrive)

;****************  Read sector register   **********************

rsecreg:

    move.w #srsec,dmamode       ; select sector reg
    bsr read1772                ; and read
```

```
         and.w #$ff,d0              ; only lower byte
         move.w d0,6(a5)            ; into FDC array
         move.w #srcmd,dmamode      ; select command reg
         rts

;******************  read track register  *********************

rtrkreg:

         move.w #srtrk,dmamode      ; select track reg
         bsr read1772               ; and read
         and.w #$ff,d0              ; lower byte only
         move.w d0,4(a5)            ; into FDC array
         move.w #srcmd,dmamode      ; Select command reg.
         rts
;*******************  read status reg  ***********************

rstareg:

         move.w #srcmd,dmamode      ; select status reg
         bsr read1772               ; and read
         and.w #$ff,d0              ; status in lower byte
         move.w d0,12(a5)           ; into FDC array
         rts

;******************  write track reg  ********************

wtrkreg:

         move.w #srtrk,dmamode      ; select track reg
         move.w 4(a5),d7            ; get track number
         and.w #$ff,d7
         bsr wrt1772                ; and write
         move.w #srcmd,dmamode      ; select command reg
         rts

;******************  Set DMA transfer address  ****************

setdma:

         move.l d7,20(a5)           ; save start address in FDC array
         move.b d7,dmalow           ; first the low byte
         lsr.l #8,d7
         move.b d7,dmamid           ; then the middle byte
         lsr.l #8,d7
         move.b d7,dmahigh          ; and last the high byte
```

```
        move.l 20(a5),d7        ; get start address back
        clr.l d6
        move.w 8(a5),d6         ; number of bytes to transfer
        add.l d6,d7             ; add the two
        move.l d7,24(a5)        ; =expected end address
        rts

;*** Read DMA status; calculate number of transferred bytes ***

readstat:

        move.w dmamode,d0       ; read DMA status
        and.w #$7,d0            ; take lower 3 bit only
        move.w d0,14(a5)        ; to fdcout

        clr.l d1                ; read DMA end address
        move.b dmahigh,d1
        lsl.l #8,d1
        move.b dmamid,d1
        lsl.l #8,d1
        move.b dmalow,d1

        move.l d1,24(a5)        ; end address into array
        sub.l 20(a5),d1         ; end addr minus start addr
        move.w d1,18(a5)        ; =number of bytes
        rts

;****************       Write FDC register       *******************

wrt1772:

        bsr wait
        move.w d7,dmascnt       ; write FDC reg or DMA sector count reg
        bsr wait
        rts

;****************       Read FDC register        *******************

read1772:

        bsr wait
        move.w dmascnt,d0       ; read FDC reg or DMA sector-count reg
        bsr wait
        rts
```

```
;***************   Wait until FDC is ready   ******************

fdcwait:

   move.l #$180,d5              ; wait until Busy is set
litlwt:
   dbra d5,litlwt

   move.l #$40000,d5            ; d5 as timeout counter
   cmp.w #$9,0(a5)              ; READ-ADDRESS command?
   bne readmfp
   move.l #$28000,d5            ; yes, shorter timeout

readmfp:

   btst #5,mfp                  ; is command done?
   beq fdcready                 ; yes
   subq.l #1,d5                 ; no, decrement timeout counter
   beq timeout                  ; if timedout

   TST.W DMA-STart(A3)          ; COMMAND W/ DATA TRANSFER?
   beq readmfp                  ; no, keep testing

   MOVE.B DMAHIGH,TEMP+1-STart(A3)   ; EXPECTED END DMA ADDRESS
   MOVE.B DMAMID,TEMP+2-STart(A3)    ; REACHED?
   MOVE.B DMALOW,TEMP+3-STart(A3)
   MOVE.L TEMP-STart(A3),D7
   cmp.l 24(a5),d7
   blt readmfp                  ; no, keep testing

   bsr force                    ; if so, then terminate command
   MOVE.W #0,DMA-STart(A3)      ; CLEAR DMAFLAG
   bra fdcready                 ; and end routine normally

timeout:

   move.w dmascnt,d0            ; read status before termination
   and.w #$ff,d0                ; mask out top byte
   move.w d0,12(a5)             ; and into array
   bsr force                    ; terminate command
   move.w #1,16(a5)             ; set timeout flag
   rts

fdcready:

   move.w dmascnt,d0            ; read status
   and.w #$ff,d0                ; mask out top byte
```

```
  move.w d0,12(a5)            ; and into FDC array
  rts

;************ Wait until motor is off *****************

motoroff:

  move.w #srcmd,dmamode       ; select status reg
test:
  bsr read1772                ; and read
  btst #7,d0                  ; Motor on set?
  bne test                    ; yes, keep waiting
  rts

;***********************    Wait    *****************************

wait:
  move.w sr,-(a7)             ; save status
  move.w #$20,d5              ; d5 as counter
wt2:
  dbf d5,wt2
  move.w (a7)+,sr             ; get status back
  rts

;*****************  Select drive and side  ****************

setdrive:

  clr.l d7
  move.w 2(a5),d7             ; get drive number
  bne set
  bsr motoroff                ; if 0, delselect when motor off
  MOVE.W #1,VBLFLAG-STart(A3) ; SET VBL RESET flag
set:
  eor.b #7,d7                 ; invert bits for hardware
  and.b #7,d7                 ; only the lower 4 bits are affected
  move.w sr,-(a7)             ; save status
  or.w #$700,sr               ; turn off interrupts
  move.b #$e,giselect         ; select port A of the sound chip
  move.b giselect,d0          ; read port A
  and.b #$f8,d0               ; clear bits 0-2
  or.b  d0,d7                 ; set new bits
  move.b d7,giwrite           ; write to port A
  move.w (a7)+,sr             ; restore status
  rts
```

```
;***************************************************************
;****************** Variables and tables *********************
;***************************************************************

     align

SAVREG:    ds.L 16,0
savprm:    dc.l 0
savstack:  dc.l 0

vblflag:   dc.w 0
dma:       dc.w 0
temp:      dc.l 0

FUNCTAB:   DC.L RESTORE-STart,SEEK-STart
           DC.L STEP-STart,STEPIN-STart
           DC.L STEPOUT-STart,READSECTOR-START
           dc.l writesector-start,readtrack-start
           dc.l writetrack-start,readaddress-start
           dc.l force-start,setdrive-start
           dc.l rsecreg-start,rtrkreg-start
           dc.l rstareg-start,wtrkreg-start

     align

;*************************** END ****************************

     end
```

Now we come to the listing of the BASIC program `FDCCREAT.BAS`. This program creates the file `FDCINTER.IMG`, which can later be bound into a BASIC program. This works with other versions of BASIC, such as GfA BASIC©, in addition to ST BASIC.

```
10   '***************    FDCCREAT.BAS          A.S.   **************
15   '
20   ?:fullw 2:clearw 2:gotoxy 0,0
25   ? "File >> fdcinter.img << is being created":?:?:?
30   dim c%( 688):cs#=0
35   for i=0 to  688
40   read a$:c%(i)=val("&H"+a$)
45   check#=check#+(c%(i))
50   next i
55   if check#= 2458472.96 then  70
60   ?"Something is wrong with the DATA."
65   goto 80
```

Abacus
Atari ST Disk Drives Inside and Out

```
70   bsave "fdcinter.img",varptr(c%(0)), 1378
75   ? "The program >> fdcinter.img << has been written."
80   ?:?:?:?"Press a key":a=inp(2):end
85   '
90   '********* DATA for fdcinter.img *********
95   '
100  DATA 6042,0001,0011,0031,0051,0071,0090,00B0
101  DATA 00C0,00E0,00F0,00D0,0000,0000,0000,0000
102  DATA 0000,0000,0000,0000,0000,0000,0000,0000
103  DATA 0000,0000,0000,0000,0000,0000,0000,0000
104  DATA 0000,0000,4A6F,0004,6600,0074,47FA,FFB2
105  DATA 48EB,7FFF,04D2,42A7,3F3C,0020,4E41,5C8F
106  DATA 2740,0516,4BEB,0018,33FC,0001,0000,043E
107  DATA 3B7C,0000,0010,377C,0000,051C,377C,0000
108  DATA 051A,302D,0000,0280,0000,000F,E588,49EB
109  DATA 0522,2034,0800,4EB3,0800,4A6B,051A,6700
110  DATA 000A,33FC,0000,0000,043E,202B,0516,2F00
111  DATA 3F3C,0020,4E41,5C8F,4CEB,7FFF,04D2,4E75
112  DATA 33FC,0080,00FF,8606,3E2B,0002,6100,02EA
113  DATA 6100,0306,4E75,33FC,0086,00FF,8606,3E2D
114  DATA 0004,6100,02D4,33FC,0080,00FF,8606,3E2B
115  DATA 0004,6100,02C4,6100,02E0,4E75,33FC,0080
116  DATA 00FF,8606,3E2B,0006,6100,02AE,6100,02CA
117  DATA 4E75,33FC,0080,00FF,8606,3E2B,0008,6100
118  DATA 0298,6100,02B4,4E75,33FC,0080,00FF,8606
119  DATA 3E2B,000A,6100,0282,6100,029E,4E75,3E2B
120  DATA 0016,6100,0274,3E3C,0100,51CF,FFFE,4E75
121  DATA 2E2D,0020,6100,0202,377C,0001,051C,33FC
122  DATA 0090,00FF,8606,33FC,0190,00FF,8606,33FC
123  DATA 0090,00FF,8606,3E3C,000C,6100,023C,33FC
124  DATA 0084,00FF,8606,3E2D,0006,6100,022C,33FC
125  DATA 0080,00FF,8606,3E2B,000C,6100,021C,6100
126  DATA 0238,6100,01E0,4E75,286D,0028,2E2D,0024
127  DATA 6100,01A6,33FC,0090,00FF,8606,33FC,0190
128  DATA 00FF,8606,33FC,0090,00FF,8606,3E3C,0001
129  DATA 6100,01E6,33FC,0080,00FF,8606,382D,000A
130  DATA 0244,007F,3E2B,0010,6100,01CE,6100,01EA
131  DATA 18C0,4A6D,0010,56CC,FFEC,6100,0188,4E75
132  DATA 2E2D,001C,6100,0152,377C,0001,051C,33FC
133  DATA 0090,00FF,8606,33FC,0190,00FF,8606,33FC
134  DATA 0090,00FF,8606,3E3C,000E,6100,018C,33FC
135  DATA 0080,00FF,8606,3E2B,0012,6100,017C,6100
136  DATA 0198,6100,0140,4E75,2E2D,0020,6100,010A
137  DATA 377C,0001,051C,33FC,0190,00FF,8606,33FC
138  DATA 0090,00FF,8606,33FC,0190,00FF,8606,3E3C
139  DATA 000C,6100,0144,33FC,0184,00FF,8606,3E2D
140  DATA 0006,6100,0134,33FC,0180,00FF,8606,3E2B
```

```
141    DATA 000E,6100,0124,6100,0140,6100,00E8,4E75
142    DATA 2E2D,001C,6100,00B2,377C,0001,051C,33FC
143    DATA 0190,00FF,8606,33FC,0090,00FF,8606,33FC
144    DATA 0190,00FF,8606,3E3C,000E,6100,00EC,33FC
145    DATA 0180,00FF,8606,3E2B,0014,6100,00DC,6100
146    DATA 00F8,6100,00A0,4E75,33FC,0084,00FF,8606
147    DATA 6100,00D6,0240,00FF,3B40,0006,33FC,0080
148    DATA 00FF,8606,4E75,33FC,0082,00FF,8606,6100
149    DATA 00B8,0240,00FF,3B40,0004,33FC,0080,00FF
150    DATA 8606,4E75,33FC,0080,00FF,8606,6100,009A
151    DATA 0240,00FF,3B40,000C,4E75,33FC,0082,00FF
152    DATA 8606,3E2D,0004,0247,00FF,6100,006C,33FC
153    DATA 0080,00FF,8606,4E75,2B47,0014,13C7,FFFF
154    DATA 860D,E08F,13C7,FFFF,860B,E08F,13C7,FFFF
155    DATA 8609,2E2D,0014,4286,3C2D,0008,DE86,2B47
156    DATA 0018,4E75,3039,00FF,8606,0240,0007,3B40
157    DATA 000E,4281,1239,FFFF,8609,E189,1239,FFFF
158    DATA 860B,E189,1239,FFFF,860D,2B41,0018,92AD
159    DATA 0014,3B41,0012,4E75,6100,00CA,33C7,00FF
160    DATA 8604,6100,00C0,4E75,6100,00BA,3039,00FF
161    DATA 8604,6100,00B0,4E75,2A3C,0000,0180,51CD
162    DATA FFFE,2A3C,0004,0000,0C6D,0009,0000,6600
163    DATA 0008,2A3C,0002,8000,0839,0005,00FF,FA01
164    DATA 6700,005C,5385,6700,003C,4A6B,051C,6700
165    DATA FFE8,1779,FFFF,8609,051F,1779,FFFF,860B
166    DATA 0520,1779,FFFF,860D,0521,2E2B,051E,BEAD
167    DATA 0018,6D00,FFC4,6100,FD06,377C,0000,051C
168    DATA 6000,001C,3039,00FF,8604,0240,00FF,3B40
169    DATA 000C,6100,FCEA,3B7C,0001,0010,4E75,3039
170    DATA 00FF,8604,0240,00FF,3B40,000C,4E75,33FC
171    DATA 0080,00FF,8606,6100,FF50,0800,0007,6600
172    DATA FFF6,4E75,40E7,3A3C,0020,51CD,FFFE,46DF
173    DATA 4E75,4287,3E2D,0002,6600,000C,6100,FFD0
174    DATA 377C,0001,051A,0A07,0007,0207,0007,40E7
175    DATA 007C,0700,13FC,000E,00FF,8800,1039,00FF
176    DATA 8800,0200,00F8,8E00,13C7,00FF,8802,46DF
177    DATA 4E75,0000,0000,0000,0000,0000,0000,0000
178    DATA 0000,0000,0000,0000,0000,0000,0000,0000
179    DATA 0000,0000,0000,0000,0000,0000,0000,0000
180    DATA 0000,0000,0000,0000,0000,0000,0000,0000
181    DATA 0000,0000,0000,0000,0000,0000,0000,0000
182    DATA 0000,0000,00C0,0000,00D6,0000,00FC,0000
183    DATA 0112,0000,0128,0000,0150,0000,0248,0000
184    DATA 0200,0000,02A0,0000,01A8,0000,013E,0000
185    DATA 0492,0000,02E8,0000,0306,0000,0324,0000
186    DATA 033A
```

Assuming you didn't make any mistakes when entering the listing, the machine language program `FDCINTER.IMG` should be available, which makes it possible to call all of the FDC commands and a bit more.

The comments in the listing in the next section tell how these routines can be accessed from BASIC.

Passing parameters to `FDCINTER.IMG`

Before we look at the demonstration program, we would like to get acquainted with the machine language program first. We will assume that you want to integrate this program into your BASIC programs, perhaps just because of a few individual functions. For such an application it is tedious to look through the various listings to find the information you need.

Let's start with an overview which lists which parameters must be passed to which commands and add some explanations.

Input parameters	Funct. number	Drive number	Track number	Start sector number	Number of bytes to be transferred	Number of ID fields to be read	Starting addr. of track buffer	Starting addr. of sector buffer	Starting addr. of ID field buffer	Starting addr. of ID status buffer
FUNCTION	FDC%(12)	FDC%(13)	FDC%(14)	FDC%(15)	FDC%(16)	FDC%(17)	FDC%(26) FDC%(27)	FDC%(28) FDC%(29)	FDC%(30) FDC%(31)	FDC%(32) FDC%(33)
RESTORE	00		xx							
SEEK	01									
STEP	02									
STEP IN	03									
STEP OUT	04									
READ SECTOR	05			xx (1)	xx (2)			xxxx (4)		
WRITE SECTOR	06			xx (1)	xx (2)			xxxx (4)		
READ TRACK	07				xx (2)		xxxx (4)			
WRITE TRACK	08				xx (2)		xxxx (4)			
READ ADDRESS	09					xx (3)			xxxx (4)	xxxx (4)
FORCE INTERRUPT	10									
SELECT DRIVE	11	xx								
READ SECTOR REG	12									
READ TRACK REG	13									
READ STATUS REG	14									
WRITE TRACK REG	15		xx							

Input parameters

(1) The number of the first record to be written or read is entered in `FDC%(15)`. Note that this specification always refers to the track over

which the read/write head is currently positioned. If you want to work with "logical" sector numbers, these must be converted to absolute track/ sector addresses.

(2) The number of sectors to be written or read is indirectly entered in `FDC%(16)` via the number of bytes to be transferred. At first this appears needlessly complicated, but it has the advantage that formats with varying sector sizes can be correctly written or read.

For example, if 5 Atari format sectors are to be transferred, a value of 5*512 is loaded in `FDC%(16)`. For a format with a sector length of 256 bytes, the same number of sectors would be specified as 5*256. It is also possible to use this "multiple sector access" with formats in which varying sector lengths occur in a track. If for some "copy protection format" four successive sectors are to be read whose sector lengths are 1024, 512, 256, and 128 bytes (doesn't matter which order), it is sufficient to pass 1024+512+256+128 in `FDC%(16)`. It is also possible, for instance, to read or write just half a sector. Just enter the appropriate number of bytes.

The same applies to the READ TRACK and WRITE TRACK commands. If an entire track is to be processed by the call, pass a value greater than 6300. With a lower value you can cause just part of a track to formatted, for example. Through multiple formatting you can create properties in the track which would thoroughly confound the most dedicated software cracker.

Very important: If data are written (WRITE SECTOR, WRITE TRACK), 32 ($20) must be added to the number of bytes to be transferred. The DMA controller loads 32 bytes into its internal registers in order to be ready for the data transfer. This means, for example, that the data for two sectors (2*512 bytes= $400) won't be completely transferred until DMA end address is incremented to $420 more than the start address.

(3) The number of ID fields to be read is limited to 128. This is generally enough to read all of the ID fields for even the strangest formats. The number - 1 is always placed in `FDC%(17)`. At least 3 fields must be read before the DMA controller will transfer the data to the buffer. In order to put all of the ID information into memory, the value (#ID fields*6) must be divisible by 16 (see also: FDC command description: READ ADDRESS).

(4) The start addresses of the buffers do not have to be given for each call. Generally this is done just once, as in our demo program. If the information for several tracks is to be stored at one time, simply dimension more arrays, the start addresses of which are passed before the call. Since addresses are always long words, this can be done simply with POKE. Let's say we have a second sector buffer:

```
dim sec2%(3200):def seg=0:poke fdc#+56,varptr(sec2%(0))
```

Parameters returned from FDCINTER.IMG

Naturally we get a number of parameters back from the machine language program. These are listed in the following table:

Output parameters	Track number	Sector number	FDC-STATUS	DMA-STATUS	Timeout	DMA starting address	DMA ending address	Number of bytes to be transferred
FUNCTION	FDC%(14)	FDC%(15)	FDC%(18)	FDC%(19)	FDC%(20)	FDC%(22) FDC%(23)	FDC%(24) FDC%(25)	FDC%(21)
RESTORE			xx		xx			
SEEK			xx		xx			
STEP			xx		xx			
STEP IN			xx		xx			
STEP OUT			xx		xx			
READ SECTOR			xx	xx	xx	xxxx	xxxx	xx
WRITE SECTOR			xx	xx	xx	xxxx	xxxx	xx
READ TRACK			xx	xx	xx	xxxx	xxxx	xx
WRITE TRACK			xx	xx	xx	xxxx	xxxx	xx
READ ADDRESS			xx	xx	xx	xxxx	xxxx	xx
FORCE INTERRUPT								
SELECT DRIVE								
READ SECTOR REG.		xx						
READ TRACK REG.	xx							
READ STATUS REG.			xx					
WRITE TRACK REG.								

Output parameters

In this overview you'll find the two array elements FDC%(14) and FDC%(15) again. These are the only parameters which are passed in both directions. Otherwise input and output parameters are strictly separated. This means that except for the READ SECTOR register and READ TRACK register, the input parameters are in no way changed by the machine language program.

We recommend that you see the section on status interpretation (section 4.2.2.4) for information on the FDC status [FDC%(18)]. Naturally, the general description of the FDC commands also helps.

The DMA status [FDC%(19)] is easy to explain. Only 3 bits are of interest to us. Bit 0 is set if no errors occurred in the DMA transfer. Bit 1 is set if the contents of the sector-count register in the DMA controller did not count down to zero. This register tells the DMAC the maximum number of data which may be transferred at the start address. You don't have to worry about this, though, because the machine language routine takes care of it. Bit 2 is a "copy" of the DRQ output of the FDC. After a command with a data transfer, bits 0 and 1 will be set if there were no errors. Therefore, FDC%(19) contains a 3. If this is not the case, the LOST DATA bit will also be set in the FDC status.

The DMA start address contains the current buffer address. After a READ SECTOR command the sector buffer's start address can be found here.

The DMA end address mirrors the buffer pointer of the DMA controller. This address minus the start address is output as the number of bytes transferred in FDC%(21). Special attention should be paid to the interpretation of these specifications. In the read direction, the pointer will be incremented by 16 ($10) after receiving this many data bytes, and the bytes which were stored temporarily in the DMA controller will be transferred to the buffer at this time. In the write direction, 32 ($20) bytes will be fetched into this internal storage and the buffer pointer will incremented by this value.

A timeout (FDC%(20)=1) should occur only rarely because the delay time of the machine language routine is measured generously and the FDC will have terminated the command on its own in the meantime—in case of an error. Since the FDC doesn't do this until after about 1.5 seconds, the delay time for the READ ADDRESS command is shorter. The reason for this is the following: You want to read 100 ID fields (we'll ignore the potential sensibility of that for the moment), and so you pass the value 99 in FDC%(17) before calling the READ ADDRESS command. The machine language program executes the READ ADDRESS command 100 times before it returns to BASIC. If the FDC didn't find any ID fields (and didn't find any 100 times), you would have to wait over 2 minutes for it to return. Something like this leads to turning the computer off, and we'd rather not provoke that. If the FDC can't read an ID field in the alloted time, the command will be terminated with FORCE INTERRUPT and the machine language program will return to BASIC.

The command words for the FDC

Another feature which makes our FDC interface universal has only been mentioned in passing so far. It involves the command words which are passed to the FDC. It would be too bad if we couldn't adapt to our own needs. We have provided this flexibility in our interface. This table shows where the command words are stored and to what values they are initialized.

Command word for	is found in	is initialized with
RESTORE	FDC%(1)	$01
SEEK	FDC%(2)	$11
STEP	FDC%(3)	$31
STEP IN	FDC%(4)	$51
STEP OUT	FDC%(5)	$71
READ SECTOR	FDC%(6)	$90
WRITE SECTOR	FDC%(7)	$B0
READ ADDRESS	FDC%(8)	$C0
READ TRACK	FDC%(9)	$E0
WRITE TRACK	FDC%(10)	$F0
FORCE INTERRUPT	FDC%(11)	$D0

The exact meaning of the option bits in the command words can be found in the FDC command descriptions elsewhere in this book. Note that the m-bit (for multi-sector read/write) is set for READ SECTOR and WRITE SECTOR. If you clear this bit, only one sector will be processed at a time.

8.3.2 Demo 1—All FDC commands

After so much information about a comparatively small machine language routine, it's finally time to see if it really does what we claim. As we mentioned in the previous section, this listing consists of two parts, whereby the first part is intended just to show how simple it is to include these routines in your own programs. Let's turn to the second part.

This section of the listing is a program which is designed to show how the parameters are passed to the machine language routine before the function is called. In addition, it has a real "demo character" because it allows direct access to all of the FDC commands and also displays all of the information returned, from the status to the data. It will let you experiment with the floppy disk controller to your heart's content.

The program consists mainly of an "info screen," which is divided into two parts:

1. Twenty functions are listed in the top part, of which the first sixteen (0-15) are those which our FDC interface can perform.

   Before an FDC command (functions 0-10) is called, a drive must first be selected. This is done via function 11. The values passed is as follows:

   >   2 => drive A, side 0
   >   3 => drive A, side 1
   >   4 => drive B, side 0
   >   5 => drive B, side 1
   >   or 0 => deselect

   The drives are automatically deselected when you exit the program with function 19 (end).

   Since data is transferred by some of the functions, it would be too bad if we couldn't look at it. This is the purpose of menu options 16-18. Bear in mind that you must read a track into memory before a sector can be read.

   NOTE: If you get the chance, modify this demo program to permit the buffer data to be changed. This would give you a complete disk monitor, with features that you probably won't find anywhere else.

2. The lower section of the screen contains the various parameters which will be passed to the subroutine or which are passed back by the subroutine. The start addresses of all of the buffers are also listed.

   At first glance this mass of information looks rather confusing and may make calling the machine language program seem more complicated than it really is. If you use the table of input and output parameters and look at just the parameters which are relevant for a given call, you will see that at most only two parameters beside the function number have to be passed (excluding the start addresses of the buffers). For half of the functions, the function number is the only thing that has to be passed.

The program prompts you for the parameters which are required by the individual functions, and displays the previous values. If you want to use the previous value of a given parameter, just press <Return> when asked to enter a new value.

Before we give you the program, let's go step by step through a call using `FDCINTER.BAS`. This sample will show you the contents of the disk directory in drive A.

a. Run `FDCINTER.BAS`.
b. Type <11><Return> to Select Drive.
c. Type <2><Return> to select drive A, side 0.
d. Select Seek function by typing <1><Return>.
e. Press <1><Return> to select track number 1.
f. Type <5><Return> to Read sector.
g. Type <3><Return> for starting sector of 3.
h. For the amount of bytes to be read, input <512><Return> (input here must be in decimal—hexadecimal numbers will be ignored).
i. Select <17><Return> to display the sector buffer.
j. The buffer will be displayed on the screen.

```
1000 '****************************************************************
1010 '*****    FDC interface for BASIC   (part 1)      A.S. (7/86) *****
1020 '****************************************************************
1030 If peek(systab)=1 then res=2 else res=1
1040 'There is little preparation necessary in order to use the FDC
1050 'routines. We need some memory for the routine itself and for the
1060 'data which are necessary for the disk operations. We dimension a
1070 'couple of integer arrays and get their start addresses for this.
1100 '
1110 dim fdc%(700)  :fdc# =varptr(fdc%(0))
1120 dim trk%(3200) :trk# =varptr(trk%(0))
1130 dim sec%(2600) :sec# =varptr(sec%(0))
1140 dim adr%(768)  :adr# =varptr(adr%(0))
1150 dim stat%(64)  :stat#=varptr(stat%(0))
1160 '
1170 'The disk routines will be loaded into the fdc% array
1180 '
1190 bload "a:fdcinter.img",fdc#
1200 '
1210 ' and the start addresses of the other arrays POKEd in.
1220 '
1230 def seg = 0 :' we POKE long words
1240 '
1250 poke fdc#+52,trk# :'  track buffer
1260 poke fdc#+56,sec# :'  sector buffer
1270 poke fdc#+60,adr# :'  ID field buffer
```

```
1280 poke fdc#+64,stat#:'   ID status buffer
1290 '
1300 'That was it!  The next section explains how the individual
1310 'functions are called.
1320 '
1330 '****************************************************************
1340 '*********************   PART 2   *******************************
1350 '****************************************************************
1360 '
1370 'This is just a small demo, but we still don't want to make it too
1380 'spartan. Let's start with a small menu which displays the
1390 'individual function numbers and their parameters. The functions
1400 '0-15 are those which are processed by machine language routines,
1410 'while 16-18 serve only for viewing the buffer. These functions
1420 'can naturally be made easier to use. Function 19 ends
1430 'this demo and deselects the drives.
1440 '
1450 '
1460 '
1470 fullw 2 : width 255
1480 Menu:
1490 ? : clearw 2 : gotoxy 0,0
1500 '
1510 ?" ----------------------  Available functions  --------------";
1520 ?"----------"
1530 ?" 0 => Restore          1 => Seek               2 => Step   "
1540 ?" 3 => Step in          4 => Step out           5 => Read s";
1550 ?"ector"
1560 ?" 6 => Write sector     7 => Read track         8 => Write ";
1570 ?"track"
1580 ?" 9 => Read address    10=> Force interrupt    11=> Select";
1590 ?" Drive"
1600 ?" 12=> Read sector reg. 13=> Read track reg.    14=> Read s";
1610 ?"tatus reg."
1620 ?" 15=> Write track reg. 16=> Disp track buffer  17=> Disp s";
1630 ?"ector buffer"
1640 ?" 18=> Display ID field 19=> End program"
1650 '
1660 ?" ----------------------  Display all parameters  ----------";
1670 ?"----------"
1680 '
1690 ?" Function:            FDC status  :$       Track buffer    :$"
1700 ?" Drive   :            DMA status  :$       Sector buffer   :$"
1710 ?" Track   :            Timeout     :$       ID field buffer:$"
1720 ?" Sector  :            DMA start   :$       ID field status:$"
1730 ?" #Bytes  :$           DMA end     :$"
1740 ?" #Id's -1:            #DMA bytes  :$"
```

```
1770 '
1780 main:
1790 '=================================================================
1800 gotoxy 12/res,9  :?right$("       "+str$(fdc%(12)),4)
1810 gotoxy 12/res,10 :?right$("       "+str$(fdc%(13)),4)
1820 gotoxy 12/res,11 :?right$("       "+str$(fdc%(14)),4)
1830 gotoxy 12/res,12 :?right$("       "+str$(fdc%(15)),4)
1840 gotoxy 12/res,13 :?right$("       "+hex$(fdc%(16)),4)
1850 gotoxy 12/res,14 :?right$("       "+str$(fdc%(17)),4)
1860 gotoxy 32/res,09 :?right$("         "+hex$(fdc%(18)),6)
1870 gotoxy 32/res,10 :?right$("         "+hex$(fdc%(19)),6)
1880 gotoxy 32/res,11 :?right$("         "+hex$(fdc%(20)),6)
1890 gotoxy 32/res,12 :?right$("         "+hex$(fdc%(22))+hex$(fdc%(23)),6)
1900 gotoxy 32/res,13 :?right$("         "+hex$(fdc%(24))+hex$(fdc%(25)),6)
1910 gotoxy 32/res,14 :?right$("         "+hex$(fdc%(21)),6)
1920 gotoxy 60/res,09 :?right$("         "+hex$(fdc%(26))+hex$(fdc%(27)),6)
1930 gotoxy 60/res,10 :?right$("         "+hex$(fdc%(28))+hex$(fdc%(29)),6)
1940 gotoxy 60/res,11 :?right$("         "+hex$(fdc%(30))+hex$(fdc%(31)),6)
1950 gotoxy 60/res,12 :?right$("         "+hex$(fdc%(32))+hex$(fdc%(33)),6)
1960 '
1970 gotoxy 0,15:?spc(150);
1975   gotoxy 0,17:?spc(30 );
1980 key:
1990 gotoxy 1,15:?spc(50)
2000 gotoxy 1,15:input " Which function";func$:func=val(func$)
2010 if func<0 or func>19 then menu
2020 func=func+1
2030 if func=20 then fdc%(12)=11:fdc%(13)=0:call fdc#:end
2040 '
2050 if func<17 then 2110
2060 reset
2070 func=func-16:clearw 2:
2080 on func gosub dumptrk,dumpsec,dumpid
2090 openw 2:goto key
2100 '
2110 on func gosub a,b,c,d,e,f,g,h,i,j,k,l,m,n,o,p
2120 gotoxy 1,17:?"Execute function (y/n) ?";
2130 if chr$(inp(2))<>"y" then main
2140 call fdc#
2150 goto main
2160 '
2170 '****************************************************************
2180 '****************************************************************
2190 '
2200 'Here are 16 functions which are supported by the machine language
2210 'routine. Here you see what parameters must be set for the call
2220 '"call fdc#". In many cases it is sufficient to pass the function
```

```
2230 'number in fdc%(12).
2240 '
2250 '
2260 '=================    RESTORE    =================
2270 a:
2280 fdc%(12)=0
2290 gotoxy 1,15:?"RESTORE - no parameters required";:return:
2300 '
2310 '=================    SEEK       =================
2320 b:
2330 fdc%(12)=1
2340 gotoxy 1,15:?"SEEK - Which track number (old=>";
2350 ?fdc%(14);")";:input v$:if len(v$)=0 then return
2360 fdc%(14)=val(v$):return
2370 '
2380 '=================    STEP       =================
2390 c:
2400 fdc%(12)=2
2410 gotoxy 1,15:?"STEP - no parameters required";:return
2420 '
2430 '=================    STEP IN    =================
2440 d:
2450 fdc%(12)=3
2460 gotoxy 1,15:?"STEP IN - no parameters required";:return
2470 '
2480 '=================    STEP OUT   =================
2490 e:
2500 fdc%(12)=4
2510 gotoxy 1,15:?"STEP OUT - no parameters required";:return
2520 '
2530 '================= READ SECTOR(s) =================
2540 f:
2550 fdc%(12)=5
2560 gotoxy 1,15:?"READ SECTOR-Start sector (old=>";
2570 ?fdc%(15);")";:input v$:if len(v$)=0 then 2590
2580 fdc%(15)=val(v$)
2590 gotoxy 1,16:?"Number of bytes (old=>$";hex$(fdc%(16));")";
2600 input v$:if len(v$)=0 then return
2610 fdc%(16)=val(v$):return
2620 '
2630 '================= WRITE SECTOR(s) =================
2640 g:
2650 fdc%(12)=6
2660 gotoxy 1,15:?"WRITE SECTOR-Start sector (old=";
2670 ?">";fdc%(15);")";:input v$:if len(v$)=0 then 2690
2680 fdc%(15)=val(v$)
2690 gotoxy 1,16:?"Number of bytes (old=>$";hex$(fdc%(16));")";
```

```
2700 input v$:if len(v$)=0 then return
2710 fdc%(16)=val(v$):return
2720 '
2730 '==================    READ TRACK       =============================
2740 h:
2750 fdc%(12)=7
2760 gotoxy 1,15:?"READ TRACK - Number of bytes (old=>$";
2770 ?hex$(fdc%(16));")";:input v$:if len(v$)=0 then return
2780 fdc%(16)=val(v$):return
2790 '
2800 '==================    WRITE TRACK      =============================
2810 i:
2820 fdc%(12)=8
2830 gotoxy 1,15:?"WRITE TRACK - Number of bytes (old=>$";
2840 ?hex$(fdc%(16));")";:input v$:if len(v$)=0 then return
2850 fdc%(16)=val(v$):return
2860 '
2870 '==================    READ ADDRESS     =============================
2880 j:
2890 fdc%(12)=9
2900 gotoxy 1,15:?"READ ADDRESS - Number of ID fields-1 (old=>";
2910 ?fdc%(17);")";:input v$:if len(v$)=0 then return
2920 fdc%(17)=val(v$):return
2930 '
2940 '==================    FORCE INTERRUPT  =============================
2950 k:
2960 fdc%(12)=10
2970 gotoxy 1,15:?"FORCE INTERRUPT - no parameters required";:return
2980 '
2990 '===================    Select drive     ===========================
3000 l:
3010 fdc%(12)=11:gotoxy 1,15
3020 ?"(X=drv/side): 2=A/0; 3=A/1; 4=B/0; 5=B/1; 0=deselect"
3030 gotoxy 1,16:?"Drive (old=>";fdc%(13);")";
3040 input v$:if len(v$)=0 then return
3050 fdc%(13)=val(v$):return
3060 '
3070 '===============    Read sector register  ======================
3080 m:
3090 fdc%(12)=12
3100 gotoxy 1,15:?"READ SECTOR REGISTER - no parameters required";
3110 return
3120 '
3130 '===============    Read track register   ======================
3140 n:
3150 fdc%(12)=13
3160 gotoxy 1,15:?"READ TRACK REGISTER - no parameters required";
```

```
3170 return
3180 '
3190 '================   Read status register   =======================
3200 o:
3210 fdc%(12)=14
3220 gotoxy 1,15:?"READ STATUS REGISTER - no parameters required";
3230 return
3240 '
3250 '==================   Write track register   ====================
3260 p:
3270 fdc%(12)=15
3280 gotoxy 1,15:?"WRITE TRACK REGISTER - Track number (old=>";
3290 ?fdc%(14);")";:input v$:if len(v$)=0 then return
3300 fdc%(14)=val(v$):return
3310 '
3320 '*****************************************************************
3330 '*****************************************************************
3340 '
3350 'The following functions (16-18) have nothing to do with the
3360 'machine language routine, and just display the buffer contents.
3370 '
3380 '==================   Display track buffer   =======================
3390 dumptrk:
3400 gotoxy 0,0:?"DISPLAY TRACK BUFFER (all values=>hex, (c)ontinue, ";
3410 ?"(e)nd":?
3420 ?" BUFFER   00 01 02 03 04 05 06 07 08 09 0A 0B 0C 0D 0E 0F   01234";
3430 ?"56789ABCDEF"
3440 ?" ------------------------------------------------------   -----";
3450 ?"-----------"
3460 ch$="                "
3470 '
3480 lcnt=0
3490 for id = 1 to (fdc%(16)+1)-16 step 16
3500 lcnt=lcnt+1
3510 id%(1)=id-1:?" +";right$("0000"+hex$(id%(1)),4);"    ";
3520 for by=0 to 15:def seg =id+by:id%(1)=peek(trk#-1)
3530 ?right$("00"+hex$(id%(1)),2);" ";
3540 if id%(1)=7 or id%(1)=10 or id%(1)=13 then id%(1)=20
3550 mid$(ch$,by+1,1)=chr$(id%(1)):next by:?" ";ch$
3560 '
3570 if lcnt<10 then 3610
3580 lcnt=0:dum=inp(2)
3590 if chr$(dum)="e" then id=70000:goto 3610
3600 if chr$(dum)<>"c" then 3580
3610 next id
3620 ?"Done! Pres a key...";
3630 dum=inp(2):return
```

```
3640 '
3650 '================= Display sector buffer ========================
3660 dumpsec:
3670 lcnt=0
3680 gotoxy 0,0:?"DISPLAY SECTOR BUFFER (all values=>hex, (c)ontinue,";
3690 ?" (e)nd)":?
3700 ?" BUFFER   00 01 02 03 04 05 06 07 08 09 0A 0B 0C 0D 0E 0F   01234";
3710 ?"56789ABCDEF"
3720 ?" ---------------------------------------------------------  -----";
3730 ?"-----------"
3740 '
3750 ch$="                "
3760 for id = 1 to (fdc%(16)+1)-16 step 16
3770 lcnt=lcnt+1
3780 id%(1)=id-1:?" +";right$("0000"+hex$(id%(1)),4);"   ";
3790 for by=0 to 15:def seg =id+by:id%(1)=peek(sec#-1)
3800 ?right$("00"+hex$(id%(1)),2);" ";
3810 if id%(1)=7 or id%(1)=10 or id%(1)=13 then id%(1)=20
3820 mid$(ch$,by+1,1)=chr$(id%(1)):next by:?" ";ch$
3830 '
3840 if lcnt<10 then 3880
3850 lcnt=0:dum=inp(2)
3860 if chr$(dum)="e" then id=70000:goto 3880
3870 if chr$(dum)<>"c" then 3850
3880 next id
3890 ?"Done! Press a key...";
3900 dum=inp(2):return
3910 '
3920 '================== Display ID fields   ========================
3930 dumpid:
3940 gotoxy 0,0:?"DISPLAY ID FIELDS (all values=>hex,(c)ontinue,(e)nd)"
3950 ?:?" BUFFER   TRACK  SIDE  SECTOR  LENGTH CRC1    CRC2  FDC status"
3960 ?" ----------------------------------------------------------"
3970 '
3980 lcnt=0
3990 for id = 1 to (fdc%(17)+1)*6   step 6
4000 lcnt=lcnt+1
4010 id%(1)=id-1:?"  +";right$("00"+hex$(id%(1)),2);"      ";
4020 for by=0 to 5:def seg =id+by:id%(1)=peek(adr#-1)
4030 ?right$("00"+hex$(id%(1)),2);"     ";:next by
4040 def seg=id/6+1:id%(1)=peek(stat#-1)
4050 ?"   ";right$("00"+hex$(id%(1)),2)
4060 '
4070 if lcnt<9 then 4110
4080 lcnt=0:dum=inp(2)
4090 if chr$(dum)="e" then id=1000:goto 4110
4100 if chr$(dum)<>"c" then 4080
```

```
4110 next id
4120 ?"Done! Press a key...";
4130 dum=inp(2):return
4140 '
4150 '========================= END ====================================
```

8.3.3 Demo 2—Copying disks

The following BASIC program shows you another use of our FDC machine language routines, and demonstrates how easily the floppy controller can be accessed from BASIC. The result is a copy program which can duplicate a double-sided disk in about 85 seconds!

It really isn't much work to write a program like this. The big limitation of the program is that it only works with two drives. This is because we didn't want to confuse the issue by using too many buffers. In ST BASIC the maximum array size is 32K.

This prevents us from doing something like `dim sec%(79,2303)` which would reserve enough room for half of a double-sided disk. We could reserve space with `dim sec1%(2303), sec2%(2303)`, etc., but we don't really want to. This is, after all, just a demo, and we don't want to deprive you of the fun of improving on our ideas.

We will read the information from two tracks at a time (front and back sides) and then write this at the equivalent tracks on the destination disk. If you were using just one drive, this would require 80 disk swaps, something few of us would ever care to try.

The Desktop takes about 195 seconds to copy a double-sided disk. This is about 50% more time than our program requires for the same task (130 seconds).

This percentage is astonishingly low if we take into account the fact that the current track is constantly displayed. Also, there is an "overhead" encountered each time the FDC subroutine is called (such as switching in and out of supervisor mode). Finally, the constantly changing selection status of the drives also takes some time. Despite these circumstances, 130 seconds is quite acceptable.

A real "tune up" is easy to do if we remove the `PRINT` commands from the copy loop (lines 60, 66, 76, and 102) which are extremely slow in comparison to the copy time. In this case, we gain 45 seconds at the cost of our track display. Put another way: the copy time is cut to just 85 seconds!

In this program we encounter a case which makes it necessary to change the command word, or at least write to the track register. Let's trace through the program starting with track 0. In connection with reading this track (front and back), a STEP IN is executed for drive A. The read/write head is then located over track 1 and the track register of the FDC also contains a 1.

Now we have to write the information we just read to track 0 of drive B. If we don't intervene here, things will go wrong:

> The FDC will terminate the WRITE SECTOR command with `Record not found` because the track register contains 1, but the ID fields contain 0 for the track number.

We can fix this in one of two ways:

1. In the STEP IN command for drive A we can clear the u-bit in the command word, which will prevent the track register from being updated.

2. After the STEP IN command for drive A, we can change the track register back to the previous value. In our program this could look like this:

   ```
   fdc%(12)=15 : fdc%(14)=track : call fdc#
   ```

We chose the first option. The command word for each STEP IN command must be changed, because we do want the drive B STEP IN command to update the track register. The track register only has to be loaded once for each track, but it would require an extra `call fdc#`. Even when it is executed twice, it is still faster to solve the problem by changing the command word.

One last comment regarding the number of bytes to be transferred: In the read direction, the desired number is always given. For nine sectors in a track (512 bytes/sector), this is 9 * $200 = $1200. This is completely logical. Things are different in the write direction, however. The number here is 9 * $200 + $20.

```
1 '* Copy program for two drives and double-sided disks    A.S. *
2 '
3 'We need 3 arrays, for the machine langauge program and as
4 'sector buffers for track 0 and track 1
5 '
6 dim fdc%(700),sec0%(2400),sec1%(2400):def seg=0
7 '
8 'Load the machine language program
9 '
10 fdc#=varptr(fdc%(0)):bload "a:fdcinter.b",fdc#
11 '
12 'Get the start address of the two buffers
13 '
14 sec0#=varptr(sec0%(0)):sec1#=varptr(sec1%(0))
15 'The number of bytes to transfer (read-$1200,write-$1220)
16 '
17 'and the command words for STEP-IN (with and without Update)
18 '
19 numread=&H1200:numwrite=&H1220:stpi=&H49:stpiu=&H59
20 '
21 'We start in track 1 with Sector-1 and POKE longwords
22 '
23 fdc%(15)=1:def seg=0
24 '
25 copy:
26 ?:fullw 2:clearw 2:gotoxy 0,1
27 ?"  Copy program for double-sided disks and 2 drives"
28 ?:?:?:?"  Insert source disk in drive A"
29 ?:?"  and destination disk in drive B."
30 ?:?:?:?"  c => copy  :  any other key => end program"
31 if chr$(inp(2))<>"c" then end
32 '
33 init:
34 clearw 2:gotoxy 0,2
35 '
36 '--------restore drive B and test write protect --------
37 '
38 fdc%(12)=11:fdc%(13)=4:call fdc#
39 fdc%(12)=0:call fdc#
40 if fdc%(18) < &HA7 then goto kopi
41 '
42 ?" Diskette in drive B is write-protected! Please remove";
43 ?" write protection.":?
44 ?" c => continue ; any other key => restart"
45 fdc%(12)=11:fdc%(13)=0:call fdc#
46 if chr$(inp(2))="c" then init
47 goto copy
```

```
48  '
49  kopi:
50  '---------------- Drive A Restore ------------------
51  fdc%(12)=11:fdc%(13)=2:call fdc#
52  fdc%(12)=0:call fdc#
53  '
54  '------Copy track 0 through track 79 ----------
55  '
56  for track = 0 to 79 : fdc%(16)=numread
57  '
58  '--------- Read side A/0 and display status ---------
59  fdc%(12)=5:poke fdc#+56,sec0#:call fdc#
60  gotoxy 10,2:?"Track";track;"Reading side 0          "
61  gosub checkstat
62  '
63  '------ Read side A/1 and display status ------
64  fdc%(12)=11:fdc%(13)=3:call fdc#
65  fdc%(12)=5:poke fdc#+56,sec1#:call fdc#
66  gotoxy 10,2:?"Track";track;"Reading side 1          "
67  gosub checkstat
68  '
69  '---------- Drive A step-in without 'Update' ---------------
70  fdc%(12)=3:fdc%(4)=stpi:call fdc#
71  '
72  '----------- Write side B/0 and display status ----------
73  fdc%(16)=numwrite
74  fdc%(12)=11:fdc%(13)=4:call fdc#
75  fdc%(12)=6:poke fdc#+56,sec0#:call fdc#
76  gotoxy 10,4:?"track";track;"Write side 0  "
77  gosub checkstat
78  '
79  '---------- Write side B/1 and display status ----------
80  fdc%(12)=11:fdc%(13)=5:call fdc#
81  fdc%(12)=6:poke fdc#+56,sec1#:call fdc#
82  gotoxy 10,4:?"Track";track;"Writing side 1          "
83  gosub checkstat
84  '
85  '-------------- Drive B step-in with pdate ---------------
86  fdc%(12)=3:fdc%(4)=stpiu:call fdc#
87  '
88  '----------- and select A/0 again ------------
89  fdc%(12)=11:fdc%(13)=2:call fdc#
90  '
91  next track
92  '
93  fdc%(12)=11:fdc%(13)=0:call fdc#
94  ?:?:?"Done !    ......(r)estart or (e)nd ?"
```

```
95  if chr$(inp(2))<>"r" then end
96  goto copy
97  '----------------------------------------------------------------
98  checkstat:
99  if fdc%(18)=&H80 and fdc%(19)=3 and fdc%(20)=0 then return
100 gotoxy 0,7:?" FDC STATUS  :$";hex$(fdc%(18))
101 ?" DMA STATUS  :$";hex$(fdc%(19))
102 ?" #DMA BYTES  :$";hex$(fdc%(21))
103 ?" TIMEOUT     :$";hex$(fdc%(20)):?
104 '
105 ?" Copy terminated because of an error."
106 ?:?" Press a key..."
107 fdc%(12)=11:fdc%(13)=0:call fdc#
108 key=inp(2):goto copy
```

8.3.4 Demo 3—Creating standard and foreign formats

The following program, designed to create various formats on disks, illustrates another use of the FDC machine language routines.

The program has two uses. The first shows how a track buffer (which is written to the disk by means of WRITE TRACK and represents the "format") is prepared, and the second formats disks so that they can be read and written by other computer systems (assuming that their drives are also controlled by a WD1772 or a compatible device). The reverse is also possible. A format may not satisfy the requirements of the FDC, which will refuse to transfer sectors in this format. The following warning should be kept in mind:

> **IMPORTANT!** Creating a format is a task which requires precise knowledge of the WRITE TRACK command. Parameters are to be changed only with the greatest of care. A number of things work, but not everything. In short: Read carefully the description of the FDC commands. There you will find information on what changes can be made to the individual components in the track.

This program offers the following features:

1)   A track buffer, influenced by a number of parameters, can be prepared. To give you an overview of the values that are normally

used, the parameters default to the values of the Atari format. The parameters can be reset to these values at any time.

The buffer is large enough to hold all of the parameters entered in addition to the track format. Naturally, the prepared buffer cannot be complete. There are some values which differ from track to track or from side to side. For example, the track number is inserted as the track specification in the ID field. Such information must constantly be updated while a disk is being formatted. The necessary address in the ID fields are placed in the track buffer.

2) A formatted buffer can be saved as a file on the disk so that you don't have to re-enter a set of values every time you want to format a disk in a special format. You can use this feature to create your own "format library" with standard and copy-protected formats.

3) A format file that has been saved to disk can be loaded back into the buffer later.

4) Naturally, it is also possible to format a disk. This formatting routine takes care of updating the track number in the ID fields. You can specify an offset which will be added to the track number. Generally, this is useful only for copy protection.

```
10   '****************************************************************
12   '*****   Extended disk formatting             A.S. (7/86)   *****
14   '****************************************************************
16   dim fdc%(700) :fdc# =varptr(fdc%(0))
18   dim trk%(3200):trk# =varptr(trk%(0))
20   bload "a:fdcinter.b",fdc#
22   def seg=0:poke fdc#+52,trk#
24   '****************************************************************
26   gosub default:'Read standard values for ATARI-FORMAT
28   menu:
30   ?:fullw 2: clearw 2:gotoxy 0,0:width 80
32   '
34   ?" a) GAP1 change                              |"
36   ?" b) GAP2 change                              |"
38   ?" c) GAP3 (Part 1) change                     |"
40   ?" d) GAP3 (Part 2) change                     |"
42   ?" e) GAP4 change                              |"
44   ?" f) DATA-FIELD change                        |"
46   ?" g) SYNC-Bytes (for the ID-field) change     |"
48   ?" h) SYNC-Bytes (for the Data-field) change   |"
50   ?" i) DATA-ADDRESS-MARK change                 |"
```

```
52   ?" j) START-SECTOR change                    |"
54   ?" k) SECTOR-LENGTH (in ID-field) change     |"
56   ?" l) RECORD-NUMBER change                   |"
58   ?" m) GAP5 change                            |"
60     '?" ======================================================";
62     '?"========================="
64   ?" n) Prepare track-buffer                   ";
66   ?" q) Set values to ATARI-FORMAT "
68   ?" o) Load track-buffer from disk            ";
70   ?" r) Format diskette"
72   ?" p) Save track-buffer as file              ";
74   ?" s) End"
76     '
78     for prm=0 to 15 Step 2
80     gotoxy 40,prm/2:?"Number:";trk%(3150+prm);"    "
82     gotoxy 55,prm/2:?"Value:$ ";hex$(trk%(3151+prm));"    ":next prm
84     for prm=16 to 20
86     gotoxy 55,prm-8:?"Value:$ ";hex$(trk%(3150+prm));"    ":next prm
88     '
90     keypress:
92     gotoxy 0,16:?spc(60):gotoxy 0,16:?" Which function?";
94     key=inp(2):if chr$(key)<"a" or chr$(key)>"s" then 94
96     choose=key+1-asc("a")
98     if choose=19 then end
100    if choose<9 then goto twovalues
102    if choose<14 then goto onevalue
104    choose=choose-13:
106    on choose gosub prepare,loadit,saveit,default,formatit
108    goto menu
110    '
112    '=============== Input number and value =====================
114    twovalues:
116    gotoxy 0,16:?spc(60):gotoxy 0,16
118 ?" >> ";chr$(key);" << Enter new value: ";:input amt$
120    if len(amt$)=0 then goto two
122    trk%(3148+choose*2)=val(amt$):gotoxy 21,choose-1:?"Number:";
124    ?trk%(3148+choose*2);"     "
126    two:
128    gotoxy 0,16:?spc(60):gotoxy 0,16
130 ?" >> ";chr$(key);" << Enter new value: ";:input w$
132    if len(w$)=0 then goto keypress
134    trk%(3149+choose*2)=val(w$):gotoxy 30,choose-1:?"Value;$";
136    ?hex$(trk%(3149+choose*2));"    ":goto keypress
138    '
140    '=================== Input value ============================
142    onevalue:
144    gotoxy 0,16:?spc(60):gotoxy 0,16
```

```
146 ?" >> ";chr$(key);" << Enter new value: ";:input w$
148 if len(w$)=0 then goto keypress
150 trk%(3157+choose)=val(w$):gotoxy 30,choose-1:?"Value:$ ";
152 ?hex$(trk%(3157+choose));"    ":goto keypress
154 '
156 '==================== PREPARE TRACK BUFFER ====================
158 prepare:
160    clearw 2:gotoxy 12,0:?"Prepare track buffer    ":?
162    '-------------------- Test entire length ---------------------
164    complete=0
166    for i=3152 to 3164 step 2:complete=complete+trk%(i):next i
168    complete=(complete+9)*trk%(3169)+trk%(3150)
170    if complete <= 6234 then goto goahead
172    if complete >6250 then ?:?:?" Track information too long":goto fail
174    ?:?" There are only ";6250-complete;
176 ?" bytes remaining in the track sector.":?:?" Too small!"
178    fail:
180    ?:?" Please press a key...":key=inp(2):return
182    goahead:
184    '-------------------- WRITE BUFFER --------------------
186    offset=1:?"    Track offset (";trk%(3150);"Byte )
188    amount=trk%(3150):value=trk%(3151):gosub bufpoke:'    GAP1
190    for record = 1 to trk%(3169):?"    Record:";record
192    amount=trk%(3152):value=trk%(3153):gosub bufpoke:'    GAP2
194    amount=trk%(3162):value=trk%(3163):gosub bufpoke:'    SYNC
196    def seg=offset:trk%(3170+record)=offset:'ID-Adr. merken
198    poke trk#-1,&Hfe:'                                   ID-AM
200    poke trk#+2,record-1+trk%(3167):'                    START-SECTOR
202    poke trk#+3,trk%(3168):'                             SECTOR-LENGTH
204    poke trk#+4,&Hf7:offset=offset+6:'                   ID-CRC
206    amount=trk%(3154):value=trk%(3155):gosub bufpoke:'    GAP3
208    amount=trk%(3156):value=trk%(3157):gosub bufpoke:'    GAP3
210    amount=trk%(3164):value=trk%(3165):gosub bufpoke:'    SYNC
212    def seg=offset:poke trk#-1,trk%(3166):'              DAM
214    offset=offset+1
216    amount=trk%(3160):value=trk%(3161):gosub bufpoke:'    SECTOR-DATA
218    def seg=offset:poke trk#-1,&Hf7:offset=offset+1:'    DATA-CRC
220    amount=trk%(3158):value=trk%(3159):gosub bufpoke:'    GAP4
222    next record
224    ?"    Track offset (";6250-offset;"Byte )"
226    amount=6300-offset:value=trk%(3170):gosub bufpoke:'    GAP5
228    '
230    ?:?:?"   Buffer is ready!":pready=1:return
232    '-------------------------------------------------------------
234    bufpoke:
236    For i = 0 to amount-1:def seg=offset+i:poke trk#-1,value:next i
```

```
238    offset=offset+amount:return
240    '
242    '=============== STANDARD VALUES FOR ATARI FORMAT ===============
244    default:
246    restore 406:for i=3150 to 3170:read standard:trk%(i)=standard
248    next i: pready=0:return
250    '
252    '================= WRITE TRACK BUFFER TO DISK ==============
254    saveit:
256    clearw 2:gotoxy 12,2:?"Write track buffer to disk":?:?:?
258    if pready=1 then goto speich2
260 ?" Track buffer is still empty.Prepare the buffer before ";
262 ?"saving!":?:?" Please press a key ...":key=inp(2):return
264    saveit2:
266    ?:?:?" Save buffer data as a disk file (y/n) ?":?:?
268    if chr$(inp(2))<>"y" then return
270    input " Please input filename for the format data:",file$
272    bsave file$,trk#,6402:return
274    '
276    '================= LOAD TRACK BUFFER FROM DISK ==================
278    loadit:
280    clearw 2:gotoxy 12,2:?"Load track buffer from disk":?:?:?
282    ? " What program name is the format";
284    ? "saved under? ":?:input file$
286    open"R",1,file$,1:test=lof(1):close 1
288    if test=6402 then bload file$,trk#:pready=1:return
290    ?:?:? " This is no data file !!! Please press a key...."
292    a=inp(2):return
294    '===================== FORMAT A DISKETTE ===================
296    formatit:
298    clearw 2:gotoxy 12,2:?"Format a diskette":?:?:?
300    if pready=1 then goto frmt2
302 ?" Track buffer is still empty. Please prepare the track ";
304 ?"first!":?:?" Please press a key":key=inp(2):return
306    frmt2:
308 ?" Format a diskette (y/n) ?"
310    if chr$(inp(2))<>"y" then return
312    '
314    ?:?:?" Please put the disk to be formatted in Drive A.":?
316    input " From which track?",a$:a=val(a$):if a<0 or a>82 then 316
318    input " To which track?",a$:b=val(a$)
320    if b<0 or b>82 then 318:if b<a then 316
322    ?:?"Which offset should contain the track numbers in the ";
324 ?"ID fields?":?" A value between 0 and ";244-b;" is valid."
326 ?" Normal offset is >> 0 <<":?
328    input " Offset? ",a$:if val(a$)<0 or val(a$)>244-b then 328
330    off=val(a$)
```

```
332    ?:?" Which side should be formatted?"
334    ?:?"    (0)=Front or (1)=Back"
336    key=inp(2)
338    if chr$(key)="0" then drive=2:goto format
340    if chr$(key)="1" then drive=3:goto format
342    goto 336
344    format:
346    ?:?" Last chance to abort! (f)ormat (q)uit"
348    key=inp(2):if chr$(key)="q" then goto formatit
350    if chr$(key)<>"f" then 348
352    '--------------------- formatit ----------------------
354    fdc%(12)=11:fdc%(13)=drive:call fdc#:' Select drive
356    again:
358    fdc%(12)=0:call fdc#:'RESTORE
360    if fdc%(18)<&Ha7 then goto sek
362    ?:?" *** ERROR!   The diskette is write-protected!"
364    ?:?" (r)epeat or (q)uit ?"
366    key=inp(2):if chr$(key)="q" then goto frmt
368    if chr$(key)="f" then fdc%(12)=10:call fdc#:goto again
370    goto 366
372    sek:
374    fdc%(12)=1:fdc%(14)=a:call fdc# :' R/W-head at starting track
376    '
378    fdc%(16)=6400
380    for track=a to b
382    for record=1 to trk%(3169)
384    def seg=trk%(3170+record):poke trk#,track+off
386    poke trk#+1,drive-2:next record
388    '
390    fdc%(12)=8:call fdc# :' WRITE-TRACK
392    if fdc%(18)<>&H80 or fdc%(19)<>3 then ?" *** Error!  Track:";track
394    fdc%(12)=3:call fdc# :' STEP-IN
396    next track
398    frmt:
400    fdc%(12)=11:fdc%(13)=0:call fdc#:goto formatit:'de-select
402    end
404    '--------------- data for ATARI-FORMAT ----------------------
406    data 60,78,12,0,22,78,12,0,40,78,512,229,3,245,3,245,251,1,2,9,78
```

8.4 Creating BASIC loaders

This section deals only indirectly with the disk drive. It involves a simple but very useful tool. In part it is intended as an answer to all the "hackers" who are always ready with a machine language solution to everything. Programming doesn't always have to involve a complete public domain program ready to offer to the masses. Often all somebody needs is just a little bit of help. But read for yourself.

A large number of programming problems can be solved with a BASIC program—easily and quickly. This language has its limitations when high speed is required, however. The small details usually prevent a good idea from being realized in BASIC. When the problem involves creating animated graphics for a game, the BASIC programmer has to pass. On the other hand, even a comprehensive database manager can be written in BASIC, but we still run into problems when it comes to sorting large quantities of data.

The point is this: There are assembly language programmers among us who write small, useful machine language routines. These same people also write BASIC programs. The hindrances of BASIC don't seem to exist for them. The reason for this is quite clear; the parts of the program which take too much time for the BASIC interpreter are converted into machine language. These routines are then called with a simple "call" instruction.

It would be nice if these routines were also available for those of us who don't have an assembler. A BASIC program must be written which contains the data for the machine language routine and which then either POKEs this data into memory or creates a disk file of the routine to be loaded later with BLOAD. We wrote this program to make these subroutines available to straight BASIC programmers.

The BASIC program shown here performs an assembler-to-BASIC-to-assembler conversion. After the program is started, it asks for the name of the file to be converted. Following this, two more filenames must be entered:

1. The name of the BASIC loader to be created. This program will most often be distributed to others in the form of a listing. A checksum is also included to try to reduce the number of typing errors which often occur when entering a large number of DATA statements.

2. The name of the file which the BASIC loader should later create. The loader tests to see if the checksum of the DATA read matches the checksum in the data. If this is the case, a file will be written to the disk which is identical to the original.

```
10    '****************************************************************
20    '***********     Data-Maker     A.S. 10/86     ***************
30    '****************************************************************
40    '
50    'Creates a BASIC program out of any file. This can be  started
60    'later with 'RUN', and will write a file identical to the other
70    'program.
80    '
90    '****************************************************************
100   '
110      ?:fullw 2:clearw 2:gotoxy 0,0
120      input "Which file do you want converted to DATA"; prg$
130      '
140      open"R",#1,prg$,1:bytes=lof(1):close: feldlen=cint(bytes/2-1)
150   ?"INFO -->> ";prg$;" << takes up ";bytes;" bytes"
160      ?:?
170      '
180      input "What do you want to call the output file";bas$:?:?
190      '
200   ?"A loader will be integrated as >> ";bas$;" <<, which"
210   ?"will be the equivalent of the input file"
220   ?">> ";prg$;" << but made of DATA statements.":?:?:?
230      input "Please input the final filename.";make$
240      ?:?"****************************************************************"
260   ?"The program will be loaded intop ";
270   ?"an integer array (c%) with ";feldlen;" as the array length."
280      dim c%(feldlen)
290      ?
300   ?"The input file >> ";prg$;" << will be loaded at varptr(c%(0))."
310      bload prg$,varptr(c%(0))
320      '
330      ?:?"The output file >> ";bas$;" << is now being opened."
340      open"O",1,bas$
350      '
360   ?"The contents of the  c%-array will now"
370   ?"be written in to this file in DATA form."
380   ?"Working....."
390      '
400      check#=0:z=0:zl=100
410      '
420      if z mod 8 =0 then print #1:print #1,str$(zl);" DATA ";:zl=zl+1
430      '
```

```
440     print #1,right$("0000"+hex$(c%(z)),4);
450     '
460     check#=check#+c%(z):z=z+1
470     if z=feldlen+1 then 510
480     if z mod 8 <> 0 then print #1,",";
490     goto 420
500     '
510     ?:?:?"Loader program now being appended...."
520     '
530     print #1
540     print #1,str$(10);" '********  File-Maker    A.S.   *********"
550     print #1,str$(15);" '"
560     print #1,str$(20);" ?:fullw 2:clearw 2:gotoxy 0,0"
570     print #1,str$(25);" ? ";chr$(34);"File >> ";make$;
580     print #1," << now being created";chr$(34);":?:?:?"
590     '
600     print #1,str$(30);" dim c%(";str$(feldlen);"):cs#=0"
610     '
620     print #1,str$(35);" for i=0 to ";str$(feldlen)
630     '
640     print #1,str$(40);" read a$:
        c%(i)=val(";chr$(34);"&H";chr$(34);"+a$)"
650     '
660     print #1,str$(45);" check#=check#+(c%(i))"
670     '
680     print #1,str$(50);" next i"
690     '
700     print #1,str$(55);" if check#=";str$(check#);" then ";str$(70)
710     '
720     print #1,str$(60);" ?";chr$(34);"Can't go any farther;";
730     print #1,"something wrong with the DATA.";chr$(34)
740     print #1,str$(65);" goto 80"
750     '
760     print #1,str$(70);" bsave";chr$(34);make$;chr$(34);
        ",varptr(c%(0)),";
770     print #1,str$(bytes)
780     '
790     print #1,str$(75);" ? ";chr$(34);"The program >> ";make$;
800     print #1," << is now written.";chr$(34)
810     '
820     print #1,str$(80);" ?:?";chr$(34);"Please press a key";
chr$(34)";";
830     print #1,":a=inp(2):end"
840     print #1,str$(85);" '"
850     print #1,str$(90);" '******** DATA for ";make$;" **********"
860     print #1,str$(95);" '"
870     '
```

```
880 ?"...closing the output file..."
890   close #1
900   '
910   ?:?"The program >> ";bas$;" >> is ready."
920   ?:?"Please press a key":a=inp(2):end
```

Appendices

Appendix A: BASIC loader for DISK EDITOR

```
10      '********  DISKMON.BAS     A.S.    ********
15      '
20      ?:fullw 2:clearw 2:gotoxy 0,0
25      ? "File >> diskmon.tos << now being created":?:?:?
30      dim c%( 9711):cs#=0
35      for i=0 to  9711
40      read a$:c%(i)=val("&H"+a$)
45      check#=check#+(c%(i))
50      next i
55      if check#= 84462342.4 then  70
60      ?"Can't go any farther;something wrong with the DATA."
65      goto 80
70      bsave"a:\diskmon.tos",varptr(c%(0)), 19424
75      ? "The program >> diskmon.tos << is now written."
80      ?:?"Please press a key";:a=inp(2):end
85      '
90      '********* DATA for diskmon.tos **********
95      '
100     DATA 601A,0000,3752,0000,0DC8,0000,9D28,0000
101     DATA 0000,0000,0000,0000,0000,0000,2A4F,2A6D
102     DATA 0004,202D,000C,D0AD,0014,D0AD,001C,D0BC
103     DATA 0000,1100,220D,D280,C2BC,FFFF,FFFE,2E41
104     DATA 2F00,2F0D,3F00,3F3C,004A,4E41,DFFC,0000
105     DATA 000C,4EB9,0000,0044,2F3C,0000,0000,4E41
106     DATA 4EB9,0000,30DA,4EB9,0000,3642,4EB9,0000
107     DATA 354E,4EB9,0000,006A,4EB9,0000,02BE,4EB9
108     DATA 0000,016C,4E75,4EB9,0000,359C,4EB9,0000
109     DATA 354E,33FC,0000,0000,452A,33FC,0000,0000
110     DATA 452E,33FC,0000,0000,4530,33FC,0001,0000
111     DATA 452C,303C,0000,33FC,0006,0000,4538,33FC
112     DATA 0001,0000,453A,33FC,004F,0000,4534,33FC
113     DATA 0009,0000,4536,33FC,0009,0000,45A2,13FC
114     DATA 0030,0000,3A17,13FC,0039,0000,3A18,33FC
115     DATA 05DC,0000,453C,23FC,0000,B362,0000,45A8
116     DATA 4EB9,0000,00EC,4E75,4EB9,0000,3642,33FC
117     DATA 0014,0000,454A,33FC,000A,0000,454C,4EB9
118     DATA 0000,35DA,207C,0000,37DE,4EB9,0000,30AC
119     DATA 33FC,0014,0000,454A,33FC,000C,0000,454C
120     DATA 4EB9,0000,35DA,207C,0000,3810,4EB9,0000
121     DATA 30AC,33FC,0014,0000,454A,33FC,000E,0000
122     DATA 454C,4EB9,0000,35DA,207C,0000,3840,4EB9
123     DATA 0000,30AC,4EB9,0000,3676,4EB9,0000,354E
124     DATA 4EB9,0000,3642,4E75,4EB9,0000,361A,4A80
125     DATA 67F6,4840,B03C,0044,6700,0048,B03C,004B
```

```
126   DATA 6600,000A,4EB9,0000,01EC,60DC,B03C,004D
127   DATA 6600,000A,4EB9,0000,0218,60CC,B03C,0050
128   DATA 6600,000A,4EB9,0000,01DA,60BC,B03C,0048
129   DATA 6600,0008,4EB9,0000,01C8,60AC,DFFC,0000
130   DATA 0008,4E75,23F9,0000,4560,0000,4526,4EB9
131   DATA 0000,024A,4E75,23F9,0000,4564,0000,4526
132   DATA 4EB9,0000,024A,4E75,2039,0000,4522,90BC
133   DATA 0000,0001,6700,000C,23C0,0000,4522,6000
134   DATA 000C,23F9,0000,451E,0000,4522,4EB9,0000
135   DATA 32CC,4E75,2039,0000,4522,D0BC,0000,0001
136   DATA B0B9,0000,451E,6E00,000C,23C0,0000,4522
137   DATA 6000,000C,23FC,0000,0001,0000,4522,4EB9
138   DATA 0000,32CC,4E75,4EB9,0000,3642,2079,0000
139   DATA 4526,2039,0000,4522,5380,E588,2270,0800
140   DATA 4ED1,33FC,000A,0000,454A,33FC,0002,0000
141   DATA 454C,4EB9,0000,35DA,4EB9,0000,3540,302F
142   DATA 0004,4440,B07C,001D,6D00,0006,303C,001D
143   DATA E548,227C,0000,430E,2071,0000,4EB9,0000
144   DATA 30AC,4EB9,0000,3676,4EB9,0000,3540,4EB9
145   DATA 0000,35C2,205F,548F,4ED0,4EB9,0000,354E
146   DATA 23FC,0000,0007,0000,451E,23FC,0000,0001
147   DATA 0000,4522,23FC,0000,376E,0000,451A,23FC
148   DATA 0000,3752,0000,4560,23FC,0000,3752,0000
149   DATA 4564,4EB9,0000,32CC,4E75,4EB9,0000,354E
150   DATA 23FC,0000,39EC,0000,451A,23FC,0000,0008
151   DATA 0000,451E,23FC,0000,0005,0000,4522,23FC
152   DATA 0000,39AC,0000,4560,23FC,0000,39CC,0000
153   DATA 4564,4EB9,0000,32CC,4EB9,0000,35AA,207C
154   DATA 0000,3A3D,4EB9,0000,30AC,4E75,23FC,0000
155   DATA 0006,0000,451E,23FC,0000,0004,0000,4522
156   DATA 23FC,0000,3AAA,0000,4560,23FC,0000,3AC2
157   DATA 0000,4564,23FC,0000,3ADA,0000,451A,4EB9
158   DATA 0000,32CC,4EB9,0000,35AA,207C,0000,3A50
159   DATA 4EB9,0000,30AC,4E75,4EB9,0000,354E,23FC
160   DATA 0000,38B2,0000,451A,23FC,0000,3872,0000
161   DATA 4560,23FC,0000,3892,0000,4564,23FC,0000
162   DATA B362,0000,45A8,23FC,0000,0008,0000,451E
163   DATA 23FC,0000,0005,0000,4522,4EB9,0000,32CC
164   DATA 4EB9,0000,35AA,207C,0000,3973,4EB9,0000
165   DATA 30AC,4E75,4EB9,0000,0E5C,4EB9,0000,0EC8
166   DATA 23FC,0000,0008,0000,451E,23FC,0000,0003
167   DATA 0000,4522,23FC,0000,3B52,0000,451A,23FC
168   DATA 0000,3B12,0000,4560,23FC,0000,3B32,0000
169   DATA 4564,4EB9,0000,35AA,207C,0000,3B9F,4EB9
170   DATA 0000,30AC,4EB9,0000,32CC,4E75,4EB9,0000
171   DATA 354E,23FC,0000,3EDC,0000,451A,23FC,0000
172   DATA 0008,0000,451E,23FC,0000,0003,0000,4522
```

```
173    DATA 23FC,0000,3E9C,0000,4560,23FC,0000,3EBC
174    DATA 0000,4564,4EB9,0000,32CC,4EB9,0000,35AA
175    DATA 207C,0000,4212,4EB9,0000,30AC,4E75,4EB9
176    DATA 0000,354E,23FC,0000,41A6,0000,451A,23FC
177    DATA 0000,0007,0000,451E,23FC,0000,0001,0000
178    DATA 4522,23FC,0000,416E,0000,4560,23FC,0000
179    DATA 418A,0000,4564,4EB9,0000,32CC,4EB9,0000
180    DATA 35AA,207C,0000,422C,4EB9,0000,30AC,4E75
181    DATA 23FC,0000,0006,0000,451E,23FC,0000,0004
182    DATA 0000,4522,23FC,0000,400A,0000,4560,23FC
183    DATA 0000,4022,0000,4564,23FC,0000,403A,0000
184    DATA 451A,4EB9,0000,32CC,4EB9,0000,35AA,207C
185    DATA 0000,4098,4EB9,0000,30AC,4E75,3039,0000
186    DATA 4530,B079,0000,4538,6D00,000A,303C,0000
187    DATA 6000,0004,5240,33C0,0000,4530,D03C,0030
188    DATA 13C0,0000,38DA,4EB9,0000,32CC,4E75,3039
189    DATA 0000,4530,B07C,0000,6F00,0008,5340,6000
190    DATA 0008,3039,0000,4538,33C0,0000,4530,D03C
191    DATA 0030,13C0,0000,38DA,4EB9,0000,32CC,4E75
192    DATA 3039,0000,452E,B07C,0001,6D00,000A,303C
193    DATA 0000,6000,0006,303C,0001,33C0,0000,452E
194    DATA D03C,0030,13C0,0000,38E4,4EB9,0000,32CC
195    DATA 4E75,3039,0000,452E,B07C,0000,6F00,000A
196    DATA 303C,0000,6000,0006,303C,0001,33C0,0000
197    DATA 452E,D03C,0030,13C0,0000,38E4,4EB9,0000
198    DATA 32CC,4E75,3039,0000,452A,B079,0000,4534
199    DATA 6D00,000A,303C,0000,6000,0004,5240,33C0
200    DATA 0000,452A,48C0,80FC,000A,D03C,0030,13C0
201    DATA 0000,38EF,4840,D03C,0030,13C0,0000,38F0
202    DATA 4EB9,0000,32CC,4E75,3039,0000,452A,B07C
203    DATA 0000,6F00,0008,5340,6000,0008,3039,0000
204    DATA 4534,33C0,0000,452A,48C0,80FC,000A,D03C
205    DATA 0030,13C0,0000,38EF,4840,D03C,0030,13C0
206    DATA 0000,38F0,4EB9,0000,32CC,4E75,3039,0000
207    DATA 452C,B079,0000,4536,6D00,000A,303C,0000
208    DATA 6000,0004,5240,33C0,0000,452C,48C0,80FC
209    DATA 000A,D03C,0030,13C0,0000,38FC,4840,D03C
210    DATA 0030,13C0,0000,38FD,4EB9,0000,32CC,4E75
211    DATA 3039,0000,452C,B07C,0000,6F00,0008,5340
212    DATA 6000,0008,3039,0000,4536,33C0,0000,452C
213    DATA 48C0,80FC,000A,D03C,0030,13C0,0000,38FC
214    DATA 4840,D03C,0030,13C0,0000,38FD,4EB9,0000
215    DATA 32CC,4E75,3039,0000,4292,323C,0001,B07C
216    DATA 0400,6600,0006,323C,0002,3F01,3F39,0000
217    DATA 452E,3F39,0000,452A,3F39,0000,452C,3F39
218    DATA 0000,4530,42A7,2F3C,0000,B362,3F3C,0008
219    DATA 4E4E,DFFC,0000,0014,4A40,6B00,000A,4EB9
```

```
220    DATA 0000,0786,4E75,3F00,4EB9,0000,0266,4EB9
221    DATA 0000,35AA,207C,0000,3973,4EB9,0000,30AC
222    DATA 4E75,33FC,0000,0000,4550,23F9,0000,45A8
223    DATA 0000,453E,33FC,001F,0000,455C,33FC,0012
224    DATA 0000,455A,33FC,0000,0000,45EC,33FC,00D0
225    DATA 0000,45EE,3039,0000,4292,B07C,0400,6600
226    DATA 001A,33FC,0200,0000,45EC,33FC,02D0,0000
227    DATA 45EE,33FC,003F,0000,455C,4EB9,0000,07E6
228    DATA 4E75,4EB9,0000,35C2,4EB9,0000,3642,33FC
229    DATA 0000,0000,4550,33F9,0000,4550,0000,454E
230    DATA 4EB9,0000,3342,4EB9,0000,3642,4EB9,0000
231    DATA 35C2,4EB9,0000,361A,4840,B03C,0019,6700
232    DATA 00C4,B03C,0048,6700,0032,B03C,0050,6700
233    DATA 006E,B03C,001C,6700,001A,B03C,004B,6700
234    DATA 0012,B03C,004D,66CA,4EB9,0000,0218,6000
235    DATA 0008,4EB9,0000,01EC,4E75,3039,0000,4550
236    DATA B07C,0000,6700,0034,B079,0000,45EE,6700
237    DATA 0018,0479,0100,0000,4550,04B9,0000,0100
238    DATA 0000,453E,6000,0014,0479,00D0,0000,4550
239    DATA 04B9,0000,00D0,0000,453E,6000,FF5A,3039
240    DATA 0000,4550,B079,0000,45EE,6700,0034,B079
241    DATA 0000,45EC,6600,0018,0679,00D0,0000,4550
242    DATA 06B9,0000,00D0,0000,453E,6000,0014,0679
243    DATA 0100,0000,4550,06B9,0000,0100,0000,453E
244    DATA 6000,FF14,33FC,0000,0000,415E,48F9,38F8
245    DATA 0000,45AC,2A7C,0000,38D2,3E3C,002D,101D
246    DATA 3F00,4EB9,0000,365C,51CF,FFF4,2A7C,0000
247    DATA 3B72,3E3C,000D,101D,3F00,4EB9,0000,365C
248    DATA 51CF,FFF4,4EB9,0000,356A,4EB9,0000,356A
249    DATA 2879,0000,453E,2A4C,33F9,0000,4550,0000
250    DATA 454E,363C,000F,3803,3A39,0000,455C,3604
251    DATA 4EB9,0000,33F8,4EB9,0000,3422,3604,284D
252    DATA 3E3C,0005,3F3C,0020,4EB9,0000,365C,51CF
253    DATA FFF4,4EB9,0000,3450,DBFC,0000,0010,0679
254    DATA 0010,0000,454E,4EB9,0000,356A,51CD,FFC0
255    DATA 4EB9,0000,3642,4CF9,38F8,0000,45AC,33FC
256    DATA 0002,0000,415E,6000,FE6A,4E75,4EB9,0000
257    DATA 35AA,207C,0000,3987,4EB9,0000,30AC,33FC
258    DATA 0000,0000,454A,33FC,0004,0000,454C,4EB9
259    DATA 0000,35DA,4EB9,0000,3580,3039,0000,4292
260    DATA B07C,0400,6600,0016,33FC,0200,0000,45EC
261    DATA 33FC,02D0,0000,45EE,6000,0012,33FC,0000
262    DATA 0000,45EC,33FC,00D0,0000,45EE,33FC,0012
263    DATA 0000,455A,23FC,0000,B362,0000,45A8,4EB9
264    DATA 0000,0A6E,4EB9,0000,01EC,4EB9,0000,01EC
265    DATA 33FC,0002,0000,454C,4EB9,0000,35DA,4EB9
266    DATA 0000,3540,4EB9,0000,35AA,207C,0000,3973
```

```
267   DATA 4EB9,0000,30AC,4EB9,0000,359C,4EB9,0000
268   DATA 0786,4EB9,0000,3642,4E75,48E7,1F1E,23F9
269   DATA 0000,45A8,0000,453E,33FC,0000,0000,4550
270   DATA 33FC,0000,0000,454E,4EB9,0000,3342,4EB9
271   DATA 0000,3642,33FC,0007,0000,454A,33FC,0004
272   DATA 0000,454C,4EB9,0000,35DA,4EB9,0000,358E
273   DATA 2F3C,0000,455E,4EB9,0000,3680,4EB9,0000
274   DATA 359C,4A79,0000,455E,6B00,0056,3039,0000
275   DATA 454C,5940,E948,3439,0000,454A,947C,0007
276   DATA 48C2,84FC,0003,D042,3239,0000,455E,2679
277   DATA 0000,453E,1781,0000,4EB9,0000,3488,0C79
278   DATA 0034,0000,454A,6D00,000A,33FC,0004,0000
279   DATA 454A,5679,0000,454A,4EB9,0000,35DA,608A
280   DATA 2039,0000,45F4,4840,B03C,004B,6700,0042
281   DATA B03C,004D,6700,0066,B03C,0050,6700,008A
282   DATA B03C,0048,6700,0142,B03C,0052,6700,01F4
283   DATA B03C,0072,6700,01EC,B03C,001C,6700,01E4
284   DATA 4EB9,0000,3488,4EB9,0000,35DA,6000,FF3C
285   DATA 3039,0000,454A,B07C,0007,6E00,000A,33FC
286   DATA 0037,0000,454A,5779,0000,454A,4EB9,0000
287   DATA 35DA,4EB9,0000,3642,6000,FF10,3039,0000
288   DATA 454A,B07C,0034,6D00,000A,33FC,0004,0000
289   DATA 454A,5679,0000,454A,4EB9,0000,35DA,4EB9
290   DATA 0000,3642,6000,FEE4,4EB9,0000,359C,3039
291   DATA 0000,454C,B07C,0016,6D00,0098,3039,0000
292   DATA 4550,B079,0000,45EC,6600,0040,0679,00D0
293   DATA 0000,4550,06B9,0000,00D0,0000,453E,33F9
294   DATA 0000,454A,0000,4558,4EB9,0000,3342,33F9
295   DATA 0000,4558,0000,454A,33FC,0005,0000,454C
296   DATA 4EB9,0000,35DA,6000,0056,B079,0000,45EE
297   DATA 6700,004C,0679,0100,0000,4550,06B9,0000
298   DATA 0100,0000,453E,33F9,0000,454A,0000,4558
299   DATA 4EB9,0000,3342,33F9,0000,4558,0000,454A
300   DATA 33FC,0006,0000,454C,4EB9,0000,35DA,6000
301   DATA 000E,5279,0000,454C,4EB9,0000,35DA,4EB9
302   DATA 0000,3642,6000,FE24,4EB9,0000,359C,3039
303   DATA 0000,454C,B07C,0004,6600,0092,3039,0000
304   DATA 4550,B07C,0000,6700,0090,B079,0000,45EE
305   DATA 6700,0040,0479,0100,0000,4550,04B9,0000
306   DATA 0100,0000,453E,33F9,0000,454A,0000,4558
307   DATA 4EB9,0000,3342,33F9,0000,4558,0000,454A
308   DATA 33FC,0013,0000,454C,4EB9,0000,35DA,6000
309   DATA 0048,0479,00D0,0000,4550,04B9,0000,00D0
310   DATA 0000,453E,33F9,0000,454A,0000,4558,4EB9
311   DATA 0000,3342,33F9,0000,4558,0000,454A,33FC
312   DATA 0013,0000,454C,4EB9,0000,35DA,5379,0000
313   DATA 454C,4EB9,0000,35DA,4EB9,0000,3642,6000
```

```
314     DATA FD6A,33FC,0000,0000,454A,33FC,0004,0000
315     DATA 454C,4EB9,0000,35DA,4CDF,78F8,4E75,48E7
316     DATA 1F1E,33FC,0000,0000,454A,33FC,0002,0000
317     DATA 454C,4EB9,0000,35DA,207C,0000,3925,4EB9
318     DATA 0000,30AC,267C,0000,38D2,363C,002D,101B
319     DATA 3F00,4EB9,0000,365C,51CB,FFF4,207C,0000
320     DATA 3941,4EB9,0000,30AC,4EB9,0000,3642,4EB9
321     DATA 0000,3676,B03C,0079,6700,000A,B03C,0059
322     DATA 6600,006C,3039,0000,4292,B07C,0400,6700
323     DATA 04E4,323C,0001,3F01,3F39,0000,452E,3F39
324     DATA 0000,452A,3F39,0000,452C,3F39,0000,4530
325     DATA 42A7,2F3C,0000,B362,3F3C,0009,4E4E,DFFC
326     DATA 0000,0014,4A40,6B00,0046,4EB9,0000,3540
327     DATA 4EB9,0000,3642,4EB9,0000,35AA,207C,0000
328     DATA 3973,4EB9,0000,30AC,4CDF,78F8,4E75,4EB9
329     DATA 0000,3540,207C,0000,3953,4EB9,0000,30AC
330     DATA 4EB9,0000,3642,4EB9,0000,3676,60BC,3F00
331     DATA 4EB9,0000,0266,60B2,3039,0000,4530,3F39
332     DATA 0000,4530,3F3C,0007,4E4D,588F,4A80,6600
333     DATA 000E,3F00,4EB9,0000,0266,6000,0046,2040
334     DATA 33D8,0000,457C,33D8,0000,457E,33D8,0000
335     DATA 4580,33D8,0000,4582,33D8,0000,4584,33D8
336     DATA 0000,4586,33D8,0000,4588,33D8,0000,458A
337     DATA 33D8,0000,458C,33D8,0000,4596,33D8,0000
338     DATA 4596,4E75,3F39,0000,4530,3F39,0000,4586
339     DATA 3F39,0000,4584,2F3C,0000,6542,3F3C,0002
340     DATA 3F3C,0004,4E4D,DFFC,0000,000E,4A40,6B00
341     DATA 0004,4E75,3F00,4EB9,0000,0266,60F4,3F39
342     DATA 0000,4530,3039,0000,4584,E348,5240,3F00
343     DATA 3F39,0000,4582,2F3C,0000,4602,3F3C,0002
344     DATA 3F3C,0004,4E4D,DFFC,0000,000E,4A40,6B00
345     DATA 0004,4E75,3F00,4EB9,0000,0266,60F4,3039
346     DATA 0000,4534,B07C,0063,6D00,000A,303C,0000
347     DATA 6000,0004,5240,33C0,0000,4534,48C0,80FC
348     DATA 000A,D03C,0030,13C0,0000,405E,4840,D03C
349     DATA 0030,13C0,0000,405F,4EB9,0000,32CC,4E75
350     DATA 3039,0000,4534,B07C,0000,6F00,0008,5340
351     DATA 6000,0006,303C,0063,33C0,0000,4534,48C0
352     DATA 80FC,000A,D03C,0030,13C0,0000,405E,4840
353     DATA D03C,0030,13C0,0000,405F,4EB9,0000,32CC
354     DATA 4E75,3039,0000,4536,B07C,0063,6D00,000A
355     DATA 303C,0000,6000,0004,5240,33C0,0000,4536
356     DATA 48C0,80FC,000A,D03C,0030,13C0,0000,406F
357     DATA 4840,D03C,0030,13C0,0000,4070,4EB9,0000
358     DATA 32CC,4E75,3039,0000,4536,B07C,0000,6F00
359     DATA 0008,5340,6000,0006,303C,0063,33C0,0000
360     DATA 4536,48C0,80FC,000A,D03C,0030,13C0,0000
```

```
361    DATA 406F,4840,D03C,0030,13C0,0000,4070,4EB9
362    DATA 0000,32CC,4E75,4EB9,0000,0E5C,4EB9,0000
363    DATA 0EC8,4EB9,0000,0F02,4EB9,0000,106A,4EB9
364    DATA 0000,01EC,4E75,33FC,0004,0000,454C,33FC
365    DATA 000A,0000,454A,4EB9,0000,35DA,207C,0000
366    DATA 40B0,4EB9,0000,30AC,33FC,002A,0000,4598
367    DATA 33FC,0006,0000,454C,33FC,000C,0000,454A
368    DATA 4EB9,0000,35DA,207C,0000,3CDD,4EB9,0000
369    DATA 30AC,4EB9,0000,3608,3F39,0000,457C,4EB9
370    DATA 0000,316C,5279,0000,454C,33FC,000C,0000
371    DATA 454A,4EB9,0000,35DA,207C,0000,3CF2,4EB9
372    DATA 0000,30AC,4EB9,0000,3608,3F39,0000,457E
373    DATA 4EB9,0000,316C,5279,0000,454C,33FC,000C
374    DATA 0000,454A,4EB9,0000,35DA,207C,0000,3D0A
375    DATA 4EB9,0000,30AC,4EB9,0000,3608,3F39,0000
376    DATA 4580,4EB9,0000,316C,5279,0000,454C,33FC
377    DATA 000C,0000,454A,4EB9,0000,35DA,207C,0000
378    DATA 3D20,4EB9,0000,30AC,4EB9,0000,3608,3F39
379    DATA 0000,4582,4EB9,0000,316C,5279,0000,454C
380    DATA 33FC,000C,0000,454A,4EB9,0000,35DA,207C
381    DATA 0000,3D3A,4EB9,0000,30AC,4EB9,0000,3608
382    DATA 3F39,0000,4584,4EB9,0000,316C,5279,0000
383    DATA 454C,33FC,000C,0000,454A,4EB9,0000,35DA
384    DATA 207C,0000,3D4D,4EB9,0000,30AC,4EB9,0000
385    DATA 3608,3F39,0000,4586,4EB9,0000,316C,5279
386    DATA 0000,454C,33FC,000C,0000,454A,4EB9,0000
387    DATA 35DA,207C,0000,3D6C,4EB9,0000,30AC,4EB9
388    DATA 0000,3608,3F39,0000,4588,4EB9,0000,316C
389    DATA 5279,0000,454C,33FC,000C,0000,454A,4EB9
390    DATA 0000,35DA,207C,0000,3D8C,4EB9,0000,30AC
391    DATA 4EB9,0000,3608,3F39,0000,458A,4EB9,0000
392    DATA 316C,5279,0000,454C,33FC,000C,0000,454A
393    DATA 4EB9,0000,35DA,207C,0000,3DA3,4EB9,0000
394    DATA 30AC,4EB9,0000,3608,3F39,0000,4596,4EB9
395    DATA 0000,316C,5479,0000,454C,33FC,000A,0000
396    DATA 454A,4EB9,0000,35DA,207C,0000,3DB7,3039
397    DATA 0000,4596,B07C,0002,6600,0008,207C,0000
398    DATA 3DF6,4EB9,0000,30AC,4EB9,0000,3642,4EB9
399    DATA 0000,3676,4EB9,0000,35AA,4EB9,0000,3540
400    DATA 4EB9,0000,35AA,207C,0000,4098,4EB9,0000
401    DATA 30AC,4E75,4EB9,0000,1832,50F9,0000,043E
402    DATA 4EB9,0000,1912,4EB9,0000,1892,4EB9,0000
403    DATA 1A76,4EB9,0000,1348,51F9,0000,043E,4EB9
404    DATA 0000,3642,4EB9,0000,35AA,4EB9,0000,3540
405    DATA 4EB9,0000,1892,4EB9,0000,1860,207C,0000
406    DATA 4250,4EB9,0000,30AC,4EB9,0000,3676,4EB9
407    DATA 0000,1832,4EB9,0000,195C,4EB9,0000,1860
```

```
408     DATA 4EB9,0000,35AA,4EB9,0000,3540,4EB9,0000
409     DATA 35AA,207C,0000,427E,4EB9,0000,30AC,4CDF
410     DATA 78F8,4E75,4EB9,0000,1B08,33FC,0190,00FF
411     DATA 8606,33FC,0090,00FF,8606,33FC,0190,00FF
412     DATA 8606,3C3C,0004,4EB9,0000,18DA,33FC,0184
413     DATA 00FF,8606,3C39,0000,452C,4EB9,0000,18DA
414     DATA 33FC,0180,00FF,8606,3C3C,00A0,4EB9,0000
415     DATA 18DA,2E3C,0005,0000,0839,0005,00FF,FA01
416     DATA 6700,001E,5387,66F0,3F3C,FFF7,4EB9,0000
417     DATA 0266,4EB9,0000,35AA,4EB9,0000,3540,4E75
418     DATA 4EB9,0000,18F4,3039,0000,416C,0800,0006
419     DATA 6600,0004,4E75,3F3C,FFF8,4EB9,0000,0266
420     DATA 4EB9,0000,35AA,4EB9,0000,3540,4E75,303C
421     DATA 0200,C0F9,0000,45A2,33C0,0000,4576,3F39
422     DATA 0000,45A2,3F39,0000,452E,3F39,0000,452A
423     DATA 3F3C,0001,3F39,0000,4530,42A7,2F3C,0000
424     DATA B362,3F3C,0008,4E4E,DFFC,0000,0014,4A40
425     DATA 6B00,000A,4EB9,0000,15A2,4E75,3F00,4EB9
426     DATA 0000,0266,4EB9,0000,3642,4EB9,0000,3676
427     DATA 4EB9,0000,35AA,207C,0000,3A3D,4EB9,0000
428     DATA 30AC,4EB9,0000,3532,60D0,3039,0000,45A2
429     DATA B079,0000,4536,6D00,000A,303C,0000,6000
430     DATA 0004,5240,33C0,0000,45A2,48C0,80FC,000A
431     DATA D03C,0030,13C0,0000,3A17,4840,D03C,0030
432     DATA 13C0,0000,3A18,4EB9,0000,32CC,4E75,3039
433     DATA 0000,45A2,B07C,0000,6F00,0008,5340,6000
434     DATA 0008,3039,0000,4536,33C0,0000,45A2,48C0
435     DATA 80FC,000A,D03C,0030,13C0,0000,3A17,4840
436     DATA D03C,0030,13C0,0000,3A18,4EB9,0000,32CC
437     DATA 4E75,33FC,0000,0000,45EC,33FC,00D0,0000
438     DATA 45EE,33FC,0012,0000,455A,2039,0000,453E
439     DATA 90BC,0000,B362,80FC,0200,4840,4A40,6700
440     DATA 000C,04B9,0000,0100,0000,453E,23F9,0000
441     DATA 453E,0000,45A8,33FC,0000,0000,4550,33FC
442     DATA 0014,0000,454A,33FC,0002,0000,454C,4EB9
443     DATA 0000,35DA,207C,0000,3987,4EB9,0000,30AC
444     DATA 4EB9,0000,0A6E,4EB9,0000,35AA,4EB9,0000
445     DATA 3540,4EB9,0000,35AA,207C,0000,3A3D,4EB9
446     DATA 0000,30AC,4EB9,0000,01EC,4EB9,0000,01EC
447     DATA 4EB9,0000,35C2,4EB9,0000,3580,4E75,33FC
448     DATA 0000,0000,4550,23FC,0000,B362,0000,453E
449     DATA 33FC,0000,0000,4594,33FC,000F,0000,455A
450     DATA 33FC,0002,0000,454C,33FC,003B,0000,454A
451     DATA 4EB9,0000,35DA,207C,0000,3A6D,4EB9,0000
452     DATA 30AC,4240,303C,0001,3F00,4EB9,0000,316C
453     DATA 207C,0000,3A7A,4EB9,0000,30AC,33FC,0004
454     DATA 0000,454C,33FC,0000,0000,454A,4EB9,0000
```

```
455 DATA 35DA,4EB9,0000,3580,4EB9,0000,3642,4EB9
456 DATA 0000,3342,4EB9,0000,361A,4840,B03C,0048
457 DATA 6700,0038,B03C,0050,6700,00A8,B03C,001C
458 DATA 6700,0120,B03C,004B,6700,0016,B03C,004D
459 DATA 6700,0004,60CE,4EB9,0000,0218,6000,0104
460 DATA 4EB9,0000,01EC,6000,00FA,3039,0000,4550
461 DATA B07C,0000,6700,0014,0479,0100,0000,4550
462 DATA 04B9,0000,0100,0000,453E,3039,0000,4550
463 DATA E048,E248,D07C,0001,33C0,0000,45FC,33FC
464 DATA 003B,0000,454A,33FC,0002,0000,454C,4EB9
465 DATA 0000,35DA,207C,0000,3A6D,4EB9,0000,30AC
466 DATA 3F39,0000,45FC,4EB9,0000,316C,207C,0000
467 DATA 3A7A,4EB9,0000,30AC,4EB9,0000,3532,6000
468 DATA FF3E,3039,0000,4550,3239,0000,4576,927C
469 DATA 0100,B041,6700,0014,0679,0100,0000,4550
470 DATA 06B9,0000,0100,0000,453E,3039,0000,4550
471 DATA E048,E248,D07C,0001,33C0,0000,45FC,33FC
472 DATA 003B,0000,454A,33FC,0002,0000,454C,4EB9
473 DATA 0000,35DA,207C,0000,3A6D,4EB9,0000,30AC
474 DATA 3F39,0000,45FC,4EB9,0000,316C,207C,0000
475 DATA 3A7A,4EB9,0000,30AC,4EB9,0000,3532,6000
476 DATA FEBE,4EB9,0000,3642,4E75,2F0C,33FC,0002
477 DATA 0000,454C,4EB9,0000,35DA,4EB9,0000,3540
478 DATA 207C,0000,3A7E,4EB9,0000,30AC,343C,0021
479 DATA 287C,0000,38D2,101C,3F00,4EB9,0000,365C
480 DATA 51CA,FFF4,207C,0000,3A98,4EB9,0000,30AC
481 DATA 4EB9,0000,3642,4EB9,0000,3676,B03C,0059
482 DATA 6700,000A,B03C,0079,6600,0038,3F39,0000
483 DATA 45A2,3F39,0000,452E,3F39,0000,452A,3F3C
484 DATA 0001,3F39,0000,4530,42A7,2F3C,0000,B362
485 DATA 3F3C,0009,4E4E,DFFC,0000,0014,4A40,6B00
486 DATA 0024,4EB9,0000,35AA,4EB9,0000,3540,4EB9
487 DATA 0000,35AA,207C,0000,3A3D,4EB9,0000,30AC
488 DATA 285F,4E75,3F00,4EB9,0000,0266,60E0,2F3C
489 DATA 0000,0001,3F3C,0020,4E41,DFFC,0000,0006
490 DATA 4A40,6600,0016,42A7,3F3C,0020,4E41,DFFC
491 DATA 0000,0006,23C0,0000,4568,4E75,2F3C,0000
492 DATA 0001,3F3C,0020,4E41,DFFC,0000,0006,4A40
493 DATA 6700,0014,2F39,0000,4568,3F3C,0020,4E41
494 DATA DFFC,0000,0006,4E75,51CF,FFFE,4E75,4EB9
495 DATA 0000,1832,33FC,0080,00FF,8606,3C3C,00D0
496 DATA 4EB9,0000,18DA,3E3C,0028,4EB9,0000,188C
497 DATA 4E75,4EB9,0000,1832,3639,00FF,8604,4EB9
498 DATA 0000,18C8,40E7,3F07,3E3C,0028,51CF,FFFE
499 DATA 3E1F,46DF,4E75,4EB9,0000,1832,4EB9,0000
500 DATA 18C8,33C6,00FF,8604,4EB9,0000,18C8,4E75
501 DATA 4EB9,0000,1832,4EB9,0000,18C8,33F9,00FF
```

```
502    DATA 8604,0000,416C,4EB9,0000,18C8,4E75,4EB9
503    DATA 0000,1832,3039,0000,4530,B07C,0001,6E00
504    DATA 0036,5200,E308,8079,0000,452E,0A00,0007
505    DATA C03C,0007,40E7,007C,0700,13FC,000E,00FF
506    DATA 8800,1239,00FF,8800,C23C,00F8,8200,13C1
507    DATA 00FF,8802,46DF,4E75,4EB9,0000,1832,33FC
508    DATA 0080,00FF,8606,103C,0007,4EB9,0000,1938
509    DATA 4E75,4EB9,0000,1832,42B9,0000,4572,40F9
510    DATA 0000,45FC,46FC,2700,33FC,0090,00FF,8606
511    DATA 33FC,0190,00FF,8606,33FC,0090,00FF,8606
512    DATA 3C3C,0016,343C,0200,C4C6,33C2,0000,4576
513    DATA D4BC,0000,B362,23C2,0000,45A4,4EB9,0000
514    DATA 18DA,203C,0000,B362,13C0,00FF,860D,E088
515    DATA 13C0,00FF,860B,E088,13C0,00FF,8609,33FC
516    DATA 0080,00FF,8606,3C3C,00E8,4EB9,0000,18DA
517    DATA 2E3C,0005,0000,2A79,0000,45A4,303C,0200
518    DATA 51C8,FFFE,0839,0005,00FF,FA01,6700,002E
519    DATA 5387,6700,005C,13F9,00FF,8609,0000,4573
520    DATA 13F9,00FF,860B,0000,4574,13F9,00FF,860D
521    DATA 0000,4575,BBF9,0000,4572,6EC8,33FC,0090
522    DATA 00FF,8606,3A39,00FF,8606,33C5,0000,4570
523    DATA 0805,0000,6700,0018,33FC,0080,00FF,8606
524    DATA 4EB9,0000,18F4,46F9,0000,45FC,4E75,60F6
525    DATA 60F4,4EB9,0000,1832,4EB9,0000,1ACC,33FC
526    DATA 0086,00FF,8606,3C39,0000,452A,4EB9,0000
527    DATA 18DA,33FC,0080,00FF,8606,3C3C,001B,4EB9
528    DATA 0000,18DA,2E3C,0006,0000,5387,6700,000E
529    DATA 0839,0005,00FF,FA01,66F0,4E75,3F3C,FFF9
530    DATA 4EB9,0000,0266,4E75,3C39,0000,4168,CC7C
531    DATA 0003,2E3C,0005,0000,33FC,0080,00FF,8606
532    DATA 4EB9,0000,18DA,5387,6700,000E,0839,0005
533    DATA 00FF,FA01,66F0,4E75,3F3C,FFF9,4EB9,0000
534    DATA 0266,4E75,203C,0000,B362,13C0,00FF,860D
535    DATA E088,13C0,00FF,860B,E088,13C0,00FF,8609
536    DATA 4E75,48E7,1F1E,4EB9,0000,35AA,4EB9,0000
537    DATA 3540,4EB9,0000,35AA,207C,0000,3A50,4EB9
538    DATA 0000,30AC,33FC,0012,0000,455A,4EB9,0000
539    DATA 1832,50F9,0000,043E,4EB9,0000,1912,4EB9
540    DATA 0000,1892,4EB9,0000,1A76,4EB9,0000,1976
541    DATA 4EB9,0000,1976,4EB9,0000,1892,4EB9,0000
542    DATA 1860,4EB9,0000,1BAA,4EB9,0000,1832,4EB9
543    DATA 0000,195C,51F9,0000,043E,4EB9,0000,1860
544    DATA 4CDF,78F8,4E75,33FC,0000,0000,4550,23FC
545    DATA 0000,B362,0000,453E,33FC,0012,0000,455A
546    DATA 33FC,0064,0000,455C,33FC,1E00,0000,45EC
547    DATA 33FC,1ED0,0000,45EE,4EB9,0000,35C2,4EB9
548    DATA 0000,3580,4EB9,0000,07E6,4EB9,0000,3642
```

```
549  DATA 4E75,4EB9,0000,35AA,4EB9,0000,3540,207C
550  DATA 0000,430A,4EB9,0000,30AC,3039,0000,4530
551  DATA B07C,0002,6E00,00B0,4EB9,0000,1832,4EB9
552  DATA 0000,1912,4EB9,0000,1892,4EB9,0000,1A76
553  DATA 4EB9,0000,1A76,4EB9,0000,1B08,4EB9,0000
554  DATA 1C6C,4EB9,0000,1892,4EB9,0000,1860,4EB9
555  DATA 0000,1CD6,4EB9,0000,1832,4EB9,0000,195C
556  DATA 4EB9,0000,1860,4E75,4EB9,0000,1832,33FC
557  DATA 0090,00FF,8606,33FC,0190,00FF,8606,33FC
558  DATA 0090,00FF,8606,3C3C,0001,4EB9,0000,18DA
559  DATA 33FC,0080,00FF,8606,383C,0018,3C3C,00C8
560  DATA 2E3C,0004,0000,4EB9,0000,18DA,0839,0005
561  DATA 00FF,FA01,6700,000A,5387,6700,000A,60EC
562  DATA 51CC,FFDA,4E75,3F3C,FFFA,4EB9,0000,0266
563  DATA 4E75,4EB9,0000,35AA,4EB9,0000,3540,207C
564  DATA 0000,429E,4EB9,0000,30AC,4EB9,0000,35C2
565  DATA 3A3C,0011,267C,0000,B362,383C,0002,3F3C
566  DATA 0020,4EB9,0000,365C,101B,3F00,4EB9,0000
567  DATA 316C,3F3C,0020,4EB9,0000,365C,3F3C,0020
568  DATA 4EB9,0000,365C,51CC,FFE0,3F3C,0020,4EB9
569  DATA 0000,365C,3F3C,0020,4EB9,0000,365C,101B
570  DATA 4880,323C,0080,B07C,0000,6700,001E,323C
571  DATA 0100,B07C,0001,6700,0012,323C,0200,B07C
572  DATA 0002,6700,0006,323C,0400,3F01,4EB9,0000
573  DATA 316C,3F3C,0020,4EB9,0000,365C,207C,0000
574  DATA 42FE,4EB9,0000,30AC,101B,3F00,4EB9,0000
575  DATA 30E2,101B,3F00,4EB9,0000,30E2,3F3C,000D
576  DATA 4EB9,0000,365C,3F3C,000A,4EB9,0000,365C
577  DATA 51CD,FF48,4EB9,0000,3676,4E75,4EB9,0000
578  DATA 35AA,4EB9,0000,3540,33FC,0014,0000,454A
```

Appendix B: ASCII character set

The following table illustrates the printable ASCII character set of the Atari ST. The corresponding numeric values (ASCII values, which can be conveyed by the ASC("") function in BASIC) can be computed by combining the hexadecimal number on the top border with the number on the left border. For example, the ASCII value of the "A" character is $41.

You can print this table out on your own system with the following GFA BASIC program and a printer:

```
Cls
For I=0 To 15
   Print At(I*3+7,3);Hex$(I)
   Print At(4,I+4);Hex$(I)
   Deftext 1,0,0,13
   For J=0 To 15
      Text 92,56,"SPC"
   Next J
Next I
Deftext 1,0,0,4
For I=1 To 18
   Draw 18,I*16+15 To 424,I*16+15
   Draw I*24-7,31 To I*24-7,303
Next I
Draw 17,31 To 40,47
Repeat
Until Mousek
Edit
```

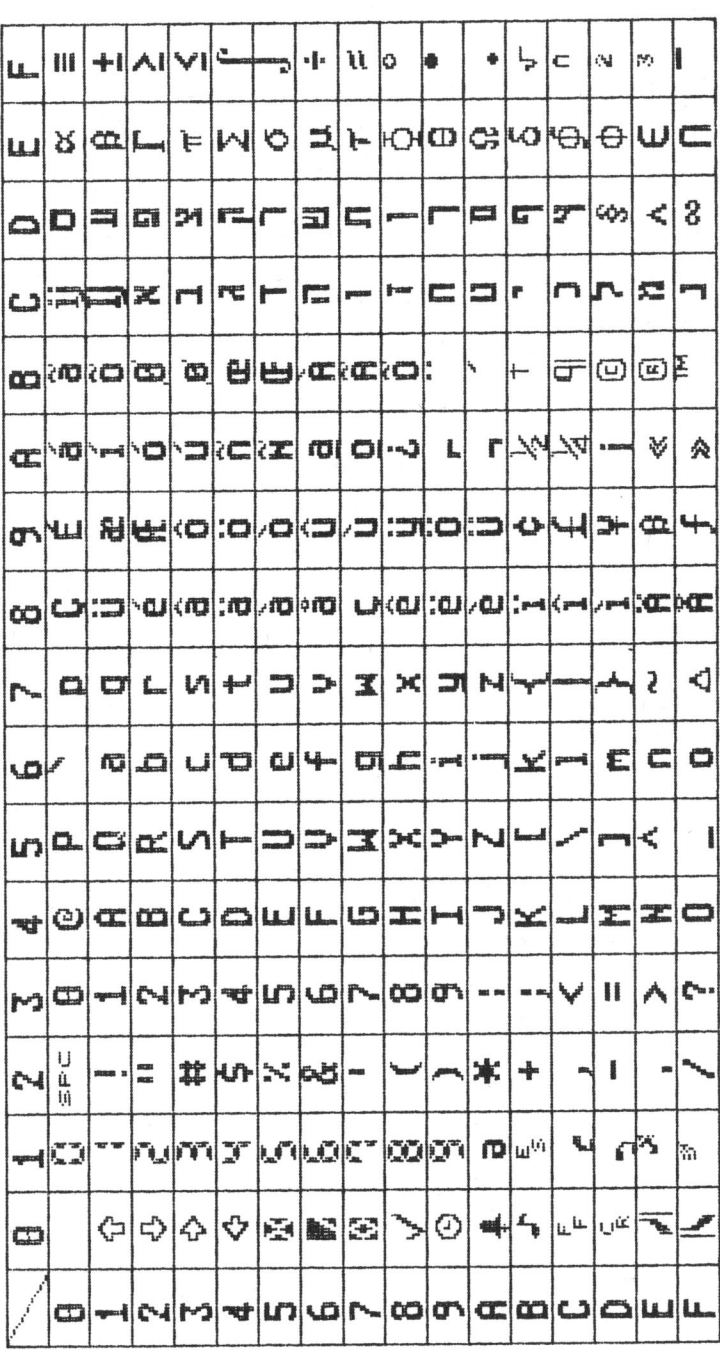

Index

`ALLDIR.TOS` program	168-175
Address mark detector	92-93,104
Arithmetic logic unit (ALU)	92
ASCII	8,12,15,17,398-399
Assembler compatibility	318
Attribute byte	312
BASIC	8,14-18
BASIC loaders	321-383,387-397
`BASIC-TOS interface` program	323-324
BASIC/FDC interface—*see* `FDCINTER` program	
`bigfmt` program	50-58
BIOS parameter block (BPB)	47,58-59,64,202-205
Boot sector	45,47-50,56,58
BPB analysis program (`BPBANA.TOS`)	59-64
C (language)	24-31
CLOSE (GEMDOS)	12
Cluster	45-46,58,65,66,68,69
Command descriptor block	141-158
CREATE (GEMDOS)	11
Cyclic redundancy check (CRC)	91-92
Data field	118-119
`Data-Maker` program	381-383
`database` program	35-38
Direct Memory Access (DMA)	79-80,144-147
Directory	65-69,153,168-172,309-312,325-328
Directory reader program—*see* `read directory` program	
Disk copying	370-374
Disk drives	77-197
`disk editor` program	210-317
BASIC loader	387-397
CLUSTER menu	278-292,306
FORMAT menu	293-297,307
GAP menu routines	297-303,307-308
main menu	215-255,303-304
OPTIONS menu	256-261,308
SECTOR menu	305-306
TRACK menu	262-269,304-305
TRACK with SYNCS menu	269-278,305
Disk monitor—see `disk editor` program	

Disk/RAM disk copying	193-198
Extended disk format program—see `bigfmt` program	
Field	9,39
`FDCINTER` program	342-370
File Allocation Table (FAT)	46,48,68-69,313-314
File extension	7-8,11,39
File handle	11
Files	7-34
random-access	9-10,16-18,22-23,29-31,33-34,202
sequential	9,15-16,19-22,27-28,32-33
Floppy disk controller (FDC)	80-118,342,361-363
Folder	65,68,168,315
FORCE INTERRUPT	90,96,99,106,126,360
Foreign formats	316-317,374-379
Format	45-47
Formatting programs	50-63,331-334
FORTRAN	11,32-34
GAP	117-118
GEMDOS	11-13,24,56,143
GETBPB	47-50,58-64,204-205
`GET_TIME in BASIC` program	340-341
Hard disk	137-175
`hard disk access` programs	144-146,153-157
Hard disk controller (HDC)	139-167
Hard disk directory printout—see `ALLDIR.TOS`	
ID field—see index field	
Index field	119-121
Interleave	149,167,207
Logical sector	310-311
LSEEK (GEMDOS)	13
Magic number	47
MS-DOS	48
Non-Atari format	316-317,374-379
OPEN (GEMDOS)	11
Partition	73-74,153,157-167
`partition analyzer` program	158-167
Pascal	11,19-23
Physical sector	310-311
Program header	70-72
RAM disk	179-192
READ (GEMDOS)	12
READ ADDRESS	89-90,96,112-113,124,130,360
`Read clock time` program	339-341

READ DATA	89
`read directory` program	325-328
`read/write sector` program	328-329
READ SECTOR	105-107,110,361
READ TRACK	81,113-115,125,130
Record	9,39
Relocation table	72-73
RESTORE	89,96,100,128,147,148,204,205
Searching data	40,318,334-336
Sector	45-50,78
SEEK	13,27,29,30,86,96,100,128, 151-152
SETDTA (GEMDOS)	13
SFIRST (GEMDOS)	13,67
SNEXT (GEMDOS)	13,67
Shugart interface	131
Sorting data	40,336-338
Status register	84,87,90,101,112,126-130
STEP	101,128,202
STEP IN	101,128
STEP OUT	101,128
Subdirectories—*see* folder	
Supervisor mode	143-144
Synchronization bytes	78,116,118
Track	10,45-46
Tramiel Operating System (TOS)	202-210
User mode	144
WRITE (GEMDOS)	12
Write precompensation	95-96,344
WRITE SECTOR	107,111
WRITE TRACK	81,115-118,123,130
XBIOS	80,202,205-210

Catalog of Abacus Products for the ATARI® ST™

Abacus, P.O. Box 7219, Grand Rapids, MI 49510

Selected Books from our ATARI ST Reference Library

GEM Programmer's Reference

Atari ST GEM Programmer's Reference is an indispensable guide if you're a serious ST programmer needing detailed information on GEM. **Atari ST GEM Programmer's Reference** is written especially for the ST and has an easy-to-follow format. The GEM routines are explained with examples written in both C and 68000 assembly language.

Topics include:

- Overview of GEM: VDI, AES, GDOS, GIOS
- Intro to programming with GEM
- The ST Development System
- Using the Editor, C-compiler, Assembler and Linker
- Inside GEM: programming the Virtual Device Interface (VDI)
- Inside GEM: programming the Application Environment Services (AES)

GEM Programmers Reference is a complete programming handbook for all ST users. 412 pages. Optional diskette available.

GEM Programmer's Reference   Suggested Retail Price: **$19.95**
Optional Diskette   Suggested Retail Price: **$14.95**

"Anyone interested in learning how to manipulate the VDI or the AES will want to have this book at their fingertips..."
—Richard Kaller
ST Applications

"Despite its title, the Atari ST GEM Programmer's Reference is really a complete programming handbook for the ST."
—Donald Evan Crabb
Byte

Optional Program Diskettes

Don't forget: optional program diskettes are available for all the books in the **Atari ST Reference Library** (except where noted). These optional diskettes contain all the program listings printed in the books, and will save you hours of tedious typing.

Each optional diskette: **$14.95**

Atari ST, 520ST, 1040ST, TOS, ST BASIC and ST LOGO are trademarks or registered trademarks of Atari Corp. GEM is a registered trademark of Digital Research Inc.

Selected Books from our ATARI ST Reference Library

Machine Language

Atari ST Machine Language is the complete introduction to the high-speed world of 68000 machine language on the Atari ST. **Atari ST Machine Language** is required reading if you're interested in getting out the full potential built into the spectacular MC68000 microprocessor used in the Atari ST line of computers. Topics include:

- Logical operations and bit manipulations
- 68000 register structure and data organization
- Fundamentals of assembly language programming
- Operating system and programs
- Solutions to typical problems
- Program development
- Step by step programming
- Program and memory structure

Atari ST Machine Language also contains many simple programs that progressively teach the fundamentals of programming in 68000 machine language. 280 pages. Optional diskette available.

Atari ST Machine Language Suggested Retail Price: **$19.95**
Optional Diskette Suggested Retail Price: **$14.95**

Tricks & Tips

Atari ST Tricks & Tips is a fantastic collection of ST programming tools and techniques that every ST user will find valuable. Teaches you how to define BASIC, assembler and C programs with the advanced programming techniques found exclusively in **Atari ST Tricks & Tips**. Topics include:

- Special ST BASIC commands
- "Safe" locations for M/L programs
- Using the VDISYS commands
- Mastering powerful GEM applications
- Producing fantastic graphics
- Building a RSC file

Program listings included in **Atari ST Tricks & Tips**:

- Super-fast RAM disk
- Time-saving printspooler
- Color print hardcopy
- Plotter output hardcopy
- Auto-starting TOS application
- Creating accessories

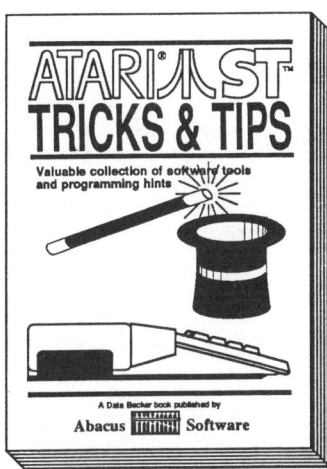

Plus much more—and all programs are included in the price of the book! Full four-color plates in appendix show you the ST's graphic capabilities. Fully indexed. 260 pages.

"...this book a best-seller and I can understand why."
—Pamela Rice Frank
Current Notes

Atari ST Tricks & Tips Suggested Retail Price: **$19.95**
Optional Diskette Suggested Retail Price: **$14.95**

Selected Books from our ATARI ST Reference Library

Graphics & Sound

Atari ST Graphics & Sound teaches the ST user how to create graphics and make full use of the built-in sound capabilities of the Atari ST. Example programs listed in **Atari ST Graphics & Sound** are written in BASIC, C, LOGO and Modula-2. Topics include:

- Mirror and rotation
- Graphics under GEM
- Coordinate transformations
- Raster and vector graphics
- Principles of music synthesis
- Sound chip
- Plotting math functions in 2D & 3D

- Moire patterns
- Bar and pie charts
- Fractals
- Waveform generation
- The ST as a synthesizer
- MIDI control of musical devices

Atari ST Graphics & Sound is a must for the ST owner who wants an in-depth look at creating sophisicated graphics and surprising music and sound with the ST. 255 pages. Optional diskette contains dozens of graphics and sound programs.

Atari ST Graphics & Sound   Suggested Retail Price: $19.95
Optional Diskette   Suggested Retail Price: $14.95

LOGO User's Guide

ST LOGO was designed specifically to take full advantage of the Atari ST's fantastic graphic capabilities. LOGO's English-like words may be extraordinarily easy to learn, yet LOGO programs are actually built along the lines of advanced artificial intelligence languages like LISP. **Atari ST LOGO User's Guide** gently introduces the reader to the fundamentals of ST LOGO with numerous examples, dozens of actual screen illustrations and exercises that optimize the ST's features. Then it moves on to work with the more advanced features LOGO has to offer—readers will soon be programming highly complex tasks on their STs under LOGO. Topics covered:

- Thorough introduction to GEM, windows, and the mouse
- Randomizing and repetition
- Programming with recursion
- LOGO words & lists
- Data structures in LOGO
- Error output
- Computing with LOGO
- ST LOGO system, input and output commands
- Programs as lists

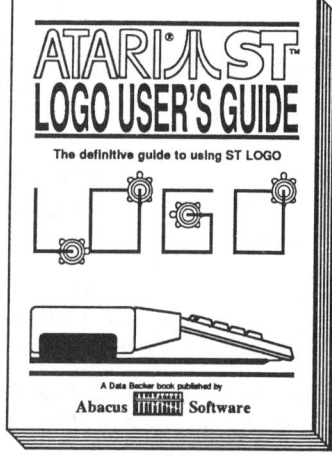

" A worthwhile addition to your reference library... contains many examples & demonstration programs in the LOGO language."
—Bruce Laubenheimer
Computer Shopper

Atari ST LOGO User's Guide covers everything your customers need to know about this acclaimed teaching and graphics language. 370 pages.

"For those folks who have been waiting for an excuse to start playing with LOGO, this may be it!"
—Steve Tearle
Atari Journal

Atari ST LOGO User's Guide   Suggested Retail Price: $19.95
Optional Diskette   Suggested Retail Price: $14.95

Atari ST, 520ST, 1040ST, TOS, ST BASIC and ST LOGO are trademarks or registered trademarks of Atari Corp. GEM is a registered trademark of Digital Research Inc.

Selected Books from our ATARI ST Reference Library

Peeks & Pokes

PEEK and POKE commands act as bridges between the user and the Atari ST's operating system through ST BASIC. **Atari ST Peeks & Pokes** enhances the user's knowledge of the ST and programs with numerous PEEK and POKE examples.

Atari ST Peeks & Pokes clearly explains a number of the most important PEEKs and POKEs and their application to common programming problems. At the same time, this book gives you an excellent look at the architecture and operation of the exciting Atari ST. Topics include:

- The ST's configuration and interfaces
- The "intelligent" keyboard
- The mouse as a paintbrush
- Pointer and stack
- Customizing the desktop
- Important PEEKs & POKEs
- Making your own fill patterns
- ST communications
- Direct disk access
- Internal memory configuration

Atari ST Peeks & Pokes unlocks the secrets hidden within the ST with an excellent collection of "quick hitters" and information. 200 pages.

Atari ST Peeks & Pokes	Suggested Retail Price: **$16.95**
Optional Diskette	Suggested Retail Price: **$14.95**

BASIC Training Guide

Atari ST BASIC Training Guide for the Atari ST is a functional, educational and well-written introduction to ST BASIC. Quickly teaches you the fundamentals of programming with an introduction to program analysis, problem analysis, algorithms, and BASIC commands. This systematic book makes learning programming in the popular BASIC language quicker and easier than ever before.

Quizzes throughout the book help you learn to "think in BASIC" while you'r getting a practical grounding in the language. Topics include:

- Data flow and program flowcharts
- Advanced programming techniques
- Menus
- Multi-dimensional arrays
- Sort routines
- File management
- BASIC under GEM

In addition, **Atari ST BASIC Training Guide** also contains advanced programming techniques if you already know ST BASIC. 312 pages.

BASIC Training Guide	Suggested Retail Price: **$16.95**
Optional Diskette	Suggested Retail Price: **$14.95**

"The Atari ST BASIC Training Guide is a first-class text for ST BASIC users. It is clear, thorough, well-written and remarkably free of errors and typos... does a good jog of introducing the user to ST BASIC programming fundamentals. It also provides a valuable reference section for the more advanced user."
—David Plotkin
Antic

Selected Books from our ATARI ST Reference Library

Introduction to MIDI Programming

The digital music synthesizer is the musical instrument of the 80s. You can now buy synthesizers for under $1000 (as low as $250), play at least four voices at a time, and they can be connected to home computers through the Musical Instrument Digital Interface (MIDI) for computer control. The Atari ST is ideal for MIDI interfacing, since it has a built-in MIDI port. This means it's ready to hook up to any digital electronic musical instrument equipped with MIDI ports.

ST Introduction to MIDI Programming gives you the groundwork for discovering the infinite musical possibilities of the Atari ST's MIDI interface and your synthesizer. Topics include:

- Introduction to MIDI programming
- MIDI STANDARD and MIDI LANGUAGE
- Programming your synthesizer
- How to buy MIDI software
- Using the extended BIOS
- Source code from Xlent Software's ST MUSIC BOX© AUTO-PLAYER program
- C source codes for many programs and functions

Essential reading for anyone who uses the ST's MIDI port. 256 pages.

Introduction to MIDI programming   Suggested Retail Price: **$19.95**
Optional Diskette   Suggested Retail Price: **$14.95**

BASIC to C

Atari ST BASIC to C was written expressly for those of you who've learned the essentials of ST BASIC, but are hesitant to try another language. This excellent book quickly takes you beyond the BASICs and teaches how to program in the C language—the language of choice for thousands of advanced program developers. **Atari ST BASIC to C** places simple BASIC programs and their equivalents in C code side-by-side, with clearly-written comparisons between the two languages. Now you can learn the groundwork for C programming in only one day! Topics covered:

- Development, applications and the benefits of C
- Functions and text output
- Program format
- Loops and comments
- Data input
- Arithmetic in C
- Control structures
- Data types in C
- C pointers and arrays
- Common errors made by BASIC programmers

Atari ST BASIC to C skillfully guides the BASIC programmer through the necessary steps for programming in the C language. An essential addition to the libraries of all ST users.

"Imagine—if someone took all of the BASIC commands that you knew and loved so well, and showed how those commands would look and work in C...in a step-by-step, logical sequence with lots of examples—wouldn't that be nice? Well that's exactly what Abacus had Mr. Hartwig do, and it's very effective. This book creates an effective bridge between ST BASIC and the C programming language."
—David M. Pochron
The Atari Journal

Atari ST BASIC to C   Suggested Retail Price: **$19.95**
Optional Diskette   Suggested Retail Price: **$14.95**

Atari ST, 520ST, 1040ST, TOS, ST BASIC and ST LOGO are trademarks or registered trademarks of Atari Corp. GEM is a registered trademark of Digital Research Inc.

Selected Books from our ATARI ST Reference Library

3D Graphics

Teaches how to create impressive, lightning-fast three-dimensional graphics on the Atari ST in 68000 machine language. **Atari ST 3D Graphics** covers introductory concepts and background materials, graphic animation, using the assembler and much more.

Learn real-time animation with dozens of graphic routines. 3D Graphics is an amazing book for all programmers interested in advanced level graphics.

Some of the topics covered include:

- Mathematical basis for 3D graphics
- Coordinate systems
- Scaling the axis
- Two- and three-dimensional transformations
- Hidden lines & surfaces
- Data structure for 3D objects
- Object animation
- Spatial projection
- Rotation of objects
- Light and shadows
- Introduction to 3D computer-aided design (CAD)

A must for all serious ST programmers. **Atari ST 3D Graphics** includes complete listings for a fascinating 3D pattern-maker and animator. 351 pages.

Atari ST 3D Graphics	Suggested Retail Price: **$24.95**
Optional Diskette	Suggested Retail Price: **$14.95**

The programs are clearly printed, well commented, planned in a sensible modular fashion, and contain many invaluable assembly-language 'tips and tricks.' And they work. ST programmers are fortunate to have this book."

—Douglas Weir
ST-Log

ST Disk Drives: Inside and Out

The latest title in the widely-acclaimed *Abacus Atari ST Reference Library* is the exclusive **Atari ST Disk Drives: Inside and Out**. This outstanding technical reference is <u>the</u> definitive source of information for the ST disk drives—it thoroughly discusses the floppy disk, the hard disk and RAM disk from both a programming and a technical perspective. In addition, the reader will find several full-length utilities and programming tools that enables him to further explore the ST disk drives' operations and capabilities. Topics include:

- Information of sequential and random access file structures
- Access to data files from BASIC, Pascal, C, and FORTRAN
- Data structures and management
- The boot sector and BIOS parameter bloc (BPB)
- The directory and File Allocation Table (FAT)
- Relocation table
- Hard disk format
- Details of drive construction: (DMA chip, disk controller, connector layout, and organization, etc.
- Command description, status interpretation, floppy interface, hard disk partition analyzer

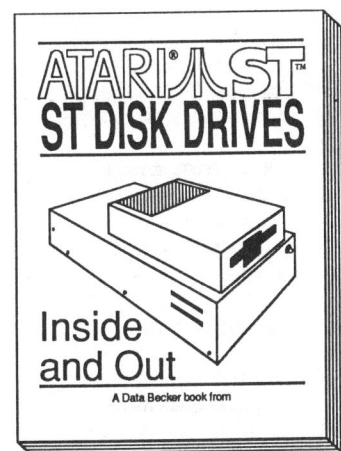

Atari ST Disk Drives: Inside and Out is literally packed with utility programs. The book includes a complete listing for an easy-to-use RAM disk, BASIC/TOS interface, BASIC/FDC interface, BASIC loaders, Floppy-to-RAM disk copy, creating standard and foreign formats, and many more timesaving programs. **Available April '87.**

ST Disk Drives: Inside and Out	Suggested Retail Price: **$24.95**
Optional Diskette	Suggested Retail Price: **$14.95**

Atari ST, 520ST, 1040ST, TOS, ST BASIC and ST LOGO are trademarks or registered trademarks of Atari Corp. GEM is a registered trademark of Digital Research Inc.

Selected Abacus Products for the ATARI ST

AssemPro
Machine language development system for the Atari ST

"...I wish I had (AssemPro) a year and a half ago... it could have saved me hours and hours and hours."
—Kurt Madden
ST World

"The whole system is well designed and makes the rapid development of 68000 assembler programs very easy."
—Jeff Lewis
Input

AssemPro is a complete machine language development package for the Atari ST. It offers the user a single, comprehensive package for writing high speed ST programs in machine language, all at a very reasonable price.

AssemPro is completely GEM-based—this makes it easy to use. The powerful integrated editor is a breeze to use and even has helpful search, replace, block, upper/lower case conversion functions and user definable function keys. **AssemPro**'s extensive help menus summarizes hundreds of pages of reference material.

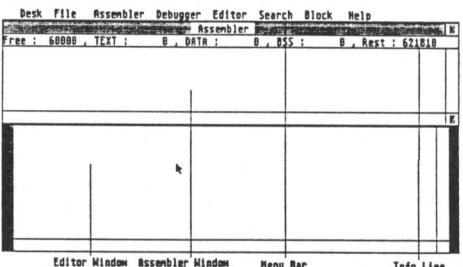

The fast macro assembler <u>assembles object code to either disk or memory.</u> If it finds an error, it lets you correct it (if possible) and continue. This feature alone can save the programmer countless hours of debugging.

The debugger is a pleasure to work with. It features single-step, breakpoint, disassembly, reassembly and 68020 emulation. It lets users thoroughly and conveniently test their programs immediately after assembly.

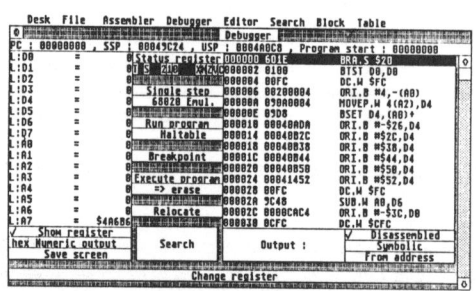

AssemPro Features:

- Full screen editor with dozens of powerful features
- Fast 68000 macro assembler assembles to disk or memory
- Powerful debugger with single-step, breakpoint, 68020 emulator, more
- Helpful tools such as disassembler and reassembler
- Includes comprehensive 175-page manual

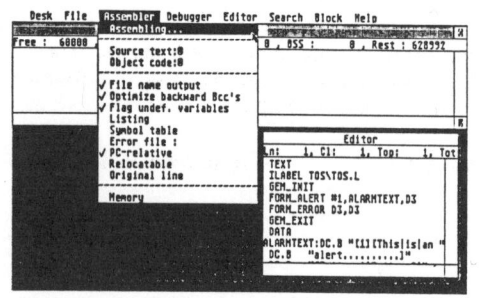

AssemPro   Suggested retail price: **$59.95**

Atari ST, 520ST, 1040ST, TOS, ST BASIC and ST LOGO are trademarks or registered trademarks of Atari Corp.
GEM is a registered trademark of Digital Research Inc.

Selected Abacus Products for the ATARI ST

Chartpak ST

Professional-quality charts and graphs on the Atari ST

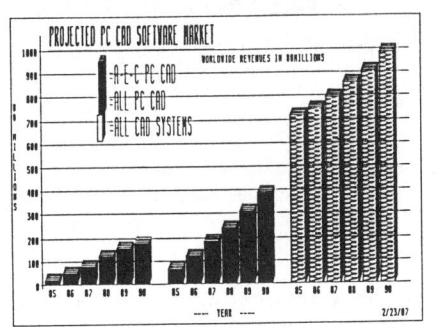

In the past few years, Roy Wainwright has earned a deserved reputation as a topnotch software author. **Chartpak ST** may well be his best work yet. **Chartpak ST** combines the features of his **Chartpak** programs for Commodore computers with the efficiency and power of GEM on the Atari ST.

Chartpak ST is a versatile package for the ST that lets the user make professional quality charts and graphs fast. Since it takes advantage of the ST's GEM functions, **Chartpak ST** combines speed and ease of use that was unimaginable til now.

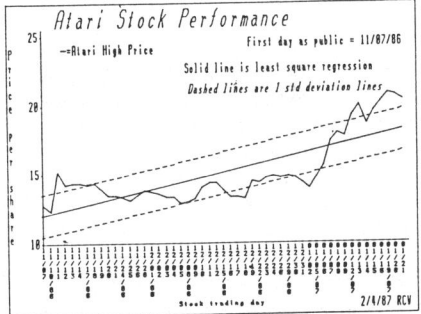

The user first inputs, saves and recalls his data using **Chartpak ST**'s menus, then defines the data positioning, scaling and labels. **Chartpak ST** also has routines for standard deviation, least squares and averaging if they are needed. Then, with a single command, your chart is drawn instantly in any of 8 different formats—and the user can change the format or resize it immediately to draw a different type of chart.

In addition to direct data input, **Chartpak ST** interfaces with ST spreadsheet programs spreadsheet programs (such as **PowerLedger ST**). Artwork can be imported from **PaintPro ST** or DEGAS. Hardcopy of the finshed graphic can be sent most dot-matrix printers. The results on both screen and paper are documents of truly professional quality.

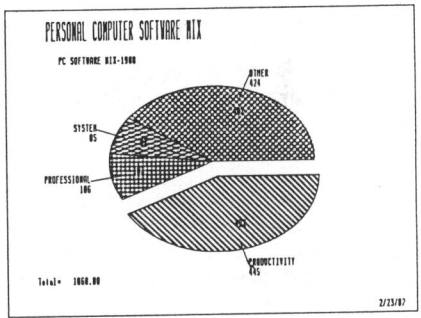

Your customers will be amazed by the versatile, powerful graphing and charting capabilities of **Chartpak ST** .

Chartpak ST works with Atari ST systems with one or more single- or double-sided disk drives. Works with either monochrome or color ST monitors. PWorks with most popular dot-matrix printers (optional).

Chartpak ST   Suggested Retail Price: **$49.95**

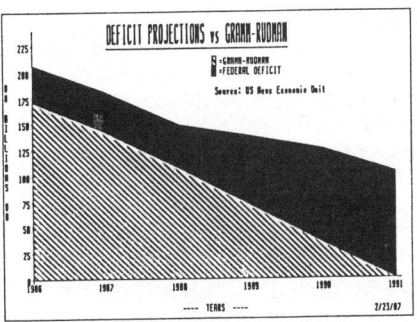

Selected Abacus Products for the ATARI ST

DataRetrieve

(formerly FilePro ST)

Database management package for the Atari ST

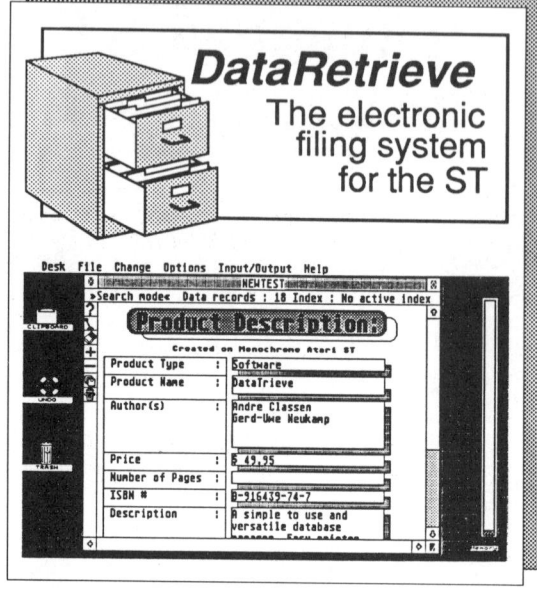

"DataRetrieve is the most versatile, and yet simple, data base manager available for the Atari 520ST/1040ST on the market to date."

—Bruce Mittleman
Atari Journal

DataRetrieve is one of Abacus' best-selling software packages for the Atari ST computers—it's received highest ratings from many leading computer magazines. **DataRetrieve** is perfect for your customers who need a powerful, yet easy to use database system at a moderate price of $49.95.

DataRetrieve's drop-down menus let the user quickly and easily define a file and enter information through screen templates. But even though it's easy to use, **DataRetrieve** is also powerful. **DataRetrieve** has fast search and sorting capabilities, a capacity of up to 64,000 records, and allows numeric values with up to 15 significant digits. **DataRetrieve** lets the user access data from up to four files simultaneously, indexes up to 20 different fields per file, supports multiple files, and has an integral editor for complete reporting capabilities.

DataRetrieve's screen templates are paintable for enhanced appearance on the screen and when printed, and data items may be displayed in multiple type styles and font sizes.

The package includes six predefined databases for mailing list, record/video albums, stamp and coin collection, recipes, home inventory and auto maintenance that users can customize to their own requirements. The templates may be printed on Rolodex cards, as well as 3 x 5 and 4 x 5 index cards. **DataRetrieve**'s built-in RAM disks support lightning-fast operation on the 1040ST. **DataRetrieve** interfaces to **TextPro** files, features easy printer control, many help screens, and a complete manual.

DataRetrieve works with Atari ST systems with one or more single- or double-sided disk drives. Works with either monochrome or color monitors. Printer optional.

DataRetrieve   Suggested Retail Price: **$49.95**

DataRetrieve Features:

- Easily define your files using drop-down menus
- Design screen mask size to 5000 by 5000 pixels
- Choose from six font sizes and six text styles
- Add circles, boxes and lines to screen masks
- Fast search and sort capabilities
- Handles records up to 64,000 characters in length
- Organize files with up to 20 indexes
- Access up to four files simultaneously
- Cut, past and copy data to other files
- Change file definitions and format
- Create subsets of files
- Interfaces with **TextPro** files
- Complete built-in reporting capabilities
- Change setup to support virtually any printer
- Add header, footer and page number to reports
- Define printer masks for all reporting needs
- Send output to screen, printer, disk or modem
- Includes and supports RAM disk for high-speed 1040ST operation
- Capacities: max. 2 billion characters per file
  max. 64,000 records per file
  max. 64,000 characters per record
  max. fields: limited only by record size
  max. 32,000 text characters per field
  max. 20 index fields per file
- Index precision: 3 to 20 characters
- Numeric precision: to 15 digits
- Numeric range $\pm 10^{-308}$ ti $\pm 10^{308}$

Atari ST, 520ST, 1040ST, TOS, ST BASIC and ST LOGO are trademarks or registered trademarks of Atari Corp.
GEM is a registered trademark of Digital Research Inc.

Selected Abacus Products for the ATARI ST

Forth/MT
Powerful Multi-tasking Language for the Atari ST

Forth is not only a programming language, but also an operating environment—the user can program, assemble and edit. Since Forth is fast, compact, flexible and efficient., it's particularly well-suited to the solution of real time problems. In use for more than fifteen years in industrial and scientific applications, Forth dramatically reduces program development time compared to programming in assembly language or other higher-level languages.

The powerful multi-tasking **Forth/MT** package was designed to make the fullest use of the ST's features for Forth programming.

Forth/MT features include:

- Over 750 words in the Kernal
- Complete TOS and LINE-A commands available
- Over 1500 words (disk accessible)
- Complete 32-bit implementation based on Forth-83 standard
- Machine language sections added for speed
- Many utilities: full screen editor, monitor, disk monitor and Forth macro assembler
- Utility descriptions stored on disk-you can change them to suit your needs
- Multitasking capability
- Machine language sections added for high-speed operation

Forth programmers will love the ease of use of this excellent package. **Forth/MT** the perfect tool for unleashing the power of the Forth programming language on the Atari ST line of computers.

Forth/MT   Suggested retail price: **$49.95**

Multi-Tasking
Full-Featured

```
POINTER NEW-MOUSE <CR>  (DEFINE BUFFER HEADER )
0 W, ( MASK COLOR ) 1 W, (MOUSE COLOR ) <CR>
BIN 0000000000000000 W, <CR>   ( 1ST MASK LINE )
    0000000000000000 W, <CR>   ( 2ND MASK LINE )
    0001111001111000 W, <CR>   ( 3RD MASK LINE )
    0001111001111000 W, <CR>   ( 4TH MASK LINE )
    0001001001001000 W, <CR>   ( 5TH MASK LINE )
    0001001001001000 W, <CR>   ( 6TH MASK LINE )
    0001001001001000 W, <CR>   ( 7TH MASK LINE )
    0000001000001000 W, <CR>   ( 8TH MASK LINE )
    0000000000000000 W, <CR>   ( 9TH MASK LINE )
    0000101010100000 W, <CR>   ( 10TH MASK LINE )
    0000011111100000 W, <CR>   ( 11TH MASK LINE )
    0000001001000000 W, <CR>   ( 12TH MASK LINE )
    0000000000000000 W, <CR>   ( 13TH MASK LINE )
    0000000000000000 W, <CR>   ( 14TH MASK LINE )
    0000000000000000 W, <CR>   ( 15TH MASK LINE )
    0000000000000000 W, <CR>   ( 16TH MASK LINE )
    0000000000000000 W, <CR>   ( 1ST MOUSE LINE )
    0001111001111000 W, <CR>   ( 2ND MOUSE LINE )
    0010000110000100 W, <CR>   ( 3RD MOUSE LINE )
    1010000110000101 W, <CR>   ( 4TH MOUSE LINE )
    1110110110110111 W, <CR>   ( 5TH MOUSE LINE )
    1110110110110111 W, <CR>   ( 6TH MOUSE LINE )
    1110110110110111 W, <CR>   ( 7TH MOUSE LINE )
    0111110111110110 W, <CR>   ( 8TH MOUSE LINE )
    0111111111111110 W, <CR>   ( 9TH MOUSE LINE )
    0011010101011100 W, <CR>   ( 10TH MOUSE LINE )
    0001100000011000 W, <CR>   ( 11TH MOUSE LINE )
    0001110110111000 W, <CR>   ( 12TH MOUSE LINE )
    0000111111110000 W, <CR>   ( 13TH MOUSE LINE )
    0000001111000000 W, <CR>   ( 14TH MOUSE LINE )
    0000001111000000 W, <CR>   ( 15TH MOUSE LINE )
    0000000000000000 W, <CR>   ( 16TH MOUSE LINE )
NEW-MOUSE TRANSFORM <CR>   ( SET NEW MOUSE )
SHOW <CR>                  ( AND DISPLAY )
```

Atari ST, 520ST, 1040ST, TOS, ST BASIC and ST LOGO are trademarks or registered trademarks of Atari Corp.
GEM is a registered trademark of Digital Research Inc.

Selected Abacus Products for the ATARI ST

PaintPro

Design and graphics software for the ST

PaintPro is a very friendly and very powerful package for drawing and design on the Atari ST computers that has many features other ST graphic programs don't have. Based on GEM™, **PaintPro** supports up to three active windows in all three resolutions—up to 640x400 or 640x800 (full page) on monochrome monitor, and 320 x 200 or 320 x 400 on a color monitor.

PaintPro's complete toolkit of functions includes text, fonts, brushes, spraypaint, pattern fills, boxes, circles and ellipses, copy, paste and zoom and others. Text can be typed in one of four directions—even upside down—and in one of six GEM fonts and eight sizes. **PaintPro** can even load pictures from "foreign" formats (ST LOGO, DEGAS, Neochrome and Doodle) for enhancement using **PaintPro**'s double-sized picture format. Hardcopy can be sent to most popular dot-matrix printers.

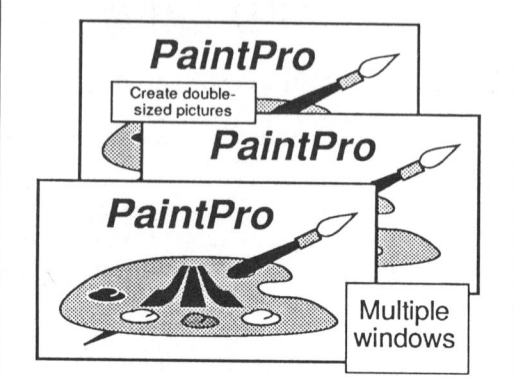

PaintPro Features :

- Works in all 3 resolutions (mono, low and medium)
- Four character modes (replace, transparent, inverse XOR)
- Four line thicknesses and user-definable line pattern
- Uses all standard ST fill patterns and user definable fill patterns
- Max. three windows (dependng on available memory)
- Resolution to 640 x400 or 640x800 pixels (mono version only)
- Up to six GDOS type fonts, in 8-, 9-, 10-, 14-, 16-, 18-, 24- and 36-point sizes
- Text can be printed in four directions
- Handles other GDOS compatible fonts, such as those in **PaintPro Library # 1**
- Blocks can be cut and pasted; mirrored horizontally and vertically; marked, saved in LOGO format, and recalled in LOGO
- Accepts **ST LOGO, DEGAS, Doodle & Neochrome** graphics
- Features help menus, full-screen display, and UNDO using the right mouse button
- Most dot-matrix printers can be easily adapted

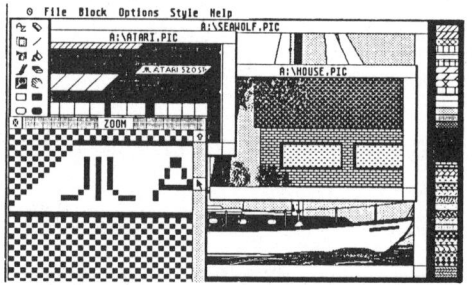

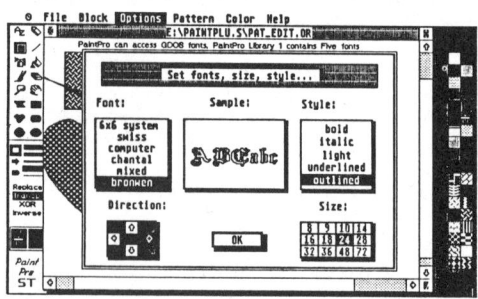

PaintPro works with Atari ST systems with one or more single- or double-sided disk drives. Works with either monochrome or color ST monitors. Printer optional.

PaintPro   Suggested Retail Price: **$49.95**

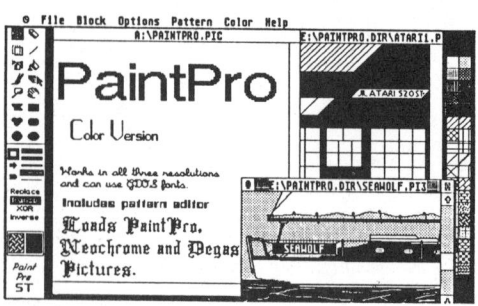

Atari ST, 520ST, 1040ST, TOS, ST BASIC and ST LOGO are trademarks or registered trademarks of Atari Corp.
GEM is a registered trademark of Digital Research Inc.

Selected Abacus Products for the

PaintPro Library #1

Fonts and Clipart for the Atari ST

The ST's excellent graphics capability make it a natural for computer art and design. To add even more flexibility and features to PaintPro we've released **PaintPro Library #1**, a companion graphics package that contains a diverse range of fonts and symbols for almost every application. It contains five new original fonts for the ST: Swiss, Computer, Chantal, Mixed and Thames. Paint Pro Library #1 also contains scores of new symbols, borders and ornamental lines. As you can see from the examples in the next column, this program fills a real need for your customers' design requirements.

PaintPro Library #1 contains five new specially designed fonts:

- Swiss
- Computer
- Chantal
- Mixed
- Thames (Old English)

Also included in **PaintPro Library #1**:

- Over 50 drafting symbols
- Over 100 electronic symbols
- Over 100 clip art symbols

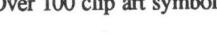

All fonts are GDOS compatible and may be used with "foreign" software that supports the GDOS. **PaintPro Library #1** also has hundreds of symbols, borders, and ornamental lines for use in your graphic designs. These libraries are DEGAS® compatible.

PaintPro Library #1 Suggested retail price: **$29.95**

Over 50 drafting symbols

Over 100 clip art symbols

Over 100 electronic symbols

And many decorative borders

Atari ST, 520ST, 1040ST, TOS, ST BASIC and ST LOGO are trademarks or registered trademarks of Atari Corp.
GEM is a registered trademark of Digital Research Inc.

Selected Abacus Products for the ATARI ST

PCBoard Designer

Interactive CAD Package for printed circuit board layout on the Atari ST

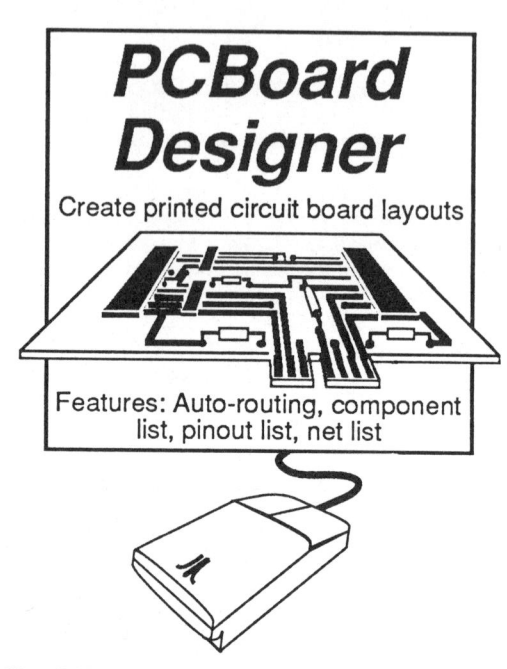

PCBoard Designer is an interactive, computer-aided design package for creating electronic printed circuit boards. It drastically reduces the cost, time and tedium of making one or two-sided pc boards. The advanced features of **PCBoard Designer** can improve a designer's productivity ten-fold.

PCBoard Designer is easy to use. Design parameters are conveniently entered and modified at the computer. The user can position the components interactively by moving them on the screen using the mouse. This lets the user compare alternative component placement with no extra effort.

As the user position the components on the screen using the mouse, **PCBoard Designer** displays the new connections! Automatic routing is fast and precise.

The most powerful feature of **PCBoard Designer** is its fast <u>automatic routing</u> capability. Traces are automatically and precisely drawn on the screen. If the user changes the design, the traces can be immediately redrawn—this feature alone can save an enormous amount of time and money. In addition, the user has options of <u>45° or 90° angle traces</u>, different trace widths, routing from pin to pin, pin to BUS, BUS to BUS, as well as two-sided boards. The <u>rubberbanding</u> feature lets you see the user-defined components during placement—and the user can reposition your components at any time during the design process.

PCBoard Designer prints the completed layout to any Epson/compatible dot matrix printer and Hewlett-Packard plotters at 2:1. The high-quality printout is camera-ready for final photo-etching. **PCBoard Designer** also prints the component layout, and lists every component and connection as well.

In conjuction with the Atari ST computer, **PCBoard Designer** is the most affordable PC board CAD package available. It boasts features that not available on systems costing thousands of dollars.

How PCBoard Designer works

There are basically four steps in creating a working pc board:

- **Specify the components:** For example, IC4 is an integrated circuit that fits in a 14-pin dual-in-line socket. You can also define custom component types, for example a 99-pin circular IC.

- **Specify the connections:** For example, pin 2 of integrated circuit IC4 is connected to lead 1 of transistor Q7. You can change the connections at any time.

- **Position the components:** Move the components to their desired position on the screen by using the Atari ST's mouse. You can reposition them at any time. **PCBoard Designer** automatically routes the connections when you're done.

- **Output the design:** The finished board can be printed on any Epson/compatible printer or Hewlett-Packard plotter. The printout is suitable for photoetching. You can also print the component layout (for silkscreening), the component list, and the list of connections.

Selected Abacus Products for the ATARI ST

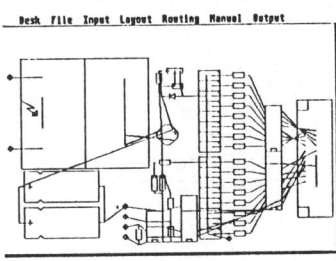

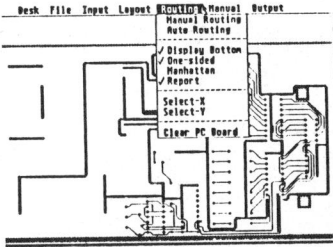

"I was thoroughly impressed... a powerful, multi-featured design tool that can be easily learned and used."

—Bill Marquardt
Input magazine

"What makes this program especially easy to use is that the components are drawn to scale on the screen. This comes in handy when it's time for the user to position the components.

*"The author invested a lot of blood, sweat and tears writing this portion of the program. **PCBoard Designer** has a wide selection of options here that allow for flexible design. Either all of the connections or an individual connection can be routed at the click of the mouse button.*

"One thing is clear, though: author Florian Sachse has produced a first-class software package. This program will undoubtedly be a godsend to the engineer and electronic hobbyist alike.

—DATA WELT Magazine
APRIL 1986

**Free PCBoard Designer
Retail Sales Kit**

Contact: Julie Carle or Jan Lloyd
(616) 241-5510

PCBoard Designer (continued)

PCBoard Designer Features:

- PC boards may be one-sided or two-sided
- Components are drawn to scale on the screen
- Custom components may be used
- Component positioning is flexible and interactive
- Components may be roatated in 90° increments
- Traces are drawn using sophisticated and fast automatic routing techniques—the user has the ability to make 45° and 90° angle traces, variable trace widths, pin to pin, pin to bus and bus to bus routing
- "Blockades" may be inserted onto the board to handle special cases
- Printout is high quality and suitable for photo-reproduction
- Features are clearly displayed and are selectable from the drop-down menus

Hardware Requirements:

Computer: Atari 520ST or 1040ST computer and monochrome monitor with one or more single-sided, double-sided, or hard disk drives.

Printers/Plotters: PCBoard Designer prints your completed layout to any Epson or Epson-compatible dot matrix printer at 2:1. Epson FX-80, FX-100, Toshiba, NEC P6 and P7 or compatible printersrequired for photo-ready traces. Also works on Hewlett/Packard plotters.

Package: Includes 100 page manual in 3-ring slipcase binder and program diskette.

Free phone support to registered users.

PCBoard Designer can dramatically improve design productivity by eliminating many redundant steps and time-consuming alterations. With all of its advanced time-saving capabilities, **PCBoard Designer** pays for itself after the first successfully designed board.

PCBoard Designer

Suggested Retail Price:
$195.00

Selected Abacus Products for the ATARI ST

PowerLedger ST
(formerly PowerPlan ST)

Spreadsheet/Graphics package for the Atari ST

"A superior spreadsheet program for weekend bookeeping to the heavyweight job costing applications, (Powerledger ST) is a definite winner."
—Judi Lambert
ST World

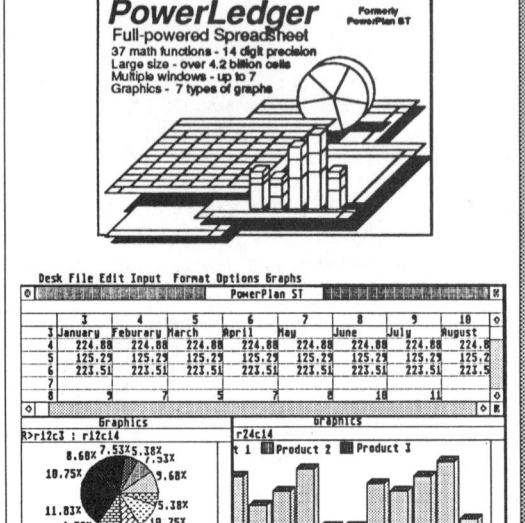

Ever since VisiCalc and Lotus 1-2-3 stormed the personal computer market, the computer has become an important planning tool. **PowerLedger ST** brings the power of electronic spreadsheets to the Atari ST line of computers—it lets the user quickly perform hundreds of calculations and "what-if" analyses for business applications, and crunch raw data into meaningful, comprehensible information, to keep track of budgets, expenses and statistics.

PowerLedger ST is a powerful analysis package that features a large spreadsheet (65,536 X 65,536 cells—over 4 <u>billion</u> data items). It also contains a built-in calculator, online notepad, and integrated graphics.

PowerLedger ST is also very easy to learn, since it uses the familiar GEM features built into the ST. And PowerLedger ST can use multiple windows—up to seven. Data from the spreadsheet can be graphically summarized in in pie charts, bar graphs and line charts, and displayed simultaneously with the spreadsheet. For example, one window can display part of the spreadsheet; a second window a different part; and a third window, a pie or bar chart of the data.

PowerLedger ST works hand-in-hand with our **DataTrieve** data management package and our **TextPro** wordprocessing package.

PowerLedger ST's extraordinary combination of data and graphic power, ease of use and low price makes it a perfect tool for every ST owner's financial planning needs.

PowerLedger ST works with Atari ST systems with one or more single- or double-sided disk drives. Works with either monochrome or color ST monitors. Works with most popular dot-matrix printers (optional).

PowerLedger ST Features:

- Familiar drop-down menus make PowerPlan easy to learn and use
- Large capacity spreadsheet serves all the user's analysis needs
- Convenient built-in notepad documents your important memos
- Flexible online calculator gives you access to quick computations
- Powerful options such as cut, copy and paste operations speeds the user's work
- Integrated graphics summarize hundreds of data items
- Draws pie, bar, 3D bar, line and area charts automatically (7 chart types)
- Multiple windows emphasize the user's analyses
- Accepts information from DataTrieve, our database management software
- Passes data to **TextPro** wordprocessing package
- Capacities: maximum of 65,535 rows
  maximum of 65,535 columns
  variable column width
  numeric precision of 14 digits
  maximum value 1.797693×10^{308}
  minimum value 2.2×10^{-308}
  37 built-in functions

PowerLedger ST   Suggested Retail Price: **$79.95**

Selected Abacus Products for the ATARI ST

TextPro
Wordprocessing package for the Atari ST

"TextPro seems to be well thought out, easy, flexible anf fast. The program makes excellent use of the GEM interface and provides lots of small enhancements to make your work go more easily... if you have an ST and haven't moved up to a GEM word processor, pick up this one and become a text pro."
—John Kintz
ANTIC

"TextPro is the best wordprocessor available for the ST"
—Randy McSorley
Pacus Report

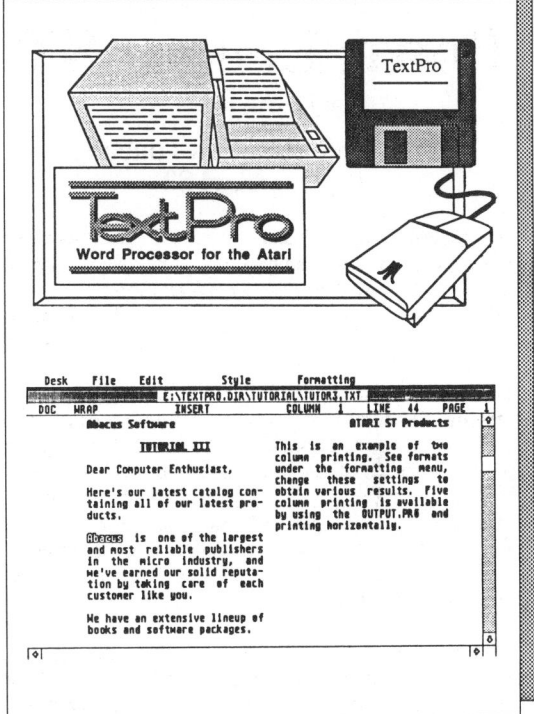

TextPro is a first-class word processor for the Atari ST that boasts dozens of features for the writer. It was designed by three writers to incorporate features that they wanted in a wordprocessor—the result is a superior package that suits the needs of all ST owners.

TextPro combines its "extra" features with easy operation, flexibility, and speed—but at a very reasonable price. The two-fingered typist will find **TextPro** to be a friendly, user-oriented program, with all the capabilities needed for fine writing and good-looking printouts. **Textpro** offers full-screen editing with mouse or keyboard shortcuts, as well as high-speed input, scrolling and editing. **TextPro** includes a number of easy to use formatting commands, fast and practical cursor positioning and multiple text styles.

Two of **TextPro**'s advanced features are automatic table of contents generation and index generation —capabilities usually found only on wordprocessing packages costing hundreds of dollars. **TextPro** can also print text horizontally (normal typewriter mode) or vertically (sideways). For that professional newsletter look, **TextPro** can print the text in columns—up to six columns per page in sideways mode.

The user can write form letters using the convenient Mail Merge option. **TextPro** also supports GEM-oriented fonts and type styles—text can be **bold**, underlined, *italic*, superscript, outlined, etc., and in a number of point sizes. **TextPro** even has advanced features for the programmer for development with its Non-document and C-sourcecode modes.

TextPro   Suggested Retail Price: **$49.95**

TextPro ST Features:

- Full screen editing with either mouse or keyboard
- Automatic index generation
- Automatic table of contents generation
- Up to 30 user-defined function keys, max. 160 characters per key
- Lines up to 180 characters using horizontal scrolling
- Automatic hyphenation
- Automatic wordwrap
- Variable number of tab stops
- Multiple-column output (maximum 5 columns)
- Sideways printing on Epson FX and compatibles
- Performs mail merge and document chaining
- Flexible and adaptable printer driver
- Supports RS-232 file transfer (computer-to-computer transfer possible)
- Detailed 65+ page manual

TextPro works with Atari ST systems with one or more single- or double-sided disk drives. Works with either monochrome or color ST monitors.

TexPro allows for flexible printer configurations with most popular dot-matrix printers.

Atari ST, 520ST, 1040ST, TOS, ST BASIC and ST LOGO are trademarks or registered trademarks of Atari Corp.
GEM is a registered trademark of Digital Research Inc.

How to Order

Abacus P.O. Box 7219, Grand Rapids, MI 49510

All of our ST products—applications and language software, and our acclaimed 14 volume **Atari ST Reference Library**—are available at more than 2000 dealers in the U.S. and Canada. To find out the location of the Abacus dealer nearest to you, call:

(616) 241-5510
8:30 am-8:00 pm Eastern Standard Time

Or order from Abacus directly by phone with your credit card. We accept Mastercard, Visa and American Express.

Every one of our software packages is backed by the **Abacus 30-Day Guarantee**—if for any reason you're not satisfied by the software purchased directly from us, simply return the product for a full refund of the purchase price.

Order Blank

Send your completed order blank to:
Abacus
P.O. Box 7219
Grand Rapids, MI 49510

Your order will be shipped within 24 hours of our receiving it

Name:
Address:
City _____ State _____ Zip _____ Country _____
Phone: _____ / _____

Qty	Name of product	Price
	Mich. residents add 4% sales tax	
	Shipping/Handling charge (Foreign Orders $12 per item)	
	Check/Money order TOTAL enclosed	

Credit Card#

Expiration date

For extra-fast 24-hour shipment service, order by phone with your credit card

VISA   MasterCard   American Express Card